Health Policy

Also by David Reisman

Adam Smith's Sociological Economics

Alfred Marshall: Progress and Politics

Alfred Marshall's Mission

Anthony Crosland: The Mixed Economy

Conservative Capitalism: The Social Economy

Crosland's Future: Opportunity and Outcome

Democracy and Exchange: Schumpeter, Galbraith, T.H. Marshall, Titmuss and Adam Smith

The Economics of Alfred Marshall

Galbraith and Market Capitalism

Health Care and Public Policy

Health Tourism: Social Welfare through International Trade

The Institutional Economy: Demand and Supply

James Buchanan

Market and Health

The Political Economy of Health Care

The Political Economy of James Buchanan

Richard Titmuss: Welfare and Society

Schumpeter's Market: Enterprise and Evolution

The Social Economics of Thorstein Veblen

Social Policy in an Ageing Society: Age and Health in Singapore

State and Welfare: Tawney, Galbraith and Adam Smith

Theories of Collective Action: Downs, Olson and Hirsch

Trade in Health: Economics, Ethics and Public Policy

Health Policy

Choice, Equality and Cost

David Reisman

Cheltenham, UK • Northampton, MA, USA

© David Reisman 2016

All rights reserved. No part of this publication may be reproduced, stored in a retrieval system or transmitted in any form or by any means, electronic, mechanical or photocopying, recording, or otherwise without the prior permission of the publisher.

Published by
Edward Elgar Publishing Limited
The Lypiatts
15 Lansdown Road
Cheltenham
Glos GL50 2JA
UK

Edward Elgar Publishing, Inc.
William Pratt House
9 Dewey Court
Northampton
Massachusetts 01060
USA

Paperback edition 2017

A catalogue record for this book
is available from the British Library

Library of Congress Control Number: 2015950299

This book is available electronically in the Elgaronline
Social and Political Science subject collection
DOI 10.4337/9781785365218

Printed on elemental chlorine free (ECF)
recycled paper containing 30% Post-Consumer Waste

ISBN 978 1 78536 520 1 (cased)
ISBN 978 1 78536 521 8 (eBook)
ISBN 978 1 78536 522 5 (paperback)

Typeset by Columns Design XML Ltd, Reading
Printed and bound in the USA

Contents

Acknowledgements		viii
1	Introduction	1
2	Good health	9
	2.1 The definition	9
	2.2 Mortality	11
	2.3 Morbidity	12
	2.4 The social context	14
	2.5 Objective and subjective	15
	2.6 Rational choice	17
	2.7 Probability	21
3	The invisible mind	25
	3.1 Questionnaires and surveys	26
	3.2 Willingness to spend	32
	3.3 Willingness to earn	35
	3.4 A representative sample	41
4	Inputs and outcomes	49
	4.1 Medical care	49
	4.2 Care beyond medicine	54
	4.3 Jurisdiction and legislation	58
	4.4 Prosperity and progress	63
	4.5 Increments and totals	67
5	The individual	71
	5.1 Needs and wants	71
	5.2 Knowledge and ignorance	73
	5.3 Information asymmetry	78
	5.4 The freedom to become	82

6	The practitioner	87
	6.1 The professional assessment	88
	6.2 The doctor knows best	91
	6.3 Payment and need	94
	6.4 Supplier-induced demand	99
	6.5 Countervailing forces	102
	6.6 Practice variation	106
	6.7 Value for money	113
	6.8 Trimming the fat	115
7	The public	117
	7.1 Social values	118
	7.2 Externalities	127
	7.3 Path dependence	130
	7.4 Political economy	132
8	The logic of insurance	139
	8.1 Risk and uncertainty	140
	8.2 Risk-rating	142
	8.3 Moral hazard	149
	8.4 Combinations and permutations	153
9	Insurance: private and public	157
	9.1 Private health insurance	157
	9.2 National health insurance	168
	9.3 The National Health Service: payment and provision	172
	9.4 Payment beyond insurance	176
10	Equity and equality	179
	10.1 Equality of expenditure	180
	10.2 Equality of contribution	180
	10.3 Equality of outcome	183
	10.4 Equal treatment for equal need	185
11	The right to health	190
	11.1 Natural rights	190
	11.2 Citizenship rights	193
	11.3 Maximin	195
	11.4 Generosity and compassion	198
	11.5 The structural imperative	200

12	Inequality and health	203
	12.1 Social distance	204
	12.2 Geographical location	214
13	Narrowing the gap	219
	13.1 Occupation	220
	13.2 Education	226
	13.3 Culture	232
	13.4 Income	238
	13.5 Inequality	244
14	Equalising medical care	254
	14.1 Payment	255
	14.2 Regulating the rules	258
	14.3 The doctors and levelling up	262
	14.4 Proportionate universalism	265
15	The cost of care	270
	15.1 Expenditure	271
	15.2 Social trends	276
	15.3 Medicine: technology and structure	280
	15.4 A fall in cost	284
16	Cost containment	288
	16.1 The demand side: price	289
	16.2 The demand side: time	293
	16.3 The supply side: purchase and containment	297
	16.4 The supply side: size and cost	306
17	State, market and cost	316
	17.1 An internal market	316
	17.2 Controls	322
	17.3 Liberalisation	325
18	Conclusion	330
References		331
Index		355

Acknowledgements

This book builds on ideas first advanced in my *Health Care and Public Policy* (Edward Elgar Publishing, 2007). It received support from the New Silk Route Fund and the Centre for Liberal Arts and Social Sciences at the Nanyang Technological University, Singapore. Sections were presented in lectures and seminars at Katsetsart University, Bangkok.

1. Introduction

Health policy is collective action. It is action undertaken by a group of people because doing nothing does not bring about the kind of society in which they wish to live. Richard Titmuss said it all: 'Social policy is about social purposes and choices between them' (Titmuss, 1974: 131). Social policy has 'no meaning at all if it is considered to be neutral in terms of values' (Titmuss, 1974: 27). Ideology is on the x-axis. Belief is on the y-axis. Stranded in between, there is thee and me. That is how health policy is made in a liberal democracy that is built upon economic exchange but upon the common identity as well.

Richard Titmuss had public policy in his blood. Adam Smith did not. Adam Smith was in favour of pecuniary self-interest, rational choice and the invisible hand of supply and demand. The consumer and the shopper, he said, could be relied upon to produce the well-being of nations. The discrete individual knows where the shoe pinches. The gain-seeking salesman knows whom he has to satisfy in order to live well: 'By pursuing his own interest he frequently promotes that of the society more effectually than when he really intends to promote it. I have never known much good done by those who affected to trade for the public good' (Smith, 1961 [1776]: I, 448).

Adam Smith looked to goal-orientated exchange to maximise people's well-being, self-perceived. Taken literally, his defence of devolution and factoring-down would suggest that health care is not a topic in public policy at all. The health-holder in need of a recommendation or a procedure buys in the intervention of the specialist even as the butcher buys in beer from the brewer and the brewer buys in bread from the baker. The doctor, the nurse and the anaesthetist serve us not out of benevolence but with a view to their own income, but they do serve us. Supply and demand are enough. Public policy is not needed. The State is not wanted. Shepherds and nannies need not apply. Richard Titmuss need not apply.

This book takes a more pragmatic view. It argues that the free market will normally negotiate a mutually beneficial compromise between supply and demand but that sometimes collective action will be the essential complement to factored-down individualism. Richard Titmuss said that pooled policies tend to 'reflect the dominant cultural and political characteristics of their societies' (Titmuss, 1974: 22). They do and they must; and one of those characteristics is 'society's will to survive as an organic whole' (Titmuss, 1963: 39). A nation has a shared and felt need for economic efficiency. It has a shared and felt need for other things as well.

Health policy, like all of public policy, is a response to the shared and the felt. It is more than the atom who hires a doctor who fixes a cough. Surrounding the nexus there is the context. There is I. There is We. There is Titmuss. There is Smith. And there is the acid test. Health policy is the acid test. The regulation of toxic banks and the denationalisation of the British Royal Mail are child's play compared with collective action to promote good health. It is a thing apart.

Health care is an unusual commodity. Its special properties make it similar but also different. This book incorporates those special properties into the broader theme of political involvement versus individual autonomy. The book asks if the unique characteristics of health make it uniquely well suited to social regulation and public administration. Perhaps apples and oranges can be left to the buyers and the sellers. Perhaps health care is different.

Definitions come first. Chapters 2, 3 and 4 describe the outcomes, the inputs and the production function.

The outcomes can be approximated by the indicators of morbidity and mortality. Good health is a sneeze arrested, a wheelchair discarded, a life-course prolonged by an organ transplant. Good health is an end in itself for the kidney patient who no longer experiences the disutility of dialysis. It is also the means to an end for the bedridden and the delusional who are empowered by better health to earn a living.

Good health is not just an objective fact but a subjective perception. It extends to the comfort of palliative care where there is no cure, the warmth of human contact where the doctor just listens to the friendless, the reintegration of the marginalised where the community nurse informs the housebound that there are welfare benefits for which they can apply.

Health status is buried in the hidden mind. Questionnaires and surveys separate the cardinal from the ordinal. Induction from willingness to pay calibrates the intervals. Each person is distinct. Each has a right to express a view. No responsible democracy formulates health policy without collecting information on what makes most of its citizens most satisfied in their own estimation.

The inputs are the jabs and the plasters, the beds and pharmacists. They are not the only ones. A tax on cigarettes paternalistically buffers the impressionable against a hospital stay. Role models encourage the couch potato to keep fit with a jog but not to slip into excessive weight loss which even the supermodels eschew. Dark chocolate contributes to good health. So does fat-free ratatouille served up by a supportive spouse. All of human life is there. All of human life has an effect on health.

People want good health. Good health, however, is not for sale. What is for sale are the inputs in the production function. The demand for health care is derived from the demand for health status which is not an economic tradeable. People have a strong resistance to pain, disease, impairment of faculties, permanent disability, premature death. They believe that health care is the wonder drug that will turn the tables on misfortune and drive the Grim Reaper from the door.

Even when there is no proof, their wishful thinking is a self-perpetuating psychological constant. Just as people believe in God, they also believe in the shaman who can make miracles happen. The appeal of the medicine man is emotive and non-rational. The doctors themselves are uncertain and the treatments not guaranteed. The link between life, death and care is imprecise, but still it is a link that is universally and eternally a source of satisfaction. No one likes to think that their life hangs by a thread or that their tremours will never stop. Health care is different from other commodities. People like to believe that someone, somewhere knows what to do.

Chapters 5, 6 and 7 say that the demand for care is a triangle of forces. It is the compromise negotiated through a continuing debate between the consumers, the producers and the community. All three constituencies believe that they have a valid contribution to make.

The liberal economics of Smith, Mill and Pareto makes the assumption that the autonomous individual is the best judge of their own well-being. Only the free-standing ego can compare the pain with the price or decide if the side-effects are compatible with one's lifestyle. Only the one-off consumer can do it. The outside observer cannot. Yet health care is a thing apart. In the case of oranges, remembered learning-by-doing has given the decision-maker a basis for rational expectations. In the case of an appendectomy, a heart attack or even a fractured clavicle the naked Adam is more likely to be on his own.

The argument for tolerance and consumer sovereignty is called into question by ignorance, uncertainty and information asymmetry. Individuals may not be in a position to distinguish their wants from their needs or to protect themselves from the supplier-induced demand of medical practitioners with a for-profit goal-function of their own.

Principals are at the mercy of their agents. Consumers do not know if they are harbouring an asymptomatic malfunction or what tests are required for von Ossobeyne's Disease or where to go for a top-quality specialist. They are too anxious to calculate the percentage change in quantity divided by the percentage change in price. They do not know what to do in uncharted territory where best practice varies, suppliers are differentiated, markets are segmented and finance makes the world go round. Intervention is instantaneous: the patient consumes the operation in the real time that it takes for the surgeon to produce it. Intervention is lagged: the patient actively invests their own time and money in keeping their body capital up to the mark. Intervention, most of all, is unbalanced. The doctor knows best. Every patient knows that.

The temptation to palm off a 'lemon' as a 'peach' is a fact of life. Yet the doctor at the same time has a professional ethic which pulls them back from lucrative mendacity. Asymmetrical information may for that reason be a greater threat when the consumer is buying a used car or deciding if a chicken is fresh than when they are being advised to take a sternum test for anticoagulants in the cortex. The doctor's role as healer and carer makes them see themself as the agent of a purposive teleology that is more than crass money-making alone. Like an emergency clinic, a medical professional will not turn away a desperate patient even if they know that the debt will go bad. The backslider who cuts corners on health and survival will experience a spoiled self-image. No sensitive doctor wants to feel bad about themself.

Medical services are often provided in a not-for-profit setting such as, in Britain, the National Health Service. They are often hedged about with regulations that circumscribe what the clinics can and cannot do. Morality restricts flexibility and licensure filters entry. Competitive pricing, manipulative advertising and entrepreneurial innovation can in the limit get a hospital delisted and a professional struck off. The butcher may have an instinct of workmanship but no one would say they had sworn a Hippocratic Oath that amplifies the law of contract. Health care, however, is different.

Society, meanwhile, has values and objectives, norms and visions, to which even the selfish dyad of market exchange is expected to conform. Consensus lays down the pitch, the court and the rules of the game. It establishes the baseline. It legitimates the patterns. The We gives the wandering self a home in time and space. It is the common bond.

Health care is other people. Fellow citizens want contagious externalities and third-party spillovers to be contained by State and not just medical intervention. Public opinion wants the ethical absolutes of social justice and Kantian respect to complement the market economist's maximand of input–output efficiency. Our central value system is what makes us teammates and integrated cooperators rather than anomic isolates whose only purpose is to turn a penny wherever a gull is to be twisted. A new hat satisfies a personal need. A linctus satisfies a personal need, but a social need as well. Health care, in other words, is not the same.

Chapters 8 and 9 discuss the business economics of third-party reimbursement. In the case of fresh fruit the transaction is complete when the buyer and the seller exchange goods for money. In the case of health care there is very often a further step. Where the nervous risk-averter has entered into a probability-sharing pool, it will be other people who will share the cost. Uncertainty is endemic to the human condition. Insurance is the rational response to the unknown and the unknowable.

There are no free-riders when the baker sells bread to the butcher. All the costs and benefits are internalised in their contract. Pre-paid care is an open door. It is socialism for sale in the capitalist market. Precisely because the use of the commons is free at the point of consumption to anyone who had the foresight to pre-purchase an entry ticket, there is a hidden temptation to translate cross-subsidisation into overconsumption. At a buffet the diners can eat as much as they like. At the margin they can continue to dine free. The diner has the peace of mind that comes from knowing it is the club that will pay.

Fire and theft are unambiguous negatives. They allow for little discretion and less judgement. Medicine is more nebulous. Policyholders look to health insurance to cover an open-ended spectrum of alternative therapies, conflicting opinions and differing amenities. Even if the small print is very small, still the contract can become a blank cheque if the patients and the practitioners demand nothing but the best.

Nor is that all. The carriers are exposed to adverse selection: the sickly will do well to sign up while the healthy will prudently save at interest instead. The carriers are vulnerable to moral hazard: the healthy will tend to debase their risk profile because the costless antidote is on the shelf. It is an actuarial jungle. The only solution is for the commercial carrier to refuse cover to all applicants likely to prove a profit-sapping drain. Money is money. Loss-makers do not balance the books. The response to the gap has, historically speaking, had to be national insurance. A national scheme ensures that no citizen, high-risk or low, is forced to pay more than he or she can afford for care.

Private cover is frequently supplied as a fringe benefit through work. Where health insurance can be set against tax, both the employer and the employee have an economic incentive to substitute insurance for pay. The tax-free status of the merit good means that it is in receipt *de facto* of a cost-inflating subsidy from the State.

Tax revenue foregone is not the only subsidy. Treatment centres will sometimes receive direct funding from the national budget because of the medical and social services they supply. In a universalist system clinical attention is delivered in citizenship-class institutions which strengthen the sense of community. In a residual system at least the deprived and the rejected are means-tested up into the medical minimum. Universalism or residualism, general or selective, the public subsidy makes possible a basic floor below which no human being can be allowed to fall. The facilities are the material embodiment of fraternal duty and a social right. No one but a beggar expects a handout when he walks into a butchery, a bakery or a pub. Health care, however, is different.

Chapters 10, 11, 12, 13 and 14 continue the discussion of membership, entitlement, equity and sharing. Equal access to cinemas, motorcars and pins is pure communism which is seldom advocated outside the family circle. A level road to the doctors and the hospitals is, however, a social objective that is more likely to command popular support.

Most people probably believe that all, irrespective of their achievement-based ability to pay, should enjoy equal access to at least a minimum medical package. There will not be universal consensus on the precise make-up of the entitlement or on the inclusion of peripheral alongside essential services. Where there will be universal consensus is on the action clause, that something should be done to level up the opportunities, the *joie de vivre* and the life-chances of all people in our nation and beyond. The moral imperative casts a long shadow before.

It does this most of all in societies with religious values that preach compassion, altruism and solidarity, with historical traditions that are imbued with responsibility, overlap and a common culture. In Britain, the nation-building impact of the Second World War was the stepping stone to the Welfare State. However, even in societies that have invested heavily in meritocracy, acquisition and living standards, there has always been an interest in fairness, access and basic health.

That commitment in itself politicises the debate. Freedom is not just freedom from the State. It is the freedom to develop, to unfold, to become truly and fully oneself. It is the freedom to attend comprehensive schools and to live in well-maintained public housing. It is the freedom to harness the amicable Leviathan in the agreed-upon interests of the All.

Mortality and morbidity are not random but patterned. Disparities in health are not just a reflection of individual assiduity versus private sloth. They are also social facts, correlated with occupational hierarchy and geographical location. Low incomes make it difficult for the deprived to pay for proper nutrition and salubrious accommodation. Subcultural mores mean that some strata are socialised into deferred gratification while other peer groups grow up with live-for-today. The job function explains why roofers have more falls and middle-ranking civil servants more heart attacks. Medical attention too is a cause of the dispersion in outcome indicators. Ability to pay can be a deterrent. People who cannot afford Disneyland do not go to Disneyland. But health care is different.

Where there is consensus that the invisible hand is letting the community down, the State will be expected to correct a market failure. Low incomes will be supplemented through housing allowances and child benefits. Subcultural conventions will be challenged through uninhibited mixing and health education. Occupational differences will be narrowed through works clinics and stringent bylaws. Medical care will be made a citizenship entitlement through community-rated insurance and a National Health Service.

The State will correct a market failure but it will also build on market success. Never sufficient but always necessary, economic growth ensures that public goods can expand without the need for private consumption to be crowded out. Continuous increase augments the taxable resources that can be devoted to the collective infrastructure. Capitalist gain and socialist cohesion can work together. The Fabian and the financier are both part of a sustainable health policy. That does not mean that they have to become good friends. The devotees of social integration and the avatars of paper appreciation do not normally go on holiday together or buy each other drinks in the bar. But they can work together; and that is enough.

Chapters 15, 16 and 17 issue a reminder that the cost of care is rising. It is rising as a share of the domestic product, a share of total public spending and a share of the household budget. $1 in every $6 spent in the United States is being spent on health. It was $1 in every $20 in 1960. What is being spent on health care is not being spent on battleships and beefsteaks. The escalation in the cost of care can impose an excessive burden on the other good things in life.

Health care has been expanding rapidly because of third-party payment, rising expectations, rising incomes, an ageing population, the development of new technology. There have been supply-side imperfections such as professional associations, local monopolies, protracted training, excess capacity, the entry barrier of capital overheads. The State, by licensing the hospitals and limiting the beds, has unnecessarily restricted the quantities and artificially inflated the price. The State has contributed to the rise. It is required nonetheless to take a lead in the containment of cost.

Relying on the free market, the government could encourage entry, rivalry and innovation. It could eliminate counter-productive restrictions that feather-bed the rent-seekers. Relying on the visible hand, it could ration demand through charges and waits. It could offer pecuniary incentives to hospitals that cut the average cost. It could employ utilisation review to expose and countervail the power to exploit. It could nationalise the treatment centres in order to minimise wasteful duplication and administrative deadweight.

Health policy could redirect total spending even as it caps the budget. Allocation in line with social criteria and not only the priorities set by the unequal ability to pay has the great advantage that effective demand will not be allowed to starve the social organism of higher-order utilities. Motorcars and cinemas do not present so great a challenge as to necessitate a collectively coordinated response. But health care is different. It is a thing apart.

2. Good health

Everyone wants good health. Along with opera, vodka, cigarettes, hang gliding, high-fat grease, tennis, serial promiscuity, university education and fast cars, it is one of the good things in life that people are observed to want. This chapter is about good health. It says that robust definitions are not easy to come by and that the end-states are a mix. It attempts nonetheless to shed some light on what is meant by a satisfactory health status. Health and health care are elusive concepts. Few, however, are so highly valued or figure so often in the eye of debate.

Section 2.1, 'The definition', states what good health is. Section 2.2, 'Mortality', and section 2.3, 'Morbidity', consider medical indicators which suggest that the body is in good shape or bad. Section 2.4, 'The social context', shows that the body is closely connected to the role. Section 2.5, 'Objective and subjective', turns from medicine and sociology to individual satisfaction, self-perceived. It is the gateway to section 2.6, 'Rational choice', which is about ignorance; and to section 2.7, 'Probability', which is about chance. Role, satisfaction, unknowledge, imagination – the message that this chapter sends to the statisticians is clear: 'One man's *explicandum* is another man's *conundrum*' (Reisman, 1993: 240). We are not all the same. That is why we need to talk: 'A market for health ... must also be a market for ideas' (Reisman, 1993: 240). There is nothing else that it could be.

2.1 THE DEFINITION

The World Health Organization (WHO) has made it all clear. Good health, it says, is 'a state of complete physical, mental and social well-being and not merely the absence of disease or infirmity' (World Health Organization, 1962 [1946]: 1). Physical well-being is the body. Mental well-being is the spirit. Social well-being is the role. The definition specifies that health, to be ideal, must be complete. Anyone whose mouth is dry, or who is feeling a bit anxious, or who suspects that his co-workers want him to move on, may be said to be a person whose health status is less than 100 per cent.

Titmuss, as always, could see that there was something wrong: 'To me this statement is meaningless as a working definition; it is a statement of an unattainable perfection of body, mind and soul. There is even something unhealthy about the perfection of the absolute ... In scientific terms, we do not know where health begins and disease ends. The lines that we draw are arbitrary ones and largely fashioned by the culture in which we live' (Titmuss, n.d.). What Titmuss is saying is that completeness itself might be a sign of illness, a symptom of obsessive-compulsive perfectionism, an exaggerated fastidiousness which suggests that the healthy themselves might be well on the way to the padded cell.

What Titmuss is implying is that most people define good health as something less than a single priceless possession of which the importance transcends any other and is insensitive to financial cost. Most people define good health not as the complete but as the acceptable, the tolerable and the satisfactory: 'The majority of people do not have totally healthy or unhealthy lifestyles: most are mixed' (Blaxter, 1990: 144). What most people want is a balanced portfolio. Good health is one of the many good things that they would like to have.

Mildred Blaxter recognises that the WHO definition is in the tradition of nirvana-like ideals such as 'the classical Platonic model of health as harmony among the body's processes, or the Galenian concept of disease as disturbance of equilibrium' that give only limited guidance to the doctor or policymaker: 'Trying to operationalize such a wide concept of health has the danger of subsuming all human life and happiness under this label' (Blaxter, 1990: 3). Nevertheless she does think that the refusal to treat health policy as illness policy is a step in the right direction: 'It does draw attention to the fact that positive aspects of healthiness ought to be considered, and not only the negative aspects of pathology. It may be that it is as important to distinguish the factors that differentiate health which is above average and that which is merely average, as it is to look at those which cause the average to become "bad"' (Blaxter, 1990: 3).

To attempt too much is to render one's holism toothless. To attempt too little, however, is to conflate freedom from constraining illness with freedom to juice the most from one's scarce endowment of body and mind. The good society is one which seeks out a compromise in between. And where, exactly, is that?

2.2 MORTALITY

Health itself is invisible. There is no single index of health status. There is no known unit in which it could be measured. Just as economists estimate felt satisfaction in non-observable 'utils', so policymakers could quantify health in hypothetical 'hels'. It would not serve any practical purpose. Hels, like utils, do not exist. Like it or not, policymakers will have to proceed on the basis of discrete indicators like the tail, the tusks or the trunk. It is simply not possible to reconstruct the elephant as a whole. It may not even exist.

The policymaker must make use of indicators. Different indicators will be used for different purposes. Different weights will reflect different priorities. The ideal index will be a measure of vitality and vigour. In practice virtually all the indices describe the things that can go wrong. One of the most salient among those indicators is death.

Mortality is useful because it is relatively straightforward. There is the problem of saying whether it must be the brain or the heart that has ceased its activity. Not everyone agrees when a foetus becomes an independent life that it would be murder to abort. These are quibbles. Most people understand what it means to be dead. Illness is more difficult to quantify. The chance of misdiagnosis or under-reporting is less. Shading and ambiguity in self-rated disparities are eliminated.

Data on deaths, moreover, are collected centrally. Not self-reported (and open to subjective miscalibration), not pluralistic (and at risk from under-reporting or double counting), data on deaths, like vital statistics on births and marriages, are assembled by a single national agency. A single Registrar General is typically charged with the task of producing a historical record that is comprehensive, reliable and accurate.

Data on deaths are attractive because they can be disaggregated to bring out the specific experience of discrete groupings. Mortality rates can be used to compare women and men, slum-dwellers and comfortable suburbanites, workers on oil rigs and workers with fast food. Towards the beginning of life there are the rates of perinatal, neonatal, infant and child mortality. In the prime working years there is adult mortality that can (weighted by life-years and earnings expected) provide a measure of future economic growth prematurely snuffed out. Towards the end of life there is adult mortality in the gradual evolution of post-retirement dependency.

The phrase 'life expectancy at ...' is a reminder of just how adaptable the information is for a researcher wishing to elucidate particular stages in the life cycle. It is also a reminder that comparisons must be age-standardised. Otherwise regions or countries with younger people will be mistaken for areas where the government has been especially astute in introducing the best possible policies.

Data on deaths are unambiguous, centrally collected and amenable to disaggregation. They are useful for another reason as well. Data on mortality are in a limited sense data on morbidity as well. People do not just die. They die for a reason. The death certificate gives the proximate cause.

The proximate cause is, admittedly, not the full medical history. A death will be put down to bronchitis when the cause of the cause will have been tobacco. Death by suicide will be misrepresented as death by misadventure when a dysfunctional family wants to avoid stigma or because suicide is against the law. Asbestos and lead, lying latent for four decades, will not be called to account when a security guard or a short-order cook develops cancer in their lungs or their bones (Bambra, 2011: 52, 55). Death is typically caused by a complex sequence and not a closed-ended affliction. The death certificate is not the blow-by-blow reconstruction that is required.

There is also the human factor. Diagnostic criteria may differ from one hospital or coroner to another. As for the patient, there is no indication of the length or painfulness of the final illness, or of the suffering that might have been alleviated by palliative care. A death certificate is black and white. Dying itself is not.

Mortality in many cases occurs without morbidity. Examples would be homicide or a car accident. Morbidity, for that matter, can occur without mortality. Illustrations would be arthritis, rheumatism, asthma or paranoid schizophrenia. Often, however, the two go together. Where they do, the fatalities can then shed light on the fall from grace which preceded the demise.

2.3 MORBIDITY

Illness is more difficult to measure. The conceptual and perceptual problems dwarf the statistical shortcomings. Yet the facts too let the observer down. There is no single data-collecting agency and no single database. Information must be obtained from a variety of sources. There is no reason to expect that the definitions will be comparable or that the records will be free from duplication.

Doctors and hospitals have information on diagnoses and treatments. Self-reporting in surveys is only the tip of the iceberg. The medicalisation of the sick role at once puts a name to the symptom and detects asymptomatic malfunctions of which the patient may not be aware. Whether the treatment centres will share what they know is a different matter. Confidentiality restricts disclosure. Business strategy makes them reluctant to reveal too much. A national system of aggregated data would at least put the broad categories in the public domain. What no system can identify are the patients who retreated into self-medication because they were deterred by the wait, or who buried their head in the sand because 'it can't happen to me'. The malfunction existed but it was never captured by the computer.

Insuring agencies complement the treatment centres when they provide information on contingencies and payouts. In some cases they will be able to add on an economic measure of work-days lost. Episodes and duration of disease will be tabulated. The number of patients will be distinguished from the number of visits. Patients often attend more than once. Hospitals know the number of visits. Insurers know the number of people with policies for whom they have had to pay.

Health-related questions are often included in the Census or in large-sample polls such as general household and family expenditure surveys. Academic investigators conduct grant-funded research of their own which fleshes out the official statistics. Little data rather than big data, such studies map a representative cross-section of health-related issues. Some of those issues never make their way to the treatment centres and the insurance underwriters. Under-reporting is reduced, but there is also the downside. Since no qualified practitioner has certified the complaint, it has never been pigeonholed into a diagnostic-related category. A sneeze could be anything.

Representative samples are amplified by blanket examinations. Compulsory screening is frequently conducted of all schoolchildren, all military conscripts and all workers in high-risk industries. The comprehensive nature of the pool nets out the risk of sampling error. Even so, microscopes as well as macroscopes will be needed to fill in specific gaps. Individual ministries supply additional pieces of the puzzle. They collect and publish focused data on narrowly defined topics such as salmonella, anthrax, road accidents, notifiable diseases and long-term disability benefits.

Raw data are necessary. They are not sufficient. Aggregated deaths are known. What is needed is an index that picks up aggregated illnesses as well. It does not exist. There is no common denominator that makes it possible to add together the heart attacks, the headaches, the hay fever and the mild rash. There is no composite 'unit of disease' that allows the length of impeded function to be summed together with the pain and inconvenience. There are no 'hels'. A picture emerges but it is not perfect. In contrast to mortality, morbidity is an overgrown administrative thicket.

2.4 THE SOCIAL CONTEXT

Symptoms give a clue as to the illness. Temperature, pulse rate, weight gain, weight loss, insomnia, hypersomnia, swollen digits, a coughing fit, indigestion, uncontrollable aggression, serious delusions, hot flushes, nausea, all suggest that something out of the ordinary may be happening. Incontinence, amnesia, confusion, inability to walk, eat, shop, hear, see, do up buttons, climb stairs or wash unaided are all indicators of a health status that falls short of the norm.

Symptoms are not, however, an illness. It is the function of the trained practitioner to certify the sick role by classifying it into a recognised medical category. At that point it acquires a name and the stamp of authority. An ache in the joints, becomes rheumatoid arthritis. An ache in the chest becomes coronary thrombosis. High blood pressure becomes an accident waiting to happen. The doctor's assessment forms the basis for the actuary's projections.

Yet there is something more. Patients are situated in time and space. The shortfall identified by the professional is a medical malfunction but also the health-holders' perception that their body is letting them down. Partly, this will be a function of their socialised expectations.

Medical opinion and public opinion might not think as one with respect to strain and fatigue. There are subcultures where everyone has unrelenting lumbar pain and where everyone is tired. The doctor, in imposing their own perception of normalcy, is in fact imputing the sick role to a patient whose peer group is telling them that they are average. The doctor says that the housewife is overworked. Her neighbours say that she is no different from all the other housewives on the street. Middle-class labelling may actually be misstating the stock of self-identified illness in the community. Occasional dizziness and lower back pain are normal, not pathological. They are 'business as usual' on our street.

Standard categories underestimate the amount of cultural heterogeneity, the plurality of perceptions in the nation. Societies have at various times labelled criminals, homosexuals, communists and capitalists as ill. Deviants like these have been handed over to the doctors for a cure. Such labelling is problematic. It reinforces the contention that good health cannot accurately be monitored.

Perceived good health has a functional as well as an attitudinal dimension. Restriction of activity must be evaluated not just by severity, duration and opportunity cost, but also by the use that specific people normally make of their faculties. A teenager playing football would regard a sprained ankle as an interference with his life plan and lifestyle. A civil servant preparing for an evening's light television viewing might regard it simply as a minor nuisance. Health for each of them is doing what they want to do when they want to do it. It is as much a perception as a condition.

What is said about leisure may be said *a fortiori* about work. Different occupations demand different capacities and different standards of fitness. A person who trades from home with a computer and a telephone can afford to be bedridden. A coal miner or a bus driver cannot. A retired person living on a guaranteed pension can ride out the bad days when he cannot leave his flat. Not so a mid-career breadwinner sandwiched between his ageing parents and his school-age dependants. Feeding them all out of his takings, there is no way that he can close his shop because he does not feel well.

A female high-flyer in a rich country may request a certified sterilisation as an investment in early promotion. An illiterate housewife in the peasant Third World will not make the same assessment of the ability to reproduce. Expected to breed labour for the family farm, childlessness would call into question her very *raison d'être*. Infertility may be the shortest route to accidental death in a cookhouse fire. Different functions as well as different attitudes differentiate the high-flyer from the peasant. They are different. Their health needs, self-perceived, are not the same.

Interpersonal signs are always a guess. Cross-cultural codes are even more difficult to read. In some reference groups it is common to 'hear voices'. In other reference groups it is only the mentally ill who distil their frenzy from the air. It would clearly be an error to divorce the clinical indicators from the targets, the imperatives, the roles and the activities in which those indicators are embedded. The sick role is not the same for all. The social role is all around.

2.5 OBJECTIVE AND SUBJECTIVE

Good health is a state of 'complete physical, mental and social well-being'. This is a definition which papers over the dispersion. Each person is unique. Each patient is unique. Different people have different notions of what it means to be well or ill. Simple enumeration is not enough. What is 'complete' for Jack is not 'complete' for Jill.

A sneeze is not a sneeze. Different people have different perceptions of the threshold that separates normalcy from malfunction. Being ill and feeling ill are not the same. The statistician's rigid categories do not pick up the meaning that Jack and Jill severally attach to their condition.

There is no single metric for a throbbing headache that is difficult to verbalise or quantify. There is no credible measure of the stabbing anguish of shingles or the shaming isolation of agoraphobia. There is no administrative magnitude that captures the secret malady plaguing the patient whom the professionals instinctively dismiss as a hypochondriac. Robust numbers on internal states do not exist. It is a major gap. 'Completeness' cannot be defined until Jack and Jill invite the Ministry into their hidden mind.

One year spent in one health-state does not yield the same satisfaction as one year spent in a different health-state. Crude life-years and calendar time do not tell the whole story: 'The difficulty is that everyone who remains alive is given the same score. A person confined to bed with an irreversible coma is alive and is counted the same as someone who is actively playing volleyball at a picnic' (Kaplan, 1995: 31). It is misleading to code death as 'No', life as 'Yes', without inquiring into the multiple gradations of the good-health continuum or the kaleidoscopic sensations of each pebble on the beach. 'Completeness' is in the eye of the body-holder. We are not a common currency that papers over the cracks.

Counting and bagging is made difficult where each atom alone can say what is 'complete' for their body, soul and role. Only the body-holders can say if, and by how much, they believe kidney dialysis to be inferior to an organ transplant, or if they fear a surgical scar to the extent that they would prefer to gamble on a herbal remedy, or if the hoped-for outcome is really worth the unpleasant and risky treatment plan. Only the discrete one-off can say if extra life-years accompanied by tinnitus, anxiety and disability are genuinely preferable to premature death; or if the fear of side-effects such as blindness or paralysis is stronger than the attraction of a 65 per cent chance of full recovery. Only the discrete one-off can know if they discount the future at a high rate or a low one; or if they are so risk-averse that they would refuse a wonder-drug still on trial. Only the discrete one-off can know it, and the Ministry cannot. Cold data must clearly be shaded by non-standard disamenity, self-perceived, if inanimate numbers are to acquire a pulse.

Liberal democracy seeks to build up an image of the good life from the perspectives and practices of separable individuals, each of them equally deserving of respect. It is easier said than done. Philosophy is about principles. Politics, however, is about action. Self-rating may be the benchmark of good health, but still, every mind is a stranger to every other. Governments will find it easier to gain a purchase on the objective and the observable than they will to tease out the qualitative and the subjective which are buried deep in each distinctive self.

The hidden mind cannot be viewed directly. The shadow is a different matter. Policymakers have used visible proxies to infer the thoughts and feelings of real-world men and women when they arrive at their private and personal definition of good health. One approach, *ex ante*, is to invite the discrete body-holders to articulate a value. Another approach, *ex post*, is to take their actions as a reliable guide to their motives.

The two approaches will be explored in Chapter 3. Before that there are the questions. Whether through words or through deeds, are people when they become patients in a position to make a rational choice? Do the consumers of medical care grasp that what they are buying is a probability and not a prediction? Liberals and democrats believe that governments have a duty to rubber-stamp the policies to which the *vox populi* has given its informed consent. The following sections ask if the consent is sufficiently informed to justify the philosophers' trust.

2.6 RATIONAL CHOICE

The assumption must be that the preference-revealers are in possession of the relevant facts and that they have the theory-driven schemata which enable them to arrive at non-random conclusions. It is a narrow gateway. If the pillars are not adequate, the definition of good health as the people's choice must be called into question.

Individuals as patients do not know if it is saccharine or magnesium sulphate that thins the amino acids. They are not perfectly informed about e-cigarettes and waterpipes. They know that high tar is more carcinogenic than filter-tipped cigarettes, but not that it starves them of precisely x years of expected life. Academic calculations based on the objective frequencies are likely to miss the mark. What is more relevant is the subjective risk factor that is applied by real-world men and women who have not bothered to find out the facts.

Guesstimates, gut reactions and loose impressions are the way in which most of us navigate our way through life. Understanding is imperfect. The citizen in the street is part of the national constituency to which public policy must respond. Yet, in contrast to the patients already afflicted and the doctors who know best, the underinformed might not know what von Ossobeyne's Disease involves or how long the vomiting is likely to last. Torrance describes the 'sticking point' in the following words: 'How do you describe, in a complete and yet unbiased manner, a particular dysfunctional health state (for example, kidney dialysis) to a healthy individual who has no experience with the condition? And how do you know when you have done it right?' (Torrance, 1986: 15).

Narratives are provided. Visual aids are employed. Treatment scenarios are simplified. Dread labels like cancer and leprosy are replaced by more neutral terms. At the end of the day, however, if the overloaded respondent does not understand the complexities, it must be questioned whether he should be asked what he thinks about von Ossobeyne's Disease. The fact is that he probably does not think about it at all.

Information asymmetry introduces a further complication. Even the afflicted might not know where the goalposts stand. Needs are not wants. The consumer's revealed preferences might not be those of an informed practitioner who knows the five-year survival rate and has made a career in schoolgirl bacteriuria. As Murray and Acharya write: 'Individuals' perception of their own health may not coincide with their actual health status ... Hence, allocation that maximizes consumer satisfaction may not actually yield the best possible health outcomes' (Murray and Acharya, 1997: 708).

Ignorance is the stuff of life. It is a reason for thinking that revealed trade-offs may not be a reliable policy platform. Yet there is another, more charitable way in which ignorance can be reconciled with democracy. Rational choice is not just the evidence but the schema as well. If careful people act logically and impartially on the basis of the defective data that they possess, they cannot be dismissed as if acting loosely on impulse. Their database may not be actuarial but at least their end-state is well defined and their reasoning good. Their information is deficient but their technology is sound.

A half-starved choice will not necessarily be an invalid one: 'What *is* important', Jones-Lee writes, 'is that if people are, for whatever reasons, more averse to risk from nuclear power generation than to an "obviously" equivalent risk from, say, a natural disaster, then this comparative aversion should be reflected in decisions concerning the allocation of resources to reactor safety and disaster prevention' (Jones-Lee, 1989: 224). People are what they are. So long as the rankings are consistent and transitive, felt satisfaction is being maximised when people get the cat that they want. The people are sovereign. The most the observer can do is to remind them that it cannot, it will not, catch mice.

People do make mistakes. Systematic errors do occur. Festinger uses the term 'cognitive dissonance' to describe the psychological discomfort that people experience when something deviates from the expected outcome: 'The presence of dissonance leads to action to reduce it just as, for example, the presence of hunger leads to action to reduce the hunger'

(Festinger, 1962 [1957]: 18). Confronted with discomfort, people either revise their assumptions in the light of the evidence or discount the evidence because it challenges their existing beliefs.

Applied to good health, revealed preference might be unmasked as an exercise in self-deception. People who see themselves as good drivers might dispense with their seat belt. People who work with toxic acids might not demand a danger differential. War correspondents will overestimate their own chances of survival. Without their optimism they would not be able to do their job. Most people find it distressing to think about their own illness or death. Wishful thinking rose-tints their risk assessment. Drinkers drink and smokers smoke. It is the others who will meet Resussianna on their way home from the tavern. Ego will not. Ego himself will beat the odds.

Salience further biases the perceptions. People are disproportionately aware of the recent, the sensational and the well publicised. They live in fear of a terrorist attack or a nuclear winter. They underestimate the far greater danger from monosodium glutamate and week-old oil in fatty *char kway teow*. They over-react to high-profile calamities such as a farmer struck by lightning or a tidal-wave that engulfs a low-lying polder. They are more sanguine about the low-profile commonplace such as a chip pan that might catch fire or a neighbour who complains about poor peripheral vision. The ubiquity of the familiar lulls them into a false sense of security. It takes a disaster to shake up their short-term memory.

Conservatism, too, makes people non-rationally defensive of a real, existing endowment. Surveys 'have consistently found that people say they would require a far larger sum to forgo their rights of use or access to a resource than they would pay to keep the same entitlement' (Knetsch and Sinden, 1984: 508). The mug once bought will only be resold for significantly higher compensation. The law of a standard price for a standard commodity is called into question not by ignorance of the alternatives but by a sentimental attachment to a bird in the hand.

A study of gases and burns confirmed that good health is often refracted through the status quo: 'Individuals were willing to pay moderate amounts for product risk reductions of 15 injuries per 10 000 bottles of insecticide or toilet bowl cleaner used per year, but when faced with a product risk increase of 1/10 000 most consumers were unwilling to buy the product at all, and those who were demanded a considerable price discount. In this context, the risky choice focused on changes in the risk from the current risk reference point to which consumers had become accustomed' (Viscusi, 1992: 143). People are afraid to surrender what they already command. One consequence is overinvestment in health insurance because good health is a status that they do not want to lose.

The willingness to acquire is not the same as the willingness to give up. Preference reversal drives a wedge between the bid and the offer. Life-saving new drugs, cost-cutting new procedures will not be licensed because people are non-rationally protective of what they already have. Misdirected novelty could take it all away.

Thalidomide did incalculable harm. Penicillin, of course, did inestimable good. Trusted barbiturates could be misused for suicides. Incomer benzodiazepines were uncharted territory, a suspect unknown. Which kind of sleeping tablet was closer to the dictionary definition of good health? History provides the answer. The delay in the United States in licensing the new and decommissioning the old led to the loss of 1200 American lives (Wardell, quoted in Peltzman, 1974: 89). It is the fear motive. Minimax meant that 1200 unhappy Americans died. As regrettable as any preventable death must be, the figure could have been many times higher if the new drug turned out to be a poison. The regulators thought it was right to be cautious. Their fellow citizens generally backed them up.

Conventions and rules of thumb are an additional reason why good health might fall short of the best attainable. Decision-making processes, Simon writes, are characterised not by global but by bounded rationality. They are dominated by a time-saving, intellect-saving reliance upon a tried-and-tested heuristic in which the health-holder has learned to place his trust: 'One could postulate that the decision-maker had formed some *aspiration* as to how good an alternative he should find. As soon as he discovered an alternative for choice meeting his level of aspiration, he would terminate the search and choose that alternative. I [call] this mode of selection satisficing' (Simon, 1979: 503). The history-dominated rubric greatly simplifies the filtering process. The cost is that new information is unimaginatively processed. The blinkered and the myopic, content with their ladder, never take it into their heads to fly.

Emotion and intuition, finally, can have an impact on rational choice. People are short-horizoned: they discount heavily the long-term consequences of obesity and tooth decay. People are stubborn: error correction is delayed because the prideful remain in denial about a mistake. People are simplifiers: because vegetarians as a stereotype are believed to be health-aware, therefore a vegetarian who wrestles with sharks will be assumed to be long-lived.

In all of this people are demonstrating psychological complexities which are at variance with the economist's dispassionate ideal of factual information in, impartial diagnosis out. Cognitive mechanisms are not a camera. If the health-holder is to be given the final say on 'completeness', then death and disease may go up or go down, but at least the respect for persons will be safe.

2.7 PROBABILITY

Good health is a destination. Life, however, is a journey. There is no route that always and everywhere leads directly to the sought-after state. Life is probability. It is not certainty. Things can go wrong. Apples have vitamins. Apples have worms. An apple a day gives the doctor his pay. Doctors grow rich because their patients mistake an apple for a one-way bet.

The health-holder will not always understand that health is choice and choice is risk. Recorded successes, regretted failures and extrapolated iterations are the essence of the human condition. The citizen when he reveals a preference might not grasp that he is gambling on a guess. The politician who acts on the basis of that revealed preference is building statistical inaccuracy into his policies. Imprecision is the price the nation must pay for its liberal democracy.

Imperfect information impedes the decision-making process. Yet there are circumstances in which perfect certainty will have the same effect. A case in point would be the highwayman's proposal of 'Your money or your life'. Faced with such a contract, there is only one maximum that would logically be articulated by a rational life-lover who does not want to die. That one maximum would be all that he has. Once the consumer has learned that he is under certain sentence of death, he would no longer have any reason to call a halt.

A dead man cannot shop: 'No sum of money is large enough to compensate a man for the loss of his life' (Mishan, 1971: 693). Assuming he is not planning ahead for his heirs, such a man would act on his certainty to run down his resources. Politicians will be strongly tempted to respect his revealed preferences and to push their own spending to the limit. It would be a fundamental error. Certain death does make it rational for the perfectly informed to live for today. Most of his fellow citizens, however, do not enjoy the certainty of the outlier. Most members of the community do not know. Their unknowledge puts teeth into consultation. It ensures that current spending will not soar into the infinite.

Where the probability approaches a certainty, each constituency fights for its own. Parents demand schools. The frightened demand policemen.

The sickly demand respirators. The bleeding demand stitches. Good health becomes one target among many in a world of selfish economising and special pleading. Certainty is conflict. Each constituency in a pluralistic democracy is revealing a preference of its own.

That is the attraction of probability. While people might know their present wants and even their needs, the future is a *tabula rasa*. Revealed preference in a form such as the willingness to pay cannot be infinite where people cannot anticipate the level of morbidity or mortality that they will one day encounter. As with all insurance, they are trading a certainty for an option on a chance. Thick ignorance may be a Rawlsian fiction but radical uncertainty about the path to come is a fact. Everyone dies of something. Will it be cancer or lead poisoning or a heart attack not treated in time? Probability allows people to say what value they would place not on a named, familiar health state but on a statistical health state. Random and unknowable, the health state may or may not be their own.

Probability shifts the focus from the known to the possible, from the factual to the imagined. The value of life becomes an economic matter of extra payment in exchange for an expected diminution in the risk of death: 'Value of life is the marginal value of a change in risk of death. It can be interpreted as an individual's value of a small change in his own probability of survival or alternatively as an individual's value of saving the life of an unidentifiable person in a large group to which the individual belongs' (Blomquist, 1982: 37n). Life is no longer Jim Jones's own life when he knows with absolute certainty that infected blood has left him with HIV. Life is less convincingly a 5 per cent probability of being crushed by a cheaply constructed building that collapses in an earthquake.

John Broome takes the view that it would be murder to act on the basis of the 5 per cent rather than the 100 per cent. Life is life, whichever way it is interpreted: 'It does not seem correct to distinguish in value between the death of a known person and of an unknown person' (Broome, 1978: 94). Hypothetically, the known life could be downgraded to the value of the anonymous statistic. Broome, for his own, part prefers to upgrade the unnamed contingency to the value of the family friend. It cannot be morally right, he says, to value a human life differently before and after the same person is been to the doctor for a cure.

Broome's recommendation is confidently utilitarian. The greatest number of survivals is the welcome result of the injunction to love one's neighbour as oneself. The problem is that human rights and human potential can cost a great deal of money. The value of life threatens to become infinite again.

It is a counsel of perfection that does not leave room for calculative optimising in a second-best environment where resources are scarce. Nor does it adequately allow for the way in which real-world individuals actually conceptualise their morbidity and mortality options. Buchanan and Faith argue that Broome is wrong to concentrate on the objective circumstances when what is more relevant is the subjective state of the individual's mind at the moment when he makes his choice: 'To say that "costs" are infinite for the person who loses his life in the draw of a lottery in which he rationally chooses to participate is to say nothing at all about the *value* that such an individual placed on life in the moment at which the choice was made. These ex post "costs" can, in no way, influence the choice behavior that created the consequences' (Buchanan and Faith, 1979: 246). The gambler stakes his money on a horse and the speculator takes a view on a portfolio. A life-holder is doing nothing different when he chooses a short-cut down a dark alley where dogs with rabies are known to lurk.

The preference revealed shadows the risk appetite of the lifeholder who owns the pulse. What happens then is merely the unfolding of a historical skein or choice-making tree that the individuals when making the choice knew that they could not precisely predict. Broome ran together the objective frequencies and the subjective perceptions. That was his mistake: 'The central flaw in his whole argument lies in a misunderstanding of *cost*. When does any attempt to *value* life arise for an individual or for a collectivity? Only when a *choice* is confronted does a valuation process become necessary. And only when choice is confronted is opportunity cost meaningful' (Buchanan and Faith, 1979: 245). Objective frequencies are a game for historians. Subjective perceptions are how real-world men and women actually choose. The government would do well to follow the example of their constituents and not that of the philosophers who stand apart.

Yet there is a problem. Contingent valuation is only meaningful for induction-based policy if the sample-subjects genuinely understand that a gamble is no more than a game. Some of the respondents will find the thought experiment comprehensible. Others will find the questions opaque, the situations unfamiliar. Even business graduates who know about trade-offs and normal distributions will find it difficult to say what a hypothetical value of 0.002 actually means to them when they buy life assurance or take out a housing loan.

Perhaps the respondents will simply pluck a random number out of the air. The investigator is expecting something and they do not have a clue. The respondents cannot be blamed for not being comfortable with the incomprehensible. Still it is a fact that a random number plucked out of the air is far from being a sensitive and robust reconstruction of good health, self-perceived.

3. The invisible mind

Liberal democracy is thee and me. Great books, great Leviathans and the doctor who knows best must defer to real-world men and women who have a preference to reveal. Their evidence is selective and their reasoning suspect. Their probabilities become their predictions and the fortuitous their facts. Real-world men and women are a handful.

Muddle-headed, frustrating and opinionated, thee and me want the law of gravity to be repealed, the care budget to be doubled and wonder drugs to be delivered as of right. Thee and me are the reason why our leaders need long holidays and become old before their time. Ordinary people are a handful. In a liberal democracy, however, they are also the *suprema lex*: 'Although it may be accepted that where public funds are involved we ought not to use a fool's valuation in deciding upon their allocation, if ... society is comprised soley [*sic*] of fools, then the valuation of these fools is the correct one to use' (Mooney, 1977: 126–7). The fellow traveller on the Clapham omnibus knows best. That is the bedrock absolute that liberal individualism came into being to protect.

The democratic order requires a good knowledge of what real-world men and women really want. That is just the problem. The contents of people's minds are not directly observable. There is no sophisticated polygraph that can measure the relevant brainwaves. There is no Clapham omnibus in which all is said and done. The hidden mind must be reconstructed brick by brick from the words and deeds that survive the passage into the public space. Without good detectives, there would be no true democracy.

Good detectives do their best to measure the consensus. It is not easy. The task is the subject of this chapter. Section 3.1, 'Questionnaires and surveys', is about words: the sample is asked to say what it wants. Section 3.2, 'Willingness to spend', and section 3.3, 'Willingness to earn', are about deeds: sometimes through spending, sometimes through earning, the sample is observed to see what it does. Section 3.4, 'A representative sample', asks if the proxies and subgroups are really representative of the wider community or are representative only of themselves. It is not very helpful to conclude from an incomplete investigation that an elephant is the same as a water-drinking tube. If that is the best the detectives can do, it might be preferable to dispense altogether with methodological individualism in favour of top-down pronouncement that does not wait for the iceberg of the people to be laboriously reconstructed.

3.1 QUESTIONNAIRES AND SURVEYS

A person-to-person approach is frequently employed to find out how the grassroots puts flesh onto the skeleton of good health. Sometimes the respondents will be asked to say how they would feel about 'for-instance' scenarios and 'what-if' contingencies. Sometimes they will be asked to make a full report on the before, during and after of the symptoms and cures that have affected the quantity and quality of their lives.

The validity of the statistic stands or falls with the sensitivity of the probe. Rosser and Kind probed the invisible mind using a using a double scale of negativities. On the horizontal axis there were eight medical outcomes: 'no disability', 'slight social disability', 'severe social disability', 'choice of work or performance at work very severely limited', 'unable to undertake any paid employment', 'confined to chair or to wheelchair', 'confined to bed', 'unconscious'. On the vertical axis there were four levels of disutility: 'no distress', 'mild distress', 'moderate distress' and 'severe distress' (Rosser and Kind, 1978: 349).

Respondents were asked to correlate their subjective sensations with the clinically measurable objective anchors, each carefully described by the interviewer. Permanent unconsciousness counted as 0. Perfect health was 1. All other states of wellness were somewhere between 0 and 1. This is not the traditional either/or of life versus death. It is an interval scale that quantifies different degrees of pain and discomfort as well.

Daly employed such an interval scale when she interviewed 63 British women in the perimenopausal years. The average age was 52.1. Using a rating scale from 1 (for perfect health) to 0 (for death), she found that, in the women's own estimation, mild menopausal symptoms reduced their satisfaction from one life-day to 0.61 life-days. Severe menopausal symptoms reduced the women's satisfaction to as little as 0.29. Things improved when they were given hormone replacement. The women reported that their satisfaction per life-day rose to 0.79 and 0.85, respectively (Daly et al., 1993: 838).

Only the women themselves were in possession of this information. Psychometrics reconstructed their felt quality of life from the preferences they revealed. What their disclosure means is no more nor less than this. If a woman with a low score of 0.29 suddenly dies, what has been extinguished is not 100 per cent of her benchmark joy from life but only 29 per cent. Assuming that the intervals give an accurate picture of the woman's actual state of mind, the two indicators of mortality and morbidity have in effect been compressed into one.

The information can be misused. In a cost-effectiveness study, the deficient and defective life-year might be recorded as less than a third of a fully satisfied life-year spent in a state of complete well-being. The discovery that one well woman admits to three times the happiness of a menopausal woman might even be incorporated into public policy on the principle that a utility monster is a better buy than an inveterate sourpuss. The information can be misused. Yet it also fills a gap. It sees good health through the eyes of the health-holder and not the detached clinician who dispassionately ticks the boxes.

Questionnaires and surveys can be employed to quantify the marginal rate of substitution that ordinary men and women subconsciously have at the back of their minds when they are being asked to choose between known resources and the risk of death. They might be asked how much more they would just be willing to pay to upgrade to an airline with a better safety record, or to install airbags and a collapsible steering column in their car. Their response, shadowing the direction and strength of their feelings, allows a finite value to be put on the economic value of a human life. The value is derived bottom-up. It comes from the implicit trade-offs of real-world people.

One such value is US$28 000. It was calculated by Acton (1973: ix) from a sample of 93 subjects from all income bands that he surveyed in Boston. Acton told his subjects that for the purposes of the study they should assume the probability of a heart attack to be 1/100 (0.01) and the probability of a heart attack proving fatal to be 2/5 (0.40). He then asked them how much they would be willing to pay for a programme such as an air ambulance service or a mobile cardiac unit that would reduce from 2/5 (0.40) to 1/5 (0.20) the likelihood that the heart attack would be followed by death. The average sum quoted was $56.

The sum of $56 was tied to the parameters of the study. A different value would have been quoted had the base level of risk or the magnitude of the reduction been different. The numbers would have been different but the steps leading to the value of life would have remained the same. As the chance of death without the intervention was (0.01)(0.40) and the chance of death following the improvement in policy was (0.01)(0.20), Acton was able to calculate the ratio of the extra cost to the extra benefit. The extra cost, derived from the sample survey, was $56. The extra benefit, defined as the decrease from 0.004 to 0.002 in the risk of death, was 0.002. Acton then solved for the economic value of an average human life. It turned out to be $56/0.002 = \$28\,000$.

Jones-Lee in Britain obtained a total of 1103 responses to a 37-question survey. Citing the hypothetical case of a safety feature that would halve the risk of death on public transport to 5/100 000, he inferred from the answers he received that the implicit value of life was approximately £1 million. It followed directly from his methodology, which was to mimic the risk appetite and the contingent valuation of those most likely to be affected: 'In the case of safety, these interests, preferences and attitudes are most effectively summarised in terms of the amounts that individuals would be willing to pay or would require in compensation for the (typically small) changes in the probability of death or injury during a forthcoming period' (Jones-Lee et al., 1985: 49).

He also found that the process of dying was itself a range of disutilities and not a single point. Financial implications held constant, when asked to say which of three forms of death they most wanted to see reduced, 11 per cent of his respondents said death in a car accident, 13 per said death from heart disease and 76 per cent said death from cancer.

One form of death is not the same as another. Jones-Lee discovered that the willingness to pay to avert a disaster in the London Underground was 50 per cent higher than the willingness to pay to reduce fatalities on the road by an equivalent amount. The prediction is not universal. He also learned from his respondents that 'the prospect of being involved in a rail accident is typically viewed with a considerably greater degree of dread ... relative to road accidents' (Jones-Lee and Spackman, 2013: 38), but that the willingness to pay for increased safety was no different. The reason might have been that the lower statistical probability of a rail accident was in effect offsetting the dread. There may have been a different reason.

The subjective and the actuarial are not the same. People are willing to pay twice as much to avoid a death from cancer as they are to avoid an instant death. A car crash is quick. Cancer leaves time for fear, anxiety, grief and pain. Sudden death is mortality. Death from cancer is mortality bundled together with morbidity. Questionnaires and surveys confirm the suspicion. Death as seen by the body-holder is not the same as death in the perspective of the impartial statistician.

Death is not death. Nor is it necessarily the lowest point on the scale of subjectivities. Being alive is not the only maximand. A good quality of life, self-perceived, is important too. Questionnaires, surveys, focus groups and face-to-face interviews show that, for some people at least, death itself is not the worst thing that can happen. Fully 6.2 per cent told Jones-Lee said that the loss of a leg was as bad as death, 2.4 per cent slightly worse than death, 1.2 per cent much worse than death, 0.3 per cent very much worse than death. As for being permanently bedridden, the percentages, respectively, were 33.4 per cent, 11.9 per cent, 11.2 per cent and 6.9 per cent (Jones-Lee et al., 1985: 54). It is a sobering thought that 10.1 per cent of the respondents thought that losing a leg was at least as bad as death, 63.4 per cent that being bedridden meant that it was better to give up and die. For some people premature death is a more satisfactory option than quadriplegia: 'In this situation, the cost–benefit policy implication is euthanasia' (Abelson, 2003: S11).

Questionnaires and surveys invite the real-world pulse-holder to quality-adjust the infinite gradations of a continuous spectrum. Sociology and economics converge on the margin, on the choice of 'a little bit more' and 'a little bit less'. Lived life is not a light switch either/or. Clearly, a survey that is stepped or bipolar will not be a reliable guide to that precise moment when ordinary people, if fully informed and thoughtful, would want their life-support to be discontinued.

Crude life-years overstate the hidden perception of what it means to be alive but under par. Being alive is not the whole story. People want a reasonable standard of well-being as well. If the respondents, quality-adjusting their statistical life-years, tell the interviewer that death is the best attainable health state, self-perceived, then that is the value that the statistician is duty bound to record. Democracy can be bad for your health. Methodological individualism can kill.

Life is consumption. It is not production alone. Questionnaires and surveys ask ordinary people for a view on their expected satisfaction and not just their earnings stream. The aspiration is noble. The evidence for all that does not always say what it means.

Questionnaires and surveys will sometimes be taken straight to the horse's mouth. They will ask old people how much they would be willing to pay for the greater comfort of a nursing home rather than a hospital ward. They will ask chronic sufferers from rheumatoid arthritis what percentage of their household income they would be willing to exchange for a complete cure if a complete cure could be found. Thompson did this. The average respondent told him it was 22 per cent. Respondents unable to climb stairs told him it was 35 per cent (Thompson, 1986: 396).

Good health is what the body-holder says it is. Better health may cost them more than a named lump sum or, to eliminate dispersion in the subjective value of effective demand, a specified proportion of unequal wealth. If it does so, then better health is not worthwhile health in the light of the next-bests that must be foregone.

Sometimes the study goes direct to the horse's mouth. Sometimes it brings in the horse's relatives and friends. Sometimes it sounds out the stable as a whole. The neighbours have attitudes and priorities which they may wish to put on record. As taxpayers they will have to sacrifice their own money for air ambulances from which they might not believe they will gain. The maximum amount cited by the bystander is not the maximum amount that was validated by the sufferer. It is the quantification of good health. Still the samples are not the same.

Studies must be carefully designed lest the survey questions suggest their own answer. Subjects can unwittingly be led into psychological pitfalls and intellectual biases. Respondents might select values at the midpoint of the scale: compromise is reassuring while confrontation is a threat. They might deliberately understate their willingness to pay: calculated deception may lead to State subsidies instead of tax. They might require prompts and explanations: step-by-step guidance can elide into slanted description. Policymakers must recognise that the survey results pick up the alarmists and the ostriches, the indifferent and the manipulative, even as they record the considered viewpoints of patients and bystanders who have a message to convey.

Subjects show a non-rational preference for outcomes that make them feel good. Language is powerful and images have consequences: 'The prospect of certainly saving 200 lives is more attractive than a risky prospect of equal expected value, that is, a one-in-three chance of saving 600 lives ... The certain death of 400 people is less acceptable than the two-in-three chance that 600 will die' (Tversky and Kahneman, 1981: 453). Because of the framing bias, Tversky and Kahneman conclude, public opinion will be less receptive to certain death than it will be to probable recovery even if the two values are actuarially the same: 'Choices involving gains are often risk averse and changes involving losses are often risk taking' (Tversky and Kahneman, 1981: 453).

It is the Bernoulli Theorem (Bernoulli, 1738 [1954]). It is Friedman and Savage (1948). It is Buchanan and Tullock (1962). It is the will of the people: 'In a question dealing with the response to an epidemic ... most respondents found "a sure loss of 75 lives" more aversive than "80 per cent chance to lose 100 lives" but preferred "10 per cent chance to lose 75 lives" over "8 per cent chance to lose 100 lives", contrary to utility theory' (Tversky and Kahneman, 1981: 455). The answers were not transitive or consistent. The framing bias altered the 'mental accounts'. The subjective and the objective values were not the same. It is not clear what the policymakers should do then.

There is also the crucial variable of time. The 'when' of a study can be as important as the 'who'. It would be a mistake to assume a stable, proportional, monotonic relationship between calendar-years and subjective disamenity. A weighting scheme might be needed to incorporate the revision in reactions and expectations. Each life-year might not be equally valued. The perception of good health might be susceptible to valuation shift. The life cycle of the condition has an impact on the stage in its evolution when the survey should be carried out.

Immediately after a life-changing intervention the patient may experience severe distress. A woman just after a mastectomy or a teenager who has lost a leg may feel that life has lost much or all of its attraction. Later on, coping strategies come onstream and the reference points are rebased. Experienced patients with long-term handicaps adapt to their wheelchairs and their insulin injections to the point where the inconvenience is a bygone that is under control. It is the new normal. In this respect they are similar to the lottery winners whose perceived happiness rises at first and then falls back to a long-established plateau.

The fox writes off the grapes that it cannot reach. It is therefore important for the investigator to conduct the survey at the correct moment in time. An assessment invited just after the loss of an endowment will elicit a quality adjustment different from the preference revealed once the sufferer has settled into the new normal. It would clearly save money if the policymakers could ground policy on the long-settled anchors and not the recent victims. Observers who concentrate on the immediate impact while ignoring the compensatory contrast and the habituation tend to 'see actors as more distressed by their misfortune than the actors see themselves ... Severe outcomes do not have as great an impact as might be expected' (Brickman et al., 1978: 926). People bounce back once the new base-point has become embedded. The self-rating of the health state might go up as the sufferers become accustomed to their disability. It might even return to 1. Time heals all wounds

It need not be so. Some people will become reconciled to the new scenario. Some will not. For them severe pain and impeded mobility might over time be perceived as progressively less tolerable. Marginal utility diminishes. At the end of some maximum endurable period, people might come to see their lives as little more than the anteroom to scrap. Becoming disheartened, they might come to rank such states as worse than death itself.

Sackett and Torrance studied dialysis patients. They found that mean daily satisfaction fell with the length of time spent in the sick-role. Home dialysis for eight years delivered only 0.65 of the satisfaction attached to perfect health. Home dialysis for life was 0.40. Hospital dialysis for life was 0.32. Hospital confinement for life for a contagious disease was 0.16 (Sackett and Torrance, 1978: 701). When the prognosis shifts from treatable to permanent, the fall in expected happiness falls too. The appropriate moment in the life cycle of the condition must be selected with care. Early, later, later still – the choice of the time has an impact on the sensations that will be revealed.

3.2 WILLINGNESS TO SPEND

Questionnaires and surveys are 'what if'. Observations are 'what is'. Observations are choices. Choices are eloquent. Actions speak at least as loudly as words. Anyone can tell an investigator that the right contribution towards a rescue helicopter is $56. The bottom line is, however, how much people actually put in when the hat is passed round. Talk is cheap and speech is free. Participant observation might in the circumstances give the better insight into the hidden mind of which no more than the shadow on the wall can ever be seen.

Market economics is the natural habitat of purposive action. Its subject matter is marginal expenditure rationally bartered for incremental utility in the light of the next-best foregone. Revealed exchanges are taken to be the observable manifestation of consumer sovereignty and respect for persons. The same emphasis on devolution and decentralisation may be carried over from the market for bread, beer and meat into the market for gold fillings, weekend surgery, home delivery to make childbirth more meaningful, and poisons purchased because a substandard existence has become an economic bad.

Payment proxies the satisfaction anticipated. Sometimes, as in the case of a famous surgeon, a brand-name drug or an aerobics class, it will be money spent in anticipation of a better health status. Sometimes, as in the case of fat, cocaine and beer, it will be money spent to purchase short-run gratification that the body-holder demonstrably ranks above a long life and a boring one. Sometimes, as in the case of health insurance, it will be money spent myopically and emotionally on inflated policies that do not track probable frequencies: 'Sometimes people's confusion and worry lead them to buy insurance at a price considerably in excess of their expected loss and in situations where they could afford to be without coverage if they were maximizing their expected utility' (Kunreuther et al., 2013: 268). Always, however, the liberal individualist will say that the realised outturn is a reasonable indicator of people's desires and intentions. Doing is not thinking. The liberal individualist is reluctant nonetheless to admit that people normally act on impulse.

Liberal individualists believe that reservation prices and self-governing negotiation flag up the consumer's secret wants and intensities. They are a way into a cave that is forever dark. They are also a tiger in the path of a national health care policy that strives to be responsive and in touch. On the one hand there is the value judgement that morbidity and mortality are objective indicators that signpost the national health. On the other hand there is the value judgement that tolerance of diversity is the highest court, the meta-indicator of revealed good health. There is no conflict so long as the information signalled through the choices made is fully in line with the objective measures of illness and death. What, however, should a bubble-up social policy aim to achieve if 'completeness' as defined by the World Health Organization leads it in one direction while good health as defined by the Clapham omnibus takes it in another?

People swim on secluded beaches because the beach with the lifeguard is crowded and noisy. They drink tap water even though they know that bottled water will better shield them from disease. They pass up organic vegetables because the pesticides and the insecticides cost them less. They buy cheap appliances that might give them an electric shock. They economise on insurance upgrades because they cannot imagine a need for expensive chemotherapy. They fail to screw on childproof safety-caps because protection for the curious uses up scarce time. They travel by motorbike, unlicensed taxis and shoestring airlines because the first-class alternative is sold at a first-class price.

People live in crime-ridden boroughs, or near firing ranges, or on flood plains, or on polluted main roads, or on fire-trap top floors, or without alarms and extinguishers, because they want to make a saving on rent. They jay-walk against the traffic lights because time is money and a wait is a nuisance. They dispense with protective goggles and cumbersome harnesses because a worker on piecework does not put safety first. They drink home-brewed moonshine. They turn down nutritious mackerel. In ways such as these they are revealing the value that they put on their good health and even their life. Yet it is not the maximum value that they could have secured if they had made up their mind to go for health and longevity and nothing else.

There are people who do not take their iron supplements or wear their crash helmets or invest in fallout shelters. There are people who go in for gang warfare, scale sheer rock faces or paraglide over crocodiles. The preferences they reveal give little support to the hypothesis that they assign an infinite value to health and life. What the evidence does suggest is that they are willing to exchange some probable survival for some present advantage in the manner described as follows by Rachel Dardis: 'Suppose 1,000 persons require a compensation of $100 due to a decrease in survival probability of 0.001, then the estimated value of a life is $100 thousand for individuals in the community ... This does not mean that any one individual will be willing to sacrifice his life for $100 thousand' (Dardis, 1980: 1078).

Choices can be made for others. Methodological individualism is not the same as egocentric selfishness. Even so, what remains constant is the mindset inferred from real-world preferences demonstrably put on display. The parent who voluntarily buys and correctly installs a safety seat for a young child is incurring both a financial cost and a time cost but is also buying a probability. The chance that the child will die in a road accident is being reduced by 4.1/10 000. The implicit value of that child's life may be as much as $526 827 (Carlin and Sandy, 1991: 196).

The value is derived from the revealed preferences of the parent. The under-four's valuation of his or her well-being is not known. Alter is not ego. Jones-Lee established that people believed the lives of friends and relatives to be worth little more than 40 per cent of their own (Jones-Lee et al., 1985: 69). Even close kin refuse to donate a kidney or share their spleen. Even devoted pensioners live self-indulgently on potential bequests. Parental love and sense of duty may raise the explanatory value of self-denying altruism. If Jones-Lee is right, it is unlikely on average to reach 100 per cent.

Preferences revealed through residential smoke detectors and child safety seats take the place of questions and answers, words and 'what ifs'. The historical record chronicles the altered probability of injury and death that was implicit when real-world shoppers were observed to spend their time and money on a given economic tradeable and to reject its next-best rival out there. The evidence may be interpreted as the equilibrium price at which they were willing to speculate on the utility of being. Morbidity and mortality to them were not exogenous variables but endogenous choices. Illness and death were self-selected at the margin by the discrete life-holder who alone can say where the shoe pinches and by how much.

Inducing the implicit from the explicit is a democratic mode of data collection. It has the advantage that people are seen to be putting resources where their mouth is. The disadvantage is the ambiguity. Yesterday's vintage is making decisions *de facto* for a later cohort that may prefer a different journey. Perry Como is not the Big Bang Boy Band. Nor is that the only blur. Death and injury, damage and destruction, are two distinct outcomes of a single decision to drink and drive. Preferences revealed are seldom sufficiently transparent for the outsider to discriminate between the two joint products. It is seldom clear if it is mortality or morbidity that is entering into the health-holders' mental calculus when they are buying an old banger with ailing brakes or drinking strong coffee with extra caffeine.

Brute life-years are not the only consideration. Individuals take into account the complementary disutilities of pain and suffering, disfigurement and unemployment, as well as the extinction of physical existence itself, when they are revealing their willingness to pay. An airbag provides data relevant to two health-related outcomes and not only one. Double-counting pushes up the profits where the airbag is taken to indicate the length but not the quality or the enjoyment of life.

Insurance complicates the interpretation of the evidence. Willingness to pay will only approximate the intensity of desire where individuals are trading their own *quid pro quo* for their own private satisfaction. Sacrifice prepaid through an insurance pool means that the payment is not the authentic metric that it would have been if the economist's full market price had had to be supported out of pocket. Because reimbursement distorts the information, it may be preferable to draw inferences exclusively from subjects who face major deductibles or pay the whole bill on their own. They are not likely to be very representative.

Reimbursement aside, there is also moral hazard. Subjects with cover may be taking risks that they would otherwise have eschewed. Their behaviour patterns may have been altered by their insurance. If this is the case, then the measured value of injury and death will not be the same.

Ironically, the very purchase of high-standard safety and security may be a cause of moral hazard as well. A do-it-yourselfer, aware that the drill is protected by a Perspex hood, no longer pays attention to the cable which gives him a shock. A motorist, lulled into overconfidence by a padded dashboard and a shatterproof windscreen, speeds recklessly through the lights. Jurisprudence and legislation in cases like these may actually be the cause of an accident or a smash. Safety regulations may reduce the old probabilities but introduce new probabilities in their stead. The new risks will make new regulations inescapable. Even in the field of health the Heisenberg Principle is all around.

3.3 WILLINGNESS TO EARN

There are no markets in certain death. The labour market does, however, deal in the risk of death. The danger differential is the monetary bribe that the risk-averse will demand in exchange for the higher probability that they will lose their life or good health. The premium is certain. The outcomes are statistical. The individual's implicit valuation of their own statistical life and capacities can be worked out by an actuary who knows how to compute the flow into a stock.

Such a computation was made by Moore and Viscusi. Using statistics on death at work in the United States, they discovered that there was 'a powerful and statistically significant positive relationship between job risks and worker wages' (Moore and Viscusi, 1988: 477). They found that the average employee required at least an extra $43.4 per annum to accept a higher chance of death of 1/100 000. The implication is that the monetary value of one life lost as seen by the workers themselves is a minimum of $4.34 million (Moore and Viscusi, 1988: 486).

Danger money quantifies the perceived hazard. Like unpleasant surroundings, unattractive locations, repellant associates and alienating tasks, the threat to life and limb is a part of Alfred Marshall's compensating variations (Marshall, 1949 [1890]: 463), of Adam Smith's 'ease or hardship' (Smith, 1961 [1776]: I, 112), that have a major impact on the hierarchy of pay. Like an extra payment for a safer product, extra remuneration is what the worker must be paid to work with a contaminated landfill emitting radon gas. There is a reference point and a final destination. The workers themselves are being asked for a minimum sum that would make them feel better off in their own estimation.

Bodyguards, police informants and deep-sea divers can earn more than well-educated graduate bookkeepers. Window cleaners on skyscraper floors can earn more than window cleaners who are afraid of heights. Between occupations or within occupations, higher pay is normally the incentive to bear higher risk. Without the carrot of $1000 a day, no one but the foolhardy and the thrill-seeking would apply to be a fisherman in the Alaskan shellfish industry (Christie, 2003). At 400 deaths per 100 000 workers, it would be safer to be a test pilot going supersonic (67 deaths) or a lumberjack wielding a circular saw (127 deaths).

Coal miners demand extra money for blasting underground. Construction workers demand extra money for working on scaffolds and roofs. The extra payment quantifies their subjective assessment of the extra risk. It is their willingness to accept, their willingness to tolerate the small but real probability that something will go wrong.

Lionel Needleman collected data on the risk premium that British building workers were requiring to chance a fall. The 'condition money' they were demanding suggested that a worker who became a scaffolder would be able to command an income some 10 to 15 per cent more than the same grade of labour on the ground. The mark-up was finely calibrated, rising in bands from 30 to 75 feet, 75 to 100 feet, 100 to 150 feet (Needleman, 1980: 235–6). The official figures put the increased likelihood of premature death due to a fall from heights at 0.52/1000. The workers themselves had only a passing need for the *Digest of Incapacity Statistics*. They were a closed community. They had learned from experience what the hierarchy of falls was likely to be. They did not need the International Labour Organization to describe to them the blood on the ground.

Deep-seam blasters dwell in one pool. Steel-erectors dwell in another. Always assuming that the locals know their own differentials, still it is not possible to select any one micro-pool and make it the sensitive indicator of the whole. A cook is not an electrician. A fireman is not a dustman. Viscusi concedes that it might be difficult to find a single value in a thicket of heterogeneities: 'The value of life is not a universal constant, but reflects the wage–risk tradeoff pertinent to the preferences of the workers in a particular sample. The mix of workers in these samples is quite different' (Viscusi, 1993: 1930). No one group is necessarily the median group that comes closest to the typical mind.

A typical mind is hard to find. Nor is it obvious that the labour market is the right place to look. The differentials might not mean what the free marketeers expect. Wages, at least in the short run, are inflexible with respect to supply and demand. Pay structures can be rigid, administered and insensitive. Institutions and precedents can perpetuate outdated relativities. Some occupations have little or no risk. Housewives and pensioners do not have the option of danger money. An exploitative monopsonist might deny danger money because the involuntarily unemployed will take up any slack. Pay that does not move with the compensating variations cannot be expected to shadow the subjective estimation of morbidity and mortality. Economists assume rationality. Ordinary people just get on with their lives.

Danger differentials might not be proportional to comparable riskiness because many submarkets will be isolated and provincial. The extrapolations might not be transferable. Within our group the incidence of black-lung disease is common knowledge. Outside our group our members do not know. Our members do not know the mortality rate associated with working with lions in the zoo. Our members do not know if laundry workers are paid enough to compensate them for the steam and the solvent. Our members do not know. Because they do not know, they will not be able to risk-rate the pay they are being offered in the next-best industry into which they might conceivably migrate.

Migration itself is not a frictionless transition. Occupational and geographical barriers restrict mobility from one subtrade to another. Change of any kind involves transaction costs. Entry may be impossible without job-specific vocational training. Exit is costly where human capital must be scrapped and new skills built up. The investment made, success is not guaranteed.

Fear of the unknown is the greatest of all exit barriers. What this means is that windfalls and shortfalls can survive even into the long run. Arbitrage cannot meaningfully be conducted where investors are stuck in a fixed habitat, in familiar terrain which a combination of anxiety and myopia makes them reluctant to quit. Real-world danger money in the instant when the economist cross-sections his hierarchy is, one suspects, more likely to be indicative of a general direction than it is to be precisely plumbed, statistically fine-tuned: 'It is a bit like asking someone what the weather is like outside – they can give a reasonable idea, but not an exact temperature ... It would be a mistake to draw sharp conclusions based on an estimate' (Cutler, 2004: 16).

Adjustments take time. That, and not transition-free comparative statics, is how markets work. Human life is a never-ending process, a 'voyage of exploration into the unknown': 'All economic problems are caused by unforeseen changes which require adaptation' (Hayek, 1948: 101). People accept a job. They find out later about the particulates, the acids and the rusty blades. After that they learn that the factory is converting to liquid plutonium stored in an unsecured vat. They revise their expectations in light of their flaking skin and their loss of hair. They move on as a consequence of what they have learned: 'Job risks raise worker quit rates ... Job risks account for as much as one-third of all manufacturing quit rates' (Viscusi, 1992: 109).

Experience leads to switch. It is optimisation through search. Either the risks go down or the pay goes up or the worker goes out. Ignorance at the beginning does not mean ignorance at the end. It does, however, mean that a social philosopher who wants to use differentials as a citizen's-eye perspective on the value of health must wait patiently for the market-clearing equilibrium moment when it will be meaningful to snap his still. It may be a long wait. In a dynamic economy where the kaleidoscope of novelty is constantly in flux, the pay and the probability may never settle into the first-year textbook's perpetual rest.

Time and space conceal the risks. Damage can be immediate when a bus goes off a cliff because of a defective clutch. It can also be drip-fed, deferred and latent. Workers who ruin their health with phosphorus might only be seen to be terminally ill when, much later and far away, they are holding a job in a hamburger restaurant. The cause of their premature death will be even more obscure where they have held a succession of jobs. If the first involved lead-based defoliants, the second asbestos fibres, the third vinyl chloride, the precise carcinogen that finished the man off may never be known. Nor it will ever be certain that the damage was actually done by low-level radiation or childhood exposure to benzene. Genes have an effect on health. So does luck. So does heavy drinking. Heavy drinking is not necessarily a reaction to eye-strain, noise or vibrating machinery nine-to-five.

Multiple causality, latency and long gestation periods make it difficult to risk-rate the competing industries. Cognitive bias means that newsworthy disasters displace upwards the perceived threat to seamen from piracy, while leaving neglected and unnoticed the high probability of heart attacks and diabetes among swanky chefs who cater for Cordon Bleu. Mind and matter, in other words, might not move in step: 'Workers' demand for extra compensation is not necessarily based on the actual risks of each job but on what they think the risks are. Most of the occupational causes of death are not obvious' (Marin and Psacharopoulos, 1982: 831).

Perceived probability can be false consciousness. True or false, still it is the perceived probability upon which actual decisions are made. Objective values can be culled from the Annuals. It is unlikely that the body-holder does much culling when they binge on chocolate or go for a swim. Paternalists know the facts. Citizens who want accuracy should fire the people and follow the paternalists instead.

Risks can be inaccurately estimated. So can rewards. As well as the pecuniary packet the workers will often receive fringe benefits. Supplementary concessions might be regarded as implied recognition of dangers and hazards in the job. Workers stationed on offshore oil rigs or in troubled war zones often enjoy lengthy periods of home leave. Workers are often given free medical insurance and a workmen's compensation scheme in the event that their pipeline is attacked or their plantation quarantined. Workers who have spent time in the field are often rewarded with promotions when they return home. The statistical risk might go up. Moral hazard can degrade the actuarial profile. Basic pay, on the other hand, might go down. Workers might be willing to accept a smaller pay differential if they knew that *ex post* they would not be left in the lurch.

Compensating differentials, both cash benefits and supplementary services, may be a way in to the subjective valuation of good health where real-world actors are deciding independently for themselves. They are more problematic where corporations and unions become active in collective bargaining. Collective bargaining produces a standardised settlement for the group as a whole. Such a block booking does not leave much room for the non-standard labour-lump to reveal a reservation price fully in line with their own private perceptions.

When corporations and unions take over the haggling role, they complement productivity with concentrated power. Monopolies and monopsonies negotiate not for the market-clearing price but for whatever they can get. It is difficult enough to interpret building workers' danger differentials in a world where smoking 20 cigarettes is twice as risky, riding a motorcycle three times as risky, as working at heights. It is even more difficult to read subjectivity into the resultant pay hierarchy when strong men hammer on the table and strong women refuse to deviate from their claim.

Olson found that union members commanded a substantially higher fatal accident premium (9.1 per cent) than did non-union members (1.6 per cent). The difference as compared with riskless occupations translates into a value of life of $8 million and $1.5 million, respectively. The weighted average might be about $3.2 million (Olson, 1981: 182, 184). The union premium can certainly be seen as a market-distorting disequilibrium pyramided upon imperfection and control. If it is, then the message it sends to the policymakers seriously overstates the contents of the hidden mind. There is, however, a different window. The premium that the union negotiates can be seen as a high-quality market signal that is conscientiously tuned to the relevant probabilities. The union is the doctor who knows what the principal requires. The union member is the patient who relies upon their agent for the facts.

Workers covered by collective agreements are likely to be better informed about chemical residues, toxic gases and odourless formaldehyde. Their unions are there to obtain accurate information and to diffuse it widely. There is also a dynamic dimension. Agreements with management often guarantee the unions a seat on the firm's safety committee. Where the accident rate subsequently falls because they have brought shop-floor knowledge to the table, the unions can pass the gains on to their members in the next pay round. The pay–productivity nexus afterwards is not the same as the pay–productivity curve before: 'Union firms are more efficient at producing safety' (Olson, 1981: 184).

However closely the differentials run parallel to the risks, still they are not compensation for risk and nothing more. They are also a proxy measure of disutility. The jointness in production resembles the ambiguity in consumption that was discussed in section 3.2. The disutility supplement is the incentive that attracts workers into dirty jobs performed in antisocial hours. It is a part of the observed differential. It is also surplus information when it is the footprints of mortality and morbidity that are being tracked. A disutility differential by itself does not trace out the perceived threat to life and limb.

Fires in the oil fields are put out by highly paid specialists. Their high pay reflects the ever-present chance of death, but also the disutility of living apart from their family and friends. Roofers who might slip demand remuneration over the odds. Their higher remuneration picks up the greater probability of a fatal fall. Yet it also mirrors the discomfort of being in the open in inclement weather and the greater likelihood of a non-fatal fall which leaves them handicapped and unable to earn: 'Jobs that are risky tend to be unpleasant in other respects' (Viscusi, 1993: 1919).

Black boxes must be unpacked if the wild animals, the loose girders and the inmate lifers are to be converted into a subjective valuation of life and limb. Not the whole of the wage differential proxies the life-or-death decision. Olson said that only 35 per cent of the top-up could in fact be attributed to the fear of a fatal outcome (Olson, 1981: 184). Of the remaining 65 per cent, an unspecified share could be attributed to non-fatal injury and a further share, also unspecified, to the rain and the sleet. It is all relevant to the subjective valuation of one job over another. Yet it is not the port in a storm where actuaries valuing life and limb would most like to dock their craft.

3.4 A REPRESENTATIVE SAMPLE

Jim Jones is on display. Photographed with his daughter and a puppy called Spot, he is not a nameless castaway somewhere in the Pacific or a faceless astronaut stranded in space. Jim Jones is a unique human being with a unique set of preferences to reveal. Jim is not a statistical frequency but a beating heart. We all know Jim. We see him every day on the number 88 bus, every night on the N19 that bypasses Clapham because it is not safe.

Jim Jones is a fully representative sample of Jim Jones. Through his words and his deeds Jim Jones has revealed what 'completeness' means to him. A liberal democracy is morally obliged to respect the standard of 'completeness' that Jim Jones has said is the right one for himself: 'The distributional issue is then: should the health service value health benefits more highly if they accrue to people who, by their behaviour, clearly value their own health more highly? Put more bluntly, should we discriminate against heavy smokers, heavy drinkers, obese people, free-fall parachutists, unclean people, etc.? ... Should we value that (most costly) benefit differently if people appear *from their own behaviour* not themselves to care much about their own health?' (Williams, 1997: 289).

Jim Jones has told us who he is. He is Jim Jones who has destroyed his liver through drink. Jim Jones has spoken. The decision that his health service must make is whether to love him precisely as he loves himself or whether it ought to love the deviant in line with the standards of the median. Jim as a body-capitalist has indicated that he is prepared if need be to impose capital punishment on himself. Should the community allow self-destroying Jim to put an above-average strain on its national health care budget? What right does the community have to assign the lexicographic priority to its revealed preferences rather than to Jim's revealed preferences? The community is putting the collective consciousness above the self-inflicted idiosyncrasy. It is saying what it thinks Jim's health status ought to be. Jim and Jim's community do not see eye to eye.

There is worse to come. If common resources are to be allocated in line with the social consensus, then it is essential for public policy to build up an accurate picture of the representative citizen on the representative omnibus. The invisible mind must be reconstructed out of shadows and hints. It is detective work. Sometimes even the detectives get it wrong.

3.4.1 The Choice of the Sample

The benchmark is unanimity. The reality is economics. Time and money make it impossible to sound out the whole. The desire to generalise must be balanced against the cost of information. A sample is inevitable. Jim Jones is a first-rate sample of Jim Jones. And who is the first-rate sample that speaks convincingly for thee and me? Should it be the snake charmer, the forest monk, the bomb disposal addict, the quarryman dicing with explosives? Should it be the roofers? Should it be the menopausal women? Advancing outward from autobiography, anthropology and psychology to political sociology and then on to public policy, what is clear is that 'completeness' can never be complete unless the subgroup selected is truly the typical subgroup that speaks for us all.

Some members of the community are so risk-averse that they lock their doors after dark and never talk to strangers. Some are so risk-loving that they go in for stock-car races and go out with promiscuous partners. The 'completeness' of the one is not the 'completeness' of the other. Generalisation only makes sense where there is a conspicuous spike in support of a modal viewpoint. If there is no spike, then there is Jim Jones and Jane Jones and that is all. The hidden mind cannot be inferred and extrapolated from the shadows on the wall. It is information overload. There are too many shadows. They are crowding out the wall.

The picture of national good health, common good health, is only as good as the choice of the sample. It must be large enough to be free from selection bias but not so large as to impose an intolerable cost. It must also be a good cross-section of the population as a whole. Relevant attributes will normally include age, income, wealth, race, education, occupation, gender, marital status and geographical location, together with lifestyle situators such as smoking. The mix is intended to cancel out the dispersion.

The sample must be sensitive to economic status. There are likely to be patterned differences in the marginal utility of income. They show up in the incremental willingness to take a chance. If not all individuals are equally risk-averse, an important reason is that not all individuals can afford the luxury.

Life and limb enjoy a high income elasticity of demand. Biddle and Zarkin, showing that 'job risk is an inferior good', situate the negative response in the range from −1.5 to −2.5 (Biddle and Zarkin, 1988: 667). Marin and Psacharopolous actually recommend that the sample should be stratified. That, they say, is how society is built up: 'If the sample is split into groups, the value of life implied for manual workers is … in the £600,000–£700,000 range, while the value of life implied for non-manual workers is over three times as high. This is expected given that safety is a superior good' (Marin and Psacharopoulos, 1982: 848). Danger is bad and safety is good. It is more likely to be the low-paid and the blue-collar who self-select themselves into the gypsum mines. It is less likely to be the senior executives and the leading accountants who mule the narcotics for the drug barons.

That is why an estimation of the value of life and limb from the danger differentials of construction workers may be partial and misleading. Even among male manufacturing workers, the roofers and the scaffolders might not be median men in the middle. The pool is disproportionately young, single and adventurous. The young, logically speaking, ought to be more risk-averse than the average. They have more life-years to lose. The stream of their expected earnings, suitably discounted, is much greater than that of an older worker nearing retirement. Logic tells only a part of the story. If they are by temperament more devil-may-care than the middle-aged and the professional, then their danger differential may be no more than that. It is their danger differential. It cannot safely be employed to quantify the risk appetite of their nation as a whole.

The trade-off may be unrepresentative because of the kind of people who are attracted onto the roof. Viscusi found a correlation between risk-intensive employments and risk-tolerant employees: 'While smokers work, on average, in industries with higher injury risk than non-smokers, smokers also are more likely to have a work-related injury controlling for injury risk. Smokers are also prone to have had a recent non-work-related injury' (Viscusi and Aldy, 2003: 16). There are many different kinds of risk. The roofers were responding to the risk of falls. They were not responding to the risk of cancer. They were focusing on their feet and not their lungs. Their peripheral vision was weak. At least they did not fall from height.

The roofers were not setting their lives at nought. They were asking for a bribe in the lottery of death that would leave their level of contentment at least the same on the roof as it was on the ground. The actual mark-up was lower nonetheless than if the sample group had been made up of teetotal clerks who obsessively washed their hands, cut the fat off their meat and reduced road-risks by walking to work. It is not certain. White-collar workers do not receive a danger differential. The comparison cannot be made.

The sample can be occupational. It can also be clinical. A subset of perimenopausal women or of kidney patients on dialysis would be a condition-specific panel. So would an ethnic group susceptible to an uncommon blood disorder that is refracted through local knowledge and a culture that is closed to tourists. The afflicted and the susceptible are informed but they are not detached. Their response rate to a general survey will be abnormally high. They are unlikely to provide the impartial intelligence that can be generalised to the community as a whole.

Insiders have local knowledge but they are also biased: 'Current sufferers ... may tend to overstate their own cases relative to other groups, thus undermining the notion of some general basis of comparison' (Loomes and McKenzie, 1989: 305). Sackett and Torrance found that patients on home dialysis assigned a higher utility to kidney dialysis than did the general public (Sackett and Torrance, 1978: 702). Dialysis patients assigned a higher utility to dialysis than they did to sports injuries or tuberculosis. They were receiving treatment. Current poor health resulted in a higher valuation of the care that was making them well. They were not suffering from malaria. Even if the statistical outcomes were the same, still they tended to think that the mosquitoes should paddle their own canoe.

The danger is blinkered obsessiveness and special pleading. Rawls draws attention to the possibility of hijacking and crowding-in on the part of utility monsters who have an abnormal capacity to be over the moon: 'Imagine two persons, one satisfied with a diet of milk, bread and beans, while the other is distraught without expensive wines and exotic dishes' (Rawls, 1982: 168). In such a case it is the complainer who is given the most precisely because deprivation to the insider would cause the greater unhappiness. Utility is maximised because the subjectively underattended get extra resourcing while the subjectively stoical feel grateful for an aspirin and a cup of tea.

Given the heterogeneity of the human experience, it is not easy to know which part may be the litmus test for the whole. The representative citizen, like the representative firm, may be a figment of the intellectual's imagination. A representative sample is hard to find. The alternative is to say that each sample is discrete and free-standing and that the anecdotes must be placed in the scrapbook one by one. It is Jim Jones again. It is as transparent as an art gallery or the animals in the zoo. So long, however, as there is no index or comparative metric, it is unlikely to contribute very much to public policy.

3.4.2 The Nationalisation of the Sample

A liberal democracy is obliged to match its policies to the preferences of its citizens. Its choices must reflect the standard of good health that its citizens believe to be right for them. How many traffic policemen will our nation need if the kill-factor on the roads is to be reduced by 10 per cent? Should we build a costly sea wall when there is a 5 per cent probability that without it 150 lives will be lost in a typhoon? What budget should we allocate to heart transplants, free school milk, street lighting and closed-circuit cameras in each deserted underpass? How much should we spend to protect the vicinity against nuclear fallout in the unlikely event that a reactor melts down? These questions involve our common resources and our shared priorities. Someone has to come up with an answer.

Moral philosophy suggests that life and health should be treated as ends that are *non est disputandum*. So does medicine, which has an instinctive revulsion to any policy that would degrade the sacred to the status of a choice. Economics, however, issues a warning that resources are finite, that even governments must be cost-conscious, and that no purchase should exceed its next-best foregone.

Not everyone is comfortable with the interpretation of good health and life itself as an economic tradeable. Willingness to pay and willingness to be paid factor down a human right to the level of utils, reservation prices, marginal benefits and rates of return. A human right becomes the marginal rate of substitution of wealth for risk. It feels sordid. Perhaps it is not. Economics, like democracy, has its roots in liberal individualism. The values that it marketises may be pecuniary but still they are the individual's own. The proprietor of the asset makes the final call. Commodities in the shops are only worth what the decision-makers think they are worth. Health and life are commodities like any other.

Economics is private choice. Politics is public choice. Unifying both is a respect for the individual and, scaling up, for the social consensus.

Governments are the agents who must satisfy their principals or hand on their mandate. A democracy cannot promulgate laws that deviate significantly from the attitudes of the typical and the representative. Revealed preferences, in words or in deeds, are the way in which governments tap into the contents of the hidden mind.

Comparison and aggregation are never easy. Interpersonal valuation is that much more difficult where people are divided into subgroups that respond to different risks with different degrees of intensity. Not all subgroups think alike or want the same thing. They differ in their knowledge of the other groups' risk profile and propensities. Roofers can be compared with scaffolders but not with office cleaners, chemotherapy patients or toddlers at risk from a plastic toy. The ideal is to compare like with like, Jim Jones with Jim Jones. Public policy, however, is condemned to across-the-board generalisation. It is obliged to decide which group, if any group, best expresses the value laid up in the hidden mind.

Generalisation is difficult. There is so much dispersion in exhilaration and discontentment that is hard to imagine what that single consensual 'completeness' would actually be. The studies reinforce the ambiguities. The value of life differs with the subgroup that reveals the preference: US$7.2 million, $9.7 million, $10.3 million, $16.2 million, $2.8 million, $1.6 million and $700 000 are only some of the values that have been recorded (Viscusi, 1993: 1926–7). Most values lie in the range between $3.8 million and $9 million. The median is about $7 million (Viscusi and Aldy, 2003: 18). It costs $1.3 million per statistical life saved to instal car side-door protection (Viscusi, 1993: 1913). Which is the 'right' value with which the $1.3 million should be compared? Which social group is the sensitive social bellwether that converts the micro into the macro because it is reliably in touch with the common mind?

Blomquist extrapolated his value of life from the 23 per cent of American drivers who voluntarily invested in car seat belts (Blomquist, 1979: 556). He did not take into account the subjective valuations of the 77 per cent who wrote off the risk. The same is true of Dardis. Although the annualised value of a smoke detector (including the battery) was a mere $4.34, only 13 per cent of American households were making the investment (Dardis, 1980: 1082). The value of life was calculated on the basis of the 13 per cent of Americans who were spending their $4.34. It would have been much lower if it had been calculated on the basis of the 87 per cent who were not safety-conscious. Then there are the roofers and the scaffolders. Do they have any idea of the statistical frequencies? Are they really the typical members of our national community?

Public policy is a public good. It is a general standard, applicable to all if it is applicable to any. It must be broadly in keeping with the attitudes of the citizenship base. The leadership must keep one ear to the ground. It can do this through questionnaires and surveys, through spending and earning. It can do this through the ballot box by means of a single-issue referendum.

A single-issue referendum has the advantage that it directly polls the citizenship pool. All citizens are invited to reveal their preferences. Unlike the preferences revealed in the economic market where incomes are not the same, in the democratic vote the spendable tokens are dead-level equal. Outcomes are determined by one person, one vote.

Equality can be a weakness as well as a strength. Simple headcounting is ordinal rather than cardinal. It quantifies the rank orderings but not the intensity of the preferences or the interval between them. What is important is not just 'which' but also 'by how much'. If a minority is more passionate than the mainstream, a policy that satisfies the place-holder in the middle might not produce the greatest happiness of the greatest number (Buchanan and Tullock, 1962). The marginal and the fringe might know better.

Nor is it only those personally affected who will be giving their view. The quality of life quantified through the vote will often relate not to ego's own expected utility but to the imagined utility of an unknown stranger. Voters are asked to imagine themselves into the health status of a diabetic, an Alzheimer's patient, a future child as yet unborn. They are being asked to discount the happiness of the wheelchair-bound when the vote is on funding for ramps and lifts at the expense of schools and swings. Even if they can manage a non-random opinion, still it is bordering on the immoral for outsiders to impose their interpersonal comparisons on unknown others. Jim Jones does not want their empathy. He wants what makes him feel better in his own personal and private estimation.

Even where the voters are informed and alert, still Jane is guessing for Jim and the results are not therefore ego-centric. If the standard of good health is to be built up from revealed preferences, then it is the individual and not the whole that must quality-adjust the life-years. It is not very satisfying. One alternative is to minimise the common sector so as to maximise the scope for Jim Jones to shape his own fate. Another alternative is to abandon the search for subjectivity in favour of medical procedures allocated through a lottery or a throw of the dice. There is a third alternative. The constitutional way would be to continue to collect revealed preferences but to collect them behind a veil.

In-period there is bound to be bias. We know who we are. Multi-period it is the void. Anything can happen. Behind the veil even the self-seeking become even-handed. Priority-setting is no longer distorted by personal interest. No one knows enough about themself to end up the judge in their own cause. Cornishman or Welshwoman, young or old, the life they save may or may not be their own.

The veil in the sense of Rawls is radical ignorance in the here and now. It is a thought experiment and a let-us-assume. The veil in the sense of Buchanan is the pure uncertainty of the history-to-come. The future is an unwritten book. A person who is healthy today does not know how he will feel if he is unhealthy tomorrow. He does not know what treatment he will need. He does not know how he will pay for it. He does not know if it will buy him good health. He does not know if he will still be alive when the bill comes in.

Clothed in unknowledge the decision-makers are in a position to make an impartial choice. Perhaps they will concentrate resources on high-cost transplants that will break the bank. Perhaps they will prefer comprehensive screening for the latent, the asymptomatic and the rare. Bunching is rational if people's fears are single-peaked. Diversification is rational since you never can tell. It is not possible to say if rational people planning ahead will opt for catastrophic care or something-for-everyone. The definition of good health only means that Jim Jones should have the chance to speak his mind.

4. Inputs and outcomes

A cow eating grass in a meadow is not the same as a nourishing beefsteak that drives away the flu. A doctor watching television in a bar is not the same as a robed crusader who whips out a tumour. The doctor, like the cow, is an input. The flu, like the tumour, is an outcome. The input is the means. The output is the end. They are not the same.

Eggs are not omelettes and wards are not cures. Still, however, there is a human propensity to treat the parts as valued contributors to the well-being of the whole. Health care leads the field in eagerness and optimism. In few other areas of social life is there a greater willingness to take spend as a proxy for success. It may be wishful thinking to assume that more means more but it is nonetheless a near-universal heuristic. Most people treat the sirloins and the surgeons as a sacred cow. Most people oppose cuts in care because economies at the margin will infect our fellow citizens with sneezes and coughs.

The link, however ill-specified, has the force of a shared conviction. It is a non-rational representation that must be treated with respect. This chapter is concerned with the principal inputs which are commonly believed to make us well. They are discussed in five sections: 'Medical care', 'Care beyond medicine', 'Jurisprudence and legislation', 'Prosperity and progress' and 'Increments and totals'.

4.1 MEDICAL CARE

The first step is to define the components. The second step is to aggregate them into a single index. Neither step is easy. Health care is slippery and ambiguous. There is no way of knowing if either step has been properly performed.

4.1.1 The List

Any list of inputs into the health status production function must include the familiar elements that make up medical care, narrowly defined. The candidates with a heartbeat will be the general practitioners, hospital doctors, radiographers, physiotherapists, pharmacists, hospital nurses, district nurses, health visitors, dentists and other certified professionals. The candidates without a heartbeat will be the hospital beds, diagnostic equipment and therapeutic facilities, together with medical complements such as gloves, ambulances, drugs, wheelchairs, dentures and walking-frames that support the fixed capital and raise the productivity of the animate and the thinking.

Figures are normally expressed as a ratio of the relevant population in order to obtain an indication of their significance. A weighted proportion makes possible sensible comparisons with the experience of other catchments and countries. The figures can be disaggregated by regional or other subgrouping in order to prevent microsocial variance from disappearing into national aggregates. They can be presented either as a numerical headcount or in the language of prices and costs. Clinical adequacy must be complemented by bookkeeping and finance in order to obtain an overall perspective.

Availability must be shaded to allow for utilisation. Structures and staff are only inert potential until they spring into action. Flow rather than stock, additional information is therefore required on patient consultations, tests performed, dressings changed, interventions delivered, vaccinations administered, full bodies scanned. Bed occupancy, bed turnover, hospital throughput, the number of doctor-hours actually devoted to patient care are all indicators that supply is indeed coming together with demand.

As well as availability, as well as utilisation, there is also quality. Comparisons can only be made where the standard of treatment is the same. Most people know that it is not. The problem is that few people can say what it is. Quality is difficult to define or to measure. There is no consensus on the nature of the beast. There is no central agency that collects and processes the data: 'We have no mandatory national system and few local systems to track the quality of care delivered to the American people. More information is available on the quality of airlines, restaurants, cars, and VCRs [videocassette recorders] than on the quality of health care' (Schuster et al., 1998: 517–8).

It is hard to be a rational shopper if there is no assurance that the product is quality-constant. It is hard to be a rational voter if the cost is being trimmed. Inconsistencies abound but the adjustment must be made. Three approaches are especially relevant to the reconstruction of essential information that is not accessible to the naked eye.

The first approach is to take the specifications of the input as a proxy for its standard. Relevant observations might include the capital commitment per staffed bed, the vintage and make of equipment, the doctor–patient and nurse–patient ratios, the number of specialists on the hospital's panel, the reliance on electronic monitoring and computerised record-keeping. Other observations will have an educational element. High-level proficiency may be inferred from involvement in research, decennial recertification, in-service training, 'conspicuous production' in the form of staff trained in the high-prestige 'Ivy League'.

Recent accreditation by a respected body such as The Joint Commission (TJC), the Joint Commission International (JCI) or the Healthcare Facilities Accreditation Program (HFAP), based in the United States, will indicate that the treatment centre has reached a known threshold. Division of labour implies a better medical encounter since group practices enable family doctors to fine-tune and specialise. Technology in the doctor's office, the practice of preventive medicine and the market value of referrals made to top-notch specialists may be taken to mean that primary doctors know their job.

A second approach to quality is to track goal attainment and not the treatments per se. The proof of the pudding is in the eating. If the patients return speedily to work, express satisfaction with the service, experience less-than-average rates of cross-infection, do not suffer from an allergic reaction or an addiction, are not readmitted precipitately with complications or a relapse, enjoy a longer life-expectancy because the affliction is gone, one inference might be that the quality of medical attention was good.

Quality in such a case is being shadowed by the outcomes. If the diagnosis is accurate, the dosage appropriate and the treatment works, then the inference is that the quality must be good. If the outcome is above average, then the quality must be above average too. If the patient is given the wrong operation or dies of complications that should have been anticipated, then the intuition is that the quality is deplorably substandard. It happens all the time: 'One study estimates that 50,000 to 100,000 people die every year of medical mistakes in hospitals, making hospital errors a leading cause of death' (Cutler, 2004: xi).

A final approach to quality is to fall back upon authority and experience. Good quality will here be defined as the quality that the wise and the certified have declared to be good. Such care will be care that has been validated by the doctors who are deemed to know best. Good quality is what the experts say it is. It is the benchmark that they impose and the expectation that they entertain. 'Good' means 'appropriate'. 'Appropriate' means 'execution in line with median medical opinion'.

'Too little' would not be good quality: underuse of inputs deprives the patients of their chance to get well. 'Too much' would not be good quality either: unnecessary tests or procedures expose the patients to discomfort, anxiety and risk without adding to full restoration of function. Situated between 'too much' and 'too little', the professional's eye-view would be that quality is conformity to the protocol. Middle-aged women should have a mammogram at least once in two years. Middle-aged men should be screened for cholesterol at least once in five years. That is the drill. Randomised controlled trials, international comparisons and tried-and-tested rules of thumb circumscribe the territory and say what is good.

4.1.2 An Aggregate Index

Inputs, like outputs, are a mixed bag. It is hard to add one doctor to one bed to one tablet. The normal method, eschewing crude numbers, is to use the common measuring rod of money. Shares of care in private and public budgets, rates of care-cost inflation and intertemporal and cross-country comparisons all make use of the monetary measure. Elections are won and lost because of the money standard.

It is a cause for concern since the data are impure. The private sector buys its inputs on the free market. The public sector buys some or all of its inputs at a notional value administered within the organisational bureaucracy. The former valuation reflects the derived demand of the final consumer and the surplus accruing to the profit-seeking business. The latter value will be an accounting magnitude that is proclaimed *ex cathedra*, often for political or social reasons, without reference to the subjective input or the competitive position. One sector is chalk and the other sector is cheese. The data obtained through simple summation of the two sectors are impure.

Total cost, moreover, is a statistical catch-all. The figure includes the fish-tank as well as the dermatologist, the prints on the wall as well as the open hearts. Not all of the outgoings are equally relevant to the core experience. Attractive as the garden and the day-room may well be, hotel services such as these should not be confused with the specifically medical nature of the clinical encounter.

Inefficiency itself artificially boosts the share. Above-average cost per case, unwarranted diagnostic tests, protracted inpatient convalescence, all become part of a bloated statistic which overstates what the nation is doing to help the sick. Unquestioned, the figures sound like ringworm arrested and hyposecretion turned round. Unpacked, they turn out to be the fish-tanks and the prints. Good surroundings unquestionably add something to the felt quality of the experience. It is, however, misleading to call them necessary stages on the road to health.

The aggregate index is used to quantify the inputs at a single point in time. It is also used to make intertemporal comparisons. Since reality is mutable and dynamic, such comparisons can be misleading. Like is not being added to like. The black box is not the same. The aggregate index aggregates different things.

Expectations change. Better-educated patients spend more time with the doctor and ask more questions. A consumer culture and a revised self-image not only put up the cost but also transform the specifications of the product. More-demanding patients derive satisfaction from the consultation itself. Previously they would have been happy to escape with some tablets.

Technology changes. New equipment pushes out the old. Today's drugs fill yesterday's void. Patients are managed differently by medical professionals who have had exposure to psychology, sociology and even economics. Generics are prescribed where formerly the aggregate would have been made up of patents and brands. The proportion of successes to total treatments may be higher.

Society changes. Inpatient stays go up because family members no longer see it as their filial duty to care for an Alzheimer's parent. Inpatient costs go down because psychiatric wards are being closed in favour of cheaper 'care in the community'. Society as well as technology is in flux. Like is not being added to like. Medicine used to be a cat. Now it is a dog. Intertemporal variations in aggregates and shares tell only a part of the story.

Cross-country comparisons are beset with problems of their own. Not only are exchange rates subject to fluctuation and the national accounts compiled using different schemata, but the medical care aggregate is not universally the same. Spas, sanatoria, optical care, a medical library, a works infirmary, pharmacist-only drugs, medical research are illustrations of elements that are included in some countries but excluded in others. In Asia there are Ayurveda, temple massage and traditional Chinese medicine. In Africa there are herbal compounds, divination and village midwives. Western definitions do not always correspond to non-Western practice. Heterogeneity makes it difficult to say that one country is spending significantly more or less on medical care than another.

Problematic though they may be, intercountry comparisons are valuable in the important sense that they demonstrate the tenuous link between outlay and outcome. The United States in 2012 spent 18 per cent of its GDP on health. It ranked first in terms of budget but 39th for infant mortality and 42nd for adult male mortality. The US is in the top three best performers for breast, prostate and colorectal cancer: 'An American diagnosed with prostate cancer has a 91 per cent of surviving at least five years, but the odds drop to fifty–fifty if you live in England' (Goldman and Leive, 2013). It is selective. Cancer is an area in which the United States scores highly in the international league table. It scores less well in motor vehicle deaths, heart disease, firearm homicides and sexually transmitted diseases.

Japan spends only 10 per cent of its GDP on health. In spite of that its life expectancy is, at 83, four years longer and its infant mortality, at 2.2, one-third the American rate. In France the figures were 12 per cent, 83 years and 3.5, respectively. The figures for Singapore were 4.6 per cent, 82 years and 2. Sierra Leone puts 15 per cent of its GDP into health. Its life expectancy is 45 and its infant mortality 109 per 1000 live births (World Bank, 2015). The scatter proves the point. There does not seem to be a strong correlation between spending and health.

There is a further complication. Even if intercountry comparisons could identify the success rates, still the mortality and the morbidity would have to be augmented with grassroots opinion to pick up the consumer's subjective satisfaction. The World Health Organization (WHO) uses expert assessment to rank the efficacy of its members' health systems. Blendon went to the end-user instead. Using surveys and interviews, he established that there was 'little relationship' between clinical performance and feelings on the ground:

> Italy is ranked second by WHO. But only 20 percent of its citizens say they are satisfied with their health care system ... Denmark is ranked sixteenth in the WHO overall performance measure, yet 91 percent of Danish citizens say they are satisfied with their health system. Once again, those who live in the country have a different perception than the WHO experts have. (Blendon et al., 2001: 15)

France was ranked first by professional assessment, third by health expenditure per capita, and sixth in the eyes of its own people. It may have been the best but its citizens may not have been the best pleased. The WHO had never waited in the queues, fought with inefficient bureaucrats or experienced allocation without respect. The rank and file had a different story to tell. It has to be told if intercountry evidence is to be more than a top-down proclamation of the input that best fits the lock.

4.2 CARE BEYOND MEDICINE

A list that is too long becomes unwieldy and even ridiculous. Sunscreen is health care because it keeps out the rays. Policemen are health care because they keep down the murders. There are few things or activities that are not related in some way to health. Yet a list that is too short will fall victim to the same charge. Health care inputs are a broad church. They are more than medical attention narrowly defined. Critics will say that too abbreviated a list may be measuring medical inputs but not the sum total of the health-influencing inputs that make morbidity and mortality what they are.

Consider household spending on perimedical inputs that branch out from the clinical trunk. The fee that consumers pay to see a doctor is included in medical spending. Their fares, travelling times and earnings lost through waits are treated as if for a trip to a football fixture. It is rather one-sided. A restful holiday can be as beneficial as a prescription tranquilliser. The benzodiazepine makes its way into the statistics. The beach resort does not.

Non-prescription drugs such as an aspirin are health-related. So are surgical stockings bought in a High Street multiple and a bracing game of cricket played on the Green. Internet searches are health-related if that is how the patient checks up on poor peripheral circulation. Explanatory manuals are health-related if that is where the patient goes for a gluten-free diet.

The statistics seldom include the non-traditional services of hypnotists, homeopathists, faith healers, acupuncturists, herbalists and colour therapists. It is an omission decided upon at the top which is radically at odds with the revealed preference of the beneficiary. Individuals pay for them out of pocket because the fringe offers the promise of a fuller health status, self-perceived. The consumer's willingness to pay marks them out as health-related. Talking market economics, they are therefore health-related. As seen by the patient if not the practitioner, they ought to be recorded as health-related in the input series.

An apple a day keeps the doctor away. A morning swim tones up the heart and lungs. Prunes and muesli keep the colon up to scratch. Early nights and sound breakfasts protect the body from wear and tear. Flossing and brushing put the root canal job to rout. Cauliflower and broccoli reduce the likelihood of prostate cancer. Beer strengthens the brittle bones of middle-aged women. Chocolate, which contains antioxidants, reduces the risk of death from heart disease. Higher rents buy access to less-polluted suburbs.

Turning from the goods to the bads, alcohol misuse is a major cause of disease and death. In terms of patient care it is costing the British National Health Service at least £20 million a year, the nation in terms of lost productivity considerably more (Department of Health, 2011: 189). Sleep deprivation increases the likelihood of premature death by 12 per cent. Bisphenol A in till receipts can cause impotence in male shopaholics. As the list gets longer, so it becomes clearer that there is more to spending than the doctors and the nurses alone. Households contribute to good health when they buy granary bread, fresh fruit and organic vegetables grown in soil fertilised by pesticide-free manure. Dark chocolate and red wine are more difficult to quantify. That does not mean that they are of no relevance to health.

Lifestyle accounts for more than 40 per cent of the difference in health status among individuals. Tobacco products are responsible for 480 000 premature deaths in the United States alone (Cutler et al., 2011a: 1175). The risk of coronary heart disease, stroke, cancer and diabetes could be cut by up to 78 per cent if Americans were to give up smoking, adopt a healthy diet, engage in 3.5 hours of vigorous physical activity per week and keep their weight within the recommended limits (Department of Health and Human Services, 2015: 118, 123). They wanted their lifestyle and they wanted good health. They must have known that the production function was shortening their life.

The simple fact of being married is itself an argument in the production function. Married men were found in one study to be 6.3 per cent less likely to die prematurely than were unmarried men. For women the figure was 3.4 per cent. The coefficient of preservation in the case of men is so great that it effectively cancels out the 5 per cent excess mortality that is the negative consequence of smoking (Gardner and Oswald, 2004: 1191, 1204).

Marriage protects. In Norway it was found that the never-married, both male and female, were 15 per cent less likely to survive 12 common forms of cancer than were the married (Kravdal, 2001: 359). It is easier to document the correlation than to explain it. Contributing factors might be the pooling of resources, the pull of children and grandchildren, a wider network of contacts, a more stable lifestyle, a reduced propensity to drink and smoke, stress-relieving companionship, greater informal care in time of illness. The association outlives the death of the partner. Even widows have a lower mortality rate than do never-married women. Divorce, in contrast, has a coefficient of aggravation. Divorced people experience 20 per cent more chronic illnesses, including cancer, than those who never marry (Hughes and Waite, 2009: 344). Divorce takes an emotional and financial toll. It imposes a burden on the body and the medical services as well.

Households can protect. So can firms. Masks and visors shield workers from viruses, fumes and sparks. Harnesses, railings and non-slip footwear restrict falls from heights. An on-site clinic provides first aid to the victim of an industrial accident. Any investment in environmental or occupational health is a private cost for the firm. It is also a social benefit. Without that private cost, the downstream drain on the medical services would be much greater.

Infrastructure too plays a part. Refuse collection and filtered drinking water are conducive to good health, just as inadequate sewers and polluted rivers are the breeding grounds for dysentery, dengue and contagious infections. Secure stores provide a dumping ground for radioactive waste. Good roads and uninterrupted refrigeration keep food fresh. Chloridation of the water supply protects the teeth and gums. Subsidies to basic science are the first step in the direction of practical applications that eliminate killer plagues.

Ranging more widely, accessible education, full employment and macroeconomic stability can be seen as inputs to the national health. Contributing to rising incomes, they are also contributing to a wholesome diet, hygienic accommodation, adequate heating and affordable health care. It is not an unmixed blessing. Rising incomes are also associated with the diseases of affluence that are brought on by a sedentary lifestyle, occupational stress and convenience foods rich in fat, salt and sugar. Middle-class women, because they start their family at a later age and have fewer children, are above average in annual mammograms but above average in breast cancer as well. More education and more income leave them at greater risk than women in the slums. These are the exceptions. The rule is that the moving staircase most of the time moves most of us up.

Where pockets of hypothermia and near starvation remain, a growing economy is better placed to provide a safety net than is one which can only finance welfare by means of Robin Hooding the successful. A growing economy generates a national dividend that is self-sustaining precisely because it is new value, incremental potential freshly being added. It may not be the sufficient condition for the transfer State but it is definitely the necessary condition. Even a well-intentioned altruist such as Anthony Crosland knew that a caring government could not spend money that it did not have: 'Rapid growth is an essential condition of any significant re-allocation of resources ... I do assert dogmatically that in a democracy low or zero growth wholly excludes the possibility' (Crosland, 1974 [1971]: 74, 75).

Economic growth is care beyond medicine. Whether health insurance is also a quasi-clinical input is less clear. Reimbursement is only a transfer payment. Where the patient pays the doctor and the insurer refunds the cost, it would be double-counting to include both the payment and the refund when in truth they are two loops in the same circular flow.

The argument is not entirely convincing. While reimbursement by itself is not an exchange, the very fact that the patient has insurance is a psychic bulwark of sorts. Peace of mind is favourable to good health.

Stress and agitation can be a threat to the nerves and the psyche. By that argument a Sunday sermon should be counted as if the equivalent of a preventive injection to ward off tetanus. Perhaps it should: if meditation in an ashram is fringe medicine, then so is the comfort afforded by a local priest who has seen it all before. At some point a line must be drawn. A list that brings in all the world is not much better than a list which stops short at the doctors and the nurses who clearly constitute only a part of the census.

4.3 JURISDICTION AND LEGISLATION

The judges who perpetuate precedents and the legislators who propound new rules are an input into the health status production function. Every courtroom, every parliament, has a direct impact on the national health. Philosopher-rulers like gifted surgeons keep us well.

Ulysses demands constraint since fallible man wants rock-solid insurance against retrograde weakness of will. Taxpayers insist on compulsion since otherwise selfish defaulters would free-ride on their consensual obligations. Patients alienate the right to decide since everyone knows that the doctor knows best. Temptation, abstention, trust – it all adds up to the proposition that often it will be rational to hire a guide. Politics and medicine cannot be kept apart. Tawney, looking backward to look forward, knew exactly what it means to say that without a nanny few of us would ever make it from cradle to grave. Unfreedom is the real freedom, he said, when the alternative is worse: 'The mother of liberty has, in fact, been law' (Tawney, 1966: 169).

Everyone likes roses. Less well liked are the thorns which can prick. Regulation can cause a social loss where politicisation crowds out individual self-reliance, social embeddedness, network capital and unorchestrated mutual aid. People will baulk at helping a neighbour to roll a log if logrolling has been made the responsibility of the Ministry of Logs. Interpersonal trust and sequential supergames may ossify for lack of exercise. Bowling alone may be inevitable in an open and mobile society where all that the citizens have in common are the laws.

The content of the laws is itself a thorn that can prick. Social democrats like Tawney put their faith in the parliamentary Samaritan because no one but a scoundrel could be indifferent to the bitter cry of the downtrodden. Ideological socialists like Marx and Engels maintained, however, that it was in the nature of the State to rubber-stamp the laws that had been handed to it on the golf course or at the Reform Club by a cabal of rent-seekers, profit-seekers and parasitical elites: 'The executive of the modern State is but a committee for managing the common affairs of the whole bourgeoisie' (Marx and Engels, 1848 [2011]: 66). The law may be the mother of liberty. Yet it may be the liberty of the few and not the many that the law is in business to enhance.

The State is licensing longer shifts and suppressing the minimum wage because it wants to save the proletariat from unemployment. The State is allowing unfiltered effluent and exhausting double shifts because strict regulation would mean even lower pay. The State may be speaking of health when secretly it is reporting to capital. Marxists and libertarians share a common mistrust of the State because they are not certain whether the throne comes with thorns attached. Social democrats like Tawney are more confident about the content of the laws. Bad governments do bad things. Good governments do good things. That is not a reason for right-thinking men and women to reprivatise the risks. The mother of liberty, Tawney said, has been proactive intervention. The State wants us to be healthy and safe. It has done its best to help.

At the level of production, Victorian laissez-faire has evolved into wise and thinking legislation. Earmuffs must be worn, smoke alarms installed, fire escapes provided, long ladders secured. Hard hats, steel helmets and bullet-proof vests must be supplied. Machinery must be made vibration-retardant. Lifeboats must be equipped with lifejackets, torches and whistles. The lunch-room must be cockroach-free. Asbestos, lead and arsenic must comply with international best practice. Maximum working hours before concentration goes must be scrupulously respected. Because of taxes, subsidies and command-and-control, in short, the costs of workplace hazards will not lie where they fall. Some people will not be made 'the social pathologies of other people's progress' (Titmuss, 1968: 157). The tort-feasors will cease and desist. The polluters will pay.

As for consumption, food products must be date-stamped. Cars must be fitted with seat belts, airbags and fog lamps. Speed limits, motorcycle helmets and hockey helmets are made mandatory. Marijuana, opium, pornography, handguns, sedition, passive smoking and the advertising of prescription pharmaceuticals are prohibited. Errors of commission are identified and neutralised. Errors of omission have an easier life. When cautious regulators red-tape away a life-saving breakthrough, passengers may be unable to escape a burning train but at least terrorists would never have been able to open the door from inside.

Laws may be paternalistic but at least they can encourage better health. Beneficent authority has made child safety seats compulsory. They have saved American lives as surely as surely as if the American government had built a new hospital or well-baby clinic: 'The mean number of infant and toddler fatalities is reduced by 39 per cent and 30 per cent respectively in states with mandatory restraint laws' (Evans and Graham, 1990: 140). In one year alone the lives of 161 children were saved because the threat of fines had modified their parents' incentive structure. Those children owe their lives to a wise leadership which rejected the libertarian credo that the consumer knows best. Laws such as the minimum drinking age and the unexpected breathalyser test contribute to preventive health. Laws that ration through taxation make at least as valuable a contribution.

The risk of being involved in a fatal car crash is 100 times greater for drivers under the age of 22 who have drunk six beers than it is for their counterparts who have drunk no beers at all. In spite of that, weak-willed young drinkers were still saddling up. Command-and-control was not stopping them from immolating themselves on the Sirens' rock. The highway patrol could not do it. The high price-elasticity of -2.3, however, could: 'A tax of approximately 35 per cent of the retail price of beer eliminates half of the alcohol-related fatalities arising from youthful drinkers, and a 50 per cent tax eliminates approximately three-quarters of alcohol-related deaths' (Phelps, 1988: 12).

The short-horizoned could successfully be nudged away from an evanescent fix by excise duties in collaboration with the elasticity of demand. The deterrent is especially effective in the case of the impressionable young. Peer pressure and herd mimicry pull the unaddicted in one direction, but low disposable incomes and the hurdle of price pulls them in the other. Excise duties are the friend in need that steers a swing constituency away from a self-inflicted habit which, acquired as an adolescent, will later on be difficult to break. They will resent the tax when young. When they are mature, they will revert from their want to their need. They will thank their lawgivers for pricing them away from a poison that could have cost them their lives.

The power to tax is the power to protect. A tax on alcohol leads to enforced abstention which leads to better health. It is the same with cigarettes. Smoking is exposed to the sensitivity of demand. Wasserman found that a 10 per cent increase in excise would lead to a 2.3 per cent fall in consumption (Wasserman et al., 1991: 56–7). Chaloupka calculated that a doubling of the duty would lead to a 6 per cent fall (Chaloupka, 1991: 736). The responsiveness is not great but it is a reduction nonetheless. High tax rates protect the wavering from themselves.

It is an intergenerational benefit. Not only will the smokers themselves be spared the heart disease and the malignant neoplasms, but expectant mothers, when forced by price to cut back, will then give birth to more robust babies: 'Pregnant women are responsive to changes in cigarette tax rates. The smoking participation price elasticity is roughly –0.50 ... Increases in cigarette tax rates have a beneficial impact on mean birth weight ... A one-cent increase in the state tax rate on cigarettes increases average birth weight by 0.16g' (Evans and Ringel, 1999: 148, 150, 152). There are important implications for social equality. In Britain 17 per cent of all mothers smoke in pregnancy. It jumps to 29 per cent for mothers in the manual occupational group. It jumps still further for teenage mothers (Boyle, 2011: 19).

Smoking doubles the risk of low birth weight. It accounts for about 20 per cent of all low birth weight babies in the United States. The external cost imposed on society by the smoking mother and the sickly baby adds up to 45 cents per packet. An excise duty of 45 cents would internalise the spillover. The buyer and the seller would then have to cover not just the private cost but the external cost as well. Healthy people would not have been called upon to pay for the antisocial.

A tax on smoking is a tax in the sense of Pigou (1932 [1920]). Its primary purpose is not to raise revenue but to reverse a market failure. Not only do non-productive sick-days go down, but also citizens with scarce skills are more likely to survive to the retirement age. They are less likely to impose a cost on the health care and health insurance systems. Smoking is 'the most important preventable cause of disease in the United States' (Ruhm, 2005: 344). It is associated with 0.5 million premature deaths annually from increased risk of cancer, coronary heart disease, stroke, respiratory illness and other ailments. If saving 0.5 million lives is a good thing, then so too is a Pigovian tax.

Like alcohol and smoking, there is problem weight. About 35.7 per cent of American adults and 16.9 per cent of American children are obese. Obesity has the same effect on 17 chronic conditions as 20 years of natural life. In terms of the health-related quality of life, the figure is 30 years. It is also expensive. Obesity in the United States is associated with an average increase in adult medical expenditures of $395 a year. The equivalent figure for smoking (current or in the past) was $230. For problem drinking it was only $150 (Sturm, 2002: 245).

Obesity imposes a total cost on the American health care system in excess of $147 billion. The seriously overweight are more likely to experience diabetes, hypertension, coronary heart disease, stroke, gall-bladder failure, respiratory problems, certain cancers, avoidable blindness or the loss of a limb. Obesity is also responsible for 100 000 to 400 000 premature deaths each year (Cutler et al., 2011a: 1175). British children who are obese between the ages of 11 and 15 are twice as likely to die before they are 50. In all, 23.7 per cent of British boys and 26.2 per cent of British girls aged 11 to 15 already count as obese (Department of Health, 2006: 26). Where will they be in less than 40 years time?

Insurance is pooled. Medicine is subsidised. Economic growth is a public good. In spite of that, productive potential is stuffing itself into an early grave. Half of all adult Americans defined to be clinically obese are spending less than 1.5 hours per week to get themselves into shape (Department of Health and Human Services, 2015: 118, 123). Their need to live is at variance with their want for food. If the epidemic is to be contained, then the most salient solution is to call upon the State.

The law cannot specify a maximum weight without intruding into what most people would define to be their personal space. Consensus aside, a ceiling would not be easy to enforce in view of the sheer size of the problem. Up to two-thirds of British men and women are already overweight. A quarter of British adults are actually obese. A passionate minority embedded in a sizeable majority cannot be put in prison simply because they like to eat.

A tax on food would be no more realistic than a prohibition: 'It is difficult to tax only excess calories; a blanket food tax affects even socially beneficial calorie intake' (Lakdawalla and Philipson, 2006: 79). A subsidy to health education, weight-loss clinics and recreational keep-fit might make more sense. Like a tax, it would alter the incentive structure precisely because it would undercut the market-clearing price. At the same time, the take-up would be opt-in. Recidivist gluttons would not be dragged from their beds by the Fat Police merely because a health-promoting community has vowed to wipe out their false tastes and deviant preferences.

Money aside, the law can mandate transparency in order to streamline the process of considered choice. Shoppers cannot give their informed consent if they are not told the sugar content of fizzy drinks or the saturated fat in a packet of crisps. Disclosure is democratic. The ignorant are not being protected from their own weathervane vacillation but from the secret darkness which prevents them from completing an intelligent shop. Disclosure weakens the case for constraint. The law ensures that the facts are in the public domain. Soft intervention gives the patrons the information they need. After that it crosses its fingers and leaves them on their own.

The law can make information more widely available. It can also prohibit disinformation lest manipulative commercialism muddy the waters of rational choice. Countries which ban the advertising of wine and beer report a lower consumption of alcohol and fewer fatalities on the road than do countries which make promiscuous hawking a part of the freedom of speech (Saffer, 1991: 77). Want creation can draw the malleable and the susceptible down the road to rowdy drunkenness that ends in death. If there is to be disclosure, then it must be truthful disclosure. The law can intervene in the market to ensure that consumers genuinely know best when they give their informed consent.

The law can prohibit misleading disclosure. It can also mitigate pollution. In that way too jurisdiction and legislation, negating the negation, can be a valuable input in the health care production function. Schwartz and Dockery discovered that a rise in air pollution of 100 micrograms per cubic metre in Philadelphia had been associated with a rise in mortality of more than 7 per cent in the general population and about 10 per cent in the over-65s (Schwartz and Dockery, 1992: 600). Industry and trade by themselves had taken little interest in the pulmonary disease, the epidemic pneumonia, the cardiovascular degeneration and the avoidable mortality that had been the negative externality of their profit-seeking behaviour. The law would do more to protect the public health.

Doctors and nurses can patch up the pathologies: 'A 1 per cent increase in the quantity of medical services is associated with a reduction in mortality of about 0.1 per cent' (Auster et al., 1969: 430). A law to contain pollution can do better than that. Government policy to cut by a quarter the volume of total suspended particulates (TSP) in Delhi saved a larger number of lives: 'The percentage decrease in deaths corresponding to a 100-microgram reduction in TSP is 2.3 per cent ... Weighing each of the 1,385 lives lost by remaining life expectancy implies a loss of 51,403 life-years' (Cropper et al., 1997: 1625, 1628). For India as a whole the loss is 2.1 billion life-years. Whether through the auctioning of licences to pollute or through enforceable limits on emissions and effluent, what is clear is that the law did what the market did not. At least in Delhi, it would appear, the law has, in fact, been the mother of liberty.

4.4 PROSPERITY AND PROGRESS

Historians have revisited the past to identify the reasons for ever-better health. One of them is Thomas McKeown. Studying England and Wales since 1750, his conclusion is that medical care, though useful, has been 'often less effective than has been thought':

> The predominant influences which led to the improvement in health in the past three centuries were nutritional, environmental (particularly control of water and food), and behavioural; the last through the change in reproductive practices which limited population growth ... The contribution of personal

> medical measures remains tertiary in relation to the predominant behavioural and environmental influences. (McKeown, 1979: vii, 9)

Medicine was tertiary. Using infant and adult mortality as his indicator of overall good health, McKeown infers that the single most important cause of longer life has been the improvement in nutrition. Rotation, mechanisation, manuring, winter feeding have all raised the productivity per acre and the meat-yield per cow. Improvements in canals, rivers and roads have meant that the food sold to the final consumer is fresher and less expensive. International trade, the relaxation of tariffs, the invention of refrigeration have globalised the supply and demand of primary produce.

Studying American data from 1700 to 1980, Robert Fogel confirmed that you are what you eat: 'Improvements in nutritional status may have accounted for about four-tenths of the mortality decline' (Fogel, 1986: 507). The effect was especially strong among infants. Food to this day retains its explanatory power. Children born in the northern hemisphere between October and December have a life-expectancy at age 50 of an extra six months because of the seasonable availability of fresh fruit and vegetables in the second and third trimester of pregnancy (Doblhammer and Vaupel, 2001).

Supply, of course, is only half of the story. Availability has to be complemented by effective demand. Rising incomes per capita have opened the door. They have given the impoverished and the undernourished unprecedented access to a balanced diet. Food has lengthened their life-expectancy. Food has improved their resistance to germs and infections.

Public investment in health-related infrastructure has made a contribution of its own. Szreter and Woolcock cite the example of Joseph Chamberlain's 'gas and water socialism' in mid-Victorian Birmingham: 'The provision of sufficient clean water and sewerage systems to preserve human health in such rapidly expanding residential centres required the effective mobilization of political will in order to solve a classic collective action problem' (Szreter and Woolcock, 2004: 658). Science and technology by themselves were not enough. Public goods such as public health must be available to all if they are to be available to any. The externalities and the spillovers are widely diffused. Only the State, never private enterprise, can mobilise the compulsory contributions raised through tax that can pay for the neighbourhood effects.

The purification of drinking water and the sanitary disposal of waste have reduced the threat from waterborne diseases such as cholera, dysentery and typhoid. The list goes on and on. Immunisation can contain the spread of measles, smallpox, polio and pertussis (whooping cough). Spraying and fogging can keep down mosquitoes in residential areas. Health education can teach people to wash their hands before handling food, to take reasonable exercise, to avoid high-risk sexual activity, to limit and space pregnancies so as to keep down maternal mortality. Health workers, often trained at public expense and many of them on the public payroll, can spread the message into the countryside. Behaviour and attitudes come in that way to reinforce income, nutrition and infrastructure in helping to raise the average level of health.

The argument for the political lead should not be pressed too far. Mortality and morbidity had already begun to decline in Victorian Britain when the State became active in the promotion of health. Household incomes had already begun to rise. Relative prosperity was empowering people to trade up from overcrowded slums to well-ventilated rental units. Airborne contagions such as tuberculosis, anthrax, pneumonia and chickenpox were becoming less of a threat. As valuable as 'gas and water socialism' undoubtedly was, private capitalism in partnership with a better standard of living was making a contribution as well. It is the same in the poorer countries today, where commerce in the form of water filters, chemical latrines and mosquito nets completes the circuit in which the State too plays a part.

Medical care in all of this has very much the character of an also-ran. Some estimates suggest that as little as 10 per cent of the decline in preventable deaths since 1900 have actually occurred in the wake of the biotechnological take-off. *Post festum* was not *propter festum*. Appearances are deceiving: 'When the tide is receding from the beach it is easy to have the illusion that one can empty the ocean by removing water with a pail' (Dubos, 1959: 23).

McKinlay and McKinlay, documenting the American experience from 1900 to 1973, showed that about 92 per cent of the marked decline in age-adjusted mortality from measles, scarlet fever, tuberculosis, pneumonia, diphtheria and typhoid had already occurred before the expensive new techniques and vaccines came into general use in the late 1940s. Only in the case of influenza, poliomyelitis and whooping cough did deaths decline by 25 per cent or more after the appropriate medical breakthroughs had been licensed for the market (McKinlay and McKinlay, 1977: 414, 420). It is all too easy to mistake association for causation. The great killer contagions have receded into history for a number of reasons. Also there, but also-ran, has been the scientific revolution: '*At most 3.5 per cent of the total decline in mortality since 1900 could be ascribed to medical measures introduced for the diseases considered here*' (McKinlay and McKinlay, 1977: 425).

McKeown confirmed the result for England and Wales: 'Immunization is relatively ineffective even today, and therapeutic measures of some value were not employed until about 1950, by which time the number of deaths had fallen to a low level' (McKeown, 1979: 54). McKeown pays tribute to the improvements in antibiotics, toxicology, anaesthetics and obstetrics that have made the medical encounter so much more successful. Joints can be replaced, hernias repaired and coronary arteries unblocked. It was not always so. McKeown does not deny that preventive and curative medicine have extended the length of life. His argument is simply that lifestyle has done even more:

> The appraisal of influences on health in the past three centuries suggested that we owe the improvement, not to what happens when we are ill, but to the fact that we do not so often become ill; and we remain well, not because of specific measures such as vaccination and immunization, but because we enjoy a higher standard of nutrition and live in a healthier atmosphere. (McKeown, 1979: 79)

The lessons for today's poorer countries could not be more stark. Improve diet and hygiene. Invest in education. Build houses. Reduce emissions. Above all, *enrichissez-vous*:

> Wealthier nations are healthier nations ... The estimated income elasticity of infant and child mortality is between –0.2 and –0.4 ... Raising per capita incomes will be an important component of any country's health strategy. The estimates imply that if income were 1 percent higher in the developing countries, as many as 33,000 infant and 53,000 child deaths would be averted annually. (Pritchett and Summers, 1996: 841, 844)

Wealth causes health. Health causes wealth. One hand washes the other. Economics is the wonder drug. The medical mystique is not. For all that, the late developers should not underestimate the clinics and the interventions merely because the first-movers are tailing off and levelling out. Where medicine is not widely available, a small increment in inputs will deliver a disproportionate improvement in status. Where the base is low, the productivity is high. The lesson of history is, however, that it will not last.

As the service becomes more widely consumed, diminishing returns will set in. The flat of the curve will harden its arteries. The marginal betterment in areas such as cardiovascular disease, malignant neoplasms and even road accidents will become progressively more modest over time: 'It is problematic whether further extension of medical care services can reduce mortality from any of these causes substantially'

(Newhouse, 1978: 81). The gains are real at an early stage in the historical trajectory. They are unlikely to be as significant once economic middle age succeeds to economic youth. The First World is not the Third.

Totals must not be confused with increments. All policy must begin with the status quo: 'Eliminating medical care services altogether could lead to a marked increase in mortality and morbidity rates, even though a further increase in medical services would show little effect' (Newhouse, 1978: 81). Looking backward, we are grateful for the medical margin that tested our blood and corrected our squint. Looking forward, we think that the golden age is behind us and that the marginal outcomes might not repay the marginal investment. Neither the aggregate budget nor its component services is likely to deliver a proportionate improvement in the outcomes. It was different when we were poor. But we start from here.

4.5 INCREMENTS AND TOTALS

Fuchs is a sceptic who has questioned the incremental effectiveness of additional care. More money, he says, will not necessarily buy better health: 'The marginal contribution of medical care to health in developed countries is very small ... Medical intervention has a significant effect on outcome in only a small fraction of the cases seen by the average physician' (Fuchs, 1974a: 64).

Some conditions such as the common cold will cure themselves given time. Other conditions such as terminal cancer will remain incurable regardless of what the doctor does. Medical intervention in cases such as these will be palliative only. It will not make a great dent in the funerals. Cochrane says that he regards such cases not as the exception but as the rule: 'One should ... be delightfully surprised when any treatment at all is effective, and always assume that a treatment is ineffective unless there is evidence to the contrary' (Cochrane, 1972: 8).

Cochrane, like Fuchs, is a sceptic. He calls it a 'myth' to assume that therapy is the same as improvement. Studying the relationship between medical inputs and mortality outcomes in 18 developed countries he calls into question the 'layman's uncritical belief' (Cochrane, 1972: 8) that the doctor is the middleman between life and death: 'None of the health service factors were consistently negatively related to mortality ... Health service factors are relatively unimportant in explaining the differences between our 18 developed countries' (Cochrane et al., 1978: 202, 204).

The causal variable with the greater explanatory power was, once again, not medicine but economics. The marginal productivity of living standards and common sense in a richer country was greater than the contribution of the doctors and the hospitals which McKeown has dismissed as 'palliative or unproved': 'Most of those who are born well will remain well, apart from minor morbidity, at least until late life, if they have enough to eat, if they are not exposed to serious hazards, and if they do not injure themselves by unwise behaviour' (McKeown, 1979: 137, 194).

Newhouse and Friedlander have tabulated the relationships between care inputs and health outcomes. Their results suggest that McKeown was right: 'The physiological measures were little affected by additional medical resources. The results are consistent with the view that what the individual does (or does not) do for himself affects health more than do additional medical resources' (Newhouse and Friedlander, 1980: 200). An apple a day should do the trick. Good parents with good genes will help. Medical services, however, are an economic deadweight. Rather than deferring to the health care budget because it is an index of national well-being, resourcing beyond the critical cut-off should be defrocked because it is not paying its way in miracles. Potential doctors and nurses should be released for more productive work in high-return activities. They can better serve their nation in banking and finance.

The RAND Health Insurance Experiment found little or no relationship between health insurance, health care and health status (Newhouse and Insurance Experiment Group, 1993). The fully insured were consuming 40 per cent more care than the uninsured. In spite of the additional outlay, the difference in health outcomes at the margin was exceedingly small.

It was exceedingly small but it was positive nonetheless. Diminishing marginal productivity does not mean zero marginal productivity. In the UK, health spending per person more than doubled between 1997 and 2013 but average life expectancy rose too. It was 76.5 years in 1997 and 80.1 years in 2013 (Economist Intelligence Unit, 2015: 3). The increment was becoming ever more costly. The bang for the buck was not what it was. Assuming, however, that health spending had made a non-trivial contribution to the rise, then the bang is a bang nonetheless. An additional 3.6 years of human life must have some value, however small.

The health care production function is widely believed to be flat. A more pessimistic assessment is, however, that of Ivan Illich. He says that the curve is not flat but forward-falling: 'A professional and physician-based health care system that has grown beyond critical bounds ... must produce clinical damage that outweighs its potential benefits' (Illich, 1977: 16). Medical care is not health-neutral but insidious. A medical consultation should come with a government health warning. Medical care can seriously damage your health.

Illich's argument begins with physical iatrogenesis and ends with psychic dependence. Doctors' waiting-rooms are a meeting-place for sick people who share their methicillin-resistant staphylococcus aureus and other bacteria. Apart from cross-infection there are the side-effects from anaesthetics and drugs. Rubella vaccinations for young girls can make it more rather than less likely that they will suffer from severe arthritis or contract the rubella virus later in life (Chantler et al., 1985: 1117). To that must be added the human error that can creep in when a surgeon is lazy, tired or simply unfortunate. The knife slips. The wrong leg is amputated. The patient has an allergic reaction. Bad blood is transfused. People's health can suffer when they fall into the hands of the professionals.

Yet it is not just the clinical disasters that Illich regards as counterproductive and pathological. He believes that the medicalisation of human life is itself of negative value. People who turn to the doctor for a helping hand are alienating their responsibility for their own suffering and survival. Dependency on the medicine man, like faith-healing by God and rote-learning at school, is a soporific and a tranquilliser. Once they have come off alcohol, people should go cold turkey off the clinic. Illness and death are inevitable. That is what life is all about.

Illich may be exaggerating his case. Concentrating on the clinical disasters, he is underestimating the greater number of episodes that end in success. It is never good to throw out the baby merely because the bathwater can scald or freeze. Illich, moreover, does not acknowledge the harm that can be done when sturdy ego is simply not able to recognise an asymptomatic malfunction like early-stage diabetes, or where self-treatment as in the case of a home-induced abortion can go badly wrong. Independence and self-determination may be ethical absolutes. Sometimes, however, even freedom must be refracted through the principal–agent relationship. Unfreedom can be a complement to freedom. It need not be at variance with individual liberty.

Dependency on the doctor is in Illich's sense the crutch of self-estrangement. Yet there are offsets. Eyeglasses improve vision. Cochlear implants improve hearing. Bunker says it would be good if medical nihilists and self-reliant stoics would recognise that the value of well-being and comfort is more than calendar-years alone: 'The miseries of depression, shortness of breath, angina, creaky and painful joints, severe pain, disabling headaches, major indigestion, urinary difficulties, toothache and sore gums, fuzzy vision, faulty hearing, paralysis, and broken bones would add up to a national disaster without the relief we are able to document' (Bunker et al., 1994: 242).

Illich has reservations about people who turn to drugs and gurus to help them cope. Another perspective would be that a hip transplant to walk unaided or a prescription that allows a public servant suffering migraine to go to work would enhance rather than circumscribe the individual's ability to define the parameters of their own life. Even if there is no cure for multiple sclerosis, simply serving as a friend in need to comfort the dying can improve a human being's felt quality of life.

The doctor–patient nexus is more than the repair of an underperforming body. It is investment in capital but it is consumer utility as well. The silent partners of reassurance and sympathy are joint products whenever the doctor sets the bone of a battered housewife or talks down a disgruntled executive on the edge. Flat-of-the-curve does not pick up the important work done by the medical professionals in helping ordinary people to get through the day: 'Paediatricians, for example, know that calming nervous mothers is often more time-consuming than treating their children. Obstetricians must deal with expectant fathers as well as their pregnant spouses. Relieving anxiety is a large part of almost every physician's stock-in-trade' (Fuchs, 1974a: 65).

Death counts. Yet it is not all that counts. Cochrane, reflecting on what he believes to be the 'relative unimportance of therapy in comparison with the recuperative power of the human body', springs to the defence of the listening ear and the bedside manner: 'I believe that cure is rare while the need for care is widespread, and that the pursuit of cure at all costs may restrict the supply of care' (Cochrane, 1972: 5, 7). Medicine is multidimensional. Cochrane is inviting the sceptics and the nihilists to redefine the function of medicine in terms of person-centred care. It is not the same as removing an appendix. That is no reason to call it flat-of-the-curve.

5. The individual

Choice in health is a triangle of forces and a compromise of constituencies. This chapter identifies the body-holder as the first of the three discussion partners. It says that the entity variously known as the patient, the client, the shopper or the customer is the bedrock initiator who harbours the preference. Reductionists and individualists will like it that way: 'Only the slave has needs; the free man has demands' (Boulding, 1966: 202). Paternalists and perfectionists think that excellence can be imposed without consultation. Believers in autonomy defend the irreducible self in the language of equal rights and respect for persons.

The individual is in pursuit of better health. Section 5.1, 'Needs and wants', suggests that revealed preference may not be the best way to improve the health outcomes. Section 5.2, 'Knowledge and ignorance', says that even the compos mentis, neither lunatics nor children, might not have the focused expertise that they require. Section 5.3, 'Information asymmetry', explains that the principal must sometimes turn to an agent to fill in the gaps. Section 5.4, 'The freedom to become', is about personhood. Personhood is more than the freedom from a sneeze or a cough.

5.1 NEEDS AND WANTS

At the base there are the physical needs: 'Human beings need vitamins, and did so before they had any notion of vitamins' (Braybrooke, 1987: 91). Survival is the precondition. Dead people do not need a doctor.

Physiology is a part but it is not the whole. Built upon the animal needs there are the cultural ones: 'By necessaries I understand, not only the commodities which are indispensably necessary for the support of life, but whatever the custom of the country renders it indecent for creditable people, even of the lowest order, to be without' (Smith, 1961 [1776]: II, 399). A stockbroker needs a bowler hat. A king needs a crown. Tastes and preferences are not things and objects. Tastes and preferences are other people (Reisman, 2002: 65).

There is the essence and there is the environment. It is not always easy to tell them apart. A physical need for nourishment elides seamlessly into the cultural need for nourishment from a traditional diet which in turn satisfies the psychological need for self-affirmation through participation in a shared ritual. Human beings have a body and they have a mind. Need does not stop short at the body. Psychosomatic illness caused by the repression of the human need for creativity, appreciation, integration and challenge is an illustration of what happens when the social health system does not service all the needs.

Good health means that all the needs are met. Economics, however, is the ideology of niggardly nature. Economics by its very charter is an invitation to the war of each against all. Scarce resources preclude the universalisation of the best: 'If the means of meeting everybody's needs are absent, needs may engender desperate, bitter struggles among human beings' (Braybrooke, 1987: 237).

Economic growth extends outward the frontiers. With it, however, comes social inclusion and widening reference groups. Once only the upper classes wore leather shoes. Now everyone does. Once a television, a computer, a telephone, a mobile phone satisfied an individual want. Now each is targeted at a conventional need since each is essential to survival in a networked role. The minimum standard of decency has gone up. What was a luxury once is a necessity now. It is a caucus race. The runners must run faster merely to keep abreast. Relativities are tough. Doctors see the failures all the time.

The freedom to choose is the freedom to translate wants into facts. Needs by that standard are a prison camp from which few escape. Wants are perceptions: a person who is mentally ill is not mentally ill if he says he is sane. Needs are absolutes: 'Whales were not fishes merely because people thought they were for centuries' (Daniels, 1985: 29–30). Wants are fleeting. They are whims that can be disregarded without irreparable damage to the human core. Needs are imperatives. They carry the implication 'that the entity asserted to be needed is actually necessary'. They convey the message that 'this needed entity ought to be received' (Culyer, 2005: 227).

Wants are preferences: the isolate alone knows if the marginal utility is worth its marginal expense. Needs are structures: 'Fiddlers need fiddles; photographers need cameras' (Braybrooke, 1987: 33). Needs are objective. The means–ends relationship has an identity of its own that has form and substance even if it is not seen, felt or heard. Wants are subjective. The assessment, all in the distinct and distinctive psyche, vanishes at the moment when the ostrich buries its sensory faculties in the sand.

Wants are *de gustibus non est disputandum*. Needs are *ne plus ultra* and *sine qua non*. Wants are what the cut-off ego rather fancies now.

Needs are the uncompromising essence of the human condition. Needs are the irreducible constraints that remain behind once the froth of inclination has been blown aside: 'People have a need for exercise regardless of what they wish, prefer, want otherwise, or choose. They have the need even if they do not much care to live or be healthy' (Braybrooke, 1987: 32).

Needs are species-constants. They are validated by natural law. They derive from the definition of what it means to be a human being: 'An imperfect satisfaction of needs leads to the stunting of our nature. Failure to satisfy them brings about our destruction. But to satisfy our needs is to live and prosper' (Menger, 1976 [1871]: 77). To live and prosper is a constitutional precondition. It is not a higgledy-piggledy of the haphazard and the ad hoc. Needs cannot reasonably be swapped at the margin by traders in the bazaar.

Jack wants alcohol because there is nothing on the TV. Jill wants psychedelics because the quick fix brings out the Jillness that the civil service does not reach. Their wants are quintessentially their own. Yet they are also *homo sapiens*. Jack and Jill are governed by an inbuilt instinct for self-preservation. It keeps them alive. Want as they will, still their needs call out to them with a single voice that they will regret their decision if they continue to chip away at their healthy life-years: 'You can need what you want, and want or not want what you need. What you cannot consistently do is not need what is required in order to avoid serious harm – whatever you may want' (Doyal and Gough, 1991: 42).

People are weak and temptation is strong. In the last analysis, however, the imperatives will have to take precedence over the preferences. If the needs are not satisfied, serious harm will result. Serious harm means that the process of want-satisfaction will lose its momentum. Eventually it will grind to a halt.

5.2 KNOWLEDGE AND IGNORANCE

The patient tends to be the first-mover in the medical sequence. There are exceptions. An accident victim might be unconscious on arrival. A schizophrenic might believe that the voices in his head are real. An insurance company might insist on a full annual check-up. A proactive doctor might call in all at-risk women for a smear test. A school clinic might check all children for vision and growth. A works clinic might screen all employees for cancerous fibres released by speed-up in the mill. Sometimes supply comes first and the individual fits in. More often than not it is the individual who makes the contact because he thinks he is ill.

5.2.1 When Something is Wrong

The problem is that the patient is seldom certain that something is wrong. The visit to the doctor will often be heralded with the personal apology of, 'I don't think it's serious but ...'. The patient cannot know in advance if the diagnosis will throw up an abnormality or whether a cure for the malfunction has actually been found. The question-and-answer tutorial costs time and money. Every patient hopes that it will be a waste. The patient is not an expert. They go in with a stomach ache and invest in the reassurance that it is not a peptic ulcer. They go in for a blood test and secure the confirmation that they are not pre-diabetic. The pay-off to the precautionary consultation is peace of mind. It could be something more. If there were indeed any indication of ulcers or diabetes, it will have been a rational choice to put time and money into a stitch in time.

Most people will have acquired some background information about health. There are biology lessons at school. There are television documentaries. There are articles on body maintenance in the quality press. Many people, moreover, are curious about health and want to find out more. Their knowledge is the unintended outcome of their hobby. It will stand them in good stead if the complaints with which they are familiar come up in their examination. The probability that general reading will be cost-effective cannot, however, be called very high.

Some bodies of knowledge are more likely to be called upon than others. Children because they are children are vaccinated against diphtheria, measles, mumps, tetanus and hepatitis B. A young couple will need to know about contraception, conception and childbirth. An older woman should expect the menopause. An older man will probably experience prostatic hyperplasmia. A worker in the chemicals industry will have a personal stake in lead.

Life cycle or occupational, in cases like these the consumer's own future is not entirely hidden behind a thick veil of unknowlege. Where the ambit is narrow, the need to know jumps off the screen. More usually, however, it does not. In most cases, the position is that it would be illogical and uneconomic to collect information on disease A if the likelihood is more or less the same that one will be struck down by disease B, disease C or disease D instead.

Once the malady has actually been diagnosed, the calculus is somewhat different. The affliction having been identified, information collected on it will be targeted and fine-tuned. Patients at that stage might conceivably have more to contribute to the competitive sift. Even so, they might reveal a personal preference to remain in the dark. Patients might be so emotional that they might not feel up to an impartial evaluation of the evidence. They might not want to amass testimony if all that it will do is to reiterate that there is no cure. They might prefer to remain in the dark if thinking about their condition is in itself a source of unhappiness and anxiety. They might have insurance. If they do, then their body is still under assault but at least they will have no financial incentive to search out the cost-effective protocol.

Besides that, there is the doctor. Once the medical practitioner has taken charge, the body-holder can go passive. The body-holder can rely on the hired gun for good advice and a balanced conjecture. There is no need to be fully informed if the prices, quantities, qualities and technical relationships can be delegated to a representative. These things change all the time. The cost of being up to date is too high to attempt the impossible on one's own, or at all. As Culyer writes: 'If information about one's health is costly to collect, it may be irrational to dispel all ignorance; i.e. it is perfect information, rather than ignorance, that is *a priori* more likely to be inconsistent with the postulates of welfare economics' (Culyer, 1971: 192).

Given the inconvenience and the expense, the patient might feel that it is enough to buy into the counsel of the specialist. The problem is that the patient does not usually know what he is being asked to select:

> The value of information is frequently not known in any meaningful sense to the buyer; if, indeed, he knew enough to measure the value of information, he would know the information itself. But information, in the form of skilled care, is precisely what is being bought from most physicians, and, indeed, from most professionals. The elusive character of information as a commodity suggests that it departs considerably from the usual marketability assumptions about commodities. (Arrow, 1973 [1963]: 18)

In the case of an everyday consumable, the shoppers will have learned from experience what to expect. They will have squeezed many tomatoes and tested many melons. In the case of information, however, they are all at sea. By definition they are asking for what they do not know. Because they do not know it, they will not know if it is accurate. They will not know if the intelligence for which they are paying is full and fair.

Where the procedure is routine and repeated, the patient has a history of trial and error. A dental patient can see the difference between one filling and the next. A Malthusian mother can compare one gynaecologist with the pregnancy before. A psychiatric patient logs in the new psychiatrists and their new concoctions. Personal contracts and self-help groups make the expectations less fanciful. Family and friends describe the nursing homes on the web. Health insurers are selected not in a medical emergency but in a moment of calm. Insurers advise on providers. Brokers advise on insurers. Neighbours advise on brokers. No one is alone.

In some cases there is a history of learning by doing. In many cases, the procedure will be once and for all. The patient will have no memory capital on which to draw. An appendectomy or a hysterectomy is not an apple that is purchased every day. Nor is a gallbladder removed like a replumbed pipe that by inspection lets the water through.

Major disasters will come to light. They are the stuff of a shouting match and sometimes a malpractice suit. The patient will know if the wrong leg has been amputated, if 0.25 mg was misread as 25.0, if full-body bruising indicates that they were dropped in theatre. It is the little things that are the greater danger. Slovenly stitching or an abandoned clip are inconspicuous enough to pass undetected. More fundamentally, not all doctors clone the standard drill. Practice variation is the essence of medicine. A patient about to complain that they were given a more expensive drug or that discretionary tissue was removed to play safe will be met with the reply, 'But that's what I *always* do'. There is no answer to that.

Disasters are not in any case a topic on which patients like to dwell. Patients who consult doctors do not want to think that something might go wrong. Psychologically, they put aside the possibility that the diagnosis was mistaken or the surgeon negligent. Medical services cannot be returned if they prove unsatisfactory. There is always the possibility of failure, mutilation and death. The market is a learning process. In the case of medicine, the learning process can take too long to be efficient. Torn between optimism and ignorance, patients close their eyes. They put their trust in the doctor who knows best.

Wishful thinking boosts the relative power of the supplier. Straightforward inertia and a non-calculative propensity to misread the evidence have the same effect. Even when people are given detailed information they still tend to make relatively limited use of the facts. As surveys have indicated, consumers' paid-for choices can let the free market down:

> The results show that quality ratings had very little impact on consumer choice of hospitals. A hospital that had twice the expected death rate had less than one fewer discharge per week in the first year, and only 116 fewer

discharges over nine years. In contrast, if there is a press report of a single, unexpected death, there is a 9 percent reduction in admissions for the next year. (Rice, 2001: 27)

Pauly, taking experience and networks into account, estimates that about one-third of personal health care decisions can be regarded as reasonably informed (Pauly, 1988: 45). Two-thirds are not. If individuals were as casual about their tomatoes as they are about their appendectomies, the enemies of consumer sovereignty would say that the invisible hand could not be trusted to maximise anyone's welfare save that of the teachers of economics.

5.2.2 Producer Sovereignty

The enemies of consumer sovereignty will deny that the shopper is the best judge of their own interest. Liberal democrats will reply that no doctor, no dictator, can ever be a match for ordinary citizens who alone can put a value on their subjective sensations. Only the patient can say where it hurts. Freedom is a means. Freedom is an end. Bottom-up is indispensable. There is no substitute for choice.

Choice, however, is a weasel-word. Choice can be exercised through a step-by-step process of in-period iteration. Choice can, however, also be exercised through a constitutional settlement, a living will or a multi-period statement of intent. Ulysses chose not to choose. His choice of precommitment over the impulse buy is the reason why he returned safely to his home. Patients may be said to be following his example when, renouncing their in-period freedom of choice, they leave it to the doctor to decide.

Bounded rationality is the choice of a heuristic. For many people, delegation to an agent is the best decision-making rule they can find. If as free individuals they have stated that they do not want to select their own pathways, if as rational investors they have instructed an agent to vote their proxies on their behalf, it is clearly a violation of their individual sovereignty to insist that their consent to an intervention should be fully and completely informed.

Freedom to them might not be the freedom to choose. Rather, it might be the freedom to choose the choosers and thereafter to waive their rights. It is the standard model in parliamentary politics. The prime minister is a doctor who does not demand a daily referendum. The doctor is a prime minister who practices slavery by consent to get the job done.

Slavery by consent might not, of course, be a considered choice. The patient, afraid of freedom and seduced by arrested development, might be demonstrating no more than Peter Pan's reluctance to commit to the responsibilities of an adult. The transfer of the poisoned chalice might be 'simply psychological denial or a process of infantilization or of giving in to the pressures of the doctor' (Dworkin, 1988: 118). The parent gets the captive consumer to eat pureed lentils, easy to digest. The parent knows best. The doctor, like the parent, marches out in front.

As with parents, doctors can blackmail and cajole. The weak-willed can be bullied. In some cases the doctor will withhold information on therapeutic grounds. Full disclosure might harm the patient's health. In other cases the doctor will practice deception. A placebo will be prescribed instead of barbiturates if an insomniac is believed to be suicidal. It is the purpose of medicine to help the sick. It is the purpose of a waiver to delegate the definition of good health. The doctor is deemed sufficiently trustworthy to act *in loco parentis*. Choice is the choice of the doctor. After that, Peter Pan should mind his own business and stick to sieved prunes.

5.3 INFORMATION ASYMMETRY

Unequal knowledge, 'information impactedness' (Williamson, 1975: 14), leaves the patient susceptible and dependent. The supplier has superior knowledge and the consumer is weak. The medical contract is not the only instance of the imbalance. The motorist must rely on the mechanic for an unbiased assessment of his brakes. The lawyer can demand unneeded documentation to garner extra fees. The greengrocer knows more about the freshness of his fruit. The rancher knows more about the hormones in his beef. Unequal knowledge is not *obiter dictum*. It is the heart of supply and demand.

5.3.1 The Double Void

The medical market may or may not be the same. What matters is perception. Medicine is widely regarded as an imbalance of a more rarefied kind. While few people are afraid of a tomato, anaesthetics, scalpels and defibrillators are at the very crossroads of life and death. Life and death magnify the asymmetry. It is an artificial distinction. The mechanic who does a slovenly job with the brakes or the grower who sprays calcium carbide on his crop can do great harm to the body and mind. Yet fear is notoriously irrational. The result is a thing apart.

The patient lacks knowledge about medicine. The patient does not know which drug will make them more talented or more energetic. The doctor, however, lacks knowledge about the patient. It is a double void. The doctor does not know that the patient sees their big nose as a shameful deformity or needs anabolic steroids for their one big chance in life. The ignorance is on both sides and not only on one. Doctors are in touch with the latest thinking on disease and cure. They know how to set a broken bone, to recognise septicaemia, to assign a statistical probability to a lump or a faint. What they do not know is the subjective meaning of the contingency for the patient factored down. Patients are unique. Their well-being, self-perceived, is not just an objective tabulation of facts. Illness is severity, duration, self-image, function. The problem is to find the right weighting scheme.

Only the purchaser can decide if the riskiness of a motorbike compensates for the miles-per-gallon of a car. Only the consumer can know if the discomfort of new fashions exceeds the vanity gratified by conspicuous ostentation. It is the same in the medical market. The patient alone is in a position to compare the pain of the metastases with the side-effects of the bicalutamide; or to know if grafting to relieve heart pains is worth the small but not insignificant risk of memory loss; or to sense if the potential complications from a transplant are greater than the anticipated gain in mobility; or to say if home convalescence is preferable to a less stressful but more costly hospital stay. The patient alone is in a position to assess the psychic value of income foregone when they have to turn down work. The patient alone knows the anxiety cost of debt incurred to finance a last-ditch procedure.

The patient knows that she will want an abortion if the amniocentesis reveals a foetal abnormality or if the child will be born a girl. The patient knows what they regard as 'full recovery' and what they see as their maximum tolerable disability. The patient alone has an idea, however loose, of the weighting scheme. The doctor does not. It is information asymmetry. The medical textbooks teach the fundamental humanness of 'normal species functioning'. The reality is the kaleidoscopic satisfaction-seeking of thee and me. We are not all standard size.

Daniels warns against the temptation to reify 'normal species functioning' into the natural law of a universal need. The truth, he says, is elusive and contingent. 'Functioning' is a function of a single ego's life-chances in a single bordered community. There is no point in giving people a way in that they do not want or cannot use. On the one hand we demand female genital mutilation. That is what we do around here. On the other hand, we reject brain surgery to improve our reading speeds. Not one of us in this village knows how to read. The inference that Daniels draws is that culture and not 'species' alone will have an impact on the 'normal' that the doctors take to be the norm: 'Dyslexia may be less important to treat in an illiterate society than in a literate one ... The social importance of particular diseases is a notion which we ought to view as socially relative' (Daniels, 1985: 34).

It is not just place that reshuffles the cards. Economists say *ceteris paribus*. It is not true. Nothing lasts forever. Forever warping the weft, there is the man in the clock who knows that change is the only constant: 'For many of us, some of our goals, perhaps even those we feel are most important to us, are not necessarily undermined by failing health or disability. Moreover, we can often adjust our goals, and presumably our levels of satisfaction, to fit better with our dysfunction or disability' (Daniels, 1985: 27). We play many parts over time.

Roles and aspirations are redefined as life-cycle personal evolution takes its never-resting course. A married person who wants children has a different sense of self from an unattached single who has no immediate plans for a family. A ballet dancer disabled by emphysema will call himself an investment banker when he next injures his hamstring. Goals change. People change. Societies change. 'Normal species functioning' is not for all seasons.

5.3.2 Consumer Sovereignty

Patient-based medicine is a difficult art to master. For all that, it remains the ideal. Doctors cannot complete their task without the template that is stored up in the patient's mind.

An architect does not ask a house if it wants to face south. A veterinarian does not ask a cat if it is planning for a family. A doctor, however, must deal with living, breathing people. They are the rawest of all raw material. Doctors are taught to treat needs. Economists are taught to satisfy wants. It is Hippocrates versus Milton Friedman. Milton Friedman may be closer to the way most people think today: 'When people's preferences run contrary to their needs, perhaps the project of meeting their needs will have to be suspended' (Braybrooke, 1987: 6).

People are reflective and self-aware. They have a need to define their space. That being the case, the medical practitioner ought ideally to consult the patient, even as the patient will normally want to consult the guide. The most sensitive agency relationship would then be one where the agent decides precisely as the principal would have done if only the principal had possessed the agent's stock of sector-specific expertise.

Medicine would become a two-way street. The doctor would not decide *for* the patient but rather *with* the patient. It would be an equal relationship between two moral entities. The objective and the subjective inputs would collaborate. The symbiosis would ensure that joint decisions will be tailored to fit. No mental patient would be sent home until the doctor had been told how they get on with their children, or whether they would prefer to be sleeping rough. The movement from producer to consumer sovereignty is an acknowledgement that even sick people like to be asked what they want.

Liberal democracy has an opportunity cost. Two-way consultation can be a mixed blessing. Telling the whole truth is open-ended and time-consuming. Resources used for discussions with insiders are resources not being used to bring outsiders into the fold. The ill-informed and the inconsistent might not be the best judges of their own welfare. A patient who is clinically depressed might not be in a fit state to debate the side-effects of convulsions. A patient unaccustomed to the language of probability might not understand that the sequence proposed is only a large-sample estimate. Discussion may not be very fruitful with patients such as these. It might be a waste.

Differentiation itself is uneconomic. There is not much point in asking patients what they want if the system, turning a deaf ear, makes it a matter of policy to offer them a standard service. If, of course, the range of choices is made to measure, then administrative costs will be incurred and economies of scale put at risk. The ins get private rooms. The outs get longer waits. Even if the clinical outcomes are not affected, there is a moral objection to putting money into amenity so long as other patients are not getting the basic service that they need.

Collective rather than one-to-one feedback might in the circumstances be the more suitable mode of consultation. Social externalities and public opinion are not likely to figure in the doctor–patient seminar. Yet figure they do in health policy as a whole. Other people are the subject of Chapter 7. It says that sometimes it will be better to determine whether there is a peaked consensus in favour of a specific option than to ask Jim Jones if he, Jim alone, would like a rectal suppository or a pill by mouth.

Consultation need not be popular. Not everyone feels a need to be perfectly informed. The propensity to rubber-stamp whatever the doctor has told them is likely to be particularly strong when they are ill and afraid: 'It is not surprising that the consumer becomes reliant upon the supplier. In fact if the anxiety costs become too high the consumer may be unwilling to participate in the choice process and default on making decisions, in which case the doctor/supplier takes over this decision-making role' (McGuire et al., 1988: 156). Consumers who want the doctor to decide will feel nervous and apprehensive when asked to speak up for themselves. They have already spoken up. They have hired an agent. It is enough. Further consultation to them seems a waste of resources. They would only be repeating what they have already heard from sage old Sir.

There is a further reason for the abrogation of responsibility. People do not want the burden of guilt if and when they make the wrong call. Richard Thaler explains the utility of choosing not to choose in the following way: 'Why do consumers want the first dollar coverage? I believe the reasons involve regret. Most consumers find decisions involving trade-offs between health care and money very distasteful. This is especially true when the decision is made for someone else, like a child' (Thaler, 1991: 16–17). Remorse is avoided when it is someone else who decides. Where the professional relationship is womb to tomb, in sickness and in health, the consumer may have confidence in the practitioner because 'the physician knows the patient well (and can thus do a good job of reflecting the patient's preferences)' (Thaler, 1991: 17). That is the attraction of a family doctor. A family friend will make a workable guess without anyone having to ask.

Consumer sovereignty will appeal to some. Others will want to be left alone. A sensitive health care policy must encourage participation on the part of the curious but must also permit the self-effacing, the indifferent and the silent to abstain. The possibility that the pushy will get more of the doctor's time than the shy is a real one. Doctors must listen with a third ear. They must decide which patient wants to talk and which wants to learn. They can get it wrong. That too is medical error.

Some clients will want to read their notes, ask supplementary questions, be told the worst. Others will leave it to sage old Sir to tick the boxes and press the buttons. If consultation is to make all customers feel better off in their own estimation then it will have to take the form of an invitation but not an obligation. It is, in other words, not only the demand for care but the demand for consultation about care that must form an important part of patient-led medicine.

5.4 THE FREEDOM TO BECOME

Aristotelians take issue with the utilitarians because liberal relativists undervalue the solid foundation even of the unseen. Their criticism of patient-led medicine would be that it puts too much emphasis on individual sensations and not enough on the underlying truth which never changes and never grows old. Freedom, the Aristotelians would say, is not just the freedom to shop. It is also the freedom to unfold an essence that makes Jim Jones by nature truly Jim. Without that freedom to develop fully into oneself the atom will feel empty, isolated and dissatisfied: 'Real guilt comes from not being true to yourself, to your own fate in life, to your own intrinsic nature' (Maslow, 1968 [1962]: 121).

Liberal marketers take little interest in the 'good life' as a value-free philosophical construct that exists independently of the unique decision-maker. Their normative standard is quintessentially microscopic, self-consciously perceptual. Aristotelians are more concerned with the basic capabilities that distinguish a human being from a rock or a tree. An Aristotelian would say that a need for health is not a need for health at all. Rather, it is the means to personal growth which is the God-given end. An Aristotelian would therefore look to wise leaders to educate people in such a way as to give them access to the single and virtuous road up.

I am what I am, but also what I have the capacity to become. An underdeveloped person is in that sense comparable to an underdeveloped country. Desert today, Dubai tomorrow – those unpromising dunes are the role-model for Jim Jones when he stops off for his injections on the way to Camden Fitness and then to school. Amartya Sen has explained the position well: 'Development consists of the removal of various types of unfreedoms that leave people with little choice and little opportunity of exercising their reasoned agency. The removal of substantial unfreedoms ... is *constitutive* of development' (Sen, 1999: xii).

In supporting good health through good care, society is facilitating personal liberation from the material roadblocks that stunt and destroy. Death is incompatible with life. Policies to preserve life must by definition be in keeping with the generic essence of a human being: 'The substantive freedoms include elementary capabilities like being able to avoid such deprivations as starvation, undernourishment, escapable morbidity and premature mortality' (Sen, 1999: 36).

Abraham Maslow writes that the body is subject to developmental laws and that the psyche is no different: 'We have, each of us, an essential biologically based inner nature, which is to some degree "natural", intrinsic, given, and in a certain limited sense, unchangeable' (Maslow, 1968 [1962]: 3). The species-being cannot be reduced to effective demand in the supermarket or the mall. Maslow sees needs as absolute and universal. He does not see them as the manufacture of the historic Jim Jones or of the culture which has moulded the malleable wax. The hierarchy of needs is not passing but eternal. It ascends through five levels of predetermined fulfillment until at the end the true and real Jim Jones emerges as that which he was always destined to be.

The lower needs must be satisfied first. Human beings must satisfy their bodily needs for food, housing, sleep and the opportunity to reproduce. One dimension of this fundamental first step would be the need to live illness-free. People cannot fly into the sky if they are enfeebled by a diet deficiency or too poor to afford life-saving surgery.

The body fed and watered, human beings then have a need to move up to safety and security. In terms of health policy this second stage might mean regulations to prevent accidents at work. It might also mean market-bending laws to protect mental health put at risk through perpetual worry about ruthless dismissals.

The third step upward will be the need for integration, fellowship, inclusion, organicism, community, social acceptance and common roots: 'The atomistic way of thinking is a form of mild psychopathology, or is at least one aspect of the syndrome of cognitive immaturity. The holistic way of thinking and seeing seems to come quite naturally and automatically to healthier, self-actualizing people' (Maslow, 1970 [1954]: xi). Applied to health, this might be an argument for a National Health Service which makes all citizens aware that they are joint tenants in a common enterprise. Privatisation would have the opposite effect. They will still be bowling but they will be bowling alone.

Blood donation is an illustration of the stage-three sense of shared attachment. Commercial donors have a pecuniary incentive to sell contaminated blood. Their myopic monetarism can cost the recipient their life. Community donors give away good blood. They do so because they are aware that the stranger gift is the biological precondition for their own psychic fulfilment: 'To "love" themselves they recognized the need to "love" strangers' (Titmuss, 1970: 239). Institutions matter. Social channels must be the appropriate ones for the satisfaction of the psychological and emotional needs and not just the physical imperatives that keep even a no-hoper alive. Inappropriate channels have the same effect in reverse. Unrestrained individualism and single-minded marketeering can damage the health of the donor and of the recipient alike.

The fourth level of need-satisfaction is the need for self-esteem and self-respect. Frustration, shame and self-loathing boost the roster of the suicides and the coronaries. Dignity and acceptance keep the melancholy and the lethargy away. If means-testing inflicts stigma and if spoiled self-image leads to illness, then one inference might be a biological need for citizen-based services as of right. The open door would protect fellow citizens from the social sanctions that are heaped upon the misfits who did not make the grade.

The fifth and highest level is self-actualisation. It is the stage at which human potential is definitively liberated through creativity, maturity and service. *Homo faber* is not the same as a satiated pig. Doctors and nurses find an outlet for their instinctual purposiveness in the meaningful work they do to alleviate the suffering of strangers they will never see again. Their sense of a vocation is intrinsic motivation that does not stop short at their cash incentive. Maslow would say that other people too should be given the same opportunity to protect their health through meaningful gratification of the higher need for workmanlike and other-orientated accomplishment. It is a sensation that people straitjacketed into the more egotistic, the more economic satisfactions will never be able to experience.

Needs, Maslow argues, are a mountain. Individuals who have not climbed the mountain might not be able to imagine the view that awaits them from the top. Health policy, like social policy in general, must be designed in such a way as to liberate the not-yet-enlightened from their own self-shackling narrowness: '*Being* a human being – in the sense of being born to the human species – must be defined also in terms of *becoming* a human being' (Maslow, 1970 [1954]: xviii).

Plato says that 'the measure of the excellence, beauty and correctness of any manufactured item, any living creature' can only be 'the use for which each is made or born' (Plato, 2012 [c.380 BC]: 348). A butterfly that never emerges from the cocoon is not a butterfly at all but a potential butterfly unnaturally suppressed: 'Nothing incomplete is a measure of anything – even though people sometimes do think they've got as far as they need' (Plato, 2012 [c.380 BC]: 229). Jim never grows beyond Jim to become fully Jones. Arrested in his development, he is not satisfying the full range of his needs when he stops short at beer.

It is not an easy journey. People know who they are. They are less likely to know what they have the capacity to become. Bottom-up, they have the option of the self-guided discovery process that leads them through life to the file marked 'Jones, Jim' in God's high-speed computer. Top-down, they can fall back on the professional expertise of sage old Sir. Empowerment through leadership is often the road to emancipation that is selected. It will often be medical attention narrowly defined, social policy as a whole, that ordinary people will prefer when they seek to satisfy needs of which in their blinkered underdevelopment they are not yet aware.

Yet even sage old Sir needs to listen and learn. Precisely because self-esteem is a need, therefore good health must involve self-determination as well. Individual preferences, revealed through purchases or recorded through votes, must be treated with respect. Most self-conscious human beings want to have a say. Denied control, they succumb to heart attacks because exclusion is incompatible with the need to be fully I: 'Disease rates are powerfully affected by the social environment' (Marmot and Bobak, 2000: 1128). The doctor knows the objective parameters but the patient alone has the personal input. Even the doctor must accept that the freedom to become implies an affirmation of voice. Even an Aristotelian must accept that autonomy and dialogue are core elements in the 'good life' that a sensitive leadership sets out to enhance.

The hip bone and the thigh bone are constants that the philosopher-rulers cannot dialectic away. The quality of life, on the other hand, is well suited to an exchange of views. Martha Nussbaum is confident that it was precisely this uninhibited give-and-take that Aristotle had in mind when he said that the quest for the absolute can be refracted through a symposium between friends:

> This is how the Aristotelian approach works – hanging on to a general (and open-ended) picture of human life, its needs and possibilities, but at every stage immersing itself in the concrete circumstances of history and culture ... Thus the Aristotelian virtue-based morality can capture a great deal of what the relativist is after, and still make a claim to objectivity. (Nussbaum, 1993: 259)

It is a lesson that every medical professional should take to heart.

6. The practitioner

Rawls writes as follows about the doctor who makes an interpersonal comparison of a dish that the diner had never ordered:

> On birthdays we give things that we know are wanted, or that will please, to express affection; our gifts are chosen in the light of intimate knowledge and shared experiences. But doctors are expected to assess the situation of their patients, and teachers to judge their students, on an entirely different basis ... Doctors consider their patients' medical needs, what is required to restore them to good health and how urgent their treatment is. (Rawls, 1982: 172)

On birthdays we go by wants. The metric of goal attainment is the recipient's personal preference. Surgery, however, depends on need. Need is a structural imperative that cannot be skimped if the function or role is to survive. Need is the precondition for want. Doctors are skilled specialists schooled in need-satisfaction. The consumers are not. It is the duty of the physician to fill the epistemological vacuum.

Medical paternalists have asserted that health care is too important to be delegated to the body-holder: 'Only the doctor knows what good doctoring is' (Horder, quoted in Johnson, 1977: 74). Liberal individualists are less convinced that the division of labour must inevitably mean delegation and dependence. Even the ill-informed have ideas and perceptions which they can bring to the table. Even the well-informed can slip into waste and beyond that into duplicity.

This chapter is about the well-informed. It has eight sections: 'The professional assessment', 'The doctor knows best', 'Payment and need', 'Supplier-induced demand', 'Countervailing forces', 'Practice variation', 'Value for money' and 'Trimming the fat'. The reader who is about to have surgery will find some of the sections more upbeat than others. Money is not the root of all evil. It is, however, a great temptation at the margin.

6.1 THE PROFESSIONAL ASSESSMENT

The ideal is the detached scientist. Faithful to the laws of nature and the balance of the body, doctors are not playing God or imposing their own view: 'The idea of professional need always rests on some definition of homeostasis or state maintenance of the client, his property or his environment. The professional defines a certain state of his client and his related systems as a state of "health" which he has a professional interest in maintaining' (Boulding, 1966: 204).

Good health is all in the body. The textbook benchmark is the blood count and the heartbeat. Yet good health is also in the utility-function. The ultimate success indicator can only be the protection and enhancement of the autonomous patient's own well-being. Rational beings want to get well and to live well. There are exceptions. The psychotic, the senile, the new-born, the unconscious and the self-destroying do not normally approach the electrician with a voiced request for better wires. Most problem-solving people do. Their 'oughtness' is similar to the doctor's 'oughtness'. The practitioner and the individual both want the body to return to its 'normal species functioning'.

The previous chapter shed light on the darkness. Ignorance is not bliss. Because of their ignorance, even wise and thinking patients can make what any impartial scientist would deem to be an inappropriate choice. The traveller wishes to go to London. The traveller ends up at Luton instead. The patient, as John Harsanyi explains, does not necessarily know best:

> All we have to do is to distinguish between a person's manifest preferences and his true preferences. His manifest preferences are his actual preferences as manifested by his observed behaviour, including preferences possibly based on erroneous factual beliefs or on careless logical analysis, or on strong emotions that at the moment greatly hinder rational choice. In contrast, a person's true preferences are the preferences he *would* have if he had all the relevant factual information, always reasoned with the greatest possible care, and were in a state of mind most conducive to rational choice ... In my opinion, social utility must be defined in terms of people's true preferences. (Harsanyi, 1982 [1977]: 55)

The final appeal is to the body-holder alone. Yet the body-holder can get it wrong. The traveller's true preference is make their way to London. They do not understand that they have boarded the train to Luton instead. Individualism is not necessarily the best means to the end where floundering subjects approach the crossroads without a map. That is a fact of life: 'One does not know what visiting the Taj Mahal is going to be like' (Mirrlees, 1982: 69). One does not know what defeating cancer is going to be like. One does not know. All that one knows is that one wants to take the chance.

One does the best one can. Sometimes one ends up at Luton instead:

> People sometimes have mistaken conceptions of their well-being. At least the conception must somehow be purified of obvious errors of foresight or memory. More, one ought to be willing to entertain the possibility that some experiences are not usually correctly valued by the individual: that, in certain respects, people do not know what is good for them. (Mirrlees, 1982: 64)

They know that they want to enjoy good health. Yet they take the train to Luton instead.

Moral agents have an incomplete picture of what is good for them. If they genuinely want to reach their self-targeted destination, then they would be well advised to let themselves be mentored by a guide. Such a guide is the medical professional. It is the doctor's role to mediate between the whole truth and the semi-deluded gut reaction. It is the doctor's function to impose order on revealed preferences that are random, knee-jerk, impulsive or intransitive. It is the doctor's duty to tell the less experienced if the resourcing proposed is likely to procure the improvement intended. That is all. London or Luton, the consumer is king.

The ideal physician is the principal's perfectly enlightened clone. Accessing both the objective facts about the body and the subjective sensations of the sentient, the ideal physician marries up the evidence. He does so without any trace of himself. The ideal doctor is 'as if' the patient. The voice of the one is the voice of the other.

The patient-led ideal is for supply to follow demand. Ignorance and information asymmetry modify the nature of the game. Face-to-face with a sick person who says they do not have a clue, sometimes the doctor will be expected to show initiative and influence the choice: 'The medical service market cannot be simply dichotomized into demand side and supply side, with price serving as the only nexus between the two; rather we must allow for shifts in the demand curve itself in response to supplier behaviour' (Evans, 1974: 163–4).

Prices are determined by supply and demand. Demand, however, is shaped by supply. That is precisely what the doctor–patient relationship is all about. Patients approach doctors to learn if wants are needs. Even if the principal is not up to date, well-informed, logical and detached, his bailiff will ideally do the economising on his behalf. No one would expect a doctor to conceal a malignant carcinoma merely because the patient did not spot it first.

Seen from the perspective of the practitioner, the patient's need is whole and uncompromising. Translated into economics, it is 'the expenditure required to effect the maximum possible health improvement or, equivalently, the expenditure required to reduce the individual's capacity to benefit to zero' (Culyer and Wagstaff, 1993: 436). It is one doctor acting on behalf of one patient to bring about the 'maximum possible'. Nothing less than the 'maximum possible' will do.

The individual comes before the practitioner. Chapter 5 comes before Chapter 6. It seems like patient-centred excellence. In fact it is an elephant trap. Chapter 7 introduces yet another constituency. The third constituency is the public. The third constituency looks the 'maximum possible' unashamedly in the mouth. It informs the doctor and the patient that the medical dyad is not alone.

Society is stern. It states that the 'maximum possible' in medicine does not take into account the 'maximum possible' in education, defence, manufacturing and marketing. A less blinkered interpretation of need would be that health care should not be taken in isolation but rather weighed at the margin against the 'capacity to benefit' in competing areas of social life. For general balance to be established, the 'maximum possible' might have to be compressed into the 'minimum that is adequate' lest the practitioner on behalf of the patient crowd out valued tracts of the good society of which both the doctor and the patient are a part. Infinite spending is as bad as no spending at all. To leave allocation by need to the well-drilled medical practitioner is to manoeuvre the nation into an elephant trap.

The medical practitioner is in any case never a detached technician aside. Doctors like all other members of their society are imbued with attitudes and expectations that are situated in time and space. It is other people and not the beating heart per se that give the practitioners their licence to cut and paste: 'The moral force of the word "need" when applied to health care stems from the moral force of the goals associated with health itself' (Culyer and Wagstaff, 1993: 435). Good health is a social fact. Situated and not universal, the doctor is always and everywhere a 'cultural dope'. The doctor returns the patient to the standard of good health that not they but their social consensus defines to be the norm.

Doctors are in that sense an agency of social control. They enforce the definition of the 'sick-role' that they share with their fellow citizens. They issue the certificate that validates the claimant as unfit for work. They ensure that malingerers do not free-ride on the income transfers of the Welfare State. They see to it that healthy young men do not feign debility in order to avoid national service. They attend at executions to certify that the law-breaker is genuinely dead. They perform lobotomies on political dissidents and report drug addicts to the police. They advise aberrant gays on an early return to beneficial heterosexuality.

Practitioners socialise and are socialised. They are a conduit through which public opinion is transmitted. Doctors do sociology whenever they tell the victims of racial discrimination that they have a persecution complex or the over-64s that a depleted once-was has no real need for a new kidney. Doctoring is what the doctors do. Chapter 7 as well as Chapter 6 is what doctors do. To think otherwise is to think oneself into an elephant trap.

6.2 THE DOCTOR KNOWS BEST

The doctor knows best. They know their objective parameters and their comparative probabilities. They know their normal, their standard, their acceptable, their minimal and their average. They also know their patients. They are in a position to give their opinion of their patient's opinion. Doctors do not need the questionnaires and the surveys, the seat belts and the danger differentials, to gain a purchase on the invisible mind. They visit the invisible mind every day in their office and in the patient's home.

The practitioner, in short, has access both to the clinical hard core and to the utility-sensitive sensations which are essential if the self-reported symptom is to be formalised into a diagnosis and after that into a cure. It is a holistic perspective which encompasses the person and not just the disease. That is why not just the patients but also the policymakers will often turn to the experts and the professionals for an authoritative assessment of person-centred good health. Who has a purchase on the common denominator, the rock-solid numéraire, that can compare acid reflux with palsy? The answer is clear. The doctor knows best.

The ideal doctor is one who can estimate the probable discomfort of the median sufferer or guess at the unrevealed preferences that from long experience they know to be latent within the hidden mind. The real-world doctor may not, however, be content with the follower's role. In such a case a gulf may open up between the counsellors and the counselled. Weak-willed Ulysses wants to steer his craft onto the rock. His strong-willed doctor replaces Ulysses' want with the doctor's own need because a divided self needs a father figure if he is to put Luton above London, which was always a foolish choice.

Kind and his colleagues compared doctors with their representative fellows. They found that the gatekeepers making the life-or-death decisions were not in tune with the rest of us: 'Doctors place relatively less emphasis on the importance of death in comparison with other states; i.e. regard *more* states as worse than death. Doctors also place more emphasis on the importance of subjective suffering' (Kind et al., 1982: 163).

Doctors, the investigators found, were soft and warm-hearted. Their aversion to disability and distress was greater than that of the median citizen. Doctors were more willing than the median to put resources into the relief of pain. Dressings have been ranked above appendectomies, hip replacements above coronary artery bypass grafting. Required to choose, it is common for doctors to rank felt happiness above life-expectancy. Williams asked five general surgeons at Guy's Hospital, London, to say which of 22 conditions was most deserving of one hour in the operating theatre. Male bilateral inguinal hernia topped the list (Williams, 1997: 259).

The bias was in favour of tea and sympathy and not the stiff upper lip. It could have been the other way round. It was the other way round in a study of family doctors in America. About 40 per cent of them pushed chronic alcoholics to the bottom of their list. Cirrhosis was a condition that they treated last. Not only was this a violation of the patient's freedom to choose, it was also at variance with the charter of liberal democracy. Only 17 per cent of the general public sampled were equally resistant to self-inflicted conditions (Neuberger et al., 1998: 174). The citizen in the street tended to think that even a convicted criminal or a drug addict could be a blood relative of Hippocrates. The doctors preferred instead to treat the responsible and the upstanding first. And the doctor knows best.

Doctors have knowledge. Still, however, there are gaps. The doctors might not be able to put a precise value on the lives they triage, or state in so many words what criteria they apply. Medical people rely on conditioned responses, knee-jerk reflexes, half-conscious reactions and the autopilot of second-nature automaticity to guide them efficiently through any emergency that might arise.

Philosophers verbalise. Doctors get on with the job. It leaves the policymakers in a quandary. The doctors know best. Yet the doctors will often be unable to articulate their general bestness in a way that can be codified into guidelines or extrapolated into policy. Doctors will seldom be able to put into words their reaction to the substandard life-years that they pare away, the terminally ill that they do not resuscitate, the potential human beings that they abort at the mother's request, the mothers' lives that are lost because of the abortions that they refuse to perform, the feeding-tubes that they disconnect because the coma is expected to be permanent. The Hippocratic Oath precommits them to help the sick. It does not encourage them to say when a human life in their care is spoiled beyond the point of redemption.

Doctors are not philosophers. It is not entirely true. Reacting quickly as they must, still the philosophy is encoded in their practice. What this suggests is that the policymaker seeking to ascertain the doctors' numerical valuation of life and limb should forego the detached intellectuality of correspondence and interviews in favour of *ex post* inference from revealed practice:

> The doctor who stays in theatre to finish a long and difficult operation and consequently misses an outpatient clinic is probably relying – implicitly or explicitly – on some sort of theory of justice whereby he can fairly decide to override his obligation to his outpatients in favour of his obligation to the patient on the table. So is the general practitioner who spends 30 minutes with the bereaved mother and only five with the lonely old lady who has a sore throat. (Gillon, 1985: 86)

The methodology is the fly on the wall. The observer might find that the median doctor has a cut-off point beyond which treatment is discontinued. The spy might discover that food and water are withdrawn after a known number of days in a vegetative state. Repeated and replicated, the policymaker will be able to infer *post festum* the quality of life and the cost of care that the doctors had at the back of their mind when they supplied the miracle drug or discontinued the antibiotics.

Doctors do philosophy even if they do not talk philosophy. It is their deeds and not their words that allow the inductivist to arrive at the maximum price that they by implication are willing to pay. It will not necessarily be the same price that the patient would judge to be fair. The doctor who incorrectly estimates the insider's own sensation-stock will be exposing the client to undertreatment or overtreatment, self-perceived. Nor will it necessarily be the same price that public opinion would put on a procedure. The community believes in stem cell research and euthanasia on demand. The doctor says that bone marrow transplants and murder as a supermarket choice cannot be reconciled with entrenched precedents and the professional code.

The patients, the public and the practitioner are in dispute about costs, benefits and sell-by dates. They seem not to agree on the precise meaning of good health and bad. Someone will have to give way. The patient and the public will have to give way. The doctor knows best.

6.3 PAYMENT AND NEED

The doctor's duty is to help the sick. Yet doctors are human too. Apart from their service ethic they also have private and personal objectives which bring them closer to their bill-paying, tax-paying fellow-citizens. Among those private and personal goals are job satisfaction, security, autonomy, prestige and income. Doctors respond to incentives. Incentives are multiple. Motivation is mixed. Money is not the only reason why doctors chose medicine over covetous Wall Street's 'greed is good'.

Yet doctors are human too; and that means that few of them will be entirely indifferent to cash. The task of the policymaker is to design a remuneration package which will bring out the best in service professionals while not marginalising the empathy and trustworthiness which differentiate the medical encounter from stock market speculation and arbitrage.

In some industries the customer pays for results. We pay the plumber when they repair our pipe. We pay the cobbler when they patch our sole. The medical nexus is different. Doctors are not contracting to make the patient well. The body, the environment and random luck all put in their oar. All that the doctors can guarantee is that they will do their best. So long as there was no proven fraud or negligence, the principal must pay the agent even if their illness gets worse. Even if they die in theatre, their estate must settle the debt.

The medical relationship is by its very nature loose and imprecise. The expectations of the patient and the practitioner might not coincide. Asymmetric information and conflicting economics give the patient an incentive to complain, the doctor an incentive to boast. There is always a penumbra of doubt: 'How successful is a treatment that saves a person's life but renders him permanently disabled? How does one measure a treatment that relieves, but does not eliminate, a particular set of symptoms? How successful is a treatment that prolongs a life for two months, or three, or four?' (Culyer, 1971: 197).

Plumbing and cobbling lend themselves to payment by results. Health care does not. More common in the field of health are the following three ways in which quantity supplied can be made a function of the pecuniary inducement.

6.3.1 Fee for Service

Fee for service is the piecework system. In piecework textiles production the economic manufacturer will multiply the pieces in order to maximise the take. In piecework medicine the avaricious peddlar will perform redundant surgery because of billable hours. People respond to monetary incentives. Even medical professionals cannot live on ethics and altruism alone.

This is not to say that economics makes all doctors liars and cheats. Strictly in economic terms their time and ancillary costs might exceed the meter fare. What is more likely is that at the margin the material doctor will add on further tests and scans; or supply precautionary medication through an in-house pharmacy; or perform unfamiliar interventions that ought ideally to be referred on; or shorten necessary consultations in order to force through the peak-paying footfall.

Patients themselves are partly to blame. If consumers demand comfort drugs or home-visit follow-ups, it not entirely the producers' fault if they deliver a higher-quality product in order to put sick people's minds at rest. Pass-through reimbursement is a sound medical reason to err on the side of more and not less. It does not prove that a sitting target is being taken for a ride. Yet the temptation to overprovide is always there. A healthy appendix can be removed to pay for a new car. It does not do much for the patient's confidence to know that the doctor may be cost–benefitting him as an asset to be bled.

There is no robust statistic on the extent of medically unjustifiable overuse. Since best practice is itself imprecise and problematic, it cannot be known if doctors who exceed the average are cynically fleecing the gullible or simply going the extra mile to restore the patient to health. All that can be said is that fee for service makes it easier for a gain-seeking entrepreneur to take the money and run. Consider the burden of health care expenditure (HCE) in Germany: 'Gross earnings for private doctors and some specialists (e.g. radiologists) are twice or three times those of salaried hospital doctors. Physician expenditures in Germany amount to about 25 percent of total HCE, the highest share in Europe' (Culyer, 1989: 30). Consider the cost-cutting capitations and salaries elsewhere in Europe: 'It is striking that the four countries that do not use fee for service as the principal means of payment (Denmark, Italy, Sweden, and the United Kingdom) have the four lowest ratios of average doctor income to GDP [gross domestic product] per capita' (Culyer, 1989: 30).

The costs went up. So did the risks. Overtreatment is bad for your health. A pill for every ill makes some people even more ill. Because of the perverse incentives, fee for service is frequently monitored by the insuring agencies. They contain the cost but they themselves cost money as well.

6.3.2 Salary

Where doctors are employed by an institution such as a hospital, they are not an independent contractor who enjoys admitting privileges but a cog on a scale whose workbench is nine-to-five. Their remuneration is not a function of the patients they see any more than it is of the recoveries they manage. Doctors on salary know how much they will be paid. The employing institution knows the wage bill for which it should plan. It helps them to contain their costs.

Doctors on salary have no financial incentive to multiply their services in order to maximise their incomes. Their economic incentive is not to oversupply discretionary interventions but rather to undersupply whatever is in the spirit but not the letter of the law. Time-servers on salary have no pecuniary incentive to deal with e-mail inquiries or monitor patients' medication. Bench-warmers have no financial reason to volunteer for weekend rostering or to perform their own night visits. The easy option is an outside locum.

Where quantity supplied is responding to a never-changing price, the economic expectation would be that the standard of workmanship will be adequate but not excellent. The tendency will be for patients to be treated as a necessary evil and a means to an end. So long as poor bedside manner does not lead to a formal complaint or legal action, the economic expectation would be that doctors on salary can afford to be abrupt, rude or slipshod. Moderate indifference will not be a serious threat to their remuneration. Especially will this be so where an institution makes seniority a proxy for productivity. Being pedestrian is no obstacle to being promoted where advancement is guaranteed and the hierarchy age-related.

Institutions know the risks. They also know that it is a simplification to think of the salary system as payment decoupled from performance. Salary can be compatible with inertia. It need not be. Where there are supplementary incentives, the doctors will less predictably regress to the baseline that was fixed in their contract.

Thus salary scales can make provision for annual reviews, accelerated promotion and performance bonuses. Hurdles such as these build in a flexible component that tops up the minimum guaranteed. Often doctors on salary will be given day-release to attend a refresher course. On-the-job updating is made that much more attractive to them by the fact that salaried staff do not incur an opportunity cost while they upgrade their human capital.

Appraisals can improve productivity. They can also favour mediocracy at the expense of service. Where the evaluation is biased towards shorter waits, faster turnover and fewer deaths, doctors will have an economic incentive to turn away the chronic because they impose a cost. Doctors will concentrate on itemised billing because that way their profit-sharing lies. They will devote less time to the confused and the concerned who want their condition to be explained in full.

Selective criteria can contain costs. They can also have the opposite effect. A doctor who receives extra points for shortening the queue will *de facto* be speeding up the flow of expensive operations. A doctor being monitored for recoveries might prescribe defensive medicine and expensive tomography out of fear that one bad mistake will block his increment. Continuous reporting and a personalised printout pick up the deviants who, exceeding the norm because they know their success indicators, are imposing an above-average burden on their institution.

6.3.3 Capitation

In the case of the capitation the doctor, an independent contractor, receives an annual sum from the patient or the patient's insurer. In exchange for this single fee the generalist undertakes to meet the patient's specified needs for the period in question.

The interests of principal and agent need not be the same. On the side of income, doctors will have a financial incentive to increase their registrations so as to maximise their per-capita fees. On the side of outgoings, doctors have no economic reason to supply services that have not been requested. Like salary and in contrast to fee for service the doctors on capitation have good time-and-effort grounds to deliver as little as they can. Doctors will want to select healthy young patients who will require fewer consultations and referrals. They will be less keen on bad risks like the anorexic, the autistic, the obese, the incurable and the high-maintenance. Problem people are a strain and a drain. No economic doctor wants that.

Money talks. Economics works both ways. While budget-holders are free to economise on top-quality service because it exhausts the surplus retained, their patients are just as free to transfer their capitations to a more generous competitor. Transparency is an essential part of rational choice. Patients need to know who is above average in the prescription of psychotropics and below average in referrals to specialists. A laggard who is seen from published statistics to be less generous than his rivals must expect that in the long run his clients will exit an unsatisfactory relationship.

Exit is economic. Yet loyalty is economic too. Where the patient is expected to remain for an extended period on the list, the capitation provides a non-medical reason to practise preventive medicine. Stress management, advice on hypertension, hepatitis injections mean extra work and marginal cost in the here and now. They are, on the other hand, an investment which will pay returns through fewer presentations over a succession of renewals.

Discounting, of course, makes business sense. The patient might not re-register with the same doctor or health maintenance organisation. Illness prevented or wellness assured might become an external economy to a neighbouring shop. Some slippage must be allowed for in the calculation. Doctors who continue to please their clients should nonetheless be confident that a critical mass of their caseload will not jump ship.

6.3.4 Mix and Match

Capitation is the third mode of payment, salary the second, fee for service the first. Conceptually, the three are distinct. In reality they can be mixed and matched. A doctor who is remunerated preponderantly by one mode can be paid a minority supplement under another. It is the task of the paying agency to put in place a combination of economic incentives that maximise the targeted state of health.

Earmarked fees are a case in point. Doctors may be on salary or capitation but they can still be offered special payments for electronic record-keeping, nose-to-toes physicals or minor surgery performed in the office. They can be paid a productivity bonus where they test a targeted proportion on their list for blood glucose and blurred vision or deliver vaccinations, mammograms or cervical smears to a threshold percentage. They can be thanked with a finder's fee where they register the hard-to-reach.

Doctors can be given extra payments if they invest in preventive medicine; if they visit the over-75s in their homes; if they attend a refresher course culminating in a relicensing test; if they supervise trainee doctors and neighbourhood paramedics; if they play their part in health awareness campaigns and community networks; if they provide out-of-hours cover or form multi-speciality group practices. Their basic pay is the salary or the capitation. The peripheral top-up is the fee.

Baseline remuneration can itself be used as an economic sweetener. Doctors can be attracted into deprived areas like the villages and the slums with the promise of lump sums, university scholarships, higher pay, subsidised housing and exemptions from military service. Such add-ons are an economic means of correcting a geographical imbalance.

Special capitations can be offered where the patient is chronic, elderly or in a high-risk occupation. In that way the practice budget ceases to be the underwriter of last resort. Shopkeepers will be less likely to turn away the customers most in need of their wares. Nor, however, should they accept more business than they can comfortably accommodate without voluntary overwork or lightning consultations. The paying agency for this reason has been known to protect general practitioners from themselves by imposing a ceiling limit to the doctor's list.

Not all incentives are financial incentives. Some doctors only want to help the sick. Some doctors strongly prefer to help themselves. Different doctors respond in different ways to different incentives. Health policy must build with the raw materials that it has. It is the great attraction of mix and match that the combination of incentives appeals successfully to a wide spectrum of personality types.

6.4 SUPPLIER-INDUCED DEMAND

The bias can go either way. Doctors can supply too little or they can supply too much. Diagnosis and treatment should not fall short of the medical optimum. Nor should they be so lavish as to suggest that the nation is being surcharged for superfluous self-indulgence. Supplier-induced demand is a layer of fat. It is a departure from clinical excellence that results when the profit motive causes higher quantity and quality to be provided than the patients themselves would have demanded had they been perfectly informed.

6.4.1 Excessive Medical Care

Supplier-induced demand is unnecessary attention unleashed by rapacious predators with an economic incentive to exaggerate and embellish. It is not the same as supplier-shaped demand, that is the unique and disinterested contribution of the trustworthy mentor who knows best. Trust is essential in the doctor–patient relationship where 'know-what' is as unequal as 'know-how' and where consumer sovereignty is so often delegated to the seller. Information asymmetry means that the supplier is free to test the limits of the fiduciary bond. The supplier has discretion. Discretion is a temptation to supply.

The starting point is Milton Roemer. He found a positive correlation between the supply of beds and the demand for stays: 'The level at which need is recognized is heavily influenced by the supply of beds available for its satisfaction ... The number and type of hospital beds materially influenced the practice of medicine' (Roemer, 1961: 37, 41). More beds were correlated with more admissions. Built beds were filled beds. Filled beds were billed beds. Billed beds were making the hospital go round.

Roemer's law is the Say's Law of inpatient attention. Say's Law says that supply creates its own demand. Fuchs found Say's Law at work even in the operating theatre when the census of surgeons increased and existing surgeons had to fight more aggressively for share: 'Where surgeons are more numerous, the demand for operations increases. Other things being equal, a 10 per cent higher surgeon/population ratio results in about a 3 per cent increase in the number of operations and an *increase* in price' (Fuchs, 1986 [1978]: 147).

More surgeons meant more surgeries. The quantity of operations went up. The price per operation went up as well. The downward-sloping demand curve predicts that it ought to have gone down instead. The inference is that underemployed professionals were using their influence to manipulate the vulnerable into paying more for more. They were able to defend and even augment their target incomes by turning to their own advantage the fact that the demand for elective surgery is not independent of the supplier's good counsel. Increasing the supply of surgeons would clearly do little to contain the cost of care. The supply curve shifts to the right. The demand curve shifts to the right. The money-minded have things all their own way.

6.4.2 Assessing the Surplus

The facts do not speak for themselves. It is never easy to falsify a hypothesis when the numbers that are required are all in the mind. On the side of demand, and because patients are never fully informed about their abnormalities and scenarios, the counsel of perfection is always as unobservable as the ideal-typical frictionless fall. On the side of supply, since few people like to admit to unadulterated avarice, the professionals in an interview will rationalise their demand-management as doing all they can to meet a genuine but unarticulated need.

The debate between demand-led supply and supply-led demand should ideally be settled with empirical evidence. As hard facts on the invisible mind are not easy to find, it must be settled instead by an appeal to a prioris and conjectures. The speculations can surprise. Logic augmented by experience does not necessarily confirm that the money-minded are having things all their own way. What it confirms is that in psychology nothing is ever as it seems.

Sometimes the optimum will be as easily recognised as a well-schooled either/or. Just as often it will be an ambiguity hidden behind a veil. Yip cautions that medicine is more than the mimicry of a knee-jerk routine: 'There are circumstances of clinical uncertainty in which individual judgment is necessary. It is under those circumstances that financial incentives would play a role in clinical decision making' (Yip, 1998: 692).

Where there is no obvious way forward, the supplier might be led by his more business-like self to induce marginal demand from which he himself stands to make a gain. A cardiologist might be led by his financial incentives to err on the side of more tests, more grafts and more ancillary services. He will deviate from standard practice but some certainty will set some limits. It is possible but less likely that he will bypass entirely healthy vessels merely because his integrity has been marginalised by his economics.

Time as well as unknowledge makes it difficult to read intentionality into the observations. Supplier-induced demand is longitudinal and history-dominated. It is not an instantaneous adjustment. The longer the time period, the less realistic it is to assume that other causal variables will remain constant. The number of doctors rises. So too do income and education. They have an independent influence of their own. People who demand more care will get more care. The supplier alone cannot be blamed if the consumers are insisting that something must be done.

People who need more care should be given more care. It is no defence of fewer treadmill tests and fewer exploratory biopsies to say that stoic acceptance and premature death keep the demand curve in its kennel. Underserved areas will have a backlog to make good. The correlation between more doctors and more doctoring might mean nothing more sinister than the relief of an existing backlog that had previously been rationed into silence by long waits and costly travel. The statistics might record not supply-induced demand but demand-induced supply. Neglected people might be getting what they need. No one should blame the doctors for that.

The principal–agent relationship itself complicates the interpretation of the evidence. Supplier-induced demand is the autonomous, exogenous pressure of the medical professional. The supplier moves first. It might, however, be just what the patient wants. Ignorance is not bliss. It is hard to believe that the patient derives no satisfaction at all from an elective procedure such as tonsillectomy, haemorrhoidectomy, hernia repair, varicose sclerotherapy or laser in-situ keratomileusis (LASIK) correction, merely because the initiative for cold surgery came from supply and not demand. If, however, the patient's well-being, self-perceived, goes up, then it would be wrong to speak of supplier-induced demand. What the supplier has unearthed may in truth be an authentic but latent demand that, never articulated, was there all along.

Consumer sovereignty does not give way to control if the practitioners only recommend what the sick themselves if fully informed would have requested. Personal gain is a good thing and not an aberration where the butcher, the brewer and the baker make their customers *ex post* feel better off. Consultations and follow-ups that make people feel healthy cannot reasonably be described as the sour fruit of misrepresentation. The practitioner cannot be said to have abused the information gap or ridden roughshod over the cash cow if the patient at the end of the exchange is convinced that a genuine need has been satisfied.

If want-creation does exist, then it is still not clear from the time-series why the push occurs where it does. It is odd that money-conscious professionals do not discover the maximisation of income until new entrants cut into their workload and attack their comfortable status quo. If slack had already been squeezed from the system, it shows remarkable restraint on the part of the money-minded that they do not exploit a seller's market until outside assault shocks them from their complacency. No less surprising is the fact that they respond to increased competition by raising and not by reducing their fees. Discounting would logically be the first line of defence when demand is unchanged and new rivals are queering the pitch.

6.5 COUNTERVAILING FORCES

The curve slopes up:

> Financial incentives significantly influence physicians' supply of health care ... A two per cent increase in reimbursement rates across the board leads to a three per cent increase in care. Physicians disproportionately adjust their provision of relatively intensive and elective treatments as reimbursements rise, and they appear to invest in new technologies in order to do so. (Clemens and Gottlieb, 2014: 1347)

The ball is in play. It is more than a tendency law.

The temptation is there. Even so, no one but a misanthropic Hobbesian would suggest that all doctors are swivelled-eyed swindlers, always on the look-out for a lucrative trade. Not every doctor is a *homo economicus* whose first duty is to his bank balance. There are crooks even in the church. This section argues that there are countervailing forces in the medical marketplace that keep the abuse of trust within tolerable limits.

One of these is the bank balance itself. It is an exaggeration to say that doctors inducing demand can pull targeted quantities and prices out of the air. They can try. Whether they succeed depends, however, on the time cost of persuasion, the marketing cost of doing business, the plasticity of the response and the speed with which the deal can be closed.

There are limits. No price can be quoted which is seriously out of line with the competition. Salesmanship itself can be counterproductive. Business may be lost when regular customers, alarmed by the hyperbole, lose confidence in the medical profession. They may seek a second opinion. The second opinion may be that the first opinion was the colour of money. Once bitten, twice shy. It adds up. Supplier-induced demand is not a free good.

Doctors respond to incentives. Their bank balance, however, is not their only incentive. Many if not most will have been attracted into medicine by the belief that their first duty is to the patient who needs their help. They would suffer from a guilty conscience and spoiled self-image if they violated the normative code into which they had been socialised. Intrinsic motivation can be more powerful than extrinsic. Job satisfaction through quality of service is an end in itself for self-policing craftsmen who take pride in their work.

Like judges and teachers, doctors are valued for their professional ethic. They are respected because their Hippocratic Oath is a cassock which proclaims the gravitational pull of the best-practice absolute. Adam Smith said that every sensitive person, striving for 'not only praise, but praise-worthiness', will make every effort to be 'that thing which, though it should be praised by nobody, is, however, the natural and proper object of praise' (Smith, 1966 [1759]: 166). Psychic income is a part of the remuneration package. Sensitive doctors strive to be impartial and reliable. They know that if they created wants in violation of their internalised norms they would not be able to look themselves in the mirror while they were scraping the blood off the cash.

The patient's utility is the practitioner's utility since the doctor has a heart. There is personal pleasure in helping a crippled child to walk or in rushing unbidden to the scene of a train crash. Price discrimination and pro bono Samaritanship envelop doctors in a warm glow of altruism that makes them feel good about themselves. Business huckstering and bottom lines have the opposite effect. Feeling bad is the psychic wrench of manipulating a known Jim Jones who is not an anonymous other. It is a cost, and all cost deters. To say that doctors are able to manufacture demand is not the same as to say that they will be prepared to do so.

Besides that, the doctor does not decide in a vacuum. The doctor is a member of a professional community and subject as such to its sanctions. Peer pressure may be as informal as ostracism and rudeness. It may be as structured as exclusion from a professional association with a monopoly charter. Doctors known to be removing healthy organs for financial gain may be denied malpractice insurance by an institutional cooperative. They may be blocked out of admitting privileges. The managers will want the windfall profits. They definitely will not want the hospital's reputation to be tarnished by the excessive and the dubious.

Professional certification, relicensing and external assessment all give the ignorant some protection from the monetised. There are the minuses as well as the gains. Professional codes can be rigid and unimaginative. Barriers can wall out innovation and wall in monopoly profits. In terms of supplier-induced demand, however, familiar responses and habituated self-regulation do keep opportunistic overtreatment within bounds.

When the velvet glove fails, there is always the law. The Ministry of Health can require a practitioner to explain above-average referrals to a fully owned subsidiary. The spectre of a malpractice suit might discourage marginal surgery that could go wrong. The patient who signs a consent form may not find it easy to prove later on that the wrong supply was induced. He is more likely to be paid damages if he can show that the knife slipped because the surgeon was drunk. Even so, the mere spectre of litigation might keep down the flagrantly egregious. The supplier has no wish to deplete his reputational capital.

A good name is a commercial asset. The internet, social media, smart phones and medical apps have radically altered the sourcing and sharing of information. One third of adults with a mobile phone are already using it to educate themselves in drugs, treatments, doctors and facilities. Advice and recommendations are being passed around. The doctor knows he is being blogged, tweeted and Skyped. The Earth is flat.

Repeat business and word of mouth have a tendency to contain superfluities. Often the medical relationship will be embedded in a continuing relationship. It is hard to pull the haggis over a long-serving patient who conducts a running tally and queries an unexpected charge. A one-off walk-in is more exposed. Knowing that few customers consume an appendectomy more than once, an economic doctor has no reason to invest in a return visit from a satisfied customer. Even then, personal recommendations give the patient a shopkeeper's stake in fidelity attention. Where the service is differentiated and the end-state not guaranteed, the ailing will approach their friends and acquaintances for a brand name they can trust.

Quality in the past is extrapolated into quality in the future. Proven veracity, established competence, are signs and signals in a floating market where heterogeneous suppliers come and go, where search is costly and where 'interest-seeking with guile' (Williamson, 1975: 9) skulks in every darkness. Established networks embed choices in a matrix of interdependent contacts. Goodwill protects the consumers from gain-maximisers who do not deserve their trust. It is also a cause of price dispersion. Search is less intense since the consumer has a rational reluctance to escape from a tried-and-tested monopoly.

Prices may be higher but potential abuse might be contained. As Granovetter says, the purposive action of social individuals is 'embedded in concrete, ongoing systems of social relations' (Granovetter, 1985: 487). It is not a wise decision to rock the boat. People get jobs because of contacts. Deals are closed with a handshake. Brokers say 'my word is my bond'. It is the same with medical practitioners. Patients enjoy protection because they come to the specialist through a referral. Even if the pool of patients is self-renewing, the family doctor goes on and on.

Where the patient begins the sequence with primary care, there is an expectation that the generalist will not recommend a specialist who spots a soft touch in every revolving door. Conflict of interest and weakness of will are kept within bounds where clients are employing point-of-entry advisers who do not themselves supply the actual service. The power of a fly-by-night wit-matcher to sell a low-quality procedure at a gold-standard price is limited by the presence in the market of the referring doctor who makes the initial diagnosis and, downstream, monitors the patient's recovery. The specialist who betrays the confidence of the general practitioner knows that further referrals cannot be expected.

Doctors fall ill. That in itself is a deterrent to supplier-induced demand. A small number of well-informed professionals with insider knowledge provide umbrella protection to the great mass of otherwise-specialised consumers who lack the expertise to police prices, sample therapies and keep standards high. They are a critical mass on which the haven't-a-clue and the in-the-dark are able to travel free. Even car mechanics buy cars. Even estate agents buy houses. The sellers of the cars and the houses know this. They are afraid to describe a 'lemon' as a 'peach' lest the shopper behind the veil turn out to have an unanticipated knowledge of fruit.

Doctors see doctors and consume care. Their appendectomies and elective surgeries may exceed the national average. It is unlikely that trained professionals would knowingly be exposing themselves and their families to expense and danger merely because some other doctor was displacing their demand curve up. If anything, the doctors might be consuming the proper quantity of care. The rest of the population might be lagging behind.

It is possible. Medical practitioners often express frustration at the tendency for expressed wants to fall short of medical needs. They are convinced that their clients 'systematically underestimate the marginal product of medical care': 'All individuals use less medical care than experts believe is appropriate ... Apparently, physicians cannot even convince people to buy enough care, much less induce them to buy more than enough' (Kenkel, 1990: 594). If the doctors are right, then asymmetric information is itself a check on supplier-induced demand. If the patients are neglecting the essentials, it is less likely that they are being cozened into the fringe.

Underutilisation exists cheek-by-jowl with overutilisation. Supplier-induced extravagance is cox-and-box with supplier-induced frugality. The bias of the imperfection is a function of the institutional architecture. Doctors indemnified by fee for service will have a pecuniary incentive to go gung-ho on quantity supplied. Doctors on salary or capitation will find it in their interest to supply only what the patient explicitly demands. A health maintenance organisation that gives a bonus to procrastinators will provide less than will a coven of fee-splitters who receive kickbacks for referrals. A patient who cost-shares will be more resistant to want-creation than will a patient for whom care is free at the point of use. Institutions matter. Reforming the institutional arrangements can moderate or even reverse the sign on the supplier-influenced imperfection.

The insurance industry itself bends back the bent rod. The paying agency has an incentive of its own to keep prices and quantities within budget. Business generates its own correctives. Insurers audit bills, standardise practices, query supernormal claims, conduct preoperative examinations. They rely on prospective payment to cap the charges and pre-specify the procedures. Payers compare the prices and shop around for their clients. They are aware that providers are exposed to moral hazard when they reason that an insured patient is a patient who conscience-free can be charged more for more. They also know that it is the function of the third party not to reimburse for waste.

6.6 PRACTICE VARIATION

The doctor knows best. Yet different doctors do different things. Each doctor believes that their solution is the rightest right, their 'optimum' the *optimum optimorum*. Each doctor believes that they are following the best-possible route to an agreed-upon improvement in their patient's health. The doctor knows best. Yet the solutions are alternatives and the routes distinct. There is more than one road between London and Luton. It would clearly not be appropriate to define supplier-induced demand as a derogation from clinical best practice when revealed preference reveals that clinical best practice is itself a range and not a point.

The practitioner 107

Alexander Pope said it in poetry: 'Who shall decide, when doctors disagree?' (Pope, 2006 [1732]: 251). Anderson and Mooney said it in prose:

> Substantial variations in utilisation of modern medical care seem to be more of an overwhelming rule than an exceptional phenomenon. Practice variation has revealed to a greater extent than ever before, and in a way which denies the essentialism of modern medicine, that medical practice floats on a sea of uncertainty. (Andersen and Mooney, 1990: 7)

Andersen and Mooney were struck by the range of disagreement and ambiguity that obtains even in a science-based, evidence-based area like medicine. Much seems to depend on the doctor that one consults. It is not much comfort to a patient down for an amputation and not bed rest.

6.6.1 The Extent of the Dispersion

The mammography rate for women aged 50–64 in America is 77 per cent. In Europe it is 46 per cent. Screening for colon cancer in America is 45 per cent. In Europe it is 22 per cent (Howard et al., 2009: 1841). Someone was overscreening and someone was underspending. But who?

The age-adjusted rate of bypass graft surgery for serious heart dysfunction was 1.79 times greater in New York than in Ontario. For mild heart dysfunction it was 8.97 times greater (Tu et al., 1997: 18). A heart patient who was very ill was almost twice as likely to have surgery in New York. A patient who was only moderately ill was almost ten times as likely to go under the knife. The hysterectomy rate was 2.3 times greater in Canada than in England and Wales. The mastectomy rate was 3.2 times greater (Vayda, 1973: 1225). A representative woman was more than twice as likely to lose her womb through surgery in Canada. She was more than three times as likely to lose a breast. In spite of that, the number of deaths from cervical, uterine and breast cancer was approximately the same. The number of deaths from diseases of the gallbladder was twice as high in Canada as it was in England and Wales. It is a surprising result. Cholecystectomy in Canada is five times as common.

Inguinal herniorrhaphy was performed twice as often in New England as in Liverpool. Cholecystectomy was performed seven times as often in Uppsala as in Liverpool. It was performed three times as often in Uppsala as in New England. Tonsillectomy and adenoidectomy were performed twice as often in New England as in Liverpool. They were performed four times as often in New England as in Uppsala. In the case of pre-school children, tonsillectomy and adenoidectomy were performed ten times as often in New England as in Uppsala (Pearson et al., 1968: 563). Were pre-school children in New England really ten times more sickly than their counterparts in Uppsala?

Doctors disagree from one country to another. They also disagree within the confines of a single nation. Few health care systems have managed to harmonise the babel of randomness or to impose a guiding light. Overuse, underuse and simply different use are as much an intra-national as an international problem. Wennberg, writing of the United States, cannot conceal his frustration: 'The "system" of care in the United States is not a system at all, but a largely unplanned and irrational sprawl' (Wennberg and Cooper, 1999: 4). Age-adjusted Medicare expenditure per capita in the United States is $6781 in Bend, Oregon but $12 090 in Corpus Christi, Texas (Dartmouth Atlas of Health Care, 2015). The patients are comparable. The treatments are not.

Wennberg found that the frequency of cardiac bypass surgery among Medicare enrollees, adjusted for age, sex and race, is three per 1000 in Albuquerque, New Mexico, but 11 per 1000 in Redding, California. Beta-blockers are prescribed for 5 per cent of heart patients in McAllen, Texas, but 80 per cent in Rochester, New York. There is a sixfold variance in surgery for lower back pain. The average number of hospital days per Medicare patient in the last six months of life ranged from 4.6 in Ogden, Utah to 21.4 in Newark, New Jersey. The average number of specialist visits per Medicare patient in the last six months of life ranged from two in Mason City, Iowa to twenty-five in Miami, Florida (Wennberg et al., 2002: W100–101). The incidence of radical prostatectomy was 0.8 per 1000 Medicare enrollees in San Francisco, California. It was 1.6 per 1000 Medicare enrollees in Los Angeles, California (Dartmouth Atlas of Health Care, 2015).

Tonsillectomies varied from 13 per 10 000 to 151 per 10 000 persons within the small state of Vermont. Appendectomies varied from 10 to 32. The total surgery rate ranged from 360 to 689: 'Hospitalization rates for specific admitting diagnoses and for surgical procedures are almost ten times greater in some hospital service areas as in others' (Wennberg and Gittelsohn, 1973: 1104, 1105). Medical opinion in Vermont is not unanimous. 'Best practice' is not a single bestness. Medical 'need' is not set in stone.

The residents of New Haven, Connecticut are about twice as likely as the residents of Boston, Massachussetts to undergo a coronary bypass. Bostonians, on the other hand, are more than twice as likely to have a carotid endarterectomy. For adult and paediatric medical cases, 'the admission rates are 1.49 and 1.47 times greater, and the length of stay 1.09 and 1.16 times longer for residents of Boston than for residents of

New Haven' (Wennberg et al., 1987: 1186–7). Both Boston and New Haven have top-class medical facilities. Both are university towns. Practitioners are in touch with international breakthroughs. Demographically, the populations are comparable. Medically, however, the neighbours disagree. What is standard procedure in the one is dubious science in the other.

The United States has a decentralised medical system. A dispersion in haemorrhoid injection per 10 000 population from 17 to 0.7, in skin biopsy from 190 to 41, in knee replacement from 20 to three (Chassin et al., 1986: 287) is what one might expect where no single planner is in charge. Canada has national insurance. The hysterectomy rate nonetheless climbs from 311 per 100 000 population in British Columbia to 512 per 100 000 population in Prince Edward Island. And there is Britain. Britain has the National Health Service (NHS). The nationalised, collectivised, unified, coordinated pyramid is explicitly committed to equalising access and universalising the best. In spite of that, the different regions do things in different ways.

Christopher Ham in 1988 documented the dispersion. There were 679 operations per gynaecological consultant in Yorkshire but 1320 in Trent. There were 740 operations per ear, nose and throat surgeon in Wessex but 1211 in Mersey. Prostatectomy varied in the ratio of 3:1 (Ham, 1988: 13, 19). Revisiting the dispersion in 2011, John Appleby found that it had not gone away. Cholecystectomy was 3.3:1. Knee replacement was 3.7:1. Hip operations, age and gender standardised, were 141 per 100 000 population in Wiltshire, 72 in Leicester. The dispersion in hip operations between Shropshire at the one extreme, Kensington and Chelsea at the other, was 4:1 (Appleby et al., 2011: 1).

In the Wessex region the mean length of stay was 3.9 per cent below that which the health-related characteristics of the catchment would have suggested. In the North East Thames region the actual figure exceeded the expected figure by 4 per cent. For the over-65s the mean length of stay was 18 per cent longer in Oxford than it was in Wessex (Martin and Smith, 1996: 285). The national standard was a moveable feast. It still is.

For emergency admission of children with asthma the dispersion between areas was 25:1. For emergency admission of patients with liver disease it was 16:1. For accident and emergency attendances it was 19:1. The mean length of stay for elective breast surgery varied from 0.3 days to 7 days. The variance was 25:1. The rate of bariatric surgery varied from 0.4 to 41.3 per 100 000 population. The dispersion was 93:1. Expressed in terms of spending, the dispersion in neurology was 2.8:1, in mental health 3:1, in dermatology 3.3:1, in learning disabilities 8:1 (Department of Health, 2011: 24, 25, 65, 66, 74, 91). Medically speaking the numbers by themselves mean very little. One hospital's 'excessive' is another hospital's 'inadequate'. All that the data says is that there is nothing so non-standard as the standard practice. And this is the *National Health Service*.

6.6.2 The Reasons for the Variance

There is nothing so non-standard as the best-possible best. The reasons for the dispersion are themselves a moveable feast of possibilities and conjectures.

On the demand side, there are the patient's own articulated preferences. Clients might be requesting specific procedures and convalescent stays. They may be making their choice in light of localised expectations, socialised risk-appetite and their own past experience in a local treatment centre. It is demand-led supply. Elective procedures follow the patient's choice. It may be the more expensive option but at least it is not manipulation for gain.

Demand, needless to say, must be effective demand. Practice variation might in that way shadow regional contrasts in income, savings and family support. Dispersion could be correlated with socio-economic deprivation. Patients with little net wealth will turn to bed rest, chicken soup and informal carers. Patients with first-dollar coverage will be under less compulsion to discharge themselves from hospital.

The doctors for their part might be tailoring their interventions and their charges to the patient's estimated ability to pay. Whether this accounts for inter-regional as well as interpersonal variance is an empirical matter. It will depend on the geographical bunching of the rich and the poor. International comparisons are more conspicuously a function of spendable resources. The median American and the median Bangladeshi cannot afford the same services and drugs.

Effective demand is correlated with insurance coverage, private and national. Even the government is not equally generous in all regions. In the US the state-by-state variance in the Medicare spend is 3:1. In England some primary care trusts are 10 per cent below their age-standardised target, others 24 per cent above (Appleby et al., 2011: 4). If they have less money, they will be purchasing fewer procedures. They will be prioritising their interventions in keeping with local public opinion. The voice of the people is the voice of God. It is not much comfort to those with a minority condition in which the mainstream takes little or no interest.

Areas differ not just in spendable resources but also in occupational, demographic and cultural make-up. Lifestyle will differ. A coal-mining community will not have the same medical needs as a leafy suburb. A deprived area will have more illness than a prosperous area. A peer group that stigmatises alcohol will be different from a peer group that lives in the pub. An ethnic group which has critical mass in an area will require the specific services for which it has an above-average need. One reason why the geographical dispersion of kidney transplants from deceased donors in England stands in the ratio of 2:1 is that Afro-Caribbeans, three times more likely to need a transplant, are geographically concentrated (Department of Health, 2011: 181).

On the supply side there is the availability of inputs. If the beds and the doctors are there then Roemer's Law comes into play. Medicare spending in Miami was $8414 per enrollee. It was $3341 in Minneapolis. Fisher, studying disparities such as these, concludes that local reserves are the best predictor of the interventions supplied: 'The greater-than-twofold differences observed across U.S. regions are not due to differences in the prices of medical services or to apparent differences in average levels of illness or socioeconomic status. Rather, they are due to the overall quantity of medical services provided and the relative predominance of internists and medical subspecialists in high-cost regions' (Fisher et al., 2003: 273, 284–5).

Inputs influence treatments. The ratio of coronary artery bypass graft in the US compared to the UK is five times higher (Brook et al., 1988: 750). A plausible reason for the variance is the larger number of acute care beds in the United States and the higher proportion of specialists to generalists within the doctoring stock. More eggs lead to more omelettes. More beds and more surgeons lead to more bed-stays and more surgery: 'Variations in the rates of hospitalization for most conditions are driven by supply, rather than need ... Capacity, not medical science, drives the rates of hospitalization, even in regions served by distinguished teaching hospitals' (Wennberg and Cooper, 1999: 69, 88).

A built bed is a filled bed. In Sun City, California, about 49 per cent of the cohort is admitted to intensive care in the last six months of life. In Sun City, Arizona, the proportion drops to 14 per cent. Wennberg and Cooper say that a robust predictor of death in hospital as compared with death at home is the local supply of beds. It is a better predictor than the patient's own preferences. Admissions per 10 000 population were higher in Boston than in New Haven. There were also 55 per cent more hospital beds in Boston. Whether the beds were proactively inducing their own occupants or whether unsatisfied demand had long been queuing for relief, what is clear is the association. If there is no bed, there is no choice.

Variance is influenced by availability. If there is no scalpel, there is no incision. The rates of cardiac bypass surgery 'are strongly correlated with the numbers of per capita cardiac catheterization labs in the regions but not with illness rates as measured by the incidence of heart attacks in the region' (Wennberg et al., 2002: W101). Cardiac bypass is more common in California than in Ontario. In Ontario the number of open-heart units is capped. In California it is not. More units go with more surgeries. California 'has three times the population of Ontario but ten times the number of bypass surgery facilities ... As a result, a typical heart attack patient is many times more likely to get bypass surgery or angioplasty in the United States' (Cutler, 2004: 58).

Variance is influenced by availability. It is also influenced by training. Different medical schools inculcate different responses. Some favour a discretionary tonsillectomy or a precautionary hysterectomy. Others are cautious about unnecessary tests and premature interventions. Some recommend admission for asthma or gastroenteritis. Others have a long-established practice of non-emergency cases sleeping at home.

Vintage is relevant. Different cohorts will have been exposed to changing techniques and shifting fashions in the course of their education and career. Not all doctors will have made an effort to keep up with the latest developments. Just as consumers can suffer from ignorance and tunnel vision, so can suppliers when they settle into a rut. Their code, in the language of the street, is 'If it ain't broke don't fix it'. A time-stamped reliance on the know-how that has performed well in the past seals in the practice variation.

Professional bodies in different regions replicate distinctive norms and specific conventions. They promulgate guidelines in an honest attempt to keep local standards up. Each hospital will have a practice subculture of its own. A physician granted admitting privileges would be well advised to respect the local way. Doctors who practice in more than one hospital may have to conform to more than one institutional consensus. They snowball their hospital's done thing because they do not want to be criticised or asked to go.

Conformity is common in the world of health. While it may be rational for a medical entrepreneur to seek out a low-cost innovation, it is at least as rational for a cautious conservative to depend on the crutch of the best-possible reflex. Health care is fraught with uncertainty. The patient can die if the doctor takes a risk. Given the subjectivity and the doubt, doctors often perpetuate the tried-and-tested because the knee-jerk has served them and their peer group well in the past. There is safety in numbers. If the patient does not make a full recovery, the doctor can blame the surgical signature, the learned response and the traditional routine. Mimicry gives the practitioner confidence. No one wants to feel guilty or to take the blame alone.

The herd instinct explains a part of the practice style but so does the doctor's own personality. Westert in Holland found that the average inpatient stay for hernia repair was a very similar 5.9 to 6.7 days. Hospitals converged. Doctors did not. The spread widened to 3.9 to 7.1 days when allowance was made for the human factor (Westert et al., 1993: 835). Doctors differ in their ability to think in terms of probability, in their aversion to risk, in their willingness to explore a short-cut, in their readiness to trade excellence for cost. They differ in the extent to which they will forego reimbursable interventions in order to be a listening ear. They differ in their capacity to spot the early symptoms of diabetes or a heart attack. They differ in their responsiveness to patients' preferences even when the expressed wish seems to them to be trivial or self-indulgent.

They also differ in their response to economic incentives. Capitation and salary can keep the interventions down. Fee for service can turn loose the demon of supplier-induced demand. Practice is influenced by the medical efficacy of different scenarios. It is also influenced by the opportunity to mine vicarious choice and voluntary delegation for whatever the traffic will bear. The patient who goes in for an aspirin might come out with a transplant. Economics brings out the worst in people.

6.7 VALUE FOR MONEY

In Boston about 16 per cent of the local domestic product was invested in health. In New Haven it was only 9 per cent. In Boston total spending per capita on inpatient care was $889. In New Haven it was $451: 'The 685,400 residents of Boston incurred about $300 million more in hospital expenditures and used 739 more beds than they would have if the use rates for New Haven residents had applied' (Wennberg et al., 1987: 1185). The residents of Boston were committing $300 million more to beds. The real question is whether they were enjoying better health in return. If they were, then it was an investment. If they were not, then it was money down the drain. There is more. The evidence does not exist that can blue-line the improvement and red-line the waste. No one can see the big picture. Individual procedures may nevertheless be used as the litmus that proves the test. The litmus does not always suggest a strong correlation between money and health.

Wennberg found that surgery for benign prostate removal in the United States varied in the ratio of 10:1 but that the outcome indicators were more or less the same. For most men, surgery did not lengthen life-expectancy (Wennberg and Cooper, 1999: 225). For some men life-expectancy might even have gone down. Where there is theatre there is death. Side-effects like incontinence and impotence affect the quality if not the quantity of life. Patients, if fully informed, might not have taken the chance. Medicare reimbursements for prostate removal exceeded $1.8 billion. Wennberg estimated that 1.6 billion hospital days were involved. It is a substantial overhead if there is little or no improvement in felt well-being.

Greenspan, asking expert cardiologists to peer-review treatments based on medical records, found that 20 per cent of the permanent pacemakers implanted in Philadelphia County were likely to have been medically unnecessary. Each implant costs $12 000 (Greenspan et al., 1988: 161). Chassin discovered that 17 per cent of the coronary angiographies, 17 per cent of the upper gastrointestinal tract endoscopies and 32 per cent of the carotid endarterectomies performed on a cross-section of the elderly were not medically justified (Chassin et al., 1987: 2533, 2535). Winslow, conducting a further study of endarterectomies, estimated that 32 per cent were inappropriate, 32 per cent were equivocal and only 35 per cent were essential. The risk of major complications was 9.8 per cent (Winslow et al., 1988: 724). The risks may have outweighed the benefits. The procedure may have been overexpanded. In terms of medical efficacy, it may have been money frittered away.

Schuster estimated the proportion of medical services in the United States that should not, professionally speaking, have been delivered at all. The figure, he said, could have been as high as 30 per cent for acute care, 20 per cent for chronic (Schuster et al., 1998: 521). Cutler, concentrating on surgery, confirmed the general impression that some Americans were getting too much: 'About one in ten people undergoing a major operation does not meet the clinical criteria for that operation' (Cutler, 2004: xi).

The difference in lifetime Medicare spending between a typical 65-year-old in Miami, Florida and one in Minneapolis, Minnesota was more than US$50 000 (Wennberg et al., 2002: W97). As much as 20 per cent of the Medicare budget could be saved if Miami were to convert to Minneapolis's medically effective practice style: 'Debates over the need for further growth in medical spending and expansion of the medical workforce are largely based on the assumption that additional services will provide important health benefits to the population served. Our study suggests that this assumption is unwarranted' (Fisher et al., 2003: 298).

Waste of 20 per cent translates into potential savings of $1000 per person. It is a great deal of money, and for not much additional health in return. Ontario rations its bypasses. It seeks out the cheaper alternatives instead. California does not. It goes for the more expensive therapy: 'And yet, survival after a heart attack is virtually identical in the two countries' (Cutler, 2004: 58). If the Canadians had got it right and the Americans had got it wrong, the inference is that a considerable sum of money could be freed up.

6.8 TRIMMING THE FAT

Depression can be seen as a sadness which, like pain, is a part of life. It can also be regarded as an intolerable abnormality that cries out for tablets and counsellors. A limp can be regarded as a minor inconvenience with which the sufferer will have to live. It can also be seen as an unacceptable disappointment that must be corrected through surgery. Perceptions differ. Doctors differ. Patients differ. We are not all the same.

A standard protocol compresses the amplitude. Medicine, however, must allow for the ups and downs in the terrain. There might not be a single right answer. There might be nothing more than a spectrum of trade-offs. Your want is not a need in this office. We prescribe backbone and red meat. Your want *is* a need in the office next door. They believe that even a hypochondriac has a condition that must be acknowledged. The wants that are validated as needs depend on the buzzer that the client presses. That might be what dispersion means.

Dispersion can be extravagance but it can also be freedom. Because human beings are not all the same, there is always a case for letting 1000 flowers bloom. Opinion should be respected but it should also be informed. Evidence-based medicine need not mean a single production function. What it does mean is that choices are made on the basis of targeted information and not in the dark.

Medicine is not an exact science. Knowledge will always be imperfect. Even so, success rates can be tracked and comparative performance monitored. Randomised control trials, hospital league tables, utilisation reviews, peer assessments, medical audit all shed light on what makes sick people feel well.

Decennial recertification forces the doctors to keep up with the medical literature. Consensus conferences give practitioners a focus group within which they can share their clinical excellence. Independent institutes make recommendations on best-practice drugs, tests and equipment. Websites and short courses diffuse information on the state of the art. Paying agencies, private and public, reward compliance and penalise the exceptional.

Yet the consumer too has a role to play in making the market perform. Patients need to know the risks and probable outcomes. Deductibles and cost shares give them a pecuniary incentive to make an intelligent choice. Referrals rather than self-referrals set limits to the overimaginative exercise of wishful thinking. There is no reason to think that this will eliminate practice variation. It does mean, however, that the supplier will not be imposing a single standard without consulting the body-holder who alone knows what it means to feel well again.

7. The public

There is individualism: it maintains that the patient alone can recognise a healthy mind in a healthy body. There is professionalism: it insists that the doctor must have clinical freedom since the clinician alone can identify a need. Then there is social-ism. Social-ists believe that the patient and the doctor are only cells in an organism, atoms in a structure. The patient and the doctor are only parts. The truth is the whole.

Social-ists situate the I in the context of the We. They believe that the embedding collectivity is an entity *sui generis*. They believe that the social cake is qualitatively different from the discrete ingredients that mix and meld. Social-ists argue that the internalised norms, the shared mores and the common conventions add up to mutual constraint by agreement and consensus: 'We may say that what is moral is everything that is a source of solidarity, everything that forces man to take account of other people' (Durkheim, 1984 [1893]: 331). The mapped coordinates emancipate the unrooted and the homeless from meaningless egotism and anomic detachment. It is their function to integrate the rudderless self in meaningful interdependence with its teammates and its fellows. They are, Durkheim says, the *sine qua non* if the Hobbesian *bellum* is to be kept at bay: 'Cause all social life to vanish, and moral life would vanish at the same time, having no object to cling to' (Durkheim, 1984 [1893]: 331).

Where there is a social mould the patient and the doctor are not free to make their own contract. Where there is a social need a third party must sit in judgement to ensure the social stake. Society has a leasehold in Jack's liver and a freehold in Jill's spleen. The property is encumbered. Jack and Jill are not free to do as they like with their own. T.H. Marshall saw precisely what the lien entailed: 'Your body is part of the national capital, and must be looked after, and sickness causes a loss of national income, in addition to being liable to spread' (Marshall, 1981 [1965]: 91). Your body belongs to us and not just to you. Your cigarettes and alcohol are our value-added foregone. You should pay your tax. You should do your homework. You should eat an apple a day.

You should also consume 'merit goods'. These are an area of social life where wise and thinking paternalists have prescribed the medicine that protects all of us from harm. Musgrave says that merit goods have a 'social stamp' that overrides the individual's whim. Where there is a social stake, and even in a market society, 'interference is not accidental':

> The existence of merit goods thus defined may be taken to suggest that our society, which considers itself democratic, retains elements of autocracy, which permit the elite (however defined) to impose their preferences. Or, it may be interpreted as adherence to community interests and values by which individual preferences are overridden. Either explanation contravenes free consumer choice, the otherwise accepted principle of resource use. (Musgrave and Musgrave, 1980: 85)

Normal economic goods are an individual choice. Merit goods are supra-economic goods which the isolated individual does not have the right to refuse.

This chapter, going beyond demand and supply, brings in the spectators, the examiners, the inspectors and the anonymous other. It says that society as a whole situates the consumer and the provider in a seamless web of cultural norms, standard-size roles and close-knit interests which only the criminal and the psychopath will have any wish to disregard: 'Needs arise by virtue of the kind of society to which individuals belong. Society imposes expectations, through its occupational, educational, economic, and other systems, and it also creates wants, through its organization and customs' (Townsend, 1979: 50). I am I because We are We. Health care is a social fact.

This chapter is concerned with public opinion and meddlesome choice. It suggests that there are four dimensions to the social stake. Each is captured in one of the four sections: 'Social values', 'Externalities', 'Path dependence' and 'Political economy'. It concludes that tolerant coexistence is less frequently found in the market for health than it is in the market for apples. Hell is other people. We cannot live with them. We cannot live without them. That is the way it is.

7.1 SOCIAL VALUES

Citizens who share their imperatives will be prone to underwrite some departures and to stigmatise others. Their unregimented choices are idiosyncratic but also overlapping. Their revealed preferences are intrinsic but also habituated. *De gustibus* is *We gustibus*. It is not, as Kenneth Boulding says, just another name for a normative Immaculate Conception: 'Even personal tastes are learned, in the matrix of a culture or a subculture in which we grow up, by very much the same kind of process by which we learn our common values' (Boulding, 1969: 1). Even High

Street purchases are the self-magnifying absolutes of self-aware communicants. They pray with greater conviction because they pray in concert as a church.

The past conditions the present and the environment moulds the mind. No free-standing ego, self-sufficient and inviolable, ever sets off without baggage in pursuit of his or her life plan: 'We must be governed by canons of reasoning, norms of conduct, standards of excellence that are not themselves the products of our choices. We have acquired them at least partly as the result of others' advice, example, teaching' (Dworkin, 1988: 12). We live by customs and institutions, tacit agreements and 'accepted understandings'. There is no other way that we can live: 'It makes no more sense to suppose we invent the moral law for ourselves than to suppose that we invent the language we speak' (Dworkin, 1988: 36). Liberty is not unbounded. My way of life is our way of life too.

Autonomy is exercised within a ring. Self-determination is circumscribed by the rules of the game. Although rugged frontiersmen like to think that they are carving out their own health, the truth is that they are starting from here and not *ab initio*. The sick role is situated in time and place. Slavery by consent is all around. The neighbours behind their lace curtains are watching the sick person's every move. They are volunteering their diagnosis as soon as the sick person stands up and says 'I don't feel well'.

7.1.1 Needs, Wants and Consensus

Economists use the construct of a 'social welfare function' (Bergson, 1938) to identify the consensual optimum in a given society. Such a function, easily accessed by the omniscient and the beneficent and with more difficulty by normal human beings, maximises the felt well-being that a bordered economy can squeeze from its productive possibilities. The welfare function is social and specific through and through. It is the property of a 'reference population', a 'self-governing linguistic subset', a nation, a State (Braybrooke, 1987: 62). It has a home on the map: 'The communitarian would argue for individuals being valuers as long as these individuals are allowed to reflect their history and their community ... Values, in other words, are context specific' (Mooney, 1991: 51). The public interest is here and now. It is thee and me. He and she will have to fit in.

Social values separate the needs from the wants. They decree that the ecstatic trance of the drug addict is neither a real need nor a valid want. They in that way violate the consumer sovereignty of the self-defining monad to purchase opium even as they purchase fruit. Social values also specify when one validated want must be subordinated to another because scarce common resources have an opportunity cost. Not everything that contributes to perceived well-being can be funded by a society that has more than one need.

A need is defined by the end. The rule is that 'N needs x in order to y': 'Nothing that cannot be fitted into the relational formula can be regarded as a need' (Braybrooke, 1987: 30). Cup-and-mug is necessary. It is not sufficient. Required as well is a collective choice as to whether the completion of the circuit will justify the time and money that it will cost the All. A Cambridge professor 'needs larger house-room, more quiet, lighter and more digestible food, and perhaps more change of scene and other comforts than will suffice for maintaining the efficiency of unskilled work' (Marshall, 1966 [1907]: 324–5). That is his need. The fact that he has a need does not mean that his fellow citizens will rubber-stamp his demand. Social values are what they are. They might put the satisfaction of other needs first.

Beliefs and attitudes spotlight the increments that ought to be put first. Two miners trapped underground have an urgent need. A thousand children requiring the polio vaccine also have an urgent need. Neither need has the lexicographic priority. Neither need has a superior claim merely because it is rooted in the imperative to survive. Need satisfaction in the one case, as in the other, is contingent upon social values. Choices have to be made. Ongoing values minimise the resentment, frustration and felt exclusion by ensuring that consensual rankings are respected when the outliers are moved to the end of the queue.

7.1.2 Achievement and Ascription

Public policy in a liberal democracy must be 'as if' an implicit referendum on the characteristics and criteria that are the gatekeeper to the common endowment. Equity must be seen and felt. The hidden mind must be gauged. The hidden median must be identified.

A castaway on an uninhabited island can act on the basis of his own particular interest. A government has to reconcile the intellectual and material interests of a cacophony of players. Since different groupings will have different priorities, public policy will often have to incorporate elements from each of the disparate world views. Consistency and accountability might not be compatible. Public opinion might be public *opinions*. Social cohesion presupposes that a skilful government puts together a mixed manifesto that keeps the disparate world views on side.

Some citizens will put economic growth first. Judgmental and econo-mystic, they will find it correct that health care should be skewed towards well-paid high-flyers with good practical qualifications who will repay the investment. People who earn more must be worth more. It is all a question of human capital, discounted cash flow, expected pay-back and the back-scratching quid pro quo. The collective need and not the individual want becomes the selective standard. Discriminating in favour of the footballer who is consistently scoring goals on behalf of the team, a consensus that puts economic growth first will treat the untimely liquidation of the heart and the brain 'more as a loss of livelihood than as a loss of life' (Schelling, 1973 [1968]: 295).

A consensus that puts economic growth first will want to skew its health care endowment towards male business and engineering graduates who earn over the odds. It will condemn low-grade office cleaners and the deadweight down-and-out to the vestigialism of the back ward. Although recognisably human, the disabled, the autistic and the over-the-top are a means that does not maximise its end. The value-add tips the balance. Taxpayers who are funding the service say that they have a democrat's right to call the tune.

Kantians will disagree. Philosophy is the last resort of the well-meaning when public opinion lets them down. It is a moot point whether governments should act on ethical absolutes when the consensus defines the body-holder to be a leaseholder whose wasting tenure has run out. Respect for human needs and respect for constituents' opinions may point the decision-maker in two different directions at once. The vestigialism of the back ward is often the only compromise that a materialistic consensus will grudgingly permit.

Some citizens will put economic growth first. Other citizens, concerned about basic needs and unrelieved distress, will have a non-rational antipathy to the idea that the defeated and the forgotten should die where they fall. Compassionate and altruistic, they will demand a steady stream of dignity and belonging, cohesion and solidarity, even if the price of the geriatric beds, the HIV hospices and the village clinics is high taxes that dent the incentives of Bad Samaritans who do not want to share.

Relying on philosophy, such societies will say that productive potential can never be the entry ticket to a human right. Relying on economics, they will say that if a money value of life must be calculated, then it should follow the proxy willingness to pay and not the expected value of the lifetime differential. Either way, such societies will believe, the senile, the retarded and the disabled must not automatically be dispatched to the knacker's yard merely because they are not covering the cost of their stable and their feed.

It is not certain how much citizens in a market society will be willing to sacrifice in order to help others whose pool of life-years, quality-adjusted, is not as great. A sample of university students in Sweden revealed that healthy respondents were prepared to trade as much as one quality-adjusted life-year of their own to purchase 0.58 quality-adjusted life-years for unknown strangers who, in the donors' estimation, had the greater need (Johannesson and Gerdtham, 1996: 366). It was all words. What they would have done on the day is not known. What is clear, however, is that inequality counts and that some people do care. The over-50s can still hope for a kidney transplant and the chain smokers for a heart.

So self-denying, so redistributive a 'conscience collective' lends support to the Rawlsian 'difference principle'. Rawls anticipated that rational people would want to see an allocation of basic claims that worked 'to the greatest benefit of the least advantaged' (Rawls, 1972 [1971]: 302). The assumption was interest and the veil was ignorance but the end-state was sharing nonetheless. The Swedish students went further. Even without a veil they were prepared to split their innings.

Every taxpayer, every blood donor, is a Swedish student in that respect. Titmuss on social interaction as a brotherhood of gifts should evidently not be written off too soon. Possibly the Swedish students, like the rest of us, do have a 'biological need to help' (Titmuss, 1970: 198). There is no point in making policy on the assumption of selfishness if it is generosity that the citizens really want.

The citizens may want health care to be allocated on the basis of common humanity and not economic growth. Yet that does not mean that they believe the entitlement to be infinite. Valuing generosity but acknowledging scarcity, they know that they have to make a choice. Very often that choice will be to show some preference for the young who have their whole life before them, even if the nation then has to cut back on history's has-beens who have exhausted their three score years and ten.

It sounds like growth. In fact, it is equity. A society has to be fair to its seniors. It has, however, to be fair to its juniors as well. A senior official who refuses to retire is depriving a junior official of a long-delayed promotion. Just as in work, so in health, the principle of dead men's shoes is alive and kicking:

> The fair innings argument takes the view that there is some span of years that we consider a reasonable life ... The fair innings argument requires that everyone be given an equal chance to have a fair innings, to reach the

> appropriate threshold but, having reached it, they have received their entitlement. The rest of their life is the sort of bonus which may be cancelled when this is necessary to help others reach the threshold. (Harris, 1985: 91)

Few decent people would go on record in support of racism, sexism, caste-ism or religion-ism. Ageism, however, is the new taboo that dare not speak its name: 'While it is always a *misfortune* to die when one wants to go on living, it is not a *tragedy* to die in old age: but it is, on the other hand, both a tragedy and a misfortune to be cut off prematurely' (Harris, 1985: 93). A 'fair innings' is a fair deal: 'Those who get less than this are entitled to feel unfairly treated, whereas those who get more than this have no cause to complain on equity grounds when they eventually die' (Williams and Cookson, 2000: 1876). Everyone dies sometime. All that the consensus is doing is expressing a considered opinion on who dies when and why.

It puts the British National Health Service (NHS) in a difficult position. On the one hand it is Bevanite from top to bottom: it has committed itself to the provision of best-quality care on the basis of 'real need' and 'real need' alone. On the other hand it is consensual and democratic: it has to copy its Patient's Charter and its Patient's Constitution from the great groundswell of public opinion. On the one hand it has to save Bill because Bill has a want and a need to live. On the other hand it has to kill Bill because Bill's neighbours believe he has had his life. A National Health Service is trapped between its morals and its ethics. It is a bit hard on Bill. If Bill had the money to go private his fellow citizens would never be able to sell him for scrap.

When all is said and done, the NHS does not provide a defined list of contractual entitlements. Bill and his fellow geriatrics will not find it easy to sue the Secretary of State for Health for violating rights that were always left loose. Research on cancer is 13 times better funded than research on Alzheimer's. The British public seems prepared to write off dementia as an inevitable part of growing old. British or brutish, that is how it thinks. Governments are always on shaky ground when they elect to dismiss the consensus and vote in another. Defeat is inevitable. Bill will not be given time to finish *War and Peace*. He should go for *The Remains of the Day* instead.

A survey in Cardiff established that 94 per cent of the respondents ranked saving a five-year-old above saving a 70-year-old. About 80 per cent put a 35-year-old above a 60-year-old (Murray, 1996: 55). Shakespeare's ages of man had poisoned their minds. In ranking the sunrise above the sunset, they were revealing their preference that innings are scarce and no one should be allowed to hog the bat forever. Perhaps they were also revealing an implicit quality adjustment of the life-years enjoyed by the cohorts. Old people are *sans* eyes, *sans* teeth, *sans* everything. Life cannot be much fun when an old buffer dodders on to 50. If resources were to be transferred to the fresh and the promising, the intergenerational correction would then increase the gross national happiness of our people as a whole.

A study in Sweden confirmed that undocumented prejudice was in the air. It revealed that one life-year for an energetic 30-year-old was widely believed to be the equivalent of 7.7 life-years for an off-peak 50-something (Johannesson and Johansson, 1997: 595), One quality-adjusted life-year lived from start to finish by a 50-year-old *sans* everything was believed by the Swedes to be worth only 13 per cent of a quality-adjusted life-year enjoyed by a 30-year-old in their prime. Even patients on dialysis score better. A life-year on dialysis was found to be 75 per cent as good as a life-year made whole by a kidney transplant (Klarman et al., 1973 [1968]: 232). The results of the implicit referendum are out. Old people are squeezing less happiness from a standard day than are young people. The 40-plus would be well advised to gloss over their encroaching decrepitude when next they see their doctor. Otherwise they might never see their grandchildren again.

The stable is assessing its horses for gums and wind. As with creeping dementia, so with present-day disability. The physically handicapped are visibly *sans* as well. Some surveys imply that the blind, the deaf and the discouraged can reasonably be deprived of all but a maintenance dose since their neighbours believe them to have a dull and damaged existence: 'The results are quite consistent ... that individuals prefer, after appropriate deliberation, to extend the life of healthy individuals rather than those in a health state worse than perfect health' (Murray and Acharya, 1997: 726). The molars are given extra. The bipolars are sent away. It is all a matter of economics. We should be maximising our gross national happiness. We are limited by a budget constraint. Someone has to be thrown to the wolves.

Sans-ness is madness, but there is method in it. Drummond collected evidence on the quality of a life-year. He found that the cost of one British life-year, quality-adjusted, was £270 if the money went on general practitioner (GP) advice to stop smoking, £7840 on heart transplantation, £21 970 on hospital haemodialysis, £107 780 on brain surgery for cancerous tumours (Drummond et al., 1993: 34). A health budget of £21 970 produces one quality-adjusted life-year if spent on kidney dialysis in hospital. It produces 81 quality-adjusted life-years if spent on practitioners' advice to give up smoking.

The inference is clear. Resources should be channelled to treatments which produce more quality-adjusted life-years per dollar, pound or euro. They should be channelled away from underperforming treatments for which the quality-adjusted pay-off is less. More satisfying years count more. Second-rate life-years count less. It is not physical survival alone that a society values but years of a reasonable standard. Social values dictate that money should be allocated in such a way as to maximise the subjective return.

Local consensus may itself be a reason for practice variation. The dispersion in surgery for breast cancer in women aged 65 and above stands in the British NHS in the ratio of 37:1. The surgery rate declines sharply in the sixties although the incidence of breast cancer peaks at 85+. For hip replacements the dispersion is 10:1. For bowel cancer it is 6:1. There are 1147 cataract operations per 100 000 population in North Lancashire but only 247 in South Reading (Borland, 2013). It is a coded message. More than half of the over-65s suffer from cataract. Each operation costs the NHS £932. Without it they could go blind.

The President of the Royal College of Surgeons called the scale of the dispersion 'very worrying' (Donnelly, 2014). He expressed the fear that it was age discrimination and not the capacity to benefit that was accounting for the difference. If so, then it might have been the variance in the local consensus that was making some regions more ageist than others. Embedded within the national consensus there is the subnational consensus. It makes a difference where you live.

There is no guarantee that the old codger *sans* everything will in the end get the kidney transplant for which he is willing and able to pay. Together with his co-morbidities and his general infirmity the old codger is likely to be exhausting his neighbours' patience. The consumer is the king and the doctor knows best. Validating both are, however, social values. Sometimes they will say that extra need should be relieved with extra funding. Sometimes they will say the opposite. Achievement or ascription, no one should be too confident that his neighbours will accept that his want is a need rather than a luxury for which his community no longer sees any need to pay.

7.1.3 The Individual Versus the Tribe

Society holds strong views on the end of life. People take positions on organ sales, assisted euthanasia, the 'do not resuscitate' label, the switching off of the life-support machine where the patient has no reasonable hope of an early recovery or a decent quality of life. Decency is in the eye of the beholder. The views of society need not be the views of the individual. The body-holders might feel that they have no wish to go on. Their fellow citizens might feel that, while they do not want them to live, they cannot bring themselves to let them die. Criminals are sentenced to death. The innocent are sentenced to life. Social values move in mysterious ways.

As with the end of life, so with the beginning. Abortion, surrogacy, stem-cell research, artificial insemination, the cloning of an embryo, the preselection of a child's gender, the morning-after pill, the prescription of contraceptives to underage schoolgirls, all are areas in which public opinion demands to be heard. Economics and not just emotion will often play a role. The failure to abort the severely disabled is the decision to impose a lifetime burden on the National Health Service and the Welfare State. A ban on contraception can lead to a labour surplus, mass unemployment and rampant AIDS. Social values can damage both your wealth and your health.

Social values to the social-ists are the median mind and the group consensus. The truth, less reassuring, is that they are an elephant trap dressed up as a social contract. Social-ists, stating that I am We, underestimate the extent to which I remain I as well. The nation does not speak with a single voice. Majority rule is not unanimous concord. The majority gets what it wants. The minority puts up and pays. Democracy leaves some citizens bitter and unrepresented. It is the rule of the people. To the excluded it still feels like the rule of the dictator who has no need to consult.

Government by groundswell can prevent minority patients from obtaining procedures that they believe to be in their own best interest. It can oblige the doctors to betray the confidentiality of the confessional in order to acquit their social control obligation. People have attitudes. Values become laws. Government by groundswell is a good thing for those who are on the winning side. It can appear distastefully priggish and self-righteous to the subcultures and the fringes who say that the democratic middle should not be allowed to throw its weight around.

Mill was speaking for all such outsiders when he told his neighbours that his liver and spleen belonged to himself alone:

> The only purpose for which power can be rightfully exercised over any member of a civilized community, against his will, is to prevent harm to others. His own good, either physical or moral, is not a sufficient warrant ... Over himself, over his own body and mind, the individual is sovereign. (Mill, 1974 [1859]: 68–9)

The patient knows best. The practitioner knows second-best. The public does not know anything at all.

7.2 EXTERNALITIES

Pigou was a Cambridge economist and a moderate interventionist. Generally in favour of free market choice, he saw that there could be a discrepancy between marginal private cost (or benefit) and marginal social cost (or benefit). The passenger and the railway make a contract from which each expects a net increase in well-being. The position of the third party who experiences collateral damage is less attractive. Neither the passenger nor the railway has a budget for the unpriced transfer of sparks that sets a neighbouring farmer's crop ablaze (Pigou, 1932 [1920]). Neither the demand side nor the supply side has any incentive to compensate the looker-on for their loss. Without the visible hand the market failure would be condemned to lie where it falls.

7.2.1 The Physical Externality

Third-party spillovers are a topic in social values. It is values alone that determine whether the side-effects are costs or benefits, good or bad. External costs might be noxious effluent dumped in a creek, or value-creating, tax-creating days lost through illness. External benefits might be medical research into cystic fibrosis or a cross-border campaign to eradicate mosquitoes in stagnant pools. Costs or benefits, social values make us aware that there is more to a contract than dyadic exchange and the equilibrium price.

A contagious disease affects non-contracting individuals who have not given their consent. Germs and epidemics are a violation of their personal integrity. Public bads are an invasion of their personal space. Mill stated that, even if the norm is laissez-faire, an exception could still be made where it is required 'to prevent harm to others'. Mill's exception is a serious door. It is often taken to legitimate State intervention when the truth is that government failure might make the market failure worse.

There is legislation. Speed limits, restrictions on gun ownership, curbs on passive smoking, chest X-rays for new immigrants, the compulsory filtering of chemical emissions, are all ways in which command-and-control can protect innocent bystanders against two-party exchange.

There is provision. Squatter colonies can be replaced by public housing. A health promotion board can warn against street food and accidental injuries. The schools can promise priority admission to the existing children of sterilised parents who have defused the population explosion.

There is legislation. There is provision. There is also price. Taxes internalise the spillovers from alcohol, tobacco and leaded petrol. Subsidies reduce the burden of preventive mammograms, dental check-ups and medical research. Nannying taxation and hypothecated grants are a middle-ground compromise that takes elements from both market freedom and Stalinist compulsion. Fiscal management targets the price but leaves the quantity to supply and demand. The numbers are different but the game is the same. The neighbourhood interest is safeguarded by thinking men and women who introduce a subjective dimension into the quantification of the externality.

7.2.2 The Humanitarian Spillover

Externalities are a topic in social values. They are also a topic in non-rational affects. It is not just communicable disease but a troubled soul that keeps the Good Citizen awake at night when he tallies up his balance sheet for the day:

> One individual is not affected merely by the possibility of another passing some disease on to him ... but also, and much more importantly, by the state of health of the other in itself. Individuals are affected by others' health status for the simple reason that *most of them care*. (Culyer, 1976: 8, 9)

Not a sparrow falls but his neighbours regret that they had not done more. Human beings experience genuine distress at the thought that their fellow creatures, at home or abroad, are suffering from preventable blindness, treatable cancer or the loneliness of the geriatric ward. Alter's frustrated essence becomes an argument in ego's happiness function. Human beings reap gains from trade when they have the opportunity to make a stranger-gift.

Interest blends into compassion. Egotism merges with altruism. Socialised beings are inseparable and interdependent. The evidence, Culyer says, confirms the conjecture that the humanitarian spillover is hardwired into the incentive structure: 'If this were not the case, who other than the very poor would ever advocate subsidising the health care of the very poor? The remarkable fact is that almost the only people who do not actively advocate such subsidies are the poor themselves' (Culyer, 1982: 40).

Private medicine in such circumstances might not so much promote economic efficiency as impede it. Private provision, Culyer observes, makes no allowance for the caring externality: 'It immediately follows that the market will *undersupply* health (and/or health care) by failing to allow for the additional value placed upon it by people other than the direct consumer' (Culyer, 1982: 40). The National Health Service is able to avoid the market's inadequacies. Social-ist in its inspiration and its function, it adds the collective valuation to the one-dimensionality of effective demand.

The quantity supplied is adjusted upward because the national community cares. Ethics and emotions aside, the provision of the caring externality can be essential for the perpetuation of the group. The National Health Service protects the national health. Even the waits are an investment. The queue for socialised medicine is a personal cost borne for the greater good. It may be compared to the watching deer who sounds the alarm but attracts the predator to itself. Self-immolation ensures the survival of the fittest. It is the fittest We and not the fittest I that survives.

Evolution is on the side of the biological imperative. It protects and perpetuates the herd. Without altruism there would be no one left to study their Hobbes. In the words of Alfred Marshall: 'The struggle for existence causes in the long run those races of men to survive in which the individual is most willing to sacrifice himself for the benefit of those around him' (Marshall, 1949 [1890]: 202). Those races which are the least willing to donate their blood, support the paraplegic, bag their litter, volunteer their tax and tell the truth are the ones most likely to sink without trace.

The privatisation of free-on-demand services, Titmuss writes, can cause far-ranging harm. The externalities spill over into all areas of social life: 'It is likely that a decline in the spirit of altruism in one sphere of human activities will be accompanied by similar changes in attitudes, motives and relationships in other spheres ... Economists may fragment systems and values; other people do not' (Titmuss, 1970: 198). Hobbesians are made and not born. The same is true of social-ists. In the one case as in the other, what matters most is getting the institutions right.

In Switzerland, at Wolfenschiessen, 50.8 per cent of the residents said they were willing to take upon themselves the sins of their nation and to welcome in a nuclear dump. That would be without payment. As soon as they were offered money, the number fell to 24.6 per cent (Frey and Oberholzer-Gee, 1997: 749). Their incentive structure differed from that of the neoclassical economics. It confirmed Sandel's contention that economic exchange over time must eat away at the foundations of civic duty: 'Markets leave their mark on social norms. Often, market incentives erode or crowd out non-market incentives' (Sandel, 2012: 64). It is a reason why parents should not pay their children for doing household chores. Their mindset is formed in their early years. If it is the quid pro quo when they are young, it will be the quid pro quo for life. Public-spiritedness at Wolfenschiessen cannot be expected to last forever.

The repression of other-orientated sympathy, in the view of Titmuss and Sandel, is an economically inefficient choice. Nor is it necessarily the mode of conduct that will deliver the greatest happiness, self-perceived. The free-rider does not pay for their ride. Yet it is not really the most satisfying ride that they could have experienced. As Hirschman puts it: 'There is much fulfilment associated with the citizen's exertions for the public happiness ... To elect a free ride under the circumstances would be equivalent to declining a delicious meal and to swallow instead a satiation-producing pill that is not even particularly effective!' (Hirschman, 1982: 90, 91). It is fair to do one's part. It is satisfying to get involved. That is when most people feel most at peace with themselves.

7.3 PATH DEPENDENCE

The constitution of a new society is a blank sheet of paper. The founding architects have the first-mover's freedom to mould and shape. We today are the footsoldiers who follow behind. They started from there. We start from here. Our institutions are in place. We must live in a structure that we never designed.

Social codes are yesterday's legacy. Trend-dominated, history-driven, the cumulative sequence of habituated momentum bestows upon the present a viable blueprint. Repetition is not rational choice but it is social stability. Without the inherited roadmap it would be the anarchy of the drawing board and the *ab initio* again.

People know no thing but the done thing. Their need for clothing is a need to perpetuate a social rite: 'Custom ... has rendered leather shoes a necessary of life in England. The poorest creditable person of either sex would be ashamed to appear in public without them' (Smith, 1961 [1776]: II, 399–400). Their need for food is a need to do what their culture instructs: 'A Masai drinks the blood of cattle; an Eskimo eats blubber; a Buddhist monk needs a bowl of rice with some vegetables' (Braybrooke, 1987: 12). Their need for health care systems is no less convention-driven.

People grow up under free enterprise health or under State-sponsored health. Personal dissatisfaction and intellectual reappraisal sometimes make them question the status quo. Even so, they are what they are: 'Human beings naturally live by conventions; so they must be said to have a natural need for some minimum familiarity with the conventions of the society in which they find themselves' (Braybrooke, 1987: 92). Socialism or capitalism, it is social-ism cradle to grave. Stamped identity reinforced by remembered iteration has them in its grip.

Path dependence can be the handing on of the factored-down. Utility-seeking atomism might be sealing worshippers into its communion because it is a familiar old catechism that they have replayed time-out-of-mind: 'Purely personal tastes ... can only survive in a culture which tolerates them, that is, which has a common value that private tastes of certain kinds should be allowed' (Boulding, 1969: 1). Such a culture will have an established bias towards independent calculation and accomplishment-based self-reliance. Antecedent socialisation will legitimate individual autonomy. Respect for persons will legitimate a market-oriented health system: 'The characteristic feature of action through political channels is that it tends to require or enforce substantial conformity. The great advantage of the market, on the other hand, is that it permits wide diversity' (Friedman, 1962: 15). Patient-led self-determination is our way. We like it because wide diversity for us is an article of faith.

The past reached consensus on the meta-ethic of ego sovereignty. The social ideal was the free-floating isolate, self-sufficient and self-creating. The present inherits the going concern. People learn by living. The tyranny of the status quo ensures that decentralisation and enterprise will be self-perpetuating. Citizens will have an unthinking tendency to demand more of the same. Private insurance and private provision are all that they know.

Path dependence can mean the replication of the factored-down. It can also mean the perpetuation of the collectivized and the organic. People who have grown up in a culture which treats social actors as parts of a bigger whole will expect their social institutions to embody the team thinking which is their window on the world. Their team spirit leads them to create a National Health Service. The National Health Service in turn reinforces the conservatism of the collective. People accustomed to the as-of-right umbrella of free-on-demand State universalism will feel confused and surprised if they are told that in Lilliput sick people who cannot pay are not given the care their condition demands. Whatever may be the system in Lilliput, they will say, Lilliput is not the NHS. Lilliput is not the way we do things around here.

Titmuss said that the gift of blood was not about blood alone but about moral fibre. Making a stranger-gift that would save the life of an unknown other, integrated communitarians were demonstrating their desire to do their share and not just to take their share. Their warm-hearted compassion had a latent function in that it ensured the integrity of their club. Without the social compact each stand-alone would be returned to the minus-sum dystopia of the war of each against all: 'If the bonds of community giving are broken the result is not a state of value neutralism. The vacuum is likely to be filled by hostility and social conflict' (Titmuss, 1970: 199).

Man is a political animal. It is in his nature to live in a *polis*, a community, a nation. Out of that long-accustomed interdependence there emerged what Titmuss calls 'society's will to survive as an organic whole' (Titmuss, 1963: 39). Each human being has in their make-up a 'biological need to help' (Titmuss, 1970: 198) which induces them, individually and with their fellows, to eliminate any 'allocation of resources which could create a sense of separateness between people' (Titmuss, 1970: 238). All roads lead to the NHS. Path dependence does the rest. Once you find your way in, you will never find your way out again.

The NHS is a school. It inculcates the social values of fellowship, compassion, community, empathy and generosity. Citizens become accustomed to the classlessness and communalism which shared wards and non-discriminatory services embody. They come to think of themselves as members of a platoon and not customers in a shop. Solidarity is the cause. Solidarity is the consequence. As Bevan says: 'Society becomes more wholesome, more serene, and spiritually healthier, if it knows that its citizens have at the back of their consciousness the knowledge that not only themselves, but all their fellows, have access, when ill, to the best that medical skill can provide' (Bevan, 1961 [1952]: 100). The medical system transmits and reinforces the central value system. The NHS heals a broken society. Broken bones are only a part of the story.

7.4 POLITICAL ECONOMY

Politics, Braybrooke says, is the art of combining structure with decoration: 'We are certainly not licensed to disregard one another's preferences; but needs make a claim on us more compelling than mere preferences do ... The most fundamental issues of politics arise as aspects of the general social task of reconciling attention to needs with attention to preferences' (Braybrooke, 1987: 7, 8). Society wants to satisfy its wants. Society needs to satisfy its needs. Politics is the art of identifying the basics and ensuring the mix.

7.4.1 Consensus

Titmuss uses the language of agreement and concord. All collectively provided services, he asserts, are manifestations 'of the expressed wish of all the people to assist the survival of some people' (Titmuss, 1963: 39). 'All the people' describes an unshakeable coalition. If all the people agree, then not one of the people does not.

The consensus model is the vision of Rousseau on the general will (Rousseau, 2012 [1762]) and Wicksell on the unanimity of consent (Wicksell, 1958 [1896]). It is the logic of Tönnies on other-regarding *Gesellschaft* that complements the atomised *Gemeinschaft* of the self-interested swap (Tönnies, 2001 [1887]). The consensus model assumes that we all want the same. The problem is how to measure the common mind.

Elections sample opinions on salient issues. Representatives and activists probe their constituents at grassroots sessions. Surveys provide feedback and so do users' councils. Complaints mechanisms are an ever-present deterrent to deviance. A free press, an independent civil service and an active Opposition publicise waits, deaths, league tables and trends on which it is felt that the public will have a view. Standing committees, audit commissions and parliamentary debates are built-in stabilisers which shame underperformers into eliminating an unpopular shortfall. Gradually a picture is built up.

Attitudes and predilections emerge. There is no guarantee that they are the consensus. The future does not have a vote: does this mean that cure will be oversupplied relative to prevention that could save a greater number of lives? The creaking hinge gets the oil: who speaks for the silent, the self-effacing, the Alzheimer's iceberg that has lost its short-term recall? A majority is not an 'all': will summed happiness go down if the disutility of the tails exceeds the felt satisfaction of the median? Consciousness can be manipulated: could a conspiracy of rent-seekers interlocked with a scheming political elite mould public opinion in its own class image? Consensus makes each of us feel good about our national family. Pluralism makes us wonder how it all adds up.

7.4.2 Following the Consensus

Pluralism assigns considerable power to politicians. It is they who must reconcile the different opinions and moderate the conflicting pressures.

Ideally they will promise a mixed portfolio in which there will be something for everyone. Politicians have to please the electorate. Their legitimacy is tested by the vote mechanism. Winning an election does not mean Titmuss's 'all'. It does, however, mean the compromise solution of 'first past the post'.

Politicians in a British democracy have to follow the will of the 'first past the post'. Like merchants in the economic market, salesmen in the political market would go out of business if they did not supply the vote-winning package. It is in their narrow self-interest, Tullock writes, to please the customers upon whom their repeat business must depend. The vote motive is a guarantee that, in a two-horse race, 51 per cent at least will get what they want:

> The market operates by providing a structure in which individuals who simply want to make money end up by producing motor cars that people want. Similarly, democracy operates so that politicians who simply want to hold public office end up by doing things the people want ... There is no reason why we should be disturbed by this phenomenon. (Tullock, 1976: 25)

Anthony Downs, like Tullock, makes election and re-election the sole maximand. In Downs's economic model the incumbent is in competition with the Opposition for the five good things that every politician craves: power, prestige, income, conflict and access to the parliamentary game (Downs, 1957). Other theorists in the public-choice tradition have extended the self-seeking orientation backwards from the leaders to the bureaucrats: 'As students of political economy have long recognized, producer interests tend to dominate consumer interests, and the producer interests of government employees are no different from those of any other group in society' (Buchanan, 1975: 160).

Bureaucrats want to build empires. Reputation, power, fringe benefits, are all, Niskanen writes, 'a positive monotonic function of the total *budget* of the bureau' (Niskanen, 1971: 41). They want pay and promotions, security and job satisfaction. They want a quiet life even where mould-breaking innovation would better satisfy the social need. Max Weber viewed the cogs in the organisational chart as dispassionate computers who store their self-interest in the cloakroom when they clock in for work (Weber, 1948 [1922]: 228). Thinkers like Tullock, Downs, Buchanan and Niskanen prefer a unitary model of human striving. In the Shop of State as in the Shop of Shop, it is the maximising posture all the way to the bank.

7.4.3 Taking a Lead

The maximising posture need not be at variance with the *vox populi*. Tullock's reference to the 'things people want' is a reminder that market liberals put revealed preference first. Their politics is their economics and their economics is consumer choice.

Sometimes the leaders will see themselves as faceless automatons who take it on trust that public opinion alone can define the public interest. It need not be so. Sometimes the leaders will interpret their role as that of the proactive initiator who shepherds the consensus into their own most-favoured vision. There are many careers that pay well in terms of power, prestige, conflict and income. Politics is all that but it is also something more. The commanding heights give zealots the opportunity to impose their world view on their community as a whole:

> Within what he treats as his feasible set, the politician will choose that alternative or option which maximizes his own, not his constituents', utility. This opportunity offers one of the primary motivations to politicians. In a meaningful sense, this is "political income", and it must be reckoned as a part of the total rewards of office. (Buchanan, 1975: 157)

Leaders whose maximand is 'political income' will assign primary importance to what they take to be basic needs. They will argue that revealed preferences are only the ill-informed pipe-dreams of a 'good life' that is neither desirable nor attainable. The philosopher-ruler knows best. The ignorant should trust to their philosopher-ruler. They should leave their guidance to their ideologues who rule parent-like to ensure that individual and collective imperatives will not be sacrificed to the short-horizoned temptations of the dog track and the smoke-filled pub. It is politician-induced demand. It is in bound Ulysses' self-interest, rightly understood. It corrects the weakness of will that is so often encoded in citizen sovereignty and bubble-up choice.

The people lead. The leaders lead. Superficially the two perspectives are different. In practice they might converge. One of the 'things people want' will, after all, frequently be a responsible State that makes sense of the contradictions and ties up the loose ends. People have a want: they want to smoke. People have a need: they need not to smoke. People have a want: they want women to stay at home. People have a need: they need industrial womanpower and an expanded labour force. People have a want: they want to be left alone. People have a need: they need fraternal fellow-feeling and common, collectivised provision. In cases such as these the paternalists will have to take the initiative. They will have to educate the electorate to want what they need. They will have to induce the demand that later on becomes self-sustaining. They will have to trample underfoot the popular choices that are resulting in tooth decay and road accidents.

Reconditioning takes time. Long before the intellectual engineering – the brainwashing – has begun to bear fruit, the paternalists who put needs before wants may well be voted out by an electorate that simply does not want to live on soya beans and milk. A clique that wants to be re-elected will often have to choose the easy way to short-term popularity. Invisible needs and unseen imperatives all too often condemn the principled visionary to the back benches where no journalists ever go.

7.4.4 Dissensus and Democracy

Rawls, who is not an Aristotelian, says that justice as fairness accepts the liberal presupposition that 'there are many rational conceptions of the good':

> The consequence is that the unity of society and the allegiance of its citizens to their common institutions rest not only on their espousing one rational conception of the good, but on an agreement as to what is just for free and equal moral persons with different and opposing conceptions of the good. (Rawls, 1982: 160)

The claims it is appropriate for citizens to make must be filtered through good procedures agreed upon in advance: 'Justice is prior to the good' (Rawls, 1982: 184).

It is not unanimity of consensus on the policies so much as unanimity of agreement on the processes that keeps savage Hobbes from the door. The poor might have different preferences from the rich, the manual from the professional, the devout from the agnostic, the doctor from the patient and from the community and from other doctors because every doctor knows that every doctor knows best. The different groups, subgroups and unique one-offs might not see eye to eye: 'Although home dialysis may be more cost-effective than hospital dialysis from the societal point of view, the reverse may be true from the viewpoint of some patients and their families' (Torrance, 1986: 7).

Aggregation and generalisation are less difficult where there is a bunched distribution of preferences with minimal dispersion in the tails. It can happen. In a war virtually the whole of the citizenry stands as one against the enemy aggressor. In the case of rheumatoid arthritis the concord between the sufferers and the bystanders in San Diego, Oregon, the United Kingdom and Arizona is not far short of 100 per cent: 'The evidence for differential preference is weak at best ... Overall preferences for health states appear to be quite similar ... Preference differences across groups appear to be small and are not sufficiently large to justify their use in influencing policy decisions' (Kaplan, 1995: 51, 52, 60).

It is ideal and idyllic. The suffering and the non-suffering all gravitate to a single protocol. Where, however, they do not, then the government is faced with the problem of imposing a single policy on a plurality of heterogeneities.

It can return the poisoned chalice to the people through liberalising its regulations and privatising its provision. Market competition would then, as the economics textbooks preach, ensure that Jack could buy a red hat and Jill a blue one. Not wishing to go so far, the State could continue to legislate and supply but could also diversify its menu so as to cater to a variety of appetites: 'A more sophisticated approach would be to plan different styles of care to satisfy the preferences of people who, for example, place different emphasis on the relief of disability relative to the relief of distress' (Rosser and Kind, 1978: 357).

One man's meat is another man's poison. To maximise felt consultation the rule might therefore be to differentiate and diversify within a unifying structure. Where the different preferences are concentrated in different localities, fiscal federalism would factor the health services down to the constituent regions while preserving the citizenship guarantee and the productive economies of a national system. Where the arthritis, the abortions and the gallstones are distributed over the whole of the national territory, the democratic option would be for different clinics to provide different services in recognition of the fact that their clients themselves are different.

Democratic accountability means that responsible decision-makers must satisfy their constituents. They must not, however, be permitted to do this at the cost of instability and inflation. In health care as in other areas, 'it is rational to *have a constitution*' (Buchanan and Tullock, 1962: 81). Whether its territory is to be unitary or devolved, the rules must be prespecified, multi-period and long-lived. The rulers themselves must be bound by the rules. Rules-utilitarianism does not have much utility if the leaders are allowed to sway with short-term caprice and the in-period electoral cycle.

Unanimity on policies is not required so long as there is unanimity on the processes that grind out the policies. Celtic wants to win. Fulham wants to win. They are divided by their inperiod interest. They are united by their precommitment to the statutes and precedents of their game.

They are in full agreement that the rule-makers were impartial and fair when they defined the playing-field, the goalposts, the free kick and the foul. The definitions can be revisited. Crucially, they should not be changed in-period once the ball is in play.

A constitution is conservative. Because a change in the rules necessitates a high degree of convergence, legitimacy depends on uncertainty and uncertainty is a function of time. The future is an unknown country. Consensus will be that much easier to secure if particular interest, special pleading and voter-buying discretion are blocked off by a veil of ignorance so thick that no individual or group of individuals can know at the rule-making stage what they personally stand to gain or lose from the laws. Celtic or Fulham, arthritis or gallstones, childhood or retirement – we may not agree on the policies but at least we agree on the decision-making processes that are administering the game. And we start from here.

8. The logic of insurance

Health care costs scarce resources. The mode of payment influences the quantity that changes hands and the price that is agreed. It also has an impact on the extent of sharing and redistribution in society. The mode of payment is a topic in 'who' and not just in 'what'. Effective demand is social interaction. It is not just the differential calculus of demand and supply.

Effective demand always takes the lead. Money makes the market go round. True in all exchanges, the proposition is doubly true in the market for health. The reason is that the market for health is very frequently not single but twinned. The final market is care: patients pay doctors to make them well. The intermediate market is protection: a third party is prepaid to share the cost.

This chapter examines the contribution of the insuring agency to the market for care. Its theme is communism for sale. Communism is 'to each according to his needs'. Communism for sale is 'to each according to his needs provided he has bought full-cover reimbursement in advance'. Capitalism is an economic system which sells full-cover communism at a price.

Rationing by price becomes secondary, marginal and even irrelevant. What takes its place is allocation by qualified experts. So long as the doctors certify that the wants are needs, the third party will settle the bills. Although it is the market economy it resembles the free National Health Service. Insured user-charges and costless access enable the consumer to shift medical costs on to the collectivity or group. It is communism as an economic tradeable. It is sharing for sale in the capitalist market.

This chapter examines the contribution of the insuring agency to the purchase of medical attention. Section 8.1, 'Risk and uncertainty', shows how the pooling of contingencies can convert uncertainty into risk. Section 8.2, 'Risk-rating', asks what information a rational insurer would want to collect about its policy-seekers. Section 8.3, 'Moral hazard', explores how the risk profile might change as a direct consequence of the policies that are sold. Section 8.4, 'Combinations and permutations',

140 Health policy

shows that the range of contracts is a kaleidoscope of possibilities. Insurance is not one animal. Insurance is a zoo.

8.1 RISK AND UNCERTAINTY

In the beginning there was fear. The future is unknown and unknowable. Monsters and ghouls lurk in the *terra incognita*. No one-off individual can know in advance what his or her life-course will be. Confronted with the hooded judge of history-to-come, it is rational to be very, very afraid.

The future cannot be known until it is a fait accompli. That is the logic of health insurance. People are fearful both that their good health will go and that they will be exposed to financial burdens which will exhaust their net worth. Few other areas of social life cause more sleepless nights than do the possibility of illness and the costliness of care. Wishing to purchase peace of mind, people therefore pay a known sum upfront in order to protect themselves against the greater loss caused by an unanticipated calamity that might never occur. It is just in case. Insurance is an unusual industry in that few people really want ever to enjoy the doctoring and the surgery on which they have bought a lien.

Ignorance is purchased because of ignorance. People do not know if or when ever-watching ill health will strike. If the insurers and their clients had perfect knowledge of the date and the amount, those certain to be afflicted would not buy insurance at all. They would put the earmarked sum in an interest-bearing account with a fixed maturity date. It would not be rational for them to buy prepayment for a known and predictable drain such as an annual check-up or a repeat prescription. After the deduction of surplus and administration, the policy, charging premiums that reflect the reimbursements, would give them back less than they had originally put in.

Unknowledge is the rock on which the industry is built. Those certain that the germs and the earthquakes will pass them by will have no reason to buy insurance. It would be a waste of money to cross-subsidise a swimming club if they themselves will never swim. Those certain that a catastrophic illness has already singled them out will, on the other hand, have a strong incentive to seek out a partner willing to reimburse their loss. Their problem is that no loss-averting agency will sell the contract to the certain.

No rational bookmaker will accept bids from well-informed insiders who know in advance the outcome of a takeover bid or which boxer has been bribed to take a fall. No insuring fund that wishes to remain solvent can by the same token promise reimbursement in excess of the premium to omniscient loss-makers who know today precisely what they will take out tomorrow. Anticipated outlays will have to be settled out of pocket or out of savings. The intermediary can take deposits and invest money left on account. What it cannot do is to quote odds on a race that has already been won.

Insurance exists because foreknowledge is imperfect and the road ahead mapped out with fog. As Shackle puts it: 'What is the future but the void?' (Shackle, 1972: 122). Each individual is an entrepreneur condemned to gamble on a *tâtonnement* that is little more than a stab in the dark. No one knew better than Frank Knight that it is not possible to guess the outcome of an imagined journey into a void-to-come that is yet to be: 'Productive arrangements are made on the basis of anticipations and the results actually achieved do not coincide with these as a usual thing' (Knight, 1971 [1921]: 272). Knight was never convinced by the maximising paradigm: 'The limitations of foreknowledge are of course more sweeping than those of knowledge' (Knight, 1997 [1935]: 43). Individuals muddle along as best they can. It is not a guarantee: 'Life is mostly made up of uncertainties' (Knight, 1971 [1921]: 235).

Uncertainty in the sense of Knight corresponds to the precautionary motive in the sense of Keynes (1973 [1936]: 170–74). It means 'I haven't a clue'. Fortunately for purposive beings, there is also risk. Risk to Knight is the equivalent of Keynes's speculative motive. It means, 'I believe I know the probable outcome'. The future is not the present and the decision-makers might later regret their choice. Even so, cautious extrapolation is an epistemological orientation that allows them to make credible inferences about the world that is yet to come.

Cautious extrapolation is at the root of the insurance industry. Insurance is Knightian and Keynesian through and through. Insurance is a sausage machine. It inputs radical uncertainty and outputs actuarial risk. It is able to convert unknowledge into knowledge because it makes use of the law of large numbers. Whereas the one-off cannot pinpoint the low-probability, high-cost eventuality that they will be attacked by a housebreaker this Friday evening at ten, the insurer can predict the likely incidence of assault and theft on the basis of recent frequencies that it expects to recur. Circumstances might change; and each subscriber has more than a single risk-related characteristic. Even so, the insurer generalising for an established pool cannot be compared to a gamester who picks random numbers out of the air.

The ideal premium for the subscriber would be a value corresponding to the mean of the probability distribution. It is not a price which an economical insurer will be able to accept. Apart from the mathematical expectation of the payout distribution, the insurers must cover the transaction costs of marketing and claims-processing, the utilisation review that is a part of their cost containment, and (in the case of a commercial intermediary) the profits and capital gains that their shareholders expect. For that reason all insurance has a built-in deterrent. The premium is always and everywhere above the actuarial mean. The risk-indifferent will see no reason to pay over the odds; and the risk-loving by temperament will never insure at all. It will only be the risk-averse who will regard it as money well spent to subscribe to a scheme which to them is actuarially unfair.

The logic is the diminishing marginal utility of income. As so many in the deductivist tradition of Bernoulli have hypothesised, the loss of an endowment normally occasions unhappiness in excess of the marginal pleasure that the acquisition of an identical endowment would have brought. Chapter 3 described their fear. People who buy lottery tickets are revealing a willingness to exchange a small amount in advance for the small chance of a big win later on. Their psychology in the market for health insurance is the same. Buying health cover, they are revealing a preference for low-cost protection against the small but non-negligible probability of a disproportionate loss.

Discouraged by the surcharge but frightened nonetheless by what it means to be on their own, the most the risk-averse will do is to pay their subscription but to economise on the content. They might choose a budget policy with an exclusion clause for low-likelihood 'acts of God'. They might self-insure through a high-deductible plan that requires them to pay the first tranche themselves. They might reserve health insurance for medical catastrophes while relying in the first instance on over-the-counter aspirins and out-of-pocket plasters. Thresholds and selectivity would keep their premiums affordable.

Yet there will always be some people who, despite the odds, will opt for comprehensive and first-dollar contracts. They will pay what it costs irrespective of the cold calculus. Subjective salience is not the same as statistical frequency. A widely reported plane crash causes the nervous to play safe and travel by car. The statistical likelihood of a fatal accident is many times greater on the road.

8.2 RISK-RATING

Insurance is redistributive. This is true by definition. If all the members pay their premiums but only the unfortunate few ever put in any claims, it is clear that there will be a transfer of pooled resources from the healthy to the ill. Bunching and bias go hand in hand. The promise of mutual aid is the very reason why the anxious give up a certainty in order to pay for a probability. They are sacrificing good money for a contingency that might never arise. There is a large chance that they might lose their investment. There is a small chance that they might sweep the stakes. Chance does strange things to people. They buy insurance because the risk of loss makes them afraid.

8.2.1 Lemons and Peaches

The client is trapped between two risks. Yet the carrier too is trapped. On the one hand its premiums must be high enough to cover the expected outgoings which it has promised to make good. On the other hand it must keep its package attractive and its pricing keen. The result is that the insuring agency is compelled by the logic of market competition to choose the right pond. It is uneconomic to water the wine with bad risks like long-term heroin addicts and end-stage renal cases. It is far more lucrative to mix gold with gold in the form of young graduates who eat healthily and get plenty of sleep.

The good risks will be creamed off into low-premium policies. Some contracts may even dispense with a risk-sharing component. The known losers are the ones who will band together for support and protection. The drowning will be expected to buoy up the drowning. There will be no strong swimmer to lend support to the cohort that is going down. Premiums will rise and services will be curtailed as Gresham's Law drives out all but the desperate. In the end the mixed-risk pools will become economically unsustainable.

The non-smokers and the non-drinkers will not regard the price quoted as money well spent. They will be reluctant consistently to cross-subsidise the losers and the loss-makers. The rejects and the residuals will not, however, be able on their own to afford an ever-rising price for an ever-shrinking club. Soon the shop will be empty: 'The less healthy naturally prefer more generous insurance than the healthy ... Healthy people, in turn, will want to avoid those plans, to keep from subsidizing their less healthy brethren. If adverse selection is large, it may destroy the market for the generous insurance entirely' (Cutler and Reber, 1998: 434). Commercial insurance is not abolished. Beset with contradictions, it simply withers away.

Adverse selection means that the worst crowd in and the best drop out. It is not a viable business model. In the market for used cars, some cars are high-octane 'peaches' but others are low-quality 'lemons'. Asymmetry of information makes it difficult for a would-be owner to distinguish a top-notch sedan from a clapped-out wreck: 'Good cars and bad cars must still sell at the same price – since it is impossible for a buyer to tell the difference' (Akerlof, 1970: 489). Aware that he is in danger of being sold a dead parrot dressed up as a live parrot asleep, the buyer must protect himself by discounting the price of the black box. Sellers who know that their car is a 'peach' will exit the market. Sellers who know that their parrot is dead will take their place. Ultimately all that will be for sale will be dead parrots and 'lemons' which no rational car-owner would be prepared to drive.

Cars are like insurance. Information is asymmetrical. Self-selection is self-destruction. The insurance industry is doomed since the 'peaches' are refusing to pay over the odds while the 'lemons' are taking out more than they put in. Yet there is a solution. The insurance industry, aware of the threat posed by adverse selection, can pick and choose. The insurers, fearful lest one big eater gobble up the whole buffet that was costed for all, can save themselves from bankruptcy by means of segregating the pools.

The rational insurer in a competitive market has no alternative but to select and target. Sometimes it is easy: a polio sufferer in an iron lung looks like what he is. Sometimes it is not: an old Etonian in a bespoke outfit is not conspicuously a sniper on loan to the Central Intelligence Agency (CIA). Yet there is something more. The very act of applying for insurance sets off the alarm bells. A proactive candidate who fills in all those forms must be suspected of knowing something about their health status or their lifestyle that they have a strong incentive to conceal. The sickly applicant faces a conflict of interest in that they know their drip will not be reconnected if they tell the truth. Moral thou-shalt-nots give way to competing absolutes if a mother knows that her baby has a hole in the heart.

Information asymmetry makes rational filtering into a business game of bluff and probe. Unable to put its faith in honour-system self-declaration, the cost-conscious insurer will have to ferret out the concealed pluses and minuses for itself. The applicant says: 'My name is Khan'. Beyond that, what is he really saying? Whom is he *really* trying to khan?

The insurer is obliged to protect its interests. It collects the information it requires in a variety of ways. It may insist upon a full medical history: disclosure will reveal pre-existent conditions such as diabetes, haemophilia, hypertension, arthritis, agoraphobia, anorexia, asthma, premature senility and muscular atrophy. It may approach the police to see if there is a record of drink-driving or fist fights. It may interview a former employer to learn if a redundancy was caused by bad health or carelessness at work.

It may also conduct its own physical examination. Expensive as it is to put each body on the monitor, there is less opportunity for concealment when naked Adam is asked for a blood test, a DNA sample, a psychological profile, an electrocardiogram of the heart, an angiogram of the head and neck, an arm X-ray for bone disease. A ticking time-bomb will have a financial incentive to disguise some or all of these pathologies. He may not even be aware that breathlessness when climbing stairs may be the harbinger of something worse.

Patients complain that the procedures and the paperwork are costly and humiliating. They say that their genes are confidential and that disclosure violates their civil rights. They may object to profiling based on the life and death of parents and siblings. A man of 39 will feel badly treated if his application is turned down merely because all the males in his family have experienced heart failure in their early forties. The fact that they imposed a cost does not mean that he will impose a cost. The probe, he will say, is not only inquisitorial but irrelevant.

It is hard to know which side to take when an applicant rejected for a company plan is no longer able to keep secret from their employer that in-service training might not pay off since they are HIV-positive, have incipient kidney failure or are receiving treatment for pancreatic cancer. Looking at the tests and the investigations from the perspective of the insurer, the position is more encouraging. At least the insurer will have had a chance to inspect the goods. It will have been able to see the named body for itself. It will have been able to make an informed guess about the likelihood that naked Adam will take out an unwarranted share.

Less accurate but less intrusive is risk-rating on the basis not of named bodies but of broad categories. There are more numbers stored up in past, present and future than the limited computational capacity of even the highest artificial intelligence can ever crunch. Herbert Simon, arguing for realistic aspirations and 'bounded rationality', has warned that 'satisficing' and not 'optimising' will typically be the best that fallible man can do: 'The decision-maker's model of the world encompasses only a minute fraction of all the relevant characteristics of the real environment' (Simon, 1959: 272). Tunnel vision is unavoidable. Even so, the rules that have survived the battlefield of natural selection have proven through their track record that they are superior to any competitor lens. The insurance industry is condemned by its 'bounded rationality' to discriminate on the basis of stereotypes, preconceptions and prejudices that have proven themselves to be successful in separating the sheep from the goats.

Risk-profiling pigeonholes the applicants using tried-and-tested rules of thumb such as gender, ethnicity and marital status. Lifestyle identifiers like smoking, drinking, violent crime or extreme sports spotlight the applicants thought likely to impose an above-average strain. Postal district can be used as a proxy on the assumption that the typical squatter in an inner-city slum will be radically deprived, unemployed, undereducated and underfed. Applicants who state that they have requested an AIDS test are taken to be lifting the curtain on promiscuity, homosexuality, bunga bunga parties and the sharing of needles. Applicants who give their occupation as heavyweight boxer might, statistically speaking, be singled out for a higher premium or perhaps be excluded altogether.

Classification by characteristics is a blunt instrument as compared with Savile Row made-to-measure. In some cases, as with age, the heuristic can actually be a self-fulfilling prophesy: 'Adequate health is a precondition for employment. At the same time this means that medical insurance is least available to those who need it most, for the insurance companies do their own "adverse selection"' (Akerlof, 1970: 494). The older worker turned down for insurance will complain that his citizenship right to health and employment has been violated. The insurance company will reply that it will not be able to earn competitive profits if it is not in a position to fine-tune its prices to its costs. Risk-rating by broad categories has the attraction that it allows the insuring agency to separate the good risks from the bad without the high economic overhead of a medical examination.

There is another option. The insurance contract might be written in such a way as to induce the applicants to risk-rate themselves into multiple and differentiated pools. A no-claims bonus will tend *ceteris paribus* to attract applicants who are not anticipating a self-inflicted contingency. A policy that combines low premiums with high deductibles and high co-payments will be a deterrent to applicants aware of undisclosed conditions likely to require costly surgery and long-term medication. A candidate who does not demur at an extortionate premium will cause the company to revisit his body carefully. A discount offered to the non-smoker or non-drinker both identifies the applicant less likely to make a claim and provides an economic incentive to the health-threatening to pull back from self-destruction. Insurance in this way has an active as well as a protective role to play.

8.2.2 From Efficiency to Equity

Business is business. The insurance industry would prefer experience rating. It is attracted by differential premiums geared actuarially to historical frequencies, clear-cut categories and the local cost of care.

Consensus, however, is consensus. Public opinion often calls for community rating. Arguing that a human body is superior to effective demand, it insists upon the same price and package for every citizen or resident who boasts a pulse. The latter policy will be more popular with the coughing and sneezing than it will be with the health-conscious whose premiums will go up. In the real world it is difficult to be impartial. One nation can be splintered by interest.

Or perhaps not. Constitutional political economy suggests that choices should be long-term rather than in-period. If the contract is for life, then it nets out the private and personal stake. Young people entering into the scheme cannot predict what drains they will make on the fund. Stranded behind a thick veil of unknowledge, it will be easier for the coughing to think themselves healthy and the healthy to think themselves sneezy. The premiums will rise with age since age is as predictable as death and taxes. Otherwise they will be citizen-standard since the risks relate to generalised hazards that cannot be made personal. Because of unknowledge the citizens will reach consensus in advance on what is fair. In-period, they might come to resent the differential claims that the healthy and the unhealthy make. They have no right to object. They signed up to the social compact. Only a scoundrel breaks his word (Reisman, 2015: 172–80).

Pauly writes that equity in risk-rating is seen differently depending on the nature of the risk that is being underwritten:

> If we were discussing fire insurance – and the financial impact of a fire is surely many times larger than that of illness, even a serious illness – no one would object to the person with the higher expected loss paying the higher premium. But in health insurance, it may not seem fair that the diabetic should pay more than the non-diabetic and that the person with a stroke should pay the most. (Pauly, 1988: 52)

Fairness-seeming is a strange animal. It does not seem fair for the chronic to pay more than the hale. Nor, however, does it seem fair for them not to do so. While it is never good to spin general theory from casual empiricism when not every accident or illness is Cain's stigma of fault, the objection will nonetheless be raised that it is rather hard on people who exercise regularly and eat sensibly that they will have to pay over the odds because the drag-racers and the jobbing cutthroats are putting the community average up.

Where the premium is made the same by law, the insurer has the loophole of increasing its profits through differentiating its product. Where the basic package is made the same by law, the insurer may refocus its strategy on the low-hanging fruit. Cherry-picking of the healthiest specimens has the great advantage to the insurer that it reduces the cross-subsidisation and increases the surplus. Socially, however, it also allows the cream to be skimmed and the lemons to be left without cover.

The inability to purchase insurance is sometimes regarded an infringement of the right to health. Where it is, the government will be tempted to complement its policy on community rating and the basic package with a statutory insistence on an open door. The law will state that no applicant can be turned away. Provided that the subscription continues to be paid, it will also make it mandatory for all policies to be renewed.

Guaranteed renewal by itself is not enough. An employee who becomes chronically ill will not lose his insurance but he may lose his exit option. He may become subject to lock-in (with his insurer) and job-lock (with his employer). Even worse placed will be workers born with congenital defects or who have a high probability of later on requiring expensive care. Once hired, renewal is guaranteed. That is why guaranteed renewal must be accompanied by community rating and open enrolment. Premiums cannot be shaded. Access cannot be denied. After that there is the renewal. It cannot be refused.

Community rating, a basic package, open registration, guaranteed renewal – the bill mounts up and the insurer is squeezed. Having intervened in the market through legislation, the State has no alternative but to intervene a second time with subsidies and tax credits that compensate the insurers for the statutory obligation to register the bad risks at the standard rate. Risk equalisation could be a payment made directly to marginal individuals: it would give them an incentive to shop competitively for a package differentiated within the fixed points laid down by law. The top-up could also go to the employer: it would be an incentive for companies to hire bad risks who might otherwise have put up the premiums charged to the plan.

Much depends on the 'community' to which the community rating relates. It can be as big as a nation but also as local as a town. It could even be a single firm. If insurers and employees are not to be handicapped in their search for something better, it is clear that the standard provisions within the rated community cannot be absolutely standard. Nor should contracts be so narrowly based that they stand in the way of geographical mobility into sunrise constituencies.

It is a fine line. Too much differentiation makes the law an ass. Too little differentiation makes the law a brake. Too little subsidisation bankrupts the insurers. Too much subsidisation bankrupts the State. Trapped between too little and too much there are the commercial carriers. They can in the limit withdraw altogether from the business. There is not much the State can do to stop private insurance from drying up in response to legislation that corresponds to the will of the people. The threat is especially real in countries where the bad-risk old-elderly are representing an ever-growing proportion of the population. Medicare in the United States became essential because the private insurers were not able or willing to fill the market niche.

8.3 MORAL HAZARD

Once the applicants have purchased insurance, they no longer face the same imperative to protect their good health. The rules of the game have changed: 'Careless behavior increases the probability of a loss' (Kunreuther et al., 2013: 81). Their risk profile alters as a direct consequence of the insurance they have bought. The phenomenon is known as moral hazard: 'By moral hazard, we mean the tendency for an insured individual to incur larger losses, take less care, and/or take additional risks than if the person had no coverage. Premiums will then be raised to reflect the higher risk' (Kunreuther at al., 2013: 80–81). Commercial premiums are always behind the times. Third-party payment can make individuals take less responsibility for their health. It can make the nation's health status fall. It can put up the cost of care.

8.3.1 Communism through Effective Demand

Once the individual has bought insurance, the economic logic is that they will become more accident-prone. Actuarially speaking, all bets are off. Where the seat belts and the vitamins cost money but the visit to the doctor is co-paid by the pool, the tendency will be to economise on prevention because care and cure cost so much less.

The neglect is a tendency. It is not a prediction. Precisely because good health is investment and consumption in itself, it would be premature to say that life-holders will inevitably cut back on maintenance merely because avoidable repairs have become more affordable. It is hard to believe that many more people will go out in the sun merely because their cancers can be treated free on the National Health Service. Yet the tendency is there. People might not look both ways when crossing the road, check the sell-by dates on their food or refrain from smoking in bed. They know that any consequent liability will be a collective one.

The implications for overall well-being are ambiguous. People who drive fast are more likely to crash but will save money-making time that will increase their capital stock. People who drink heavily are more likely to damage their liver and nerves but will have had such convivial evenings in the pub. A short life can be a merry one. All that is certain is the logic. Insurance can cause people at the margin to revise their estimation of cost and benefit. They might not be the same people before and after they sign.

Moral hazard alters the risk profile that lands the well-insured in the ward. Moral hazard also affects their attitude to the medical attention on which they have pre-purchased a claim. Rights having been secured, rational consumers will want to make the most of their entitlements. They will present more frequently and request more costly services. There is no need to call out the clergymen to protect *homo economicus* from the slippery slope of moral decay. Moral hazard is not moral decay. All that it means is that purposive men and women will prefer more to less: 'The response of seeking more medical care with insurance than in its absence is a result not of moral perfidy, but of rational economic behavior' (Pauly, 1968: 535).

The textbooks teach that marginal utilisation proceeds to the point at which marginal utility is proportional to marginal sacrifice. Money is not the whole of the payment. Time lost is opportunity cost. Pain is a deterrent to overuse. Demand aside, a responsible doctor might refuse to validate a frivolous request. Even so, there is an intuitive logic in the expectation that goods without prices will be consumed in greater quantities than will non-merit goods that have to stand on their own two feet.

Where there is no cost-sharing or when the annual out-of-pocket ceiling has been reached, the price at the point of use is zero. The last unit will be free at the point of consumption. Being free, it will therefore be the unit that yields no more than zero marginal utility. The signals are twisted, medical effectiveness is ignored and the buck is passed. There is no such thing as a free buffet. What is free to the consumer must be paid for by the pool. It is a waste. It is a cost.

Some numbers are weasels and some statisticians lie. Used responsibly, however, the figures can be the shadow on the wall. Manning estimated what it would mean if all Americans under 65 were to move to insurance with a zero co-payment. He found that the welfare loss due to moral hazard would lie between $37 billion and $60 billion. That was between 14 per cent and 30 per cent of all the money households were devoting to health. No more than an indication, still an overhang of 30 per cent or even of 14 per cent cannot have been good news for the restaurants, cinemas and universities left empty because the money was being spent on a surfeit of just-in-case (Manning et al., 1987: 270).

The consumer has an incentive to shop prudently for insurance. He has less of an incentive to shop sensibly for the care that the insurance makes possible. There is no reason to search, monitor and bargain when it is the third parties who will pay. It is moral hazard again.

The providers too adapt their priorities to the new incentive structure. Even if a marginal intervention will almost certainly be flat-of-the-curve, the practitioners have the luxury of recommending further tests, referrals and prescriptions once they know that the unique human being across from them, insurance-protected, will not have to make a direct pecuniary sacrifice. More wolfish doctors will take advantage of the position to garner inflated fees for themselves. Supply will find it easier to induce its own demand where someone other than the beneficiary is settling the bills.

In the short run it will be pass-through without resistance. In the long run the premiums will go up. Self-restraint on the part of the principal or agent is no more than fighting a flood with a bucket. There is no way that a single face in the crowd can keep the streets litter-free, spend the nation out of a recession or prevent the village commons from being tragically overgrazed. It is the dilemma of collective action, the tyranny of small decisions and the fallacy of misplaced concreteness. What one can do, all cannot. One consumer's search for best-possible information, one consumer's decision to do without a marginal test, would have an insignificant impact on the price at the next renewal. One consumer's gain would be shared with crowd. Like the phlogiston theory, the dodo and von Ossobeyne's *Magnum Opus*, it would vanish without trace.

8.3.2 A Cause of Change

Insurance can shape events. It is more than knee-jerk reimbursement. It is not just a passive pass-through.

The wording of the contract may itself lead to a reordering of the treatment options. There are policies where the insurer will pay for inpatient care but not for day-case surgery. There are policies where the insurer will pay for a truss but not for a linctus. There are policies where the insurer puts a cap on the annual cost-shares. The annual ceiling is a reason to save up a mixed bag of postponable treatments for a single insurance year. In cases such as these the doctor might select the reimbursable alternative because it is cheaper for the patient or more lucrative for themselves. They might ignore the greater burden that the prepaid option puts on the pool and on the nation. It mounts up. In the long run the costs and the premiums will rise.

Insurance protects the doctor's clinical freedom. It sets the professionals free to do what their medical ethic dictates. Doctors have a Hippocratic Oath. They have a moral commitment to deliver an irreversible service even to a patient whose creditworthiness is poor. On the other hand, doctors are not a charity. They cannot afford to become the insurer of last resort by regularly supplying uncompensated attention. In order to cushion themselves against bad debt and default, doctors might choose to raise their average charges. It will then be their paying customers who will credit in the pro bono business. Insurance is the other option. It ensures that patients who cannot pay will not be turned away. It also ensures that the doctor's own time will be reimbursed.

Research and development follow the money. If insurance is prepared to reimburse for high-technology treatments, then the research laboratories and the commercial manufacturers will have an economic incentive to push back the frontiers of business. A cure for cancer pays. A cure for malaria, kwashiorkor or dementia does not. Government grants and public laboratories seek to balance out the patents and profits that do not cater to the poor.

Insurance is causing the cost of care to rise. The rise is at once a deterrent to purchase health insurance and a convincing reason to do so: 'Costly new surgical techniques such as organ transplants and artificial replacement parts spur the demand for insurance; low-cost vaccines diminish it' (Weisbrod, 1991: 534). It is a vicious circle. Precisely because of the expense, the costly new treatment must be made a part of the promise. The insurer who fails to sell the most modern entitlements will lose out to one who is touting the state of the art.

Insurers can make the costs go up. They can also intervene in history to keep the escalation down. Commercial carriers collect comparative data on doctors and hospitals. They monitor the waits, techniques, stays, inputs, recoveries and readmissions. They refuse reimbursement for mould-breaking therapies until they are given proof that novelty, clinically and economically, is better than the status quo.

Insurers scrutinise large claims. They query deviations from the mean. They insist on prospective rather than retrospective payment in order to force the treatment centre to share the risk of a cost overrun. The third party does all of this out of self-interest and not at all out of benevolence. Yet the invisible hand has made itself the fourth party to the deals. As if guided by the invisible hand, the self-interest of the insurer comes to countervail the self-interest of the provider. Insurance makes things happen. Value for money can be the result.

Insurance can generate incentives that brake the rise in cost. Yet the economic burden hinges on the services that are reimbursed and the dynamic knock-ons that they occasion. In the United States, 'if universal health coverage were achieved, the number of annual physician visits would increase by roughly 1 visit for each child who gained coverage and between 1 and 2 visits for adults' (Buchmueller et al., 2005: 20). It is a cost. There is also a benefit. Physicians provide preventive care and conduct early diagnosis. Physician visits reduce the need for expensive hospitalisation, disability and death. Insurance, in short, has an active function. Insurance, by protecting good heath, can lean against the escalation in cost.

8.4 COMBINATIONS AND PERMUTATIONS

Insurance is like a box of chocolates. They are all chocolates but they are not all the same. The differentiation in service maximises the non-median consumer's felt well-being. Heterogeneity appeals to the marginal who want to dwell at the fringe. Yet homogeneity has its constituency too.

8.4.1 The Spice of Life

Sometimes the insurer settles the bill without precommitting the ceiling. Sometimes the maximum per year, per episode, per life as a whole is prespecified. Sometimes there is a deductible: this is a lump-sum excess which the patient must pay out of pocket per episode or per annum before the insurance kicks in. Sometimes there is a co-payment: this is a fixed amount above the excess that the patient must pay at the point of consumption. Sometimes there is co-insurance: this is the percentage of the reimbursable band that must be covered personally by the insured party. Sometimes there are all three: a deductible, a co-payment and co-insurance. Sometimes there are none of the three: even rugged individualists who describe the National Health Service as the Iron Curtain and worse have been known to buy all-inclusive policies with first-dollar cover.

Sometimes the cost-sharing cuts off at a preannounced ceiling: all marginal treatment becomes free to the consumer once the threshold has been breached. Sometimes the cost-sharing is never finally suppressed: the intention is to prevent moral hazard but the byproduct is the ever-present possibility of financial ruin. Sometimes the insurer preannounces a fixed indemnity for each kind of medical service: consumers must pay the difference if their demands exceed the scale. Sometimes the insurer commits itself to a fixed number of services but not to a specific monetary total. Sometimes the subscribers are obliged to choose from a closed panel of providers. Sometimes the subscribers are allowed to select their own doctor or hospital.

Sometimes the policies protect the individual alone. Sometimes they blanket in the spouse, child dependants and elderly parents. Sometimes the policies are automatically and permanently renewed. Sometimes the prices and quantities are recalibrated at the first renewal after a chronic diagnosis. Sometimes the premiums are age-related and gender-specific. Sometimes they are set at the same flat rate for all. Sometimes the policies impose a special-risks surcharge on the motorist, the sportsman or the smoker. Sometimes they offer a good-health discount to members who perform well on a battery of tests. Sometimes the coverage is studiously non-judgemental, avowedly indifferent to deviations and idiosyncrasies.

Sometimes the contracts are restricted to major contingencies such as inpatient episodes. Sometimes the refund extends to walk-in clinics, day-case surgery, routine check-ups, physiotherapy and prescription drugs. Sometimes the insurer will pay for prevention such as a vaccination, early detection such as a mammogram, body maintenance such as an aerobics session, follow-up rehabilitation such as counselling sessions for former alcoholics. Sometimes it will pay for care in-place with complements such as a full-time home nurse or a live-in home help.

Some contracts exclude mental health. Some exclude venereal disease. Some exclude artificial insemination, gynaecology and antenatal care. Some exclude blood transfusions, organ transplants, cosmetic surgery, gender reassignment, medical tourism, self-inflicted injury or attempted suicide. Some exclude walking-frames, wheelchairs, dentistry and refraction. Some exclude self-referrals to surgeons and hospitals. Others raise no objection when the patient bypasses the gatekeeper and goes directly to a specialist.

In some cases the policyholder covers the full cost of the insurance. In other cases the employer covers the full cost. In other cases the taxpayer pays in a share. In some cases the low-income subscriber can apply to the State for means-tested support. In some cases all premiums attract tax relief as a merit good. In other cases the fiscal subsidy is confined to the lowest tax bands. In other cases the tax foregone is confined to named basics. In other cases the tax deduction is granted to the employer as a legitimate business expense. In other cases there is no access to the deductions and exemptions that Titmuss, seeing the similarity with cash transfers to the poor, termed 'fiscal welfare' (Titmuss, 1963: 44–50).

In some cases the patient is allowed to buy a top-up rider for better amenities, shorter waits, an expensive drug, a named surgeon or the abrogation of cost-shares. In other cases what is permitted is the standard package, no more and no less. Sometimes brand-name pharmaceuticals and not just generics are included on the list. Sometimes only essential and not comfort drugs will be refunded. Variety is the spice of life. All these contracts are insurance. What is insured is not, however, always and everywhere the same.

8.4.2 A Single Package?

Insurance is a restaurant with many dishes. Options are attractive where different people like different things. There is no reason to think that one-size-fits-all will satisfy their infinite complexity.

An apprehensive hypochondriac might put all-risks first. A self-reliant adventurer might prefer to make his own mistakes. An affluent saver might want low premiums accompanied by a considerable excess. The case against a uniform package is the Kantian respect for persons that in the world view of the libertarians becomes the defence of bottom-up consultation against top-down command. A system which values autonomy and choice, it is argued, ought to leave it to the individual to decide what he or she wants: 'Underlying most arguments against the free market is a lack of belief in freedom itself' (Friedman, 1962: 15).

Not only should people have the right to choose their own insurance, but they should have the opportunity to change their mind. It is not evidence of inconsistency and contradiction but of purposive personal development that the same person might be a risk-lover when single but a risk-averter when a family member becomes permanently incapacitated. The same person might find it rational to go for a low-cost, low-cover policy one year and for a high-cost, high-cover policy the next. Prudent, sensible economisers might even plan ahead. They might plan to concentrate their elective surgery in the comprehensive phase. Once there is nothing left to fix, they might plan to return to limited cover that matches the needs of the new person they have become.

The case for product differentiation is a persuasive one. Where different people put different values on different services, a single policy can distort the relative utilities and the quantities that are consumed: 'Any system which attempts to force all people to buy the same amount of health services is likely to result in a significant misallocation of resources' (Fuchs, 1973 [1966]: 163). Pauly, like Fuchs, regards it as a shortfall in perceived well-being when the cat is forced to eat the dog food and to pay for it as well:

> If individual demands for medical care differ, it is possible that the loss due to 'excess' use under insurance may exceed the welfare gain from insurance for

one individual but fall short of it for another individual. It follows that it may not be optimal policy to provide compulsory insurance against particular events for all individuals. (Pauly, 1968: 534)

Tastes can differ. Where they differ, it is not really optimal to expect even the vegetarians to eat beef. It is insensitive and intolerant to require risk-lovers to join a club designed for risk-averters merely because wise paternalists have decreed that silly Bill's revealed preferences are not very good.

The case for laissez-faire is the case for the individual: 'No exchange will take place unless both parties do benefit from it. Cooperation is thereby achieved without coercion' (Friedman, 1962: 13). Persuasive as it is, sections 9.2 and 9.3 of the following chapter show that mandatory cover with restricted choice knows some good tunes as well.

9. Insurance: private and public

Insurance can take a variety of forms. It can be provided by a variety of agencies. Section 9.1 on 'Private health insurance' and section 9.2 on 'National health insurance' discuss prepayment options in the two sectors. Section 9.3, 'The National Health Service: payment and provision', examines the double-barrelled structure that marries up the two sides of the circular flow. Finally, section 9.4, 'Payment beyond insurance', is a reminder that the money can be found even if there is no third party to share the risk.

9.1 PRIVATE HEALTH INSURANCE

Not all insuring agencies in the non-State sector are commercial and for-profit. Some are linked to private charities, professional associations, trade unions, consumer co-operatives and hospitals. Some large employers operate their own insurance funds. All are subject to financial regulation to ensure that their capital is sufficient and their investments sound. Often that is the sum total of the regulator's involvement.

9.1.1 The Individual Plan

Individuals apply for private cover either because they have no core protection or because they want incremental options. The fact that the individual applies does not, however, mean that the application will be accepted. Each one-off is a mystery. Adverse selection is always a threat. A person who has made a calculated choice to spend money in the hand on an unforeseeable outcome in the bush must always be regarded with suspicion.

Individual plans are always higher-priced plans because of the chance that the applicant is secretly anticipating an above-average claim. Personalisation of administration adds to the cost. So does the fiscal difference where a business-sponsored group plan can be set against tax but an individual plan, treated as a private consumable, is excluded from this concession. It makes the private plan more expensive.

9.1.2 The Group Plan

Not all group plans are employee-sponsored. A mutual aid society or a local community can set up its own plan. The only condition is that the pool be large enough to spread the risks and the overheads. The most common group plan is, however, the fringe benefit at work. About 90 per cent of private health insurance in the United States is provided in this way. The employer self-insures either through an in-house insurance section or through an outside carrier with which it registers its entire workforce.

Comprehensive registration is attractive to the insurer. Because the pool is brought together through employment in a named organisation and not because of individual risk, concealed or unknown, the insurer has the guarantee that it is enlisting a representative cross-section. Adverse selection is ruled out save in the minority of cases where a sick worker joins an organisation specifically to access its medical insurance. The insurer has the confidence that very bad risks would have been weeded out by the firm's own medical tests before a new worker was put on the payroll.

Large numbers enable the carrier to set an experience-rated premium based on the risk profile of the firm and its industry. Statistical deviants like older workers and the chronically ill may be charged a higher premium. Otherwise the average workers, finding the cross-subsidy inequitable, might be reluctant to join the firm.

Because the market is competitive and the sponsor always on the look-out for a better bid, each carrier must ensure that its package and premiums, and therefore its internal efficiency and declared profits, are in line with rival bids. The rigidities of competition among the few may cushion interdependent giants in the short run. In the long run, being natural enemies, they will have a strong temptation to undercut the implicit cartel. They will cheat in order to capture market share.

The employer seldom pays the whole of the premiums. In the United States in 2014 the average annual total cost of employer-sponsored family coverage was $16 834, of which the worker's share was $4823 per year. The employee's share is increasing as a proportion of the total (Kaiser Commission, 2014). Tax relief on a group plan goes some way to reducing the burden on the employer, and so does any increase in productivity which better morale and fewer days off work may engender. On the other hand, there is the pressure from the unions to keep the employee's contribution down.

Employers are especially likely to concede if they think it will be possible to shift the incidence on to the final consumer in the form of higher prices. This is a function of the elasticity of demand for the final product. If there is a shortage of skill or if there is full employment, labour will be in a stronger position to secure better benefits. If, of course, labour's bargaining position is weak, then the net increase in compensation may be negligible: 'The "employer's share" of payment for a job-related fringe benefit eventually reduces worker money wages spendable on other things by approximately the amount of the payment' (Pauly, 1994: 47). In such a case it will really be the employee and not the employer who is paying the 'employer's share'. That is why some employees consciously choose firms that offer them higher pay instead.

Aside from the shares, there is also the acumen. Professionalisation of intelligent decision-making means that fewer opportunities will be missed. Quality investment is a benefit. Because it is the employer who searches, screens and checks, the one-off employee is spared the labour of tracking down the best deal. Cost-effectiveness is too important to be left to the uninitiated. Personnel officers and vigilant unions, Paul Feldstein writes:

> develop the necessary expertise and information to evaluate alternative medical care delivery options available to their employees ... The greater selectivity of better-informed groups benefits the less-informed subscriber ... The competition among health plans for the better-informed purchasers, those who are more likely to switch plans if quality deteriorates, will help those who are less well informed. (Feldstein, 1988: 326)

The insurance companies will have an incentive to upgrade their package even if not all participants in the market are equally knowledgeable or equally willing to change. A small number of active and cost-conscious choice-makers, undeterred by retention clauses such as no-claims rebates, can be sufficient to ensure that the pool as a whole will reap the spillover benefits of allocative and dynamic efficiency. Minorities with insider knowledge or above-average curiosity are a fifth column that keeps tabs on asymmetric exploitation.

The insurer quotes a lower premium for a standard contract. This is likely to be the option that the employer selects. What is sauce for the median might not be sauce for the deviant. An unmarried member has no need for a policy that covers a non-existent spouse or child. Such a member might want to exchange redundant well-baby clauses for a better dental package, travel and repatriation insurance, spa massages, wellness treatments and the indemnification of user charges. The same is true of a two-income couple where each partner is fully covered under the other partner's group insurance plan. They might prefer an enhancement of non-health benefits in areas like superannuation and house purchase to a duplicate inpatient shield which has no economic value.

Usually the group plan is a standard package with a standard set of benefits. Sometimes, however, the employer will negotiate with the insurer for moderate differentiation within a single plan. The employer might even pay the employee's capitation to join a health maintenance organisation. Not all employees are satisfied with a group plan that only indemnifies and reimburses. Employees who want managed care or a change of menu might be given the opportunity to pay more for more. It expands their felt freedom. Wants and needs are not all the same.

The same may be said of the contributions. Members of group plans who are expected themselves to pay a part of the premium are more likely to be active, less likely to be passive, at the time of the annual enrolment. Some, Strombom found, are especially sensitive to small differences in cost:

> While significant price effects are estimated for all groups, the elasticities for individuals presumed to face the lowest switching costs – younger, recently hired employees who are in good health – are roughly four times larger than those estimated for individuals for whom switching plans is likely to be more costly – older, incumbent employees who have recently been hospitalized or diagnosed with cancer. (Strombom et al., 2002: 90)

Price sensitivity decreased with age. The elasticity of demand for an employee under 30 was twice that for an employee over 45. The result, analogous to adverse selection, was adverse retention. Adverse retention could over time increase the average risk and the fair price of the disparate offerings. Younger members move on to cheaper alternatives within the group plan. Older members seize the default option.

A fringe benefit that one is not going to use is not really a fringe benefit at all. Diversity, however, puts up the price. Tailor-made administration means that less care can be squeezed from a given overhead. Employees themselves incur transaction costs and information overload to make a reasoned assessment of the options. They may not regard the collecting and processing of marginal knowledge as an efficient use of their scarce time. In the end they might simply roll over the status quo. Perhaps this is the reason why only a third of the group plans on offer in the United States actually offer any selection at all. The number falls to only 15 per cent in group plans with less than 25 members (Rice, 2001: 25). The lack of choice might not be an imperfection. It may be what the consumers want.

Employees have reservations about a change of plan within a single group. Their reservations will be even greater when they are changing to a new job with a new policy. A change of organisation may mean a new annual excess. There may be a precautionary wait before the new policy kicks in. Medical tests might have to be repeated at an economic cost. A new medical history might have to be taken. Premiums might be higher. Continuity in the doctor–patient relationship might be disrupted where the new insurer has a closed-ended panel of doctors of its own.

Most disturbing of all is the possibility that the new insurer will refuse to continue cover for an existing condition. The old policy was binding and renewable. A chronic condition diagnosed while the old policy was in force could not be made the subject of an exclusion clause. It is different when the employee decides to move on: 'For type I diabetics, diagnosed early in the life cycle, job lock may be a very serious issue ... Having a preexistent condition may reduce the ability of young type I diabetics from switching firms to find their best employment match' (Kahn, 1998: 896). New pastures do not seem so green when insurance enters into the calculus. Even if the new job is offering a higher salary, employees might decide to stay where they are.

Employers know that occupational plans are an impediment to mobility. That is why they often offer especially attractive health benefits to key staff whom they know to have a high market value outside. Some of those outside opportunities will be in adventurous new start-ups which do not offer any insurance at all. Employees in such firms will have to apply for risk-related individual cover. The expense and the exposure are a good reason not to shake off their golden handcuffs.

Cooper and Monheit asked a sample of Americans about their golden handcuffs. About 30 per cent reported that the potential loss of occupational cover had prevented them or a member of their household from moving to a better job. Married men who stood to lose their health insurance were especially conservative. They were 23 per cent less likely than the uninsured to make the change (Cooper and Monheit, 1993: 412). It was the young, the low-paid and the unskilled who were the least afraid to try new things. Since the experienced and the educated are more likely to be the bottleneck input, the inference is that job lock is likely to lead to an inefficient deployment of the skill stock.

Occupational plans are a good reason not to indulge in voluntary unemployment. They are a cause of misallocation where quits followed by search would have led to a better use of manpower. Occupational plans also make dismissal more of a calamity. Unemployment means not just the loss of the breadwinner's income but also the exclusion of the entire family from job-related medical cover. Unemployment, transitional or long term, is a bad time to fall ill.

Occupational plans impede mobility, stunt productivity and make workers feel unfree. The response to widespread discontent has been legislation to fill in the gaps. It has taken a variety of forms. Workers between jobs have in some cases been given the right to extend their previous group plan at their own expense. They have been allowed privileged access to an individual plan where their previous job did not come to an end because of ill health. Once re-employed, they have by statute been given exemption from a new waiting period if an existing condition had been included in their previous policy. In ways such as these the government can contribute to the humanitarian spillover while also unfreezing a frozen labour market.

Well-intentioned as the policies may have been, there is always the risk of creating a failure to correct a failure. Insurance companies will find it unprofitable to carry known loss-makers. They will shift part or all of the cross-subsidy to existing policyholders through higher premiums. Existing policyholders will not necessarily welcome the *de facto* social welfare that more costly private insurance represents. Especially will this be so where the blanketing-in is not universal. Selective inclusion will be seen as piecemeal, illogical and unfair. Should the retired be allowed to retain their occupational cover or should they be offloaded onto Medicare? Should selective inclusion be extended to dependants left on their own by a divorce or the death of the breadwinner? There is no end.

A more general objection will be that occupational cover is by definition tied to an organisation. It is not portable on the model of the individual plan or national insurance. Nor is it open to part-timers, the seasonally employed or the self-employed. They must arrange individual plans or do without.

Compulsory cover is a non-wage cost. As with all supplementary benefits, it can be seen as a tax on jobs. The incidence falls most heavily on labour-intensive activities and small businesses not large enough for reasonable odds. Neither the small employer nor the low-income employee might be able to afford the premiums. In the United States 98 per cent of firms with more than 200 employees offer health insurance. The figure drops to 55 per cent for firms employing ten workers or less (Gruber, 2008: 574).

Compulsion cannot alter the basic economics of a small business struggling to get by. Mandatory cover has some of the properties of the textbook minimum wage. Trapped between bankruptcy and innovation, such a firm will have a strong incentive to mechanise its processes and reduce its labour force. An occupational plan may in that way put the most vulnerable out of work.

Well-intentioned intervention may be correcting an existing failure by creating a new one. That, however, is not how the interventionists see it. They say that a firm that expects its workers to pay it a subsidy by doing without a basic human right might be a firm that deserves to close down.

9.1.3 A Case Study: Managed Care

Both the individual plan and the group plan can be delivered in the form of managed care. In the case of the traditional indemnity, the practitioner supplies the treatment and the insurer reimburses the fee. In the case of the prepaid contract the legal entity that treats is the legal entity that pays. Risk-bearing and medical attention are two domains ruled by two different structures. Vertical integration makes the payment wing and the provision wing into one.

The best-known of the double-headed eagles are the health maintenance organisations (the HMOs) that have developed in the United States as a consequence of the Health Maintenance Organization Act of 1973. In 1988 73 per cent of American employees were enrolled in conventional indemnity plans and 27 per cent in managed care (Berk and Monheit, 2001: 11). By 2004 the 27 per cent had become 95 per cent and Cutler was declaring that 'traditional insurance is an anachronism' (Cutler, 2004: 87). The largest is Kaiser Permanente. Founded in 1945, by 2014 it had 9.3 million members, 14 600 doctors and annual operating revenues of $47.9 billion.

In the prepaid system there are a number of competing organisations. They collect an annual fee from the applicant or, very commonly, from the enrollee's employer. In return for the premium they agree to meet all the medical needs named in the contract for the specified period. About 80 per cent of the American HMOs require co-payment.

One variant is the 'staff model'. In this case the HMO operates health centres and hospitals of its own, retains its doctors full-time on salary and treats only those patients that are enrolled. Utilisation review and physician profiling are practised in-house. They ensure that referrals are in line with norms and that practice variation corresponds to organisational guidelines. This differs from the second variant, the 'group model', where the doctors remain in outside practice and have their own premises. Doctors on the panel are paid an annual capitation or receive a prespecified fee for service.

The third variant, the 'network model', is looser still. The HMO has a number of contacts and contracts with a selection of independent providers, primary and inpatient. The designated suppliers know that they are in competition for renewals. It is an incentive to keep the quality up and the cost of care down.

None of the three models is literally closed-panel. Patients can in all three models seek diagnosis and treatment from an outside supplier. Doing so, however, they might have to cost-share at a higher rate or pay the entire cost out of pocket. Their range is therefore limited by the economic deterrent.

Some HMOs are profit-seeking. Others price only to cover cost. Some give the professionals a share in the operating surplus: a move towards a socialistic producer co-operative is also a move towards interest-driven cost containment. Others see no reason to make stakeholder professionals into businessmen shareholders as well: the interests of the patient are better served if clinical freedom is not perverted by conflict of interest. Clearly, the precise arrangements can vary. The principle, however, remains the same. Similar to Britain's State-sector National Health Service (NHS), the insurance function and the delivery function in the private sector HMO make up an integrated whole.

The prepaid plan has an incentive to keep down the average cost per case. The reason is that the burden of the inefficient or the unnecessary falls on the single HMO itself. One way in which excessive care can be kept in check is by permitting the family doctor with a fixed practice budget to retain the unspent surplus as a bonus. A second way is by requiring the primary care physician to act as the gatekeeper to more expensive consultant and hospital attention. A third way is by requiring pre-authorisation from the paying arm before a non-emergency hospital sequence is launched. Not only do the general practitioner and the hospital specialist have to validate the choice, but the insurance wing must do so as well. Even major emergencies are not spared. After the patient has been admitted the insurance wing may insist upon concurrent authorisation for each test or treatment in turn. The less that is delivered, the lower will be the bill.

The HMO is led by its balance sheet to economise on its medical non-essentials. Simple procedures will be performed in the doctor's office. Referrals will be kept to the minimum. Sedatives will be preferred to psychotherapy. Waits will be used to ration and delay. Bed occupancy will be kept high. Equipment and operating theatres will not be left idle. Throughput is productivity. Productivity keeps the HMO lean.

Cost-consciousness extends to prevention as well as cure. The delivery wing invests in health capital through flu injections, educational input and early detection. Doing so, it is speculating with the insurance wing on a lower incidence of expensive treatments later on. It is not certain.

The patient might die prematurely or move on to a competitor. An HMO is not the NHS, where out-migration is minimal. Even with the discount, an HMO might nonetheless reason that preventive medicine is a business asset. A satisfied customer is more likely to extend.

Managed care is strategic interaction. Rivalry forces the HMOs to market a competitive product. The prepaid system must bargain hard with its suppliers for cost-effective contracts. It must make full use of the internal economies that accrue to the concentration of administration, billing and communication in a unified structure. It must pass the gains on to its enrollees in the form of shorter waits and more attractive premiums. It must entice them to register and renew by means of convenient opening hours, well-situated premises, ungrudging referrals and a generous package. Desertion at the next annual renewal is 'exit'. Exit gives the rank-and-file 'voice'. Premiums are the ultimate feedback in the marketplace for insurance.

It must also keep the quality of its inputs and its outcomes high. In aggregate, the track record of managed care is not very different from the survivals and recoveries in traditional insurance: 'Fears that HMOs uniformly lead to worse quality of care are not supported by the evidence ... Hopes that HMOs would improve overall quality also are not supported' (Miller and Luft, 1997: 8). Medical indicators in aggregate are broadly the same. Within the sector, however, there are the good performers and there are the butchers. Transparency means that competitors have not merely to slim and trim but also to demonstrate that their service is better than the average.

Less attractive in a competitive market is the manipulation and the salesmanship. Razzle-dazzle does not go well with helping the sick. These things should be kept in perspective. Factual information has long been disseminated by private business. In some if not all cases it has been in the consumer's interest to be kept up to date with the prices and the products. The HMO is selling a product like any other. So long as medicine is commodified into the marketplace, it is a fudge to make it an exception that may not cry its wares. Either it is for sale or it is not for sale. Concealing relevant information is not the appropriate way to make the commercialism go away.

It might be difficult to be detached and calculative in the heat of a cardiac arrest. Insurance, however, is seldom sold in the back of an ambulance. Consumers normally enroll or re-enrol on an annual basis. The fact that they shop only once a year means that they have the time to study the prospectuses, performance and online postings. They will have the time to discuss the options with advisers, employers, brokers and friends. When they do make their choice, it is less likely to be an impulse buy. Besides that, want-creation will cut no ice with the administrators of a company plan. Where the employer selects the HMO, value for money rather than the undignified endorsement of a Hollywood starlet is more likely to sway the balance.

The prepaid plan must have an effect on the doctor–patient relationship. The nature of the effect is not, however, clear-cut. On the one hand, in contrast to fee for service, the patient knows that the doctor has no financial incentive to overtreat. On the other hand, the paying wing putting pressure on the providing wing, confidence is eroded by the knowledge that the doctor might be treating too little. There is, in other words, a recognisable conflict of interest within the multi-product HMO between its profit-seeking and its health-maximising objectives.

The trade-off between economic returns and clinical freedom will be especially acute where doctors on profit-share are paid a bonus if they curtail appointments to pack more passengers in. They may even fear that their own contract might not be renewed if they treat marginal conditions that the fund would prefer them to conceal. Deselection would interrupt the doctor–patient relationship. The possibility of deselection is a reminder to the patient not to trust the doctor too far.

Provision is threatened not just by avarice but also by resourcing. A prepaid plan is self-financing. It is dependent on premiums and not public finance for its budget. It cannot spend more money than it has. Radical default will lead to litigation. Small savings and studied discretion will probably pass unseen. Most contracts in any case have a ceiling limit. Once the ceiling has been reached, all but life-saving treatment will be suspended. The contract runs for no more than a year. Unless there is a statutory obligation to renew, the provider might simply postpone the tests and delay the transplants until the potential loss-maker goes off the books.

9.1.4 The Multiple-Pool Market

Whether they are selling indemnity plans or whether the product is an HMO, private insurers cannot afford to carry ballast. The very fact that an applicant falls into a high-risk category, irrespective of their own current state of health, might be enough to invite a refusal.

The advertising campaign of an HMO might sell an image of sport and athletics with which the sickly and the wheelchair-bound might find it difficult to identify. The receptionists, the doctors and the nurses might make the very ill feel like unwelcome gatecrashers. Prospectuses might be written in small type that older applicants cannot easily read. An HMO might be situated on a high floor without a lift. It might be located in a gold-standard mall hours away from the Sowetos and the *favelas*. It might specialise in a portfolio of services that screens out the addled and the addicted in favour of the suburban and the professional: 'For example, a health care plan might recruit an outstanding pediatrics department, to encourage the enrollment of healthy young families, but offer a weak cardiology program, to discourage the enrollment of people with heart problems' (Enthoven, 1980: 120–21). The co-payments themselves might be moulded into a deterrent. A high cost-sharing ratio for insulin and syringes self-selects the diabetics out.

Risk segmentation is the rule. Low-severity patients are 'creamed'. High-severity patients are 'skimped'. Very high-severity patients are 'dumped' (Ellis, 1998: 538). The insurance market is failing to meet the needs of the sick. Some observers criticise gain-maximising capitalism for targeting medical insurance at the prosperous who can pay. Others, more cautious, will reflect that the imbalance might be due not so much to free enterprise per se as to misguided regulation that has made free enterprise dysfunctionally unfree.

Dowd and Feldman lay the blame for 'skimping' and 'dumping' at the door of ill-advised legislation that has made mandatory a standard charge:

> The true culprit in this theory is neither multiple competing health plans, nor even risk-based health plan choice ... Instead, it is the constraint, commonly imposed by both public and private purchasers, that health plans must charge the same premium to enrollees regardless of their health risk ... The problem could be solved, or at least attenuated, by allowing plans to risk-rate enrollees within a market. (Dowd and Feldman, 2006: 142)

Price differentiation, the authors argue, would improve the sensitivity of the market. It would ensure that the very high-severity cases could buy their way into the pool. It might encourage product differentiation in place of a reversion to the median. The downside is obvious. Beyond some trigger price the very high-severity cases will not be in a position to pay.

In a multiple-pool market, the insurer has to be tough to be cost-effective. The HMOs have been accused of dumping their high-cost cases on to the traditional insurers who must then raise their charges in self-defence: 'Above some threshold level, the net effect of increased HMO activity is to raise traditional insurers' premiums' (Baker and Corts, 1996: 389). Baker and Corts, conducting a nationwide survey in the United States, found that adverse selection had made traditional insurance even less of a close substitute. Only in areas with less than 15 per cent HMO penetration was there any evidence of lower premiums being quoted by the traditional insurers in order to defend their market share. Otherwise the premiums went up as the competitors flooded in. It is all too easy for the very sick and the very poor to be trampled underfoot.

9.2 NATIONAL HEALTH INSURANCE

The State foregoes tax revenues when it zero-rates the employer-sponsored plan. It subsidises private hospitals where otherwise an inaccessible island would be underbedded and understaffed. It regulates the standards and makes mandatory the coverage. The State is already a part of the mixed health economy. National health insurance is no more than more of the same.

Knitwear and software, car insurance and house insurance, are obliged to support themselves in the unforgiving marketplace. Health insurance is different. It is an exception to the rule. Even where the provision of care is left in the private sector, the payment function is frequently taken over by the State.

A national scheme is a socialised scheme. That does not mean that it has to be centralised and standardised as well. In some countries the word 'national' will mean what it says. Democracy will demand the unitary command-structure of Westminster and Washington in preference to the opinionated disparity of fringe and periphery. It is the same principle as in free schooling with a national curriculum. In other countries the 'national' element will be decentralised and devolved. Different provinces, states, districts, regions and townships will be given every opportunity to tailor their contributions and their packages to the voiced preferences of the subnational unit.

Some will chose high premiums and comprehensive entitlements. Others will be satisfied with shorter lists and longer waits. Within limits they can put flesh on their own unique needs and wants. Beyond some point they cannot. National insurance is a national commitment. At the end of the day it is the duty of the national government to keep the spillovers under review. It must ensure that the national minimum is a universal minimum and that no resident cannot make good on his rights.

9.2.1 The Self-Funding Model

Contributions to fully funded national insurance are hypothecated and earmarked. There is no grant-in-aid from general taxation. Tripartism is excluded. Bipartism, however, is the norm. The employer and the employee each puts in a contribution, often identical. The contribution is seldom shaded by health status or risk. Because the superordinate principle is solidarity, not individualism, the premium tracks the average and not the unique. It can be a lump sum: fixed amounts impose a disproportionate burden on lower incomes. It can be a constant proportion: all the deciles are charged at the same flat rate but higher earners pay more in total. It can be income-linked: all the deciles pay something but higher deciles pay at a higher marginal rate for their stamp.

Where the contribution is income-related rather than lump-sum, there will often be a ceiling limit. The maximum keeps the drain from becoming a disincentive to the worker, a bottomless pit to the firm. A cap also contains costs since it limits the amount of money that can only be released for health. Besides that, a cap limits a contra-egalitarian transfer. Where the payments can be set against personal income tax, the tax shelter is of greatest value in the higher income bands. Tax avoidance compounds the pro-rich bias that is already a fact of life on the provision side. The higher bands normally enjoy more life-years. They are more vocal in claiming their benefits. The inverse care law is the result.

The employer's contribution ceases when the employee retires or is made redundant. The old and the unemployed put pressure on the health system but do not contribute to the national insurance fund which is its bloodstream. The same is true of dependent children and a stay-at-home partner. Heads of households might be required to put in double contributions to ensure that the other members of the club are not short-changed.

Rigorously self-supporting, the national insurance fund is outside electoral politics. Constitutional ring-fencing policed through independent and transparent audit ensures that the politicians will not raid the fund for activities not related to health or to prop up a marginal constituency. The health care constitution must ensure that subscriptions will not be put up without a qualified majority in Parliament.

The constitution must block off any supplementary top-up save where public funding has been expressly authorised to credit in named categories of the excluded. It must also ensure that the national insurance fund obtains permission from Parliament to issue bonds in its own name. Excessive debt could lead both to care cost inflation and an unsustainable insurance deficit. Perhaps the constitution will commit in perpetuity a 'sin tax' such as a tobacco excise. Non-fungibility is a bulwark against in-period discretion and ad hoc interference.

A multi-period constitution is minimax. Its objective is to minimise the likelihood of the worst-possible outcome rather than to maximise the outturn from the best. Precommitment is in line with the spirit of insurance in general, national health insurance in particular. Fear of loss and not hope of gain is written on every page. Critics of set-in-stone budgeting reply that, while an irresponsible Leviathan in thrall to the political business cycle and the medical mystique is inevitably a budget-buster who turns the chaos loose, the nightmare scenario is neither inevitable nor probable.

Not all politicians are short-termers and opportunists who will run the printing presses. Some are men and women of principle who will prudently supplement the national insurance fund only when they are certain that the nation can afford the increment. Politics in the form of party-political rivalries, economics in the form of fixed exchange rates, keep latent expansionism in check. The rule in hypothecation is that more must be put in if more is to be taken out. It affords some protection against weak leaders, although against wise ones as well. It is a mixed blessing. A constitutional solution might leave the national insurance fund too short of resources to do its job.

So might unrestricted exit. National insurance and private insurance are frequently open for business side by side. Some people, sensitive to information asymmetry, are more comfortable with a non-profit insurer and more comfortable still with the State. Some people, on the other hand, prefer a more individualized product. Many end up with both. The multiple pool system gives the consumer a choice. It can turn malign.

A national fund which recruits across the board is, actuarially speaking, a citizenship pool. The healthy cross-subsidise the unhealthy. The subscriptions converge on the mean. Being all-embracing and all-inclusive, the geographical disparities are evened out. An earthquake or flood can decimate the reserves of a regional micro-pool. A national fund is large enough to act as its own insurer of last resort.

A single pool is a representative pool. Multiple pools, on the other hand, are an invitation to adverse selection and cherry-picking. Where a critical mass of good risks abandons the national fund, there is a real possibility that the State system will be left with the lemons. Where there are better offers outside, only the medical catastrophes and the congenital handicaps would remain in the fund. It would always be in the red.

Defection makes the national fund unsustainable. That is why membership is so often mandatory. Compulsion is freedom. Adverse selection is not. Without a prison gate to lock in the citizens the national pool would be only one pool among many. Selective supplementation through commercial riders and parallel policies can be allowed for dental care, holiday mishaps, expensive pharmaceuticals, a private room, the reimbursement of cost shares. What cannot be permitted are top-ups that go beyond the luxuries or opt-outs to leave only the permanent loss-makers behind.

Some of them will be the genuine victims of unavoidable adversities. Some of them will be hard cases by their own free will. They will have made a decision to ride-free on moral hazard. They will have known that a citizenship entitlement once granted cannot easily be withdrawn.

The feckless can take chances with their health since there is always the citizenship port in the storm. The voluntarily unemployed can expect credited contributions since a national pool means that the whole nation is in. A social consensus committed to a health care minimum is a sitting target. Rational cost-minimisers know that their fellow citizens will not allow them to die on the street.

Few threats are more challenging to the self-image of the social democrat than that of the Atomic Bum when, wrapping himself in explosives, this blackmailing Bad Samaritan shouts, 'Your money or *my* life'. National insurance is forever at risk from the irresponsible and the idle who think that a decent commons can always support a few more sheep. Making insurance mandatory makes it more difficult for the Bum to travel free. When all is said and done, however, the Atomic Bum has got us dead to rights and there is not a lot we can do.

9.2.2 The Tax-Subsidised Model

Token contributions may be demanded. They are just for show. The tax-subsidised model does not expect national health insurance to be self-funding. Instead of ring-fencing it relies on public finance.

Direct tax tracks the ability to pay. Since income tax is levied at different rates in different bands, the prosperous put more than the less fortunate into the common kitty upon which all alike can draw. Assuming that an extra tranche yields less pleasure than the tranche that went before, graduated inequality has the additional advantage that it makes perceived sacrifice more equal for all.

Direct tax is progressive tax. The rich give up a higher proportion of their income than the poor. The lowest-income deciles are exempted altogether. Direct tax is not, however, the only source of public finance. There is indirect tax in the form of value-added tax, council tax, stamp duties and excise duties. There are social charges such as the dog licence, the television licence, the road-fund levy and the peak-hour supplement. Unlike the income tax, such payments are regressive. A prescription charge, like an aspirin bought over the counter, represents a higher proportion of a low income than it does of a high one. A poll tax is like a vote. Each poll is counted as one. A poll tax is equal in its magnitude but not equal in its bite. The incidence of a purchase tax falls more heavily on the proles who take the bus than the polls who go by yacht.

It is impossible to state with certainty if the overall incidence will be progressive, proportional or regressive. Each annual budget and each individual country will have its own story to tell. Aneurin Bevan, looking back on the first decade of the British National Health Service, said that the thrust was progressive: 'The redistributive aspect of the scheme was one which attracted me almost as much as the therapeutical ... What more pleasure can a millionaire have than to know that his taxes will help the sick?' (Bevan, 1958: Col. 1389). History reveals that he did not wait for his answer.

Henry Phelps Brown made a different judgement call. He concluded that the bias in one direction cancels out the bias in the other. The overall impact, he said, was proportional: 'Taxation, when the direct and indirect forms are taken together, does little to change relative incomes' (Phelps Brown, 1988: 331). The poor are not soaking the rich. The rich are not soaking the poor. No one, in fact, is doing much soaking at all.

Finally, there is Marmot. The higher deciles earn more but also save more. The lower deciles earn less but plunge what little they have into basic necessities that are only selectively tax-exempt. In the end the poor pay more: 'People on low incomes spend a larger proportion of their money on commodities that attract indirect tax. As a result, overall tax, as a proportion of disposable income, is highest in the bottom quintile' (Marmot and the Marmot Review Team, 2010). People in the bottom quintile pay 38 per cent of their income in tax. People in the top quintile pay 35 per cent. The tax system in Britain works to the disadvantage of those on lower incomes. £4 out of £5 going to the NHS comes out of general taxation. It is not progressive but regressive taxation that is funding Britain's socialised health.

9.3 THE NATIONAL HEALTH SERVICE: PAYMENT AND PROVISION

National health insurance pays for medical services. It funds the services but it does not deliver them. A more ambitious system is one that unifies the two wings in a single structure. In the private sector the managed plan is the two-headed eagle. In the State sector it is a national health service.

9.3.1 The Comprehensive Model

The agency that pays is the agency that provides. It is a two-pronged attack. Demand and supply, finance and attention, become integrated in a single bureaucracy. So huge will the monolith be that it will often be divided up into regional or specialism-based trusts. Even where the authorities are in competition with each other for business, still the parastatal divisions must not be mistaken for the private sector's managed care organisations (MCOs). The State holds the property rights. The State allocates the budgets. The State issues the guidelines. However much the decision-making may be devolved, at the apex of a single bureaucracy there will always be the political top-down.

The purchasing wing, even allowing for the penumbra of private insurers, has the countervailing power of a quasi-monopoly when it negotiates with the providing wing, the pharmaceutical industry and the outside clinics and hospitals with which makes putting-out contracts. Within the national service, the providing wing will operate its own hospitals and retain its own salaried physicians. It is the civil service. A national service that only reimburses outside providers but does not itself supply will not be a national health service but a national insurance fund alone.

Consumers in an NHS are offered treatment within the public system. The services in kind are provided free of charge at the point of consumption. Insurance and attention come ready-mixed. The entitlement is double. The two parts cannot be unstitched. The patient cannot spend his claims on a private doctor not on the panel. Nor are they allowed to buy a fast-track place in the NHS queue. It is not cricket, British or Bevan to push others into longer waits. Nothing is forever. Attitudes are flow. The spirit of 1948 may one day mutate into the spirit of something else.

So long as the client-citizens are in broad agreement on their wants and needs, it would be both economical and ethical for their health services to be off-the-peg, standardised, mass-produced and one-size-fits-all: 'If consensus is pretty close (as was assumed at the time the NHS was set up) one might as well adopt the consensus allocation straight away on a "free" basis' (Collard, 1978: 138). If most of the subscribers most of the time are satisfied with the uniform entitlement, there would be no need to force them into an unwanted vortex of search. The future is unknowable and information is scarce. Existing policies are at worst the devil we know.

Where the distribution of preferences is single-humped, citizens might have little interest in frivolous and petty differentiation for which they would have to pay. Left or right, black or white, we all open our umbrellas when it starts to rain. If, however, popular attitudes become more discrete and more differentiated, more divergent and more individual, then it might be the freedom of choice that public opinion puts first. If some people want apples and some want oranges, there is no unique mean that will satisfy both clusters: 'The less consensus or agreement there is, the more pressure there is to move from "free" provision to market prices' (Collard, 1978: 138). It is an empirical question. Titmuss or Friedman, history will decide.

People are different. Economies of scale are all very well if they give the consumer what he wants. Long production runs are less attractive if the consumer values diversity as an end in itself or wants an outlier service that purchase-and-provision is badly placed to deliver. Henry Ford promised the motorist a Ford car of any colour they liked so long as it was black. Galbraith, referring to central planning and not to corporate capitalism, said much the same about uniformity mixed with conformity to get the average cost down: 'This may be the problem of socialism. Planners can provide for everything but color' (Galbraith, 1958: 28).

Even if the planners do cut the cost, plain vanilla might not be the flavour that most people prefer. Their preferences might fall on stony ground. Where the funding of a national health service exceeds its hypothecated premium, non-State entrants and fresh innovators will find it difficult to mount a challenge. The National Health Service is available free at the point of consumption. Plain vanilla or fancy vanilla, few new entrants can stand up to a hegemon like that.

Much depends on what ordinary people expect. A national health service might be able to meet the urgent needs of most people in a poorer society like Britain in 1948. How far it can accommodate the multiple lifestyles of globalised affluence is less certain. Pluralism is likely to have a high income elasticity. If it does, then the same pressures that forced market capitalism upon the previously communist planned economies might force factored-down coordination on health care purchase and provision. Buchanan predicts that it will: 'If socialism fails in the large it also fails in the small' (Buchanan, 1990: 23).

It may be wishful thinking on his part. Different sectors might respond in different ways. What is true of Ford cars might not be true of health. Especially is this so since a common service has an integrative as well as a productive purpose. Its function is not to smother the individual but rather to uncork the sociability that makes us all one.

9.3.2 The Residual Supplier Model

That is why the spirit of 1948 must not be confused with the residual supplier model. The comprehensive model is intended to social-engineer backbone into the national identity. It is the Church of England in a bed. It is a sacred cow and a national religion. It is not means-tested Medicaid and not poor-law charity. It is not age-based Medicare or the service entitlement of the Veterans Health Administration in the US. Socialised universalism is a world away from the Dickensian selectivity of the residual safety-net which is the clinic of last resort.

In the residual supplier model the free-on-demand clinics are intended for the destitute and the absolutely deprived. They are given purchase and provision because they need medical attention and do not have the ability to pay. Some churches have infirmaries and some doctors do uncompensated business. Medical charities and mission hospitals look after the lepers and the haemophiliacs because no one else will. In an emergency even private hospitals do not refuse to stabilise an urgent case. Some have pro bono wards and do outreach among the destitute sleeping rough. These are the exceptions. In correcting the social failure, the State does not face much competition.

Soup kitchen medicine is basic and no-frills. Where the society regards those unwilling to achieve and unable to save as indolent pariahs who have defaulted on the work ethic of personal responsibility and earned reward, it may take the opportunity to inflict stigma, to spoil identity, precisely because the deterrent of shame is part of the system. There will be a naked light-bulb without a shade. The seats will be torn. The uninsured get the message. They put off their visit. Often when they get to the free clinic it will be too late.

Some cultures will blame the uninsured for the inability to pay that forced them to become free walk-ins at the charity clinic. Some will find it objectionable that the less-affluent will make the last resort into the first resort because the emergency ward is always there and it costs them nothing. Where, however, the society is more tolerant towards those made medically indigent by a crippling disease or long-term unemployment, the concept of contributory negligence will not be invoked. The needy will not be dismissed out of hand as idle scroungers who ought to have planned ahead.

A society that has made up its mind not to judge will offer something better than the basic minimum to all the celebrants in its community. We as an articulated symbiosis will feel that we have a common need to care. It is one of the advantages of a national health service that no one knows who has money and who came in off the streets. Clients share the same wards. They have adjacent beds. They eat the same meals. They receive the same treatment. They see the same surgeons. The sheep are not separated from the goats. Manager or worker, stockbroker or vagrant, no one is an outsider when the gloves go on and the needles come out.

The universalist entitlement is the common curriculum of an unstreamed comprehensive. Fraternal and non-judgemental, it integrates all the teammates without distinction into a homogeneous set of shared experiences. In the pubs, in the boardrooms, on the shop floor, we enjoy a common base upon which the hurly-burly of market capitalism may later be built. Like Shakespeare, the King and the national language, a national health system is the infrastructure of an interlocking destiny and a journey shared. The residual supplier model is not powerful enough to generate a sense of solidarity and cohesion. Only the universalist model can do that.

Only common pools can give malleable men and women the feel of a common soul: 'What a community requires, as the word itself suggests, is a common culture, because, without it, it would not be a community at all' (Tawney, 1964 [1931]: 43). Solidarity is Good Egg. The National Health Service is togetherness and belonging. Estrangement and segregation are driven back to the private sector. Commerce is an I that shops for utility and value. The National Health Service is a We that provides a countervailing corrective to the underlying sickness of selfish Myself-Alone.

Qualitatively as well as quantitatively, selective health and the national health are not the same. Residual supply is for the failures. Universalist health is for the independent and the dependent alike. The National Health, Richard Titmuss said, had to be part and parcel of the national health: 'We want to see a health service developing which will not be separate and aloof from the life of the nation but an expression and reinforcement of national unity' (Titmuss et al., 1964: 124).

Titmuss found little to admire in the loneliness and isolation of free enterprise health that had no time for friends and fellows. Nor did he believe it to be citizenly that a State health system should stop short at the rejects who had failed the market test. Instead of commerce and residualism he argued strongly for the mutual support of a social organism that wants to keep its We-ness and its jointness in good repair.

9.4 PAYMENT BEYOND INSURANCE

Not all of health is paid for out of prearranged insurance. There are other ways in which patients can put money into medical treatment. First and foremost, there is payment out of pocket. Not all treatment involves a CAT scan or a double bypass. Most people who are in work can afford a practitioner consultation or a routine drug. In some countries user charges represent the major source of income for a doctor or clinic. Some of the charges are unofficial and illegal. Yet people do pay. They pay out of current income, as if they were buying any other consumer durable.

Interpersonal transfers are a second source of finance. Few patients are so isolated that they maximise personal satisfaction entirely on their own. Most patients are situated in a web of friends and neighbours, workmates and fellow worshippers, parents and children. People when they are ill tend to rely most of all on the extended degrees of the family network. The patient's kinsfolk will rally around.

Stranger-gifts are a further source of support. Churches and philanthropists provide money for exceptional bills. Hospitals practice price discrimination and cross-subsidisation. Doctors discount their fees when the patient has no insurance. In some cases they do not charge at all. Their altruism is an interpersonal transfer which helps the patient get well.

Employers too put money into care. Where they do so, often as a substitute for full health insurance, they refund a prespecified amount of health-related spending each year. An alternative would be for them to maintain a free-on-demand works clinic in-house. A full-time nurse on site is a good investment. Clinics reduce travelling time and absences from work. They protect value-added and throughput. They attenuate workplace alienation and resentment. They also ensure that the employee secures access to basic care without having to pay.

Savings are yet another source of funds. For most people insurance is money paid for peace of mind. The same peace of mind might be purchased if the precautionary premium were invested in the stock market or placed in a high-interest account. Savings are the cushion upon which the individual can draw in time of adversity. Money held idle for a rainy day can be used to pay for health.

The government, realising this, will sometimes opt not just for mandatory savings but for mandatory medical savings. Such medical savings accounts (called MSAs) could be voluntary. It is more effective for them to be compulsory. If they were opt-in, and if the interest rates were attractive, they would be chosen only by healthy candidates expecting few major bills. The unhealthy would prefer generous insurance policies, especially if the premiums did not fully reflect their above-average needs.

Subscriptions to the MSAs are sometimes collected at the same time as national insurance contributions. This keeps the administration cost-effective. Individuals set aside a fixed percentage of their income each month. Normally the balance is made subject to a ceiling. This limits the health-related wall of money that is being built up. The funds are held by a commercial bank or a State-run agency. Often the interest earned is tax-free.

An MSA can only be withdrawn for approved, health-related expenditures. One of these will sometimes be a high-deductible catastrophic insurance policy. Once the deductible has been met, the cost-sharing bias of MSA-funded insurance is no different from any other third-party plan.

The individual and the family will normally be able to choose the actual provider for themselves. On the provision side at least, the model is the market. MSA holders have an incentive to shop cost-consciously in order to secure a competitive deal. The assumption is that they have enough information to do so.

MSA holders have an incentive to look after their health capital. Prevention is economic. Account holders do not want to deplete their balances. In contrast to the common resource of an insurance policy, an MSA account is strictly private. No one but the owner and later the heirs to their estate can touch the nest egg that they have put aside. No one can take out (plus interest) more than they have put in (Reisman, 2006).

MSA balances are savings and not insurance. There is no cross-subsidy within the pool and no adverse selection. There is no correction for the inequality that earnings-related savings inevitably accumulate most quickly for the higher-earning deciles. There is no Exchequer top-up apart from tax revenues foregone and occasional supplements credited ad hoc to the poor and the old. Within those parameters, personal savings in MSAs can accumulate rapidly over time. A healthy old person might be health-savings-rich but disposable-income-poor. At least the money is there if there is a medical need.

10. Equity and equality

Equity means fairness. It means that the entitlements are as they ought to be. It means that each member of society is getting his or her just deserts.

Fairness can refer to the beginning. *Ex ante* each contestant is known to enjoy the appropriate opportunities when the starting-gun goes off. Fairness can refer to the race. In-period each runner is seen to experience the same treatment within the accepted guidelines of the rules. Fairness, finally, can refer to the finish. *Ex post* each player is believed to have been accorded the prize that they deserve. No one is getting less than they deserve. No one is getting more.

Fairness is a moral absolute. It is a correct procedure or an equilibrium outcome. In that sense it is different from equality, which is merely a statement of fact. Jill is precisely as tall as Jack. John is precisely as fat as Bill. There is no suggestion that they ought to be the standard size. Equality is measuring up. That is all.

This chapter is concerned with fairness. Yet it is concerned with sameness as well. The reason is that, rightly or wrongly, equity is often the moral principle that is invoked to make equality a desired objective and not just a dispassionate yardstick. Many people attach normative significance to a levelling of interpersonal distance. Many people say that in core areas of social life it is proper for the disparities to be kept within manageable limits. Many people are at one with Tawney when he asserts that it is right for fellow citizens to have unrestricted access to the social minimum: 'Whatever their position on the economic scale may be, it shall be such as is fit to be occupied by men' (Tawney, 1964 [1931]: 108).

Political democracy is one area where equality is believed to be a desideratum. The norm there is one citizen, one vote. The police services and the law courts are built around the same even-handed impartiality. They would be unable to function effectively if they consistently sold themselves to the highest bidder. Health status and health care is another such area where equality is widely believed to be a desirable objective.

This chapter asks what, precisely, is equal about equality. One reason why policymakers approach equality with caution is that there is no real agreement as to what the term actually means. On a good day it is unclear. On a bad day it is divisive. It is curious that something so widely debated and so frequently welcomed should also be so elusive, so difficult to pin down. Four dimensions of equality in health stand out nonetheless as particularly salient. They are discussed in the four sections of this chapter, headed 'Equality of expenditure', 'Equality of contribution', 'Equality of outcome' and 'Equal treatment for equal need'.

10.1 EQUALITY OF EXPENDITURE

Each child at a school picnic is given an identical piece of cake. 'One size feeds each' is the ethical 'ought-to-be' that the teachers invoke. Per capita equality of health care spending is a horse from the same venerable stable. Whether the equality targets public spending or the whole of the health care encounter, private and public alike, the lump-sum principle is the same. Equal-share consumption is the expectation that each citizen will be putting an identical strain on the common fund.

Tawney did not think that the expectation made much sense: 'Equality of provision is not identity of provision. It is to be achieved, not by treating different needs in the same way, but by devoting equal care to ensuring that they are met in the different ways most appropriate to them' (Tawney, 1964 [1931]: 49). Different people need different treatments. Different treatments entail different costs. There is no point in promising each citizen the same pot of gold. Their illnesses and their cures will not impose the same economic burden.

Every system of risk pooling, capitalist and socialist alike, must face up to the challenge of heterogeneity. Patients who take the blue tablet cost more than patients who take the white one. Only the very hard-hearted would say that the blue tablet should be discontinued once the sickly have exhausted their dead-level pot of gold. Nor would many people say that the healthy who never see a doctor should be given shopping vouchers to make up their citizenship entitlement. Heterogeneity makes health care a thing apart. Behind the veil we contract into a network of subsidies and cross-subsidies. Once we have joined the club we have to play by the rules. We cannot ask for our money back merely because our worst nightmares never came true.

10.2 EQUALITY OF CONTRIBUTION

Equality of contribution can mean that each member pays an equal amount into the fund. Rich or poor, sick or well, each citizen each month sticks on his 2 shilling health care stamp. An identical contribution buys an identical entitlement. It is like a cup of coffee purchased from an undiscriminating automat.

Equality of contribution can mean an identical monetary debit. It can also mean the same sum of psychic satisfaction. Where equality of sacrifice is the equality that is targeted, it is a logical deduction from the diminishing marginal utility of income that the poor should pay at a lower rate than the rich. Means tests, sliding scales and progressive income taxes are said to have the advantage over a standard-size lump sum in that they put clear water between the desperate and the luxury-loving.

It need not be so. The rich might be psychologically more sensitive while the poor might be more accepting, more accustomed to a hard life. Since happiness cannot be measured directly, interpersonal comparisons are intrinsically a priori, inherently speculative. Braybrooke for his own part is prepared to make the leap of faith. Braybrooke defends a rising gradient in tax with the documented empiricism that 'the poor find it difficult to cover their basic needs, while the rich can indulge in the most frivolous preferences' (Braybrooke, 1987: 173).

The implication is that unequal payment makes the redistribution double. Not only do the healthy pay for the sick but, also, the successful subsidise the less-advantaged. Since the lower deciles are more likely to have unmet medical needs, there is a further benefit in the form of health care levelling up.

Equality of contribution can mean the same objective payment or the same subjective sacrifice. It can, finally, mean an unequal charge that tracks an unequal burden. Metering means that people pay for what they use. The sick use up a larger share of health care resources than do the healthy. There is an argument that they should put in a larger share of the funding.

Where contributions are the same for the risk-prone and the careless as they are for the health-conscious and the responsible, there is an inherent inequity. Moral hazard and self-inflicted illness can push up the payments for good citizens while allowing bad citizens to travel free. That, however, is what pooling means. Nor can it be assumed that all pooling is in and of itself an invitation to abuse. The demand for medical care is erratic, peaked and unpredictable. Often random, the need for care is not always under the control of the consumer. Citizens are nowhere more equal than in the veil of uncertainty.

Even so, some risk factors do send their shadow before. Actuarial science makes possible the matching of differential contributions to differential risks. Private insurance or social insurance, there is enough knowledge to distinguish the median from the outlier. Such knowledge makes equitable fine-tuning possible. The health-conscious can be offered a no-claims discount. The over-75s can be charged an age-related supplement. Smokers can be asked for a hypothecated surcharge actuarially calibrated to the marginal medical cost. It is money in and money out. Extra coffees feed extra automats.

In private insurance, the calculation is a familiar one. The higher risks pay higher premiums upfront since it is they who are more likely to spend more days on a drip. In social insurance the position is more complex. Statistical frequencies, necessary but not sufficient, must in social insurance be tempered by social values. It can mean a serious clash of principles. On the one hand sin fills up the beds. The deadweight of sin should not be shared with the sinless. On the other hand the tolerance of diversity is the mark of the liberal. One person's sin is another person's lifestyle. Is high-risk sexuality not as valid a choice as motoring to work or eating red meat? Should the poorest of poor be charged a high premium merely because they have to brave the sharks for pearls while low-premium plutocrats sip their tea on the lawn? On the one hand we want to balance the books. On the other hand we do not want to judge.

Our consensus has both an economical and an ethical maximand. A national health system does not know which way to turn. Thus the British National Health Service might want to recoup a part of its costs through user fees but might also want to protect the citizenship-fostering function of a single-class ward. A compromise proposal, as Julian Le Grand has suggested, might be to charge the same fees to all patients but then to rebate the payments to the poor: 'The extension of means-tested charges would raise the cost to the high income groups, hence perhaps reducing their use relative to that of low income groups, while at the same time perhaps promoting equality of cost' (Le Grand, 1982: 50).

The proposal, in the spirit of social insurance, is intended to promote equality of sacrifice. The problem is that, in violation of private insurance, it does not address the actuarial issue of risk. Even poor people have been known to drink and smoke. 'Culpable negligence' is not a term that is heard frequently in the wards and the clinics. Public opinion will not always be as open-minded as the doctors. Public opinion may take the view that it cannot be equitable for the hard-working and the self-reliant to pay for the reckless and the irresponsible who put drunkenness and crime before their social duty.

The actuarial assessment of equal contribution is a numerical calculation. The reference to social duty does, however, mean that all bets are off. Equal contribution need not be a pecuniary magnitude. It can be the equal execution of the collective commitments that are the quid pro quo for the team-based entitlements: 'Social rights imply an absolute right to a certain standard of civilisation which is conditional only on the discharge of the general duties of citizenship' (Marshall, 1992 [1950]: 26). T.H. Marshall, never averse to looking a gift cherub in the mouth, said that equal access to a service was forever contingent, not ever absolute. It was dependent on the equal recognition of other citizens' claims.

Breaking the social contract can cost the offender more than their friends. It can also have major implications for the medical care they can expect. An alcoholic who petitions for a repeat liver may be sent to the end of the queue. A criminal shot while robbing a bank may be treated after an innocent bystander who got in the way. Social values are not always context-blind. Would most people really find it fair that a murderer should enjoy the same entitlement as a policeman sent to apprehend him? Equal rights might have to be qualified by equal duties in order to ensure that equality is equity and not just a flat, level line. It would be the thesis of judgemental contractarians that the characteristics and history of the patient, and not just his current and present need, ought to be taken into account when they are being graded and prioritised for care. Equal treatment for equal need might not always be equally fair.

10.3 EQUALITY OF OUTCOME

Health status will never be the same for all. There will always be differences in quality-adjusted life years. Biology marks out the playing field. Inherited genes are an intergenerational gift. Women live longer than men. Women hold a monopoly in the reproductive function. The old man has a shorter life-expectancy than the beardless youth. We may all be equal but we are not all the same.

Some inequality, indeed, will be self-selected. It is a topic in equality of respect. Individual freedom includes the freedom to take a chance. Society cannot stop boys from playing football merely because they might break a leg. It cannot force girls to raise their profile in armed robbery merely because they are statistically under-represented in premeditated homicide. It cannot force mercenary soldiers to convert to whist merely because mercenary soldiers have rates of attrition that make the Minister of Hospitals look bad.

A society cannot prohibit hang-gliding, skateboarding or tiger-shooting merely because it has made a decision to bring the mortalities and the morbidities closer together. A society cannot force religious minorities to have blood transfusions merely because death ranked above a violation of the moral code introduces a spike into the equality of outcomes. Equal liberty in cases such as these is actually incompatible with equal outcomes, equal incomes or equal levels of satisfaction. Different people opt for different risks. They regard different amounts of health and health care as right for them.

A smoker, revealing that they are less risk-averse than a non-smoker, may be said to have made a considered purchase of their health-status differential. A misanthropist, choosing freely to reside in a remote lighthouse offshore, may be said to have waived their equal access to a world-class local hospital. Such inequalities might not be unacceptable inequalities: 'If one individual receives less than another owing to her own choice, then the disparity is not considered inequitable' (Le Grand, 1991: 87). Students who put in different amounts of effort must not expect to score equally well in a test. If some people have opted for a trade-off that damages their health, it might not be in the spirit of T.H. Marshall or even of common usage to say that they have an equal right to restorative care that makes their health outcomes equal again.

The expectation of equal outcomes loses much of its appeal where the deserts are well within the individual's grasp but the effort expended is not the same. The student who works hard should not have to share their grades with the student who is lazy. The saver who defers their gratification should not have to share their wealth with the spendthrift who dissipates and squanders. Two individuals cutting a cake might not intuitively find the rule of 'half for you, half for me' equally fair to both: 'Suppose that one of the two individuals concerned had baked the cake; might not she have a claim, on equity grounds, to a larger share? ... Equality of outcome will sometimes be equitable and sometimes not' (Le Grand, 1991: 66, 71). Equality of outcome will not always and everywhere be fair. In assessing the distance, a decision will have to be made on the chain of causality that made the more healthy and the less healthy the unequal human beings that they have become.

So must a decision on whether to incorporate the capacity to benefit. Musicians who can play the piano are given first refusal when only a few pianos are around. Linguists who can read Bulgarian are offered books in Bulgarian that Romanians could only use to make a fire. Patients who are more likely to get well are pushed up the list for surgery when not all operations can be performed. People left out and left behind will complain that their outcomes have been disregarded. They will insist that they are plants and not weeds that can legitimately be culled. Scarcity, however, is not on their side. Limited resources rule out an egalitarian solution: 'People with greater aptitude for legal studies justly gain admission to law school, while other people, however worthy in other respects, must accept rejection' (Braybrooke, 1987: 141).

Equality of outcome, if it is to be a policy goal, cannot be defined as uniformity, constancy or strict convergence on the mean. Yet it does have a meaning. It can usefully be defined as an equalisation of differences that are at once avoidable, unwanted and properly understood. An equal chance, not an equal finish, is the objective that must be pursued. Non-random, systematic, patterned pathologies should not be forcing broad categories or recognisable groups into a position on the health status map which they would not have selected had the material constraints and the unequal information not shoehorned them into degradation without hope, that was not of their own choosing. Equity means that preventable handicaps deriving from socio-economic position and political access should be made less arbitrary, less of a lottery that rides roughshod over the meritocrat's legitimation of reward. Equity does not mean that morbidity and mortality are everywhere the same.

10.4 EQUAL TREATMENT FOR EQUAL NEED

The famous professor needs radiotherapy and the unemployed labourer needs radiotherapy. When Titmuss was dying in a National Health Service hospital, he was gratified to find that both he and a young West Indian from Trinidad, aged 25, had the same access to the same expensive equipment: 'Sometimes he went into the Theratron Room first; sometimes I did. What determined waiting was quite simply the vagaries of London traffic – not race, religion, colour or class' (Titmuss, 1974: 151).

'To each according to his need' means that each should have an equal chance (whether or not they actually exercise their option) of receiving the medical attention that their condition dictates: 'What is important is not that everyone achieves the same level of health but rather that everyone has the *opportunity* to achieve the same level' (Wagstaff and van Doorslaer, 2000: 1817). This need should be met irrespective of age, income, gender, intelligence, performance, occupation, ideology, religion, class, caste, place of residence, ethnic background, insurance status or any other non-medical irrelevancy. Horizontal equity means that no one should be able to secure fast-track treatment merely because of non-need selection criteria such as influential friends or ability to pay. It might even suggest positive discrimination in order to overcome history-dominated inequities that have imposed an unjustifiable handicap.

The debate centres round the general case versus the specific exception. In the general case of pins, cars, clothes, oranges, apples and yachts, many people would argue for allocation by supply and effective demand: 'No exchange will take place unless both parties do benefit from it. Cooperation is thereby achieved without coercion' (Friedman, 1962: 13). In the specific case of PhD degrees and professional certificates many people would argue the opposite: the consensus would probably be that demonstrated proficiency and not willingness to pay should be the deciding factor in allocating an examination pass. Specific too are bedrock commodities such as basic nutrition, basic shelter, legal assistance and medical services. Like the PhDs and the certificates, these essentials are made exceptions even in an economy where most people are broadly satisfied with exchange.

Tobin has used the phrase 'specific egalitarianism' to encapsulate the notion that the distribution of 'basic necessities' cannot be left to the economist's haggling and bargaining. Bought-and-sold degrees distort the information they are expected to convey. Bought-and-sold basics are at variance with the common value core. They make us feel that we have defaulted on the social contract.

The 'social conscience', Tobin stresses, is offended by 'severe inequality in ... commodities essential to life and citizenship' (Tobin, 1970: 264, 265, 276). Moral obligation in respect of pins is not the same as moral obligation in respect of cardiac arrest. Equity, as Walzer writes, is specific to a sphere: 'The principles of justice are themselves pluralistic in form ... Different social goods ought to be distributed for different reasons, in accordance with different procedures, by different agents' (Walzer, 1983: 6). Health care is different from pins. It must be distributed in accordance with a standard that is in keeping with the nature of the beast. Social conscience provides that standard. Haggling and bargaining can price and sell the luxuries. In the case of health care, however, 'ought-ness' comes from 'need-ness' and 'need-ness' comes from 'us-ness'. 'Want-ness', good in its place, somehow leaves us hungry for another meal.

Bernard Williams says: 'Leaving aside preventive medicine, the proper ground of distribution of medical care is ill health: this is a necessary truth' (Williams, 1973 [1962]: 240). Williams expresses his regret that ill health in so many societies is a necessary but not a sufficient condition for access to professional attention: 'Such treatment costs money, and not all who are ill have the money; hence the possession of sufficient money becomes in fact an additional necessary condition of actually receiving treatment' (Williams, 1973 [1962]: 240). The right to a fair trial would not be an effective right were the litigant not able to afford a lawyer.

Williams concludes that to believe in liberty it is necessary to believe in some supported equality, a moderately supported equality, as well.

Health care is a mixed bag. The equalisation of entitlement that is picked up by Tobin's 'social conscience' and Williams's 'proper ground' relates to the hard-core essentials and not to the elective periphery. Above the citizenship minimum, equal access might be discretionary over-commitment that oversatisfies the need. Up to the basic floor, on the other hand, threshold access is a distributional imperative that cannot be refused. There at least, needs take precedence over wants and ethical absolutes marginalise the effective demand.

Basic access is just, noble, humane and impartial. Translating allocation by need into normative policy is more difficult. A list must be drawn up; and a number of health care systems have had to do this. The list would have to include access to a primary care doctor, a hospital inpatient bed, an ambulance in an emergency, a tried-and-tested generic (but not an experimental drug or a non-essential brand), palliative alleviation of intolerable pain, necessary X-rays, necessary dentistry, necessary laboratory tests. Perhaps the list would include preventive care such as a tetanus injection and health education in areas like family planning. Perhaps it would include mental health services such as counselling and psychotherapy.

Some services will be indispensable fundamentals. Emergency anti-venins and life-or-death resuscitation are basic. Other services will be top-ups. Chemical injections to look young and attractive are add-on embellishments. The problem lies with the ambiguities in between. Suppose that a standard test is called basic but that it false-negatives one cancer in 10 000. Is a battery of sequential tests basic where the outcome might have been to save the ten-thousandth human life that, snuffed out, would leave three small children penniless, orphaned and alone? Dictionaries and encyclopaedias to their discredit have no Ten Commandments that reveal the essence of basic care. It is easier to be in favour of equal access than to say what is being covered by the guarantee. What is clear is that the equality extends only to needs. Preferences and wants, however defined, will have to look after themselves.

Equal access to basic care is an end in itself. It is the passport to a more enjoyable use of leisure, a wider range of consumables, a longer and more satisfying retirement. What should not be forgotten is that basic care is a means even as it is a utility. The gateway to tolerable health, basic care is twice blessed in that tolerable health is itself a means to an end. As Daniels writes:

> Health care is "special" because of its connection to the special social good, opportunity. Health-care needs are things we need to maintain, restore, or compensate for the loss of normal species functioning. Impairment of normal functioning means that an individual might not enjoy his fair share of the range of opportunities normal for his society. (Daniels, 1985: 86)

Health care is about economic success. It is not just about getting rid of a stubborn cold.

That is why there is a strong temptation to say that the definition of 'basic' should be shaded to incorporate the equalisation of life-chances as well. Tuberculosis gets in the way of promotion. Anxiety affects concentration. Basic health is basic not least because it empowers the left-behind to obtain and retain a decent job. Basic care is levelling up. It is liberalism and it is statism. It has the same social mission as skill formation through schooling. It opens doors. It gives everyone a chance.

Basic care satisfies the standard of allocation by need. It is not, however, the only commodity to do so. Much illness is the result not so much of inadequate doctoring as of inadequate housing, poor diet, structural unemployment and a polluted environment. As strong as the case for basic health may be, the danger is that the agenda might also be open-ended, the cost a blank cheque. The concept of 'basic' implies that, at some crucial cut-off, allocation by human need must hand over to allocation by supply and demand. The operational difficulty is to triangulate the porous boundaries that demarcate the shifting sands.

Basic care is a social wage. It is equality of access as defined by validated need. Validated need, however, is a hostage to fortune. The social consensus might not be prepared to treat one as one. If person A has a 20 per cent and person B an 80 per cent chance of survival, their cost-conscious fellow citizens might argue that diagnosed needs should be recalibrated to incorporate the probability of success. It is the same cost for both. It is not the same benefit. It is not the same weighted need.

There is a further complication. Equal treatment for equal need can all too easily be confused with equal treatment for equal *needs*. It would be a mistake to assume they are the same. Where the needs as well as the costs and the probabilities differ, there is no single rubric that identifies the maximal endstock of felt felicity. If need C costs ten times as much as need D, does the principle of equal access really dictate that treatment for need C can never be discontinued? If technique E satisfies the same need as technique F, can the sovereign patient really hold out for a new hand when a metal hook would be adequate enough? Once these questions are answered, the conclusion is then inevitable: 'There is nothing egalitarian about distribution according to need' (Culyer and Wagstaff, 1993: 448).

There is one more thing to say. It is about democracy and preference. While Britain has an ideal of integration, the median American is an independent isolationist:

> Insofar as Americans attach less importance to equality in health services than do the citizens of other wealthy nations, the marked heterogeneity in health care utilization by region, socioeconomic status, insurance coverage, race, and ethnicity could represent a choice to optimize for the individual rather than to maximize an egalitarian social welfare function. (Garber and Skinner, 2008: 44)

Some people are falling through the net. That is the way it is.

11. The right to health

The charters and the manifestos state that health care is an absolute right: 'The enjoyment of the highest attainable standard of health is one of the fundamental rights of every human being without distinction of race, religion, political belief, economic or social condition ... Governments have a responsibility for the health of their peoples' (World Health Organization, 1962 [1946]: 1). The highest attainable standard is a fundamental right. Governments have a fundamental duty to raise up their citizens until they reach the bar.

The subject of this chapter is the right to health. Divided into five sections headed 'Natural rights', 'Citizenship rights', 'Maximin', 'Generosity and compassion' and 'The structural imperative', it suggests reasons why consensus might converge on the perception that, in health at least, it is equitable to be more nearly alike.

11.1 NATURAL RIGHTS

The commitment to levelling up may be derived from what it means to dwell within the 'normal opportunity range' (Daniels, 1985: 35) of the generic *homo sapiens*. It is in the nature of a human being that they should be able to move about, reason creatively and propagate their kind. It is in the nature of a human being that they should be able to forage for food, which in the market economy means holding a job. The full flowering of the human essence is more than the beating of the heart.

A being is not a human being if they do not have an adequate set of the capacities and faculties that are the norm in their species. Their humanness alone certifies their need. Even the elderly, the frail, the disabled and the incurable are human. Their humanness is their passport to their right. The mentally and the terminally ill cannot reasonably be shot merely because their economic value has gone into the red.

Locke started from the premise that 'one omnipotent and infinitely wise maker' had imposed a law of nature upon the state of nature which otherwise would have been a normless void: 'And reason, which is that law, teaches all mankind who will but consult it that, being all equal and independent, no one ought to harm another in his life, health, liberty, or possessions' (Locke, 1993 [1689]: 263–4). The right to life or liberty might legitimately be cancelled out by a crime. The right to possessions might reasonably be annulled where the property had been acquired through force or fraud. In the normal course of things, however, the claim to retain that which is my own is an irrevocable imperative. It is a *noli me tangere* that even an overwhelming majority cannot override.

Locke's criterion is the negative injunction of 'thou shalt not harm'. Taken at face value, it is a duty to abstain but not a commitment to assist. The letter of Locke need not, however, be the spirit of Locke. Locke's non-aggression pact can arguably be extended into the Hippocratic undertaking 'to help the sick'. To make this extension it is only necessary to say that the right to a body is the right to a functioning body. Possibly this is implicit in Locke's vision of the natural order. He says that men are 'all the servants of one sovereign master, sent into the world by his order and about his business' (Locke, 1993 [1689]: 264). Nature is defined to be stewardship. No steward can go about God's business if their mind and body are not up to the task.

Adequate health is the silent partner. It would make sense to interpret 'to each according to his need' as 'to each that which is the distinguishing mark of the performing agency'. The Author of Nature placed the nose above the mouth so that his stewards could enjoy the aroma of their food. The Author of Nature also made the *salus populi* into the *suprema lex* so that the generically human could carry out their duties. A non-dead body was not enough. It had to be a functioning body. The right to good health was more than simply the protection from wolves.

Robert Nozick knew all about the wolves. Inspired by Locke, he was adamant that invasion and seizure are a violation of nature's own law. Leviathan would do well to keep his hands to himself: 'Individuals have rights, and there are things no person or group may do to them ... A minimal state, limited to the narrow functions of protection against force, theft, fraud, enforcement of contracts, and so on, is justified ... Any more extensive state will violate persons' rights' (Nozick, 1974: ix). The wolves are a danger to the self. So is the government which does not respect the right of the citizen to decorate their own space.

Nozick is clear on the conflict that can arise when the government does too much: 'No one has a right to something whose realization requires certain uses of things and activities that other people have rights and entitlements over' (Nozick, 1974: 238). In calling for a minimal State, Nozick is seeking to build barriers to stifle the ill-conceived error of commission. Naked Adam's estate is not his own where arrogant Leviathan billets the homeless in his barn. The problem is that even a Lockean has to accept that omission can be an error too. A baby's natural rights will not survive for long where paediatric clinics are being closed because the natural right to untaxed wealth is being put before the natural right to life.

Nozick enlists the minimal State to protect the endowment but not to enhance the capital. A vulnerable body should be protected from aggression but a functioning body should be left to the discretion of naked Adam alone. Gillon regards the distinction as an artificial one. If the right to adequate health and not just to off/on survival were to be included in Locke's list, then even an advocate of the minimal State could accept the legitimacy of State health care for the sick and the poor (Gillon, 1985: 88). Even the sick and the poor were sent into the world by 'one sovereign master'. Even the poor and the sick have natural needs which transcend their ability to pay. *De jure* does not pay the bills. Human rights impose a duty on the community to ensure that the functioning body is empowered *de facto* to reach the bar.

Altruism is a choice. Natural rights are an obligation. They are as absolute as the laws of the tides. Even if justice is refracted through mutual agreement, still the underlying principles upon which we agree are not up for grabs. It cannot be called just for a democracy to murder Bill merely because 99 per cent of his fellow citizens do not like his face. Health and health care have some of the properties of the referendum to murder Bill. It cannot be called equitable for Bill's chemotherapy to be made contingent on preference, purchase, time and place. Natural rights are rights that have been conferred by nature. Nature, however, is niggardly. If nature had been more bountiful, natural rights would less frequently have come under threat.

Locke himself sows the seeds of doubt when he introduces a caveat into his theory of property. A natural right is created, he says, where the labourer mixes his toil and trouble with nature's free gifts. Appropriation is the first step but there is more to come. A right can only be termed natural, Locke continues, where there is 'still enough – and as good – left' for the wider community: 'Nobody could think himself injured by the drinking of another man, though he took a good draught, who had a whole river of the same water left him to quench his thirst' (Locke, 1993 [1689]: 277). It is a right absolute where 'as much' and 'as good' is left behind for the second-movers and the movers after them. It is no more than a right *nisi* if the first man's 'good draught' exhausts the whole of the endowment. It is a serious door. How then will the later-movers quench their thirst?

Nozick saw clearly what such an engrossment of the means of life might imply: 'A person may not appropriate the only water hole in a desert and charge what he will ... An owner's property right in the only island in an area does not allow him to order a castaway from a shipwreck off his island ... The rights are overridden to avoid some catastrophe' (Nozick, 1974: 180). The rights are overridden. The scarcity of resources throws the natural rights back into the melting pot. It is not obvious what will come out.

Medical attention is Nozick's 'only water hole' and 'only island'. Locke's river is a free gift to all. No one can drink dry the Thames. Guy's Hospital is not in the same giving vein. Unlike Locke's river, its medical staff can be exhausted by the never-ending struggle between life and death. Real-world resources are not infinite. There will not be 'as much' and 'as good' for all. At some point a line must be drawn and a queue must form. Patients must wait. Some of them will die.

Medical attention would seem to fall into a Lockean no-man's-land between the patient's natural right to tolerable care and the economist's natural law that the cupboard is bare. Nozick's 'only island' might not be big enough for all the castaways in the storm. Nozick accepts that supplies are never infinite. His approach, however, is to blame not niggardly nature for an obvious tautology but instead inappropriate institutions for failing to squeeze all the juice they can from the lemon that they have. The solution to the economic problem, Nozick says, is not State but market. It is not Titmuss but Smith.

The freedom of entry and libertarian laissez-faire would open the floodgates. Automaticity would relieve the shortage of beds: 'I believe that the free operation of a market system will not actually run afoul of the Lockean proviso' (Nozick, 1974: 182). The invisible hand would solve the problem. It would bring the fellow shoppers up to the threshold minimum. The proviso as always is that they can pay. A natural right to stay alive is not accepted in Harrods Food Hall. The body-holders must have cash or a credit card as well.

11.2 CITIZENSHIP RIGHTS

Nature is one way of explaining the right to health. Affiliation is another. Citizenship is 'a status bestowed on those who are full members of a community' (Marshall, 1992 [1950]: 18). All citizens are full members of the club. As such, they are all entitled to make full use of its facilities.

Citizenship rights are different from natural rights. They are entirely in tune with sociology, hardly at all in awe of nature. In the case of citizenship rights, the entitlements are derived from belonging and membership, consensus and community. They are not therefore absolute but strictly relative. They are rights which a given group of people has decided to confer on its members.

T.H. Green was in no doubt that the life in common was the sole source of reciprocal obligation. Negatively speaking, he wrote, nature has no imperative: 'If the common interest requires it, no right can be alleged against it ... There is no such natural right to do as one likes irrespectively of society' (Green, 1941 [1879]: 109–10). Positively speaking, he emphasised, human rights are other people: 'A right is a power of which the exercise by the individual or by some body of men is recognised by a society, either as itself directly essential to a common good, or as conferred by an authority of which the maintenance is recognised as so essential' (Green, 1941 [1879]: 113).

T.H. Marshall, like T.H. Green, made much of citizenship as 'a claim to be admitted to a share in the social heritage' (Marshall, 1992 [1950]: 6). Citizenship to Marshall meant not simply a cold passport legality but 'a direct sense of community membership based on loyalty to a civilisation which is a common possession' (Marshall, 1992 [1950]: 24). He made perceived integration in an evolving organism the basis for civil rights like valid contracting and political rights like adult suffrage.

He also made the ongoing collectivity the basis for social rights such as the right to health: 'By the social element I mean the whole range from the right to a modicum of economic welfare and security to the right to share to the full in the social heritage and to live the life of a civilised being according to the standards prevailing in the society' (Marshall, 1992 [1950]: 8). The rights of assembly or of speech are negative freedoms that do not cost any money. Social rights are more expensive. Where our brothers and sisters cannot pay for medical care, the social whole must tax and spend in order to make an equal right into a social fact. The national family looks after its own.

Equality is equity because our fellow citizens want it that way. Sometimes through market processes, sometimes through consultation and democracy, they name the rights that they think their fellow toilers ought to have. As in economic exchange, however, each of those teammates must do their part to make the social compact into a two-way street: 'If citizenship is invoked in the defence of rights, the corresponding duties of citizenship cannot be ignored' (Marshall, 1992 [1950]: 41). The right to education implies the duty to complete one's assignments. The right to health implies the duty to go to the gym. The right to a heart transplant implies the duty not to smoke. The right not to be infected implies the willingness to surrender one's liberty when contagious to an isolation ward.

It all sounds suspiciously like what Nozick calls a 'utilitarianism of rights' (Nozick, 1974: 28). Absolutes give way to functions. Social good is superordinated to personal preference. Nature cedes its primacy to thee and me. It is a far cry from the categorical imperative, which in Kant's sense is intended to universalise the Golden Rule: 'Act in such a way that you always treat humanity, whether in your own person or in the person of any other, never simply as a means, but always at the same time as an end' (Kant, 1961 [1785]: 86). Welfare rights are a city of glass. They make it difficult to be left alone. Even the individualist is also a steward. At least the entitlements are not eleemosynary handouts. Teammates who put in what their community expects have a social right to take out what their community says they need.

11.3 MAXIMIN

Situated in the here and now, the ill person knows that they are ill and the well person knows that they are well. Each has a vested interest in protecting their own known stake. Neither will be impartial or even-handed in their approach to social levelling. Situated in the here-and-now, we know who we are. Knowledge makes our bias predictable. We know what we should nurture and what we should shred.

The story is different when our knowledge of ourselves is taken away. Situated behind a thick veil and clueless in the maze, anything might be out there. No individual, however purposive and rational, can recognise themselves or identify their circumstances. Decision-makers are compelled to make their choice in the darkness of 'insufficient reason' where 'objective probabilities' (Rawls, 1971 [1972]: 168) are stored in secret and all the records are masked by a cloak.

Disorientated and confused, frightened economisers must choose between the great win and the great loss in a great emptiness where all the black boxes look alike. Afraid of making a mistake but obliged to make a decision, John Rawls has advanced the hypothesis that rational economisers will 'rank alternatives by their worst possible outcomes' (Rawls, 1972 [1971]: 152–3). Their rational choice will be maximin. They will strive to minimise the damage that they associate with the worst-possible outcome. It is the loss of their inflation-proof nine-to-five and not the sweepstakes scooped at Monte Carlo that most occupies their imaginings when as frightened Hobbesians they think themselves through the sealed shroud.

The hypothesis is uncompromising. The Rawlsian damage-averter is assumed to have 'a conception of the good such that he cares very little, if anything, for what he might gain above the minimum stipend that he can, in fact, be sure of by following the maximin rule' (Rawls, 1972 [1971]: 154). The Rawlsian Prufrock is not a self-denying moralist who wishes to assist the less-advantaged because their inequality is unjust. He is certainly not a fearless entrepreneur who throws caution to the winds because the mould-breaker values the excitement of new challenge above the stasis of cosseting insurance. Instead he is a self-seeking, risk-averting cost-counting go-getter who out of calculative self-interest pays progressive income tax, makes distributive justice redistributive and insists upon a generous National Health Service because he is afraid of the dark.

Levelling in the sense of Rawls is not across-the-board levelling. It extends only to what Rawls terms the 'primary goods' which equity dictates must come under the aegis of the social guarantee. The list includes income and wealth, occupational opportunity, liberty under the law, access to positions of authority. It also brings in 'the social bases of self-respect' without which people would not have the confidence to assert themselves in their own best interest: 'The primary goods are necessary conditions for realising the powers of moral personality and are all-purpose means for a sufficiently wide range of final ends' (Rawls, 1982: 166).

Rawls does not mention health care by name. There can be little doubt, however, that threshold health satisfies the primary condition that it must unblock the great waste of stunted potential. Health care is a 'primary good' in the spirit of Rawls, just as it is a 'fundamental right' in the sense of the World Health Organization (WHO). Both the World Health Organization and John Rawls are in agreement on the action clause. Both make it a fundamental duty of the government to ensure that all citizens are lifted up to the bar: 'Society, the citizens as a collective body, accepts the responsibility for maintaining the equal basic liberties and fair equality of opportunity ... If these requirements are not met, persons cannot maintain their role or status, or achieve their essential aims' (Rawls, 1982: 170, 172–3).

Rawls predicts that rational citizens behind the veil will rank alternatives by their worst possible outcome. The medical professionals will not necessarily share the Rawlsian priorities. The doctor treats a named and unique human being who has escaped from the veil into the here and now. The service ethic makes it difficult for a professional to refuse. The doctor will agree that the health status of the worst-off ought to be improved. Just as much, however, will the doctor regard it as a success indicator if the genetic head start were to get well too.

Rawls conducts his thought experiment behind a veil of ignorance. The economic men and women who are deciding what is just are absolutely in the dark about every dimension of their own identity. Politically, it is one way of saying that no person should be a judge in their own cause. Sociologically, however, it is impossible to operationalise. People already know their own identity. It is too late to close the curtain.

James Buchanan finds a way to reconcile knowledge with unknowledge. What he invokes when he derives his theory of justice is not the let-us-assume of hypothetical ignorance but the real-world uncertainty of all social actors when they plan for a future that they cannot predict. No one knows what mishaps and misfortunes the future will bring. History-to-come is a blackness in which anything can happen. Even today's captain of industry, prosperous and self-reliant, can become brain-damaged, crippled, impoverished, uninsurable and unemployable as a consequence of tomorrow's unforeseeable accident or next week's unprovoked assault.

It is rational to be afraid. Walking backwards into the future, the radical agnostic will in the circumstances favour protective rules that embody a deep-seated endowment effect: 'Citizens will act as if they were risk-averse' (Brennan and Buchanan, 1985: 55). Citizens will not vote for rules that do not provide for a precautionary cocoon: 'We need not predict that each child will fall off the cliff to justify the installation of railings. Minimax is descriptive of deeply felt human precepts of rationality' (Brennan and Buchanan, 1980: 207).

Fear focuses the mind. Logically speaking, minimax by consent can swell into the safety net, the Welfare State and the National Health Service. Minimax can make even the right wing vote left wing because the alternative is being left with no wing at all. Buchanan, in favour of balanced budgets and market capitalism, does not himself believe that the State should respond to the fear motive with an infrastructure of medical care that is better provided through profit and utility. Yet he is also a democrat and a contractarian. Minimax has a momentum of its own. If ordinary people demand income maintenance and socialised medicine because effective demand takes no hostages, then that is the package that vote-seeking politicians will be led by an invisible hand to supply.

Rawls or Buchanan, the psychological baggage is always maximin. The question is whether it will also be levelling up by default. Maximin in health is fiscal socialism through rational choice. Equal access is undeniably a tendency. Whether it is a prediction is open to debate.

Some people reveal a high degree of risk-tolerance. They deliberately fail to insure. Some people are opposed to levelling because the veil is too thin. The veil does not make their privileged head start look like their impoverished old age. Some people believe that they can extrapolate their future health needs from their family's health history and the experience of their peers. Probabilities are not predictions but they are an indication. Ignorance or uncertainty, detachment is not guaranteed. Equity behind the veil may give way to the politics of grab.

That, however, is the grubby reality. The benchmark is more idealistic. Whether people decide to level up, to level down or not to level at all, the sole test of equity can only be agreement. On this Rawls and Buchanan see eye to eye. Justice is consensus. Right or wrong are the free gift of ordinary people when they hammer out their rules in general unknowledge of their own in-period stake:

> A 'fair rule' is one that is agreed to by the players in advance of play itself, before the particularized positions of the players come to be identified. A rule is fair if players agree to it. Note carefully what this definition says: a rule is fair if players agree to it. It does not say that players agree because a rule is fair. (Buchanan, 1986: 126)

No end-state in itself can ever be right or wrong. A dispassionate verdict cannot be called into question. *The Bible* and Marx's *Capital* are great classics that come down on the side of the needy. The calculus of consent is what it is. The players may have specified in advance that the sick should be given a National Health Service. The participants may have decided that all future losers should lie where they fall. All that matters to the consistent constitutionalist is the rules.

And fear. The nervous rule-maker seeks to block out the worst even at the cost of blocking out the best. That is why there is a strong inference that maximin will come down on the side of health. It is all a question of rational choice. No rational person will want to be levelled out.

11.4 GENEROSITY AND COMPASSION

Whereas Rawls and Buchanan would derive the sharing imperative from self-seeking *homo economicus*, Titmuss would explain it in terms of attachment, responsibility, cohesion and community. Titmuss believed in the reality of ethical commitment and *pro bono publico*. He took Britain's National Health Service (NHS) as living proof that the gift made to unknown strangers could become embedded and embodied in other-regarding public policy: 'The most unsordid act of British social policy in the twentieth century has allowed and encouraged sentiments of altruism, reciprocity and social duty to express themselves; to be made explicit and identifiable in measurable patterns of behaviour by all social groups and classes' (Titmuss, 1970: 225).

The National Health Service is living proof that the community cares. Its origins may be traced back to the common purpose of a nation at war. Its function has been to reinforce the interlocking attachments by making collective health a citizenship crusade. Private alms-giving would not be enough. The individual and the piecemeal can never be the same as the Totality, the Whole and the All.

The human need for integration is both the cause and the effect of the National Health Service. It is the institutional embodiment of the instinctual propensity to band and belong. Michael Walzer writes as follows about the ritual that the species-being is performing when they worship in the same waiting room with an unbiased and representative cross-section of their fellow celebrants: 'Membership is important because of what the members of a political community owe to one another and to no one else ... This claim might be reversed: communal provision is important because it teaches us the value of membership' (Walzer, 1983: 64). Matter is in motion. History is shaping our mind: 'Goods in the world have shared meanings because conception and creation are social processes' (Walzer, 1983: 7). What we regard as just is a function of what we regarded as just. Institutions once created acquire a momentum of their own.

Health policy to Titmuss and Walzer was more than the doctors and the nurses. It was also a topic in nation-building and the transcendence of isolation. A common health service taught lonely atoms to think of themselves as members of a national family. There is a snowball effect, a caring externality that was discussed in Chapter 7, section 7.2. Good neighbours join Neighbourhood Watch schemes and water each other's plants. Mutual aid gets into their souls. They take pride in a continuing pattern of gift exchange.

It is emotion rather than logic but it does lead to the imputation of a right. People, unless they are pathologically insensitive, empathise with what they imagine to be the discomfort and apprehension of the needy sick. They suffer from spoiled identity and the pinch of conscience when they cross the road and pretend not to see. There is no veil of uncertainty but instead a real, existing human being who has collapsed in the street. The outcome is that empathetic strangers willingly sacrifice a part of their self-centred hedonism in order to ensure that a real, existing human need will not lie where it falls.

Generosity and compassion are at the root of the right. Impulse takes the place of rationality and interest. Strictly speaking, impulse is not a moral absolute but simply a self-selected preference. It is the less reliable vessel. Justice cannot be traded at the margin when wealth falls or the next-best foregone goes up. Sentiment, on the other hand, is mutable and contingent. A sick person today is promised a right because the will-of-the-wisp swings in favour of care. A sick person tomorrow loses the right because moods and whims mean that Caligula's word is never Caligula's bond. It is a reason to spend unstintingly on private insurance instead.

Generosity and compassion produce a non-market distribution that is built on sand and not on rock. Yet built it is, and that is what counts. Strong feeling satisfies the residual need once contractual entitlements have been used up. Consensus validates the concessions. Agreed-upon processes legitimate the prizes. Benevolence fills the gap when written-down rights are not enough to relieve the uncorrected distress of the widow, the orphan and the dental patient who cannot pay.

11.5 THE STRUCTURAL IMPERATIVE

Commitment is subjective and motivational. It is refracted through individual choice. Structure, on the other hand, is the logic of the system. It is stable and it is functional. Agreement is demand. Structure is supply. Both pillars are necessary if a levelling policy is to be a sustainable one.

The microscopic approach is grassroots-led and bottom-up. The structural imperative begins and ends with the aggregate. The whole is different from the sum of its parts. The public interest is an entity *sui generis*. The structural orientation derives the case for intervention from the need to ensure that the social machine functions well. Evaluative and judgemental, it calls a halt to equalisation once the engine is fuel-efficient and the brakes do their job.

Equalisation is not equality and it is not equity. Equalisation is performance. Once the social machine is seen to be functioning well, the structural approach would suggest that any further upgrading of the health-deprived would be a bad use of scarce resources. The money could more cost-effectively be channelled into education, defence or private consumption instead.

The right to health may be termed a right but it has 'yes, but' marbled into its core. It is in the structural perspective no more than a means–ends right. It is a conditional right and a fair-weather friend. Moral philosophy can be good business where it leads to more productivity and less conflict. For it to be *moral* philosophy, however, the utilitarian outcome must be unintended and unexpected. Otherwise the nation would be in the amoral position of sentencing people to death merely because they were too confused and too crippled for economics. Equality can be justified on the grounds of economics. Equity is a harder nut to crack. Fairness is still fairness even if the right-holder will never add value to thank his fellow travellers for their gift.

One illustration of the structural imperative is economic growth. The economic system requires a reliable supply of skilled and unskilled labour. The prosperity of the whole is put at risk by days lost to disease, disability, debility or death. In Britain, if the mortality rate for the lowest two occupational groups had been the same as that for the upper two occupational groups, then '74,000 lives of people aged under seventy-five would not have been lost. This estimate includes nearly 10,000 children and 32,000 men aged fifteen to sixty-four' (Townsend and Davidson, 1982a: 15). Over and above the loss to the life-holders and their relatives, the loss to the national economy in the hard currency of lost production, consumption and potential was great. It is second-rate economics and third-rate sociology to treat our own people as if they had no market value. Britain was importing labour. At the same time fully 10 000 of its children and 32 000 of its working-age males were being wiped off the slate because they never had an equal start.

Our growth is dependent on his health. We therefore invest our money in his health capital so that he can contribute to the full to our macroeconomic expansion. Even in a market economy, the most efficient distribution of entitlements need not be the allocation that is brought about by the invisible hand. Efficiency up to the possibilities frontier dictates that no one should be off work with jaundice when they could be making microchips or delivering the milk.

A second illustration of the structural imperative relates to felt integration. Ascriptive characteristics like race and age draw the fellow citizens apart. Perceived distance can be incompatible with the overlap in life experience that is necessary to make one nation out of the multiple tribes. Universalistic provision of health care services might be seen as a way of smoothing out the disparities that could otherwise lead to riots and strikes: 'Civil rights legislation in Britain ... would be a poor and ineffective substitute for the National Health Service' (Titmuss, 1968: 142).

Adjacent beds in a one-class ward, in common with national service, British Broadcasting and comprehensive schooling, bring the social groupings closer together. New affiliations take the place of old ghettos. Integration in sickness and health takes the sting out of the conspicuous Gini that is splitting the nation into Ferrari and Tube. Equalisation protects the social system against the resentment and envy, the low morale and underperformance that could throw sand into the gears.

Without the levelling up the also-rans might stone our Ferraris in Belgrave Square.

Integration is an end which is also a means. The legitimation is derived not from eternal truths but from the cash flow pay-off. There is no contention that the narrowing of the health gap is somehow right and proper in itself. The structural imperative is only concerned with the atom where the component is contributing to the edifice. The approach relies heavily on philosopher-rulers to identify the shortest distance to a popularly validated destination. Top-down and paternalistic, the structural approach takes the view that the shepherd knows better than the sheep and that the sheep are only there because mutton tastes good at lunch.

Equalisation can be the result of the social engineer's omniscient and beneficent response. The solution is simple. Social engineers who know everything they need to know and are able to sacrifice their private interest to the public good must take command. God is equal to the task. God will not let us down. Social engineers who are as good as God will never be out of a job.

12. Inequality and health

The White Paper of 1944 that led to the creation of the British National Health Service (NHS) on 5 July 1948 took equality in health to mean equal access for equal need. It built on the historic Beveridge Report of 1942 which had declared war on the 'five giant evils of Want, Disease, Ignorance, Squalor and Idleness' (His Majesty's Stationery Office, 1942: para. 456). It committed itself to the generation and perpetuation of a common entitlement. It made clear precisely what levelling as levelling up would have to mean:

> The Government ... want to ensure that in the future every man and woman and child can rely on getting ... the best medical and other facilities available; that their getting these shall not depend on whether they can pay for them, or on any other factor irrelevant to the real need. (Ministry of Health, 1944: 5)

The objective was to be the universalisation of the best. Allocation was to be driven not by the profit motive and the ability to pay but by an equal citizen's right to the most appropriate treatment as prescribed by the best available professional. Like was to be treated as like. Medical services were to be distributed on the basis of medical need alone. Filthy lucre would not be permitted to jump the queue.

Explicitly, it was to be the equalisation of the inputs. Implicitly, it was to be the equalisation of the outcomes as well. In the end there would be a national health status. Like a national language or the right of abode, it would be the badge of unpartitioned union. The common culture would extend to the common health culture. White-collar or blue-collar, Ferrari or Tube, the children of Shakespeare, England and St George would regress to the mean in their life-expectancy and their epidemiological profile. Unequal purchasing power would not be permitted to fragment the happy breed.

The aim was ambitious. The realisation was elusive. In countries as market-centred, as payment-oriented as the free-enterprise United States, one would have expected the disparities to survive. What is surprising is the extent to which they have not gone away even in the solidaristic United Kingdom that in 1948 had committed itself to high-quality care at no or low user-cost. The 10 000 children and the 32 000 males described in the previous chapter have not gone away:

> If everyone in England had the same death rates as the most advantaged, people who are currently dying prematurely as a result of health inequalities would, in total, have enjoyed between 1.3 and 2.5 million extra days of life. They would, in addition, have had a further 2.8 million years free of limiting illness or disability. It is estimated that inequality in illness accounts for productivity losses of £31–£33 billion per year, lost taxes and higher welfare payments in the range of £20–£32 billion per year, and additional NHS healthcare costs associated with inequality are well in excess of £5.5 billion per year. (Marmot and the Marmot Review Team, 2010)

Inequity is inefficiency. Social patterning is big pounds. It focuses the mind. This chapter, divided into two sections, examines first 'Social distance' and then 'Geographical location'. It shows that the differences in mortality and morbidity are still separating one nation into parallel streams that still lack a national health.

12.1 SOCIAL DISTANCE

Aneurin Bevan was the Minister of Health responsible for the introduction of the National Health Service. Negatively speaking, he regarded it as the welcome antithesis of possessive individualism: 'A free health service is pure Socialism and as such it is opposed to the hedonism of capitalist society' (Bevan, 1961 [1952]: 106). Positively speaking, he saw it as *primus inter pares* in a bundle of social services that conferred disproportionate benefits on the have-nots, the excluded and the left-behind: 'The Socialist Party ... rushes to the defence of state spending: their supporters are the poor and the defenceless who most need it' (Bevan, 1961 [1952]: 136). It is likely that he would have been bitterly disappointed by the failure of the British National Health Service to narrow the gap.

Half a century on from the establishment of the free-on-demand National Health Service, the Independent Inquiry into Inequalities in Health (chaired by Sir Donald Acheson) revealed that rising living standards backed up by the warm-hearted Welfare State had not put paid to persisting inequalities in health outcomes: 'Although the last 20 years have brought a marked increase in prosperity and substantial reductions in mortality to the people of this country as a whole, the gap in health between those at the top and bottom of the social scale has widened' (Stationery Office, 1998: v). A decade on it was wider still:

> Whilst the health of all groups in England is improving, over the last ten years health inequalities between the social classes have widened – the gap has increased by 4 per cent amongst men, and by 11 per cent amongst women – because the health of the rich is improving more quickly than that of the poor.
> (House of Commons Health Committee, 2009: 5)

Infant mortality nationwide had declined by 16 per cent. In the lowest socio-economic group it had declined by only 5 per cent. Inequalities in cancer had not changed. Inequalities in heart disease had increased (House of Commons Health Committee, 2009: 17, 62).

Relativities are not absolutes. The life-expectancy of the lowest quintile now exceeds the life-expectancy of the richest quintile as it was when Bevan turned the system to the left. Social welfare, economic growth and political democracy have lifted all but the frailest craft. Even so, some vessels have risen more rapidly than others. The health divide has widened. The national health system has not brought about a national health status. Irrespective of Shakespeare, England and St George, the plebs and the toffs are drifting further apart.

12.1.1 The Occupational Proxy

There is no single measure of the social slope. There is no accepted statistic of socio-economic status, no single 'SES' that tracks the gradient from top to bottom. Acheson used the occupational category of the primary breadwinner to proxy the layers and pigeonhole the compartments.

Acheson was able to draw upon the work-based Standard Occupational Classification that was employed by the Registrar General and the civil service to situate the peas in the appropriate pod. The hierarchy of socio-economic status extended from the high-end professionals of group I (the doctors, lawyers, accountants and managers) to the blue-collar unskilled of group V (the labourers, cleaners and messengers). In between there were the intermediate professionals such as teachers and journalists (group II), the skilled non-manual workers such as clerks and cashiers (group IIIN), the skilled manual workers such as plumbers and bus drivers (group IIIM), and the partially skilled support staff such as care assistants and security guards (group IV). While the number of groups will vary over time, and while other countries employ slightly different schemata, all somewhat arbitrary, what is constant in the socio-economic classification is the logic. Location is defined by work.

The producing role is the stem signifier. Complementary locators such as income, education, power, lifestyle, working conditions and security of employment are closely correlated with the job-function. So are perceived superiority, perceived inferiority, owner-occupied housing and positional assets such as a car and a timeshare abroad.

Even the Marxian distinction between labour and capital can be detected in the difference between the manual worker at the bottom and the professional at the top. The upper classes have stocks and shares to enrich their earned incomes. The lower classes produce surplus value to nourish the absentee investors. Occupation can be seen as the tip of the iceberg. Market capitalism can be regarded as the economic basis that lies beneath.

Complementary locators march in step with the occupational hierarchy. For that reason it is generally taken to be a useful skeleton upon which to hang the patterned inequalities in health. It is a catch-all and an amalgam. The disadvantage is that the familiar and the salient vacuum up the micro-linkages and the cross-cutting identifiers which are the real determinants of distance. The advantage is simplicity. It is a big advantage. Completeness is a counsel of perfection. Too many markers would make health policy into an overstuffed encyclopedia that can explain everything but cannot act.

The truth is multidimensional. Work is an approximation that stands in for the whole. If, however, the occupational pyramid is to be treated as a reliable heuristic, then there are a number of statistical and conceptual ambiguities that must be addressed. Only then can the measure of vertical stratification be taken to mean what it says.

First of all, there are the gaps. An occupational category by definition cannot house human beings without occupations. Unpaid carers, unpaid volunteers, the unemployed, the retired, are not included. Nor are full-time housewives. Since most people marry within their own class, it may not be an excessive distortion of socio-economic location to take the husband's occupational group as a fixed point for the family as a whole. At the same time, it might make sense to classify housewives by their own years of schooling and their own professional attachment at the time when they were last in work. Women are central to the family's health. The husband's occupation is not enough to pick up the different contributions made by different women in possession of different cultural attributes.

The black box is very black. The occupational schema does not differentiate between high earners and low earners in a single group. It does not distinguish the one-income from the multiple-income household, although intra-family pooling undeniably makes more living space, better consumer durables and high-standard medical attention more affordable. The occupational category does not identify those families where one or both breadwinners have health insurance through work. Ranging more widely, the black box cannot separate the new immigrant from the long-standing resident, spotlight the single parent or pick up the special circumstances of the disabled and the slow. Nor can the black box say if the job-holder is black. It is an omission. Race, like gender and religion, makes it difficult to single out the specifically occupational component in multifaceted starts and finishes.

Woolf in the United States found that the mortality rate for blacks was higher than that for whites. Had the age-adjusted rate of the African-Americans been levelled up to that of the Caucasian Americans, some 886 202 unnecessary deaths between 1991 and 2000 could have been averted. This is five times as many lives as were saved in the 1990s through advances in medicine per se (Woolf et al., 2004: 2079). There were more low-birthweight babies among blacks than among whites. There were more deaths in the first year of life. Occupation by itself cannot explain the whole of the variance. Race provides an additional causal variable.

Residential segregation leads to educational segregation. The median white has more years of schooling than the median black. White schools in the United States are generally believed to be of a higher quality than black schools. Medical care for the representative black is not as good. Holding income constant, black enrollees in the American Medicare system have fewer doctor visits, fewer mammograms, more amputations and higher mortality rates: 'Racial differences in treatment account for the lion's share of this mortality gap' (Cutler et al., 2011b: 150). The occupational pigeonhole is a black box. Within that black box the blacks would seem to be trapped in the vicious circle of a self-fulfilling prophesy. The occupational schema treats the blacks as if they were whites. The real world is not as colour-blind.

Work itself is differentiated. Not all manual grades face the hazards of explosions, bites and stampedes. Not all white-collar workers are exempt from physical risk or psychic wear and tear. The differences within the groups can be at least as great as the differences between them. Thus British university teachers (in occupational group I) have a standardised mortality ratio of 49, but engineering foremen (in group III) have a ratio of 47 and pharmacists (in group I) have a ratio of 116. British fishermen (in class IV) have a ratio of 171 but office cleaners (in class V) only 88 and innkeepers (in class II) fully 155 (Jones and Cameron, 1984: 43). The averages indicate a smooth gradient. It rises from 77 for the group Is to 137 for the Vs. The averages only serve to conceal the heterogeneities.

Even if the standard categories can be taken on trust, still the relative numbers within each occupational group will not be constant over time.

Upward mobility, dynamic *embourgeoisement*, the microeconomic revolution, the proliferation of technical education, all are making the lower occupational categories relatively less populated over time. In Britain in the 50 years from 1931 to 1981, groups IV and V contracted from 38 per cent to 26 per cent of the population. In the same period groups I and II expanded in size from 14 per cent to 23 per cent. Equivalent proportions for 2013 might be 15 per cent for the lower groups and 31 per cent for the higher classes (Jones, 2013). Even if the number of buses was the same, the number of passengers per bus was not.

It is clearly important to recalculate the statistics on health and illness using a weighting scheme that picks up the total number of heads of which each standard category is comprised. As with all data on migration, the figures must be age-standardised to allow for the disproportionate numbers of seniors in the population left behind. Le Grand and Rabin performed the requisite transformation for Britain from 1931 to 1981.

Other studies had shown that inequalities in health had remained broadly the same in the historic half-century from the Depression and the Second World War to the Welfare State and the National Health. Le Grand and Rabin produced a more encouraging result. Weighting the number of buses by the number of passengers per bus, they were able to improve on the sign:

> Over that time the death rates in adult males in classes I and II fell faster than those for classes IV and V, creating an impression of widening inequality. However, because of the changes in the composition of the classes, the numbers of deaths in classes I and II actually increased (in fact, nearly doubled) over the period while the numbers in classes IV and V fell (by about a quarter). Hence if inequalities in health are measured by differences in numbers rather than in rates (a not indefensible procedure), the same data show a decrease rather than an increase in inequality. (Le Grand and Rabin, 1986: 118)

Welfare was doing what it was supposed to do. The National Health was bringing the British closer together.

Time, as Alfred Marshall taught, is the centre of the chief difficulty of every social problem. Just as structural change is altering the slots available in the different occupational categories, so a discrete individual may pass through a succession of job functions and affiliations in line with ambition, achievement, accident and simple luck. Flows are not stocks. A cross-section is not a time series. Individuals go up and down.

The kaleidoscope of life has a feedback effect on the occupational measure. The occupation given on the census form or the death certificate might not be the group in which the individual had spent the bulk of their health-shaping life. A miner who contracts pneumoconiosis in group V will carry with him the baggage of neglect when he later becomes an electrician in group IIIM or a Cabinet minister in group I. Black lungs do not go away. His life-expectancy was shortened by his V that went before. It was not his IIIM or his I that made him die young. Which then is the occupational category that should be entered into the database and correlated with the inequalities in health?

The occupational taxonomy is a still photograph. Life is a moving picture. The dynamic is relevant for both destinations and origins. At the level of destinations, the ambitious and the intelligent may be able to rise into the higher occupational groups while the indolent and the incompetent may go down. At the level of origins, the intergenerational multiplier may be the accelerator or the brake that twists the individual's own life-course away from the individual's intrinsic economic value. Educated parents transmit leadership skills and coping strategies which give their children a head start and the will to win. Manual grades crowded in sink tenements on rock-bottom nutrition may be too passive to push a self-perceived dead-ender to escape from an undisciplined lifestyle. The genetic capital influences the leads and lags. So do the social determinants which are cross-correlated with the destinations and origins. Class is handed on. Health status is the result of the conditioning, the positioning, the replication and the reproduction.

There is a final ambiguity in the interpretation of the occupational grid. Just as occupation can influence health, so health can influence occupation. Reverse causality makes it difficult to put the chicken before the egg. A sickly child may not be able to concentrate at school or to obtain full educational credentials. A worker who is chronically ill, physically or mentally, will not have equal access to a full range of jobs. They might have to take early retirement on a reduced pension. They might become exhausted before they have earned a full day's pay. They might be all but unemployable because of a congenital handicap. They might be out of work long term because of industrial restructuring or macroeconomic stagnation. Their income will fall and with it the housing and diet that they can afford. It is a cumulative process. Recording their social class as their last-known occupational group might be misleading where downward social mobility has seriously degraded their life-chances.

12.1.2 Using the Grid

The Acheson Inquiry used the occupational grid as its Ordnance Survey of social location. Using that measure it concluded that health distance in Britain had increased and not decreased despite the National Health

Service. In the early 1970s, Acheson found, the mortality rate among unskilled men of working age was twice that of equivalent men in the administrative, managerial and professional grades. By the early 1990s it had become three times greater. For men in groups I and II life expectancy had increased by two years. For those in groups IV and V the increase was 1.4 years.

Infant mortality in the mid-1990s was five out of every 1000 births for the higher groups. It was seven out of every 1000 for the lower ones. In 2010 the rate of excess mortality was exactly the same (Marmot and the Marmot Review Team, 2010). In the mid-1990s, about 17 per cent of professional men reported long-standing illness. The figure for unskilled men was 48 per cent. Babies with fathers in social classes IV and V had a birthweight on average 130 grams less than that of babies with fathers in social classes I and II. Mortality from suicide for men in occupational group V was four times greater than it was for men in occupational group I.

As for hypertension, in the UK 'average blood pressure increases as social class decreases'. Nor is that all: 'At any level of blood pressure people from lower socio-economic groups appear to be more vulnerable to the associated diseases, as evidenced by their higher rates of coronary heart disease and stroke' (Stationery Office, 1998: 11, 13, 14, 66, 69). In the USA males aged 50–64 in the lowest income tercile are twice as likely to be suffering from diabetes or to be at risk from a heart attack as are males in the top income tercile. Lower-income males score significantly worse on cholesterol. They are almost five times as likely to experience a stroke (Martinson, 2012: 2053). Disparities like these are what we expect from foreigners living abroad. In Britain, however, we have the National Health Service.

Almost a decade before Acheson, the Association of Community Health Councils had been reporting that equal care for equal need had failed to deliver the equalisation in outcomes that had been intended:

> In 1987, babies whose fathers had unskilled jobs had infant mortality rates over 70 per cent higher than those for babies whose fathers had a professional occupation ... In the major killer diseases lung cancer, coronary heart disease and cerebrovascular disease, manual classes have a considerably higher risk of death than non-manual classes (comparing all non-manual classes against all manual classes). For example in the 20–54 age band, men in manual work are more than twice as likely to die from lung cancer as non-manual workers ... Nearly all the major and minor killers now affect the poor more than the rich. (Association of Community Health Councils, 1990: 3–4)

Cardiac interventions for British South Asians are less frequent than the average despite the fact that their mortality from heart disease, predicting from their ethnicity, is 40 per cent higher. Babies born to women of Pakistani origin continued to experience a death rate 'almost 50 per cent above that for the white population'. Working-class women remained 'three times more likely to suffer mental illness than professional women' (Association of Community Health Councils, 1990: 6). Only in a limited number of areas did the higher occupational groups experience a higher rate of major illness. Among those areas were, however, life-threatening conditions such as cancers of the skin, prostate and lymph glands.

A decade before the Association, the Working Group on Inequalities in Health had reported a similar, and an equally disturbing, lack of progress towards the eradication of socially proportioned gaps. Sir Douglas Black and his colleagues had found that the differential mortality rates for men aged 15 to 64 had not narrowed since 1921. The mortality gap between groups I and II and IV and V had actually widened (Townsend and Davidson, 1982b).

The mortality rate varies inversely with status group. This is true for both men and women and at all stages in the life cycle. A child born into social group V is four times as likely to die in the first year of life as a child born into social group I. A boy aged from 1 to 14 born into group V is twice as likely to die while in that age range as a boy born into group I. A person born into group I who remains in group I is likely, according to the Black Report, to have a life-expectancy five years in excess of their counterpart in group V. Five years is a lot of life to lose merely because one never managed to make the climb from blue collar to white.

In absolute terms the mortality rates for all occupational groups had declined. In relative terms the spread had survived. Morbidity is just as stubborn. Thirty years into the NHS, Mildred Blaxter reported, the prevalence rates for chronic illness in social group V, 'at over 200 per 1000 people, are well over the rate of 75 reported in class I' (Blaxter, 1976: 117). Fifty-five years into the NHS, the Ministry discovered, people in social class V as compared with people in social class I had a 60 per cent higher prevalence of long-term conditions. Each condition was on average 30 per cent more severe (Department of Health, 2012: 11). As for children, 11 per cent of the under-threes in British families with incomes over £50 000 were suffering from chronic conditions such as asthma or mental abnormalities such as attention deficit hyperactivity disorder. In families with incomes of £10 000 or less it was 23 per cent (Currie, 2009: 92).

The inequalities related to inputs as well as outcomes. Very early on in the history of the classless NHS Richard Titmuss had found that the higher occupational groups had managed to secure a disproportionate foothold in the screening, radiography, referrals, antenatal care, infant care, dental care that were supposed to be allocated on the basis of clinical need alone:

> We have learnt from fifteen years' experience of the Health Service that the higher income groups know how to make better use of the Service; they tend to receive more specialist attention; occupy more of the beds in better equipped and staffed hospitals; receive more elective surgery; have better maternity care, and are more likely to get psychiatric help and psychotherapy than low income groups – particularly the unskilled. (Titmuss, 1968: 196)

Stigler (the proposition is sometimes called 'Director's Law') used libertarian public choice to predict that the squeaky wheel would get the grease: 'Public expenditures are made for the primary benefit of the middle classes' (Stigler, 1970: 1). Brian Abel-Smith found evidence of the squeaks and the grease, the silver-spoon assertiveness and the special pleading, at the heart even of Britain's well-intentioned Welfare State. Abel-Smith concluded that the upshot of parliamentary socialism had been perverse,

> that the major beneficiaries of these changes have been the middle classes, that the middling income groups get more from the State than the lower income groups, that taxation often hits the poor harder than the well-to-do, and that in general the middle classes receive good standards of welfare while working people receive a Spartan minimum. (Abel-Smith, 1959: 55–6)

Le Grand's findings on the distribution of the social wage document the extent of the upward bias. Drawing his data from Britain's General Household Survey that samples 14 000 households and 40 000 individuals, he found that the members of socio-economic groups I and II were receiving 'at least 40 per cent more expenditure per person' than were the members of socio-economic groups IV and V (Le Grand, 1978: 132). The actual inequality was even greater. The figure of 40 per cent relates exclusively to public provision. Many of the affluent had private cover as well.

The problem has not gone away: 'While total physician contact suggested equal treatment for equal need in the UK, there was a tendency for those on low incomes to use GP [general practitioner] services and those on high incomes to use specialist services more relative to need'

(Dixon et al., 2007: 105). Those on low incomes have fewer consultations for preventive care such as cervical screening. They have lower rates of elective surgery. They have fewer referrals for cardiac and diagnostic procedures, for hip replacement and hernia repair. NHS patients in the top quintile by education wait 14 per cent less than NHS patients in the bottom three deciles by education. NHS patients in the two bottom deciles by income wait 7 per cent longer than NHS patients in the top decile by income (Laudicella et al., 2012: 1339). The entitlement is the same. The take-up is not.

It is the inverse care law, 'that the availability of good medical care tends to vary inversely with the need of the population served' (Tudor Hart, 1971: 412). The lower-income groups experience more illness and take more sick-days per annum. Their medical need is proportionately more. Somehow, however, they consume proportionately less of the health care budget than the patterned inequalities in their documented need would suggest. *De jure* has not become *de facto*. The National Health Service has not defeated the vested interest of sharp elbows and the invisible hand.

The same invisible hand appears to be in business in the United States. The number of doctor visits per 100 bed disability days was, age-adjusted, 80 per cent higher among higher-income whites than among whites below the poverty line. Lack of health insurance is a significant barrier. The insured saw a doctor 70 per cent more often than the uninsured although the uninsured, disproportionately on lower incomes, are more likely to self-report poor health (Starr, 1986: 117–18).

The outcomes parallel the inputs. The poor in America have a life expectancy that is 10 per cent less than the rich. White men with family incomes of less than $10 000 can expect to live 6.6 fewer years (for black men it is 7.4 fewer years) than white men in families with incomes of more than $25 000 (Smith, 1999: 146, 147). Black males in general have a life-expectancy at birth that is 6.8 years less, black females 5.2 years less, than that of their white counterparts.

The invisible hand has not been enough. Neither the starts nor the finishes have satisfied the social consensus. Medicare (for the elderly) and Medicaid (for the poor) have been the response of the public sector to need. Medicare was created in order to ensure that the over-65s could access medical care irrespective of their ability to pay. The intention was to draw in the needy. The outcome was the inverse care law. Medicare reimbursements per enrolled beneficiary have been greater for the higher-income elderly than for their low-income counterparts.

Targeting improves access. It is not a substitute for money. Increased allocations to Medicare and Medicaid have been essential in expanding the services that upgrade the deprived. It was money that allowed more black women to be enrolled in New Jersey's HeadStart Medicaid programme. Having fewer low-birthweight babies, they shortened the birthweight distance that had separated them from the Medicaid whites (Reichman and Florio, 1996: 471). It was money that permitted an overall increase in Medicaid eligibility for pregnant women. Currie and Gruber found that a 30 per cent increase in the income cut-off had been associated with a decrease in the infant mortality rate of 8.5 per cent (Currie and Gruber, 1996: 1276). Funding makes a difference. It is a reason for resisting cuts.

12.2 GEOGRAPHICAL LOCATION

Different countries are different. Male life expectancy (the world average is 68) is 40 years in Angola, 52 in Burundi, 79 in the UK and the USA, 80 in Japan. Infant mortality per 1000 live births (the world average is 49) is 74 in Lesotho, 55 in Laos, 6 in the USA, 3 in Singapore, 2 in Japan. Maternal mortality per 100 000 live births (the world average is 210) is 4 in Sweden, 5 in Poland, 630 in Nigeria, 1100 in Chad (World Bank, 2015).

There are 29 hospital beds per 10 000 people in the United States, but 9 in Ghana, 50 in Switzerland, 72 in Kazakhstan and 80 in Germany. There are 49 doctors per 10 000 population in Belgium, 28 in the UK, 25 in the US, 12 in Malaysia, 1 in Ghana (World Bank, 2015). Which country has got it just right? Or is each optimum the *optimum optimorum*?

There are differences between the countries. Yet there is imbalance even within a single nation. In Australia there are 376 doctors per 100 000 population in urban areas, 187 in the countryside. In France the equivalent figures are 463 and 120. In Canada they are 217 and 84. In the United States they are 210 and 113 (Organisation for Economic Co-operation and Development, 2011: 137). In the United States only 11 per cent of doctors practice in rural areas despite the fact that 19 per cent of the American population is rural (Department of Health and Human Services, 2015: 255).

The jam in America is not evenly spread. Even the public sector has its peaks and its troughs. The average Medicare reimbursement was $9033 in McAllen, Texas but $3074 in Lynchburg, Virginia. In 56 of the 306 hospital referral areas Medicare spending was at least 25 per cent below the national average. In 19 of the referral areas it was at least 30 per cent above (Wennberg and Cooper, 1999: 12). A saw-tooth of that magnitude must have some impact on outcomes. Infant mortality is 7.6 per 1000 live births in rural West Virginia. It is only 3.7 on the Upper East Side of Manhattan. The inner city is a law unto itself: 'A boy born and brought up in Harlem has less chance of living to 65 years old than a baby in Bangladesh' (Wilkinson, 1996: 158).

In the Philippines the ratio of dentists to population is 1:2533 in Metro Manila. In the Eastern Visayas it is 1:33 433. Professionals follow the money. It is one reason among many why the infant mortality rate in Metro Manila is 24 while in Northern Mindanao it is 38. In Thailand 49 per cent of all dentists and 35 per cent of all doctors practise in Bangkok. The figures for the impoverished North-East are 12 per cent and 15 per cent, respectively (World Health Organization, 2010: 19). In Malaysia the dentist to population ratio is 1:8779 on the peninsula but 1:21 346 in Sarawak and 1:25 108 in Sabah. Such dentists as can be found in Northern Borneo tend to be in the urban areas. It is a day's trip by boat if a tribesman's tooth starts to hurt.

In China the money is not the same. Health expenditure per capita in Shanghai is Y561.7. In Guizhou it is Y72. In Tibet it is Y44. The outcome indicators too seem to come from different planets. In Beijing the life-expectancy at birth is 80.1. In Yunnan it is 67.5. Infant mortality is 4.35 in Beijing, better than the United States. In Qinghai it is 32.19, on a par with Rwanda. The Gini coefficient for maternal and child health in China is 0.44. For income itself it is only slightly higher at 0.45 (Fang et al., 2010: 22, 23, 24). Comparing Sweden with Bangladesh, there are bound to be differences. Comparing America with America, China with China, it is less obvious that there should be so great a spread.

Least of all should there be significant and patterned inequalities in a country such as Britain which has a national health system. British citizens are given an explicit undertaking that each naked Adam has equal worth in the sight of God and Westminister. In spite of the promises, the end-states and the inputs have continued to reflect the residential patchwork.

Peter Townsend, 40 years into the NHS, compared the least healthy with the most healthy districts in the North of England. He found a dispersion of approximately 4:1 for lung cancer in both sexes and for female deaths from circulatory complaints (Townsend, 1987: 52). In Bristol, likewise comparing the worst with the best, he found a dispersion of more than 2:1 in the ratio of stillbirths, of infant deaths, of deaths of adults in the economically productive age band from 15 to 64 (Townsend, 1987: 52–3).

Looking at countrywide disparities in mortality rates (and taking 100 as the base for the calculation), Townsend et al. were able to identify a sizeable gap between the bad-health areas and the good: 'If Middlesbrough's age-specific death-rates occurred nationally 125 deaths, not 100, would be experienced, with the greatest percentage increase over the national rate being in the 45–64 range; whereas if Guildford's death-rates applied nationally, only 83 deaths would occur, with the largest decrease being in the 45–64 range' (Townsend et al., 1988: 27).

At every age children living in the North have more dental decay than children living in the South: 'For example, at 5 years children living in the North West NHS Region show a 59 per cent excess compared with those in the South Thames NHS Region. At 12 years there is a 75 per cent excess' (Stationery Office, 1998: 72). The North–South divide has not gone away.

In 2012 the infant mortality rate in England stood at 4.5. Within England it varied from 5.5 in the West Midlands to 3.4 in the South East. The age-standardised mortality rate for the United Kingdom as a whole was 537 per 100 000 population. In the North East it was 593. In the South East it was 483. Life expectancy at birth in Kensington and Chelsea was 84.4 years for men, 89 years for women. In Glasgow City the figures were 71.1 and 77.5 (Office for National Statistics, 2014). The lifespan difference was 13.3 years for men, 11.5 years for women. Life-expectancy in central Glasgow is the same as in Vietnam or Egypt.

Men in the most deprived wards in England have a life expectancy of 78 years and a healthy life expectancy of 52. For men in the least deprived wards the figures are 81 and 69 (House of Commons Health Committee, 2009: 17). Small pockets throw up their own variations. Men born in Middlehaven, the docklands of Middlesbrough, have a life expectancy of 67.8 years. Men born in Moreton Hall, just outside Bury St Edmunds, can expect to live to 93.4. The difference is 25.6 years. Within the London Borough of Westminster male life expectancy varies by 15.2 years. It is 67.4 years in the worst-performing ward and 82.6 years in the best (Department of Health, 2006: 83). The wards are within walking distance. They are health-miles apart.

Life expectancy in Britain has never been so high. In spite of that, the stubborn disparities in chronic disability, perinatal mortality and life-expectancy at birth have not withered away. Deaths from cardiovascular disease were 20 per cent higher in the most deprived areas: 'In England, people living in the poorest neighbourhoods, will, on average, die seven years earlier than people living in the richest neighbourhoods ... Even more disturbing, the average difference in disability-free life expectancy is 17 years' (Marmot and the Marmot Review Team, 2010). They live less and they live worse.

As for the inputs, there is the average and there is the variance. For general practitioners the average list has 1452 registrations. It is 1031 in the Oxford primary care trust but 1860 (80 per cent more) in Bexley. For acute beds the average availability per 1000 population is 1.9. It is 1.5 in the South East. It is 2.4 in the North East. There are 0.5 NHS dentists per 1000 population in the South East and London. There are only 0.4 (20 per cent less) in the East and West Midlands. Breaking up the data into the primary care trusts the spectrum is even wider. It goes from 1.16 NHS dentists in the best-provided areas to 0.34 in the worst.

Average expenditure on cancer in England is £82 per capita. The figure varies between £43 and £151. Average expenditure on mental health is £198. It fluctuates from £148 to £278 (Boyle, 2011: 232, 242–3, 323, 331, 392). The figure for London is 1.87 times that for South Central. It would only make sense if the overhang of mental distress were 1.87 as well.

The number of hospital medical staff per 100 000 population was 112 in the East. It was 200 in London (Ham, 2005: 206). It goes on. There is the diagnostic equipment, the complementary professionals, the waiting times, the ratio of specialists to clinical admissions. The ideal is supply in proportion to clinical need. The reality is difference and spread.

Doctors in stunted precincts will on average be older and less well qualified. The shortfall in formal care only reinforces the shortfall outside the medical centre. There are more accidents at work in industrial areas. Productivity and earnings will frequently lag behind. The average level of education will typically be lower. The environment will be more contaminated. Effluent, gases and emissions are together responsible for between 12 000 and 24 000 premature deaths each year in the UK: 'Poorer communities tend to experience higher concentrations of pollution and have a higher prevalence of cardio-respiratory and other diseases. Sixty-six per cent of carcinogenic chemicals emitted into the air are released in the 10 per cent most deprived wards' (Marmot and the Marmot Review Team, 2010). Fumes, dust and chemicals impair cognitive development. They retard the ability to learn. Deprived children are more likely to underperform at school. Their own children are more likely to be trapped in the same toxic dead end. Residential sorting is handed on from one generation to the next.

Health status is a topic in economic power. Townsend, decomposing his sample into the 678 electoral wards of the Northern Regional Health Authority just as others have drilled down to the six-digit postal code, found a correlation that spoke for itself:

The link between measures of health and socio-economic measures reflecting deprivation could scarcely be more firmly demonstrated. Unemployment is almost four times worse, overcrowding four-and-a-half times as likely, and car ownership and owner-occupation levels nearly three times lower, in the 10 per cent of wards with the worst overall health, as compared with the best 10 per cent. (Townsend et al., 1988: 75)

Health status is economic status. It is the economy that is letting the nation down.

Material deprivation was correlated with an above-average incidence of mortality and morbidity. The economic system had left the excluded in the lurch. The economic system and not just the medical system would have to be overhauled if British health were to become national health in line with the high ideals of Bevan's citizenship right.

13. Narrowing the gap

The World Health Organization regards the 'highest attainable standard of health' as a 'fundamental right'. It can never be just to violate a 'fundamental right'. A 'fundamental right' cannot be reduced to a market tradeable. A 'fundamental right' is more than wants and interests, competition and efficiency.

The aim is not simply to equalise the standard but, specifically, to universalise the best. That is why the desired equalisation cannot be achieved by selectively refusing treatment to candidates with above-average health status or by deliberately cross-infecting patients with above-average access to specialists and drugs. Envy and malice can easily shunt the car of levelling on to the siding that leads to *Schadenfreude* and then on to Birkenau. The focus on the human essence keeps the car on the path of reason.

To level down rather than to level up would be an inequitable violation of core personhood that is an inalienable possession of the healthy and not just of the unwell. To be equally healthy means to be equal and to be healthy. It does not mean that Peter can be robbed of life-years in order to bring him closer to Paul. To do this would be morally on a par with cosmetic surgery to reduce beautiful Jolene to the point score of average Ethel that was explored by L.P. Hartley in his Brave New World of *Facial Justice*.

The 'Darling Dictator' in *Facial Justice* gives the top-class specimens the freedom to be as one with their profoundly undecorative sisters: 'You had been reduced to a lower level and no longer felt the emanations of Bad Egg from those with under-privileged faces. You could confront them on equal terms without the gnawing sense of superiority that was haunting you' (Hartley, 2014 [1960]: 139). Facial justice is an extreme form of affirmative action. Independent schools, Knightsbridge mansions, trust funds, inherited fortunes, annual bonuses, conspicuous consumption can all be emancipated from Bad Egg through facial justice. Health care, however, is different. No one has ever recommended that levelling down be applied to the allocation of queue-tickets for the National Health.

The healthy have a 'fundamental right' to retain their good health. What the World Health Organization would say is that the unhealthy too have a 'fundamental right' to match the good health status at the top: 'It does not have to be this way, and it is not right that it should be like this. Where systematic differences in health are judged to be avoidable by reasonable action they are, quite simply, unfair' (World Health Organization, 2008: 1). The distance is excessive. The gap must be narrowed. The gap is, quite simply, unfair.

The subject of this chapter is closing up through levelling up. It is a topic which involves more than the doctors and the plasters alone:

> Inequalities in health arise because of inequalities in society – in the conditions in which people are born, grow, live, work, and age. So close is the link between particular social and economic features of society and the distribution of health among the population, that the magnitude of health inequalities is a good marker of progress towards creating a fairer society. (Marmot and the Marmot Review Team, 2010)

Action to reduce inequalities in health requires action across the whole of society. It will never be enough to fix up the walking wounded in order that economic life might knock them down again.

Inequalities in health go beyond the medical encounter. This chapter situates the medical gradient in its socio-economic context. It proceeds through five interconnected sections, each of them dealing with a prominent influence that draws the health indicators apart. The sections are headed 'Occupation', 'Education', 'Culture', 'Income' and 'Inequality'. Narrowing the gap will necessarily entail a wider range of policies than are delivered even by the free-on-demand British National Health Service.

It is the 'causes of the causes' that lead downstream to the asthma from poor ventilation and damp walls, to the liver and kidney damage that are the free gift of the rats and the open sewers. If the self-perpetuating cycle of deprivation were to be brought to an end, the doctors and the plasters would be less in demand to cure the preventable that need never occur. Care without payment will sometimes be the necessary but it can never be the sufficient condition for rescuing the left-behind. That is not to say, however, that the doctors and the plasters will have no role to play. Universalising the access to medical care is the topic of Chapter 14.

13.1 OCCUPATION

Different people do different things. Different jobs carry different risks. It cannot in the circumstances be expected that all citizens will experience the same injuries or die at the same age. Office workers suffer from carpal tunnel syndrome, dry eyes and the effects of glare. Deep-seam miners are exposed to cave-ins and dust. Drum makers working with untreated hides inhale anthrax spores. Block printers dipping fabric in dye get cancer of the bladder. Street prostitutes are vulnerable to HIV. Policemen have access to guns when they are feeling low. Pharmacists have access to poisons. Cooks face a temptation to overeat. Barmen have a tendency to overdrink. Not all members of the labour force are equally at risk from lead, mercury, sulphur dioxide, asbestos fibres, insecticides, isotopes, radioactive slurry, burning buildings and falls from height. That is what the division of labour means. We are not all average. It is a fact of life.

Different people have a different image of the state of health that they regard as right for themselves. A free society must give them the freedom to choose. Just as some people will want a safe life with an index-linked pension, so others will become test pilots, Everest explorers, mercenary soldiers, bare-knuckle boxers and stunt doubles because the adrenelin-rush of excitement combined with the lure of the danger differential will make them feel better off in their own estimation. Some people knowingly give their assent to cadmium vapours, strontium 90 and chlorine trifluoride. So long as the transaction is 'bi-laterally voluntary and informed' (Friedman, 1962: 13), so long as no prohibitive externalities are imposed on innocent third parties who are not signatories to the contract, there is a sense in which the differences in health status are an indicator of a healthy society and not the scarlet letter of intolerable inequity.

Inequality can be an individual choice. It is not necessarily an intolerable pathology. The problem arises where the choice is not free. A conscript or a convict cannot be said to have selected their own preferred level of health when they parachute onto thin ice or work on a railway in subzero cold. An indentured coolie does not have the libertarian's valued personal autonomy when they haul excessive loads or gather cockles in the face of the incoming tide. The passive who are compelled to take risks are not the same as the active who seize the day because they love the thrill.

The conscript and the convict are clearly trapped in an unfree exchange. There is an imposed gradient that, even if socially licensed, is incompatible with the touchstone standard of 'bi-laterally voluntary and informed'. Yet the same restricted autonomy may also be observed where the unbonded and the undrafted are obliged to drive buses with exhausted brakes or grow old in badly lit sweat shops because they lack the skills that would give them meaningful choices. The unemployed do what is there to be done because they are a reserve army and there are not enough good jobs to go round. They are not soldiers and they are not in prison. Only a dictionary would, however, say that they are free.

Policy in such a case must ensure at the very least that equal citizens have an equal opportunity to become occupationally unequal. It must provide enabling services like education and ensure an adequate level of total demand. If then some people continue to chose less-healthful work, at least the wider society can be confident that it was their tastes and preferences, not forced and resented exchange, that cost them the frostbite and the gangrene in the end.

Forced exchange can make the poor die young. Yet even prestigious and well-paid jobs can be bad for the health. Medical professionals not only spend their days with suffering and death but are also continually exposed at work to peer pressures, stress, exhaustion, missed meals, burnout, irregular hours, sleep deprivation, inadequate rest-periods, exceptional responsibilities, breaking bad news to the next of kin, and the unrealistic expectations of patients which in the limit can erupt into verbal and physical aggression. Doctors as perfectionists tend to be abnormally self-critical. The personality type is that they want to help and please. It takes its toll. Doctors in Britain clock more than 100 times more at-fault accidents on the road than do building society clerks (Collinson, 2014). They are three times more likely to have a cirrhosis problem. They have on average only five hours of sleep.

Doctors in Britain are more likely to be on sleeping tablets, tranquillisers and even addictive hallucinogens. One in three is overweight but only one in ten is on a diet. A quarter of British doctors do no regular exercise. Depression, divorce, eating disorders and hypertension are higher than in the British population as a whole (Brooks et al., 2011: 2). Female doctors (but not the men) have above-average leanings towards suicide (Richards, 1989). It is a rough life.

One-third of doctors in Australia are not registered with a general practitioner. One-third of doctors in Ireland have not consulted another physician in the last five years. Some feel that seeking help (especially psychiatric help) would damage their promotion prospects. When they feel ill, they self-medicate. About 92 per cent self-prescribe. Benzodiazepines and opiates on demand do not set a good example for their patients.

Doctors in the United States will more reliably be practising what they preach. Although one in five takes no exercise and 11 per cent drink alcohol every day, these figures are better than those for the general population. Doctors are less likely than the median American to be obese. On the downside, only half regularly consult another doctor about their health. Less than half (despite the ever-present threat of needle-stick) are immunised against hepatitis. While only 5 per cent of American doctors now smoke (it was 40 per cent in 1959), the proportion is 40 per cent of all doctors in Bosnia, 49 per cent of all doctors in Greece, and 61 per cent of all male doctors in China (Smith and Leggat, 2007). The prevalence of smoking among doctors in Italy, at 44 per cent, is double that of the general population. Doctors work hard. Even the role models can fall from grace.

The wise and well-informed in occupational class I can fall from grace because the job is a strain. Also at risk are the lumps of labour in class V. Not liking the job and not liking the boss, they fall into self-destructive patterns that reveal just how much they have in common with the medical professionals to whom they turn for relief.

Public policy is not in a position to reverse the division of labour. Adam Smith pointed to the 'mental mutilation' (Smith, 1961 [1776]): I, 308) that is the unintended consequence of repetitive, exhausting and unchallenging toil. Karl Marx asserted that the 'species being' is being repressed by commodification, marketisation, alienation and objectification when what it most requires is to embody itself in creative production: 'An animal only produces what it immediately needs for itself or its young ... Man produces even when he is free from physical need' (Marx, 1973 [1844]: 113, 114). Marx believed that the self could not be reunited with the self so long as the profit-seeker was grinding innate imaginativeness into a marketable thing. He predicted that the economics of repression would lead inexorably to liberation through revolution. Marx did not explain how socialism would be able to cure the disease if the disease is modern industry itself. Nor did he anticipate the extent to which the capitalist economy would be able to minimise the irritants without renouncing its free-enterprise core.

Private enterprise has found that job rotation, team responsibility, flexible hours, self-scheduling, shop-floor consultation, union representation on corporate boards can raise the productivity of the cog in the wheel. Profit-seeking itself may be able to correct the control shortfall that lies at the heart of psychosocial alienation. If so, then health policy might not be needed to curb the damage done by lassitude, boredom and bitter frustration. Perhaps the gain-seeking system will generate its own turning points. Discretion, autonomy, variety and challenge will be good for business as well as health if they reunite the workers with the work.

The name of Fredrick Winslow Taylor is synonymous in the industrial relations textbooks with scientific management and top-down centralisation. Robert Karasek has criticised Taylor's model of efficiency through regimentation for failing to draw upon the latent reserve of worker attachment: 'Redesigning work processes to allow increases in decision latitude for a broad range of workers could reduce mental strain, and do so without affecting the job demands that may plausibly be associated with organizational output levels' (Karasek, 1979: 285). It is, in Karasek's view, not overwork but underinvolvement that is the worm in the apple of good health.

Marx would not agree. If wealth is the source of class and class is the source of power, then, Marx would say, *Mitbestimmung* can never be more than repressive tolerance, fictive cohesion that papers over the contours of exploitation. Consultation or no consultation, it is the same elites who meet on the golf course to carve up an interlocking stake. It is not enough for the boss to say 'Just call me Tex' or for the canteen to be made as uniclass as a British National Health Service (NHS) ward. So long as the real stressors remain untouched, the truth will get through even to the Clapham omnibus. After that health status will return again to its natural rate.

Marx would deny that redesign and latitude can contribute to better health at work. Karasek, on the other hand, would argue that organisational sociology without an economic revolution will be enough. He would add that the evolution of the economy is itself on the side of good health. The nature of employment is changing. The satanic mills that operate round the clock without fans, heating, fire escapes or meal breaks are being marginalised by automation, robotisation and microelectronics. Manual brawn is giving way to the service sector. Technological upgrading is altering the risk profile.

Hand-knotting is bad for the eyes. Porters lift heavy cases which strain the knees and dislocate the back. Textile factories have fibres and sometimes silica in the air. Often the risk is multiple. There may be exposure at one and the same workplace to noise, accidents, vibration and carcinogens. The harm is a fact. It is not, however, the whole of the story. Even allowing for musculoskeletal conditions brought on by un-ergonomic seating, eye strain caused by the computer screen, and shift work made necessary by round-the-clock globalisation, mechanisation is undeniably reducing the physical harm that can be caused directly by work. Some workers will be displaced as a consequence of modernisation. Others, however, will move up from the residuum of unskilled hands to the white-collar proletariat that appreciates a good quiche. The new-style jobs will be more conducive to good health.

Yet the world is a big place. Some at least of the old-style risks are not being eliminated but rather outsourced. Workers who import the accidents and the fatigue should not be swept under the carpet merely because they are manufacturing the toys, the flat-packs and the mobile phones in the heat and dust of the invisible Third World. Even workers in the Punjab have a right to good health.

Nor should the far more visible 'Third World at Home' be ignored merely because it is incomer labour and not our own people who are slipping through an unsecured hatch, falling from a crane, risking tinnitus from the jack-hammers, dicing with death from the chainsaws. In many countries a disproportionate share of the labour force in construction, demolition, foundries, quarries, mines, blasting, assembly lines and road repair is made up of contract foreigners. They are a sub-proletariat of on-demand aliens with little job security, low pay, bad food, no family life, no unions, few inspections, insanitary dormitories, minimal compensation for injury or impairment. They are exhausted by piecework, long hours and negligible leave. They suffer from disturbed sleep and uncompensated sick-days. They live with the constant fear that they will be sent home if they drink to forget or if they complain. In some places troublemakers have been known to disappear. It cannot have been good for their health.

Domestic or foreign, low-class manual workers are the most exposed to physical harm at work. In the UK the rate of injury among managers and senior officials is 128 injuries per 100 000. Among process, plant and machine operatives it is 1725, or 13 times more (Bambra, 2011: 67). Because there is a social gradient in the workplace, therefore there is a social gradient in the health status of the population as a whole.

Good health is a human right. Perhaps economic evolution, post-Taylorism and technological upgrading will make physical risk at work more equal. Perhaps, however, it will have to be complemented by 'microeconomic welfare' (Reisman, 2001: 60–64) if there is to be upward equalisation in the statistics on morbidity and mortality. Law can correct a market failure. Public policy can narrow the gap.

In business, good Samaritans who put in air conditioners will always be undercut by free-riders who store lidless acids next to visorless lathes on the way to a toilet that does not flush. Legislation policed by inspection has the great attraction that it makes all competitors, egoists and altruists alike, subject to one and the same deadweight. It may also cost some IVs and some Vs their jobs. Fringe benefits are analogous to a tax on jobs. The overhead will often be as unpopular among the redundant as it will among the profit-seekers. There is no accounting for tastes.

13.2 EDUCATION

Occupation is matter. Education is mind. Work makes men and makes them money. Schooling inculcates skills and moulds functional attitudes. The school conveys the fodder to the factory. The factory does the rest. Greater equality will sometimes be the finished product that is manufactured by the process. Sometimes it will not.

13.2.1 An Important Correlate

More is more. An additional four years of education in the United States lowers the five-year mortality rate by 1.8 percentage points, the risk of heart disease by 2.16, the risk of diabetes by 1.3 (Cutler and Lleras-Muney, 2006: 4, 9). Even among nuns in a convent, the university-educated lived longer. Differential acceleration compounds the relative distance. Between the early 1970s and the late 1990s the five-year death rate for less-educated males fell by 0.5 per cent. For graduate males it fell by 2.0 per cent. The rift was widening (Cutler et al., 2011a: 1177–8). The gap in life-expectancy between Americans with tertiary education and Americans with only high school education now stands at seven years.

Education, Grossman says, is *primus inter pares*: 'Among socio-economic variables years of schooling completed is probably the most important correlate of good health in adult populations' (Grossman, 1982: 191). The relationship is multidimensional. It is nurture: incremental education is cross-correlated with a non-manual job-function and a higher earned income that leads in turn to a more healthful diet and a better standard of housing. It is nature: a superior health-stock empowers the upcoming generation to learn more at school and to perform better at work. Genetic make-up and childhood socialisation reinforce the contribution of qualifications and chalk. Brighter people enjoy more years of formal schooling and invest more in their own health capital. Endowment is skill and skill is promotion. Some people are born hunks and some people are born weeds. Nature is not fair.

Education, vocational or higher, is the funnel to the jobs and to the incomes. The suggestion that education delivers better health mainly because it delivers more money is the ultimate goodbye to Mr Chips: 'It may be more cost effective to tap the mechanism than to increase educational attainment ... If all of the education effect operated through income, and income improved health, then it would possibly be cheaper to transfer income directly, rather than to subsidize schooling' (Cutler and Lleras-Muney, 2006: 23). If the road from education to health does begin and end with money, then there would conceivably be a case for health-chances to be equalised not indirectly through the schools but directly through welfare cheques, food vouchers and credited-in health insurance.

The circuit is complex and the causality unclear. Association is not proof. It is impossible to say with certainty if additional years of schooling are the cause or the consequence of good health. The correlation might be spurious. Individuals with a bias towards disciplined assiduity and deferred gratification might be investing more both in education and in health. What is clear is that the correlation between schooling and health does exist:

> Those with no qualifications are significantly less likely to eat breakfast and those with a degree are significantly more likely to do so. The more educated are less likely to smoke, while those with no qualifications are significantly less likely to exercise than other groups. Those who have a university degree are less likely to be obese. (Contoyiannis and Jones, 2004: 979)

Body mass index has a negative education gradient. The same is true of drug abuse, heart attacks, stroke and the absence of household smoke detectors. The less educated are less likely to seek preventive care in forms such as mammograms, smears, colonoscopies and vaccinations. The less educated are less likely to complete a course of antibiotics. Compulsion would give them the freedom to enjoy health. Statistically at least, compulsory education has the property that it improves their life-expectancy.

The better educated have a healthier lifestyle. Through assortive mating in the coffee bar and the quad they are more likely to meet and marry educated people who will share their pro-health lifestyle. Their children will benefit from that lifestyle and from the educational head start that two graduate incomes can procure. Richer parents will be better placed to pay for tutors, crammers and private schooling that enhances the life-chances of success. Better health will be the result. Still, however, it might be the income differential that is doing the work.

The outcomes bear out the classrooms. Guralnik, studying retired American males, found that those with at least 12 years of education had an active (non-disabled) life expectancy 2.4 to 3.9 years longer than those with less than 12 years of education. Weighted by years of education there were no significant differences between blacks and whites. The equality is deceptive. Only 14.6 per cent of black men but fully 31.9 per cent of white men had had at least 12 years of schooling. In the case of women the educational differential has an additional dimension. Infant mortality is higher among black mothers than among whites. The differences are large but they are not immutable. The missing 2.4 to 3.9 life-years can be restored through the expansion and targeting of compulsory education (Guralnik et al., 1993: 113). Pro-poor education is pro-poor health.

Educated people have a longer shelf-life: 'An additional year of education lowers the probability of dying in the next 10 years by approximately 1.3 percentage points or even more. This could represent as much as 1.7 years of life' (Lleras-Muney, 2002: 23). Elo and Preston showed that adult mortality per 1000 working-age males was 7.41 for those with 0–8 years of schooling but only 3.33 for those with at least 16 years. They calculated that each additional year of formal education reduces the number of deaths in the United States by 7.7 per cent. The figure is broadly the same in England and Wales (7.4 per cent), Sweden (8.0 per cent), Denmark (8.1 per cent) and Finland (9.2 per cent) (Elo and Preston, 1996: 47, 48, 49, 56). In England, 'for people aged 30 and above, if everyone without a degree had their death rate reduced to that of people with degrees, there would be 202,000 fewer premature deaths each year' (Marmot and the Marmot Review Team, 2010). The returns to education clearly go beyond book learning alone. They also reduce the steepness of the social gradient in health.

At its most basic level the school teaches human biology. It imparts factual information on body maintenance. Preventive care and early detection are more likely if the patient knows what causes tooth decay, why cigarettes are bad, how to avoid venereal disease or how to recognise the symptoms of malignancy in time. Foundation knowledge makes it easier and cheaper to add on informal learning through the media and on the job.

As well as biology there will often be lessons in home economics. They give pupils background knowledge on household budgeting, the washing of vegetables, how to store meat, when water is safe, the nature of a balanced diet, the threat from cholesterol, pizza, hamburgers, alcohol, tobacco, salt, sugary drinks, saturated fats, chemical additives and aluminium saucepans. Possibly children from more privileged backgrounds will have acquired much of this knowledge in the home. They will have been given more fruit, vegetables, iron, calcium, vitamin C, wholemeal bread and dietary fibre. In such a case it is the less advantaged children who will gain the most from the academic increment that facilitates the catch-up.

All of education, moreover, has an invisible curriculum. In tandem with cognitive skills schooling can instill health-fostering habits and a goal-orientated outlook. Enlisting mainly young people at a time when their lifetime health habits have still to be formed, it conditions their reflexes and shapes their values. Formal education demands regular and punctual attendance. The intellectual stance is identical to that which makes the rhythm method of contraception a success and ensures conscientious tooth-brushing at least twice a day. Formal education rewards candidates who are willing to exchange time and effort for technique and enlightenment. The quid pro quo is the same as that which Grossman has in mind when, postulating a 'production function of healthy days', he makes use of an eggs-produce-omelettes, jugs-fill-mugs approach to derive the result that 'the level of health of an individual is *not* exogenous but depends, at least in part, on the resources allocated to its production' (Grossman, 1972: 225, 233).

Formal education requires present sacrifice in order that a future dividend might one day accrue to human capital laboriously built up through lessons. It is the valuation of disciplined sowing in order to reap, the concept of taking responsibility for oneself and one's choices, the notion of gratification deferred later rewarded by a productivity differential that leads Fuchs to conclude that 'the most likely explanation for the high correlation between health and schooling is that both reflect differences in time preference' (Fuchs, 1996: 6). Human capital or health capital, the future-facing valuation of compound interest is a transferable window on the world. It is acquired for life through early patterning and the conditioning of reflexes.

The foundations laid, better-educated people have a differential economic incentive to keep up to date. Earning more, the opportunity cost of falling ill is that much greater. It is hard to explain why, in one study, a sample of university students underestimated the additional risk of driving under the influence of at least six beers by a factor of ten (Phelps, 1988: 12). They were cream of the apex. They were university students. It is counterintuitive to assume that they knew so little about beer.

Possibly the result was an outlier and a freak. Auster found that the impact of formal education on mortality rates was double the impact of medical care (Auster et al., 1969: 434). Newhouse and Friedlander found that education was a better predictor of healthy gums than was the availability of dentists (Newhouse and Friedlander, 1980: 201). Reality may not after all be letting the pure theories down. Perhaps it really is the schoolmasters and not the doctors who make the greater contribution to the length and enjoyment of life.

13.2.2 An Intergenerational Bequest

The foundations for good health are laid in childhood: 'The concept that individuals somehow choose their socioeconomic pathway through life is too simplistic ... The health-related behaviours and psychosocial characteristics of adult men are associated with the social class of those men's parents' (Lynch et al., 1997: 815, 817). Poor people behave poorly because their parents behaved poorly. History has not gone away.

Health status is lagged outcomes replicating remembered practices. It makes choice into non-choice because memory is trapped in a cage: 'People do not choose the early life experiences that play an important role in forming their life trajectories and their future patterns of health and disease' (Spencer, 2007: 167). The intergenerational bequest makes it more difficult for education today to level up the socio-economic inequalities. Distance has deep roots in the past.

The present-day is held back by the dead hand of the once-was. Diabetes in adults can be the lagged consequence of malnutrition before the current cohort was even born. Bronchitis in children at age two is more common where the parents of the children had had a respiratory ailment in their own early childhood. The list goes on:

> Poor conditions at home during early life predict high systolic blood pressure at age 43 ... Development of schizophrenia by age 43 was related to difficulties in infancy in walking and talking ... More than half of those physically disabled by age 43 had a serious childhood illness ... Those whose parents had divorced by age 15 reported higher levels of male alcohol consumption and female smoking. (Smith, 1999: 161)

The sins of the great-grandparents are visited upon their great-grandchildren. Today's alcoholism or antisocial estrangement will often be the poisoned chalice of yesterday's socialisation or addiction. Blaming the victims is to rob the atom of its lineage and its history.

A study of middle-aged Finnish men has demonstrated vividly the continuity of the socio-physiological inheritance: 'Men born into the poorest childhood circumstances had 28 per cent lower intake of fruit, 15 per cent lower non-root vegetables, 12 per cent lower carotene, 8 per cent lower vitamin C, 6 per cent higher levels of salt' (Lynch et al., 1997: 814). Poorer nutrition as a child, like other early-life handicaps and disadvantages, never really goes away. It does not go away even in Britain, which has the NHS: 'Lower respiratory illness in the first two years of life was a significant risk for signs of adult chronic obstructive pulmonary disease' (Wadsworth and Kuh, 1997: 7). British women are more likely to be alcoholic at age 36 if their parents divorced when they were under 15. The cumulative life-course is not solely a function of the body-holder's own free will and personal preference. 'A person's past social experiences become written into the physiology and pathology of their body. The social is, literally, embodied' (Blane, 1999: 64). Individualism is not fully and freely the individual's own.

Moulding has a longitudinal and an intergenerational dimension. Today's child is tomorrow's parent. Health plays a crucial part in determining the receptiveness to education. Education plays a crucial part in breaking the orbit of the vicious circle. Education for women is particularly important if the trajectory is to be reprogrammed and the inequalities in health reduced.

Future health begins *in utero*: 'The best way to safeguard children's health may be to start with their pregnant (or prepregnant) mothers' (Currie, 2009: 115). The mother's health affects the incidence of stroke, diabetes, hypertension and personality disorders over the life-course of the foetus that becomes the infant. Good nutrition in pregnancy is an investment in the child's cardiovascular system: 'Birthweight is determined by the weight and height of the mother, which in turn reflects her own growth in childhood' (Stationery Office, 1998: 69). Height at age seven is a powerful predictor of subsequent unemployment. Shorter people are three times more likely to spend time out of work (Blane, 1999: 67). The circle is self-perpetuating. It goes round and round.

An additional year of maternal education in the United States reduces the probability of low-birthweight delivery by 10 per cent (Currie and Moretti, 2003: 1516). An additional three years of compulsory education in Taiwan reduces the infant mortality rate by 11 per cent (Currie, 2009: 97). Since educated women are less likely to smoke, they are presumably less likely to be on narcotics while they are pregnant. It is just as well. Joyce found that between 1482 and 3359 low-birthweight babies in New York City (3.2–7.3 per cent of all low-birthweight babies in that city) were born to women on cocaine. The cost to the system for excess neonatal health care was between $18 million and $41 million (Joyce et al., 1992: 312).

It is women who are the most directly involved in antenatal care, breastfeeding, vaccinations, shopping, menu planning. It is women who are with the child in the first year of cognitive development. They talk to the child. They build up patterns of acceptance and rejection that will have an impact on later success at school, on incomes that are contingent on qualifications, on the ability to interact with others. It is more often the woman than the man who takes the child to the doctor: 'Black–white differences in use of services would be dramatically altered by eliminating black–white differences in mother's schooling' (Colle and Grossman,

1978: 149). It more often the woman who sees to it that fatty crisps and low-fibre starches are consumed only in moderation. Women's education is in that sense high-powered education. The woman is being equipped with family-related as well as economically relevant skills. These skills have the character of a cohort-to-cohort transfer: 'Children and teenagers of more-educated mothers have better oral health, are less likely to be obese, and less likely to have anaemia than children of less-educated mothers' (Grossman, 1982: 192).

Better-educated women will command higher than average earnings. They are more likely to marry better-educated men who will themselves be able to command a better than average income. Because of the higher opportunity cost of earnings foregone, better-educated women will have a stronger incentive to limit family size. Education is a reliable form of family planning. The result is that more resources will be concentrated on fewer beneficiaries. The biological capital of each quality child will be higher. The mother's own health status will not be imperilled by excessive childbearing. As for the labour supply, a nation faced with a shortage because the parents have gone on strike will have to rely on machines or on immigrants to get the work out.

13.3 CULTURE

Culture is shared values and aspirations, common ideals and norms. Learned and transmitted, the cultural baggage is the sociological concomitant of the genetic inheritance. It has a close link to observed inequalities in illness and death. Health status has a behavioural component that is not self-selected but group-selected. We start from here. Health is other people.

Initially people absorb the lifestyle into which they have been socialised by their parents. Later on they internalise the attitudes and patterns that their reference group at once validates and expects. Prevalence disseminates the roles and perpetuates the models. Informal learning is all around. The freedom to choose is not 100 per cent.

13.3.1 Patterned Differences

Some peer groups make it a convention that their members should smoke and drink. They would ostracise a deviant who rejected the done thing by turning away from an unsterilised needle. Some peer groups are reckless and irresponsible. They gamble on fate and trust in luck. They eat white bread with pork fat. They abuse chocolates to calm their nerves. They do not make fresh oranges, brown rice and organic vegetables a staple part of their diet.

Some individuals lack health discipline because the peer pattern is 'live for today'. Saying 'it can't happen to me', thinking 'devil-may-care', they resist the calculative rationality that would have led them to don crash helmets or move out of flood plains. They do not wear nicotine replacement patches to shield their lungs. They do not attend meditation sessions for inner peace. Other people may do it. We do not.

It is not simply a matter of disposable income. Red meat costs more than a salad. Smoking costs more than not smoking. Logically speaking, it ought to be the prosperous professionals and not the unskilled manuals who would be the target demographic for what non-communicants would call an expensive luxury. In fact, it is the lower-income groups who are the more likely to make the investment. Cigarettes are the props and the costumes of their script. The consequence of their drama is community-inflicted illness. Culture is widening the health status divide.

Some peer groups have short horizons. Other peer groups have long horizons. They plan for the future and invest in success. They reject fried fat with greasy chips in favour of low-salt stewed fish and an occasional glass of wine. They exercise actively on the cricket pitch rather than vicariously through television sport. They value a long-term business plan over speculative immediacy. Relentless turnover might cost them acid indigestion.

Long-termers might look askance at competitive individualists whose entrepreneurship extends to quick turnover at the expense of a cooperative, consensual, communitarian culture. They might put integration above fragmentation and stability above the whirlwind. It is support rather than *anomie* but it may also be Bad Egg and Black Dog. The glums and a barbiturate overdose may be inevitable if smothering overconformity comes to be perceived as a juggernaut that stigmatises all idiosyncrasy exclusively because it is a departure from the mean.

The lesson is this. Different individuals will want different things at least in part because of the different subsets to which they belong. Culture is not always vertical. There are rich Baptists and poor Baptists. There are Fulham supporters in the Ferraris and on the Tube. Culture can be classless. It is not, however, always so.

In America in the 1990s 40 per cent of men who had not completed high school smoked. The comparable figure for male graduates was 14 per cent (Smith, 1999: 148). In 2006 the figure for the lowest income tercile was 31.2 per cent and for the highest 15.8 per cent (Martinson, 2012: 2060) In Britain in the lower occupational groups 41 per cent of the men smoke, 25 per cent of babies are still breastfed at six weeks and

25 per cent of the women are obese. The figures for the top occupational groups are 12 per cent, 75 per cent and 14 per cent respectively. Women in social class V are four times more likely to smoke in pregnancy than are women in social class I (Stationery Office, 1998: 15, 16, 22, 23, 72). Lack of self-control and poor coping strategies feed through into accidents and operations. Alcohol-related hospital admissions for men in the lower occupational groups are 2.6 times greater than for managerial and professional males (Marmot and the Marmot Review Team, 2010). The IVs and the Vs are living differently from the Is and the IIs. It should be no surprise that they are ending up with different health outcomes.

13.3.2 Cultural Imperialism

Levelling up can be cultural imperialism. The demand for a national health culture will inevitably be seen by the libertarian fringes and the pluralistic tails as a demand for homogeneity at the cost of tolerance. They will be right to be afraid. Subcultural mores, ethnic self-definition and personal choice must be treated with respect. That is the categorical imperative. It is the Golden Rule.

The differences are there. They may be what the subcultures regard as a part of their shared identity. Alpha males go in for drinking and brawling. Indians cook with ghee. The Chinese enjoy *char kway teow*. The Brazilians like giant steaks. If that is what they are and what they want, then there is a limited amount a democratic society can do to standardise the outcomes apart from making sure that the preferences revealed are bilaterally voluntary and informed.

Attitudes and conventions are resistant to social engineering. That does not mean, however, that they may not legitimately be challenged. The Russians have a want for vodka but a need to stay alive. Expectant mothers have a want for amphetemines but a need for a healthy child. In the one case as in the other, the wants pull the divided self in the direction of Mr Hyde but the needs pull the non-destructible ego in the direction of Dr Jekyll. It is the political economy of the split personality and the weakness of will. Acting on the conjecture that the Russians and the mothers would in a moment of calm and clear-sighted reflection have decided to rank their core needs above their ephemeral wants, the State will not be violating but reinforcing their own preferences when it nudges them toward the choices that they themselves would have put first.

The State is not rejecting but actualising the superordinate values of the rational Ulysses when it binds the deluded Ulysses to protect him from a subordinate course. A cultural community declares that it values promiscuity over monogamy. It also declares that it values life over death. The two most important risk factors for death from cervical cancer are first intercourse at an early age and a high number of sexual partners (Eddy, 1990: 214). The cultural community knows that it has to make a choice between licence and existence. The State acting as the subgroup's agent makes the choice on behalf of the rational Ulysses because the Sirens cannot.

Nannying by consent and consensus is the means by which Ulysses is empowered to target the health status which his representatives guess would be his own most preferred alternative. If they guess correctly, then it is not cultural imperialism. Instead, it is the acknowledgment of his own authentic needs that makes undeluded Ulysses keen to accept the breathalyser and forego the hookah.

Subcultures can be remoulded because Big Nanny is what the subcultures really want. Subcultures can also be remoulded because the wider community believes that the subcultures have violated the social contract. Tolerance has its limits. Once those limits are breached, it will be the public and not the particular interest that will speak out against the minorities and the spillovers to which their fellow citizens have never agreed.

Smoking in the United Kingdom accounts each year for 30 000 deaths from lung cancer and a further 16 000 deaths from cancers of the oesophagus, stomach, mouth and throat. It is an important cause of chronic obstructive lung disease, coronary heart disease, aortic aneurysm, respiratory disease and middle ear disease. The nation pays for the self-inflicted illness. It does so through the free-on-demand National Health Service that the British people fund to the tune of 83 per cent through tax. In 2013 there were on average 4500 adult admissions per day (4 per cent of all adult inpatients) with a primary diagnosis that could be traced back to smoking. It does so through absenteeism, lower productivity and slower growth. In 2013 17 per cent of all deaths in the 35+ cohort were estimated to have been caused by smoking (Health and Social Care Information Centre, 2015). In that sense we are all the victims of passive smoking. It is the smokers and not the non-smokers who are the true cultural imperialists. They are the ones who are imposing their externalities on their community as a whole.

The distinction is not just between the smokers and the non-smokers. It is also between the Is and the Vs. Smoking is stratified. The cultural subgroup follows the income distribution down. British households in the lowest income decile spend six times as much of their income on tobacco products as do households at the top. Such consumers might cut back on food, clothing, seat belts, motorcycle helmets, car air bags, heating and other basic necessities in order to feed their nicotine dependence, augmented by drink: 'Deaths from diseases caused by alcohol show a clear gradient with socioeconomic position, with an almost fourfold higher rate in unskilled working men compared to those from professional groups. In addition, alcohol is a contributory factor to deaths from accidents, which also show a pronounced socioeconomic gradient' (Stationery Office, 1998: 85).

The disparities are at once social and geographical. About 37.8 per cent of the households in the North East of England are economically deprived. In the South East it is only 5.1 per cent. In spite of being stranded in the poverty trap, 25.1 per cent of the residents in the North East drink heavily, 25 per cent are obese, and 888 per 100 000 are receiving treatment for drug abuse. The figures for the South East are 15.5 per cent, 20.4 per cent and 385 respectively (Department of Health, 2006: 9, 10).

The poor North East is spending more, and more than the North East poor can afford. The North East rich are less of a concern. Owner-occupiers with a car spend less on cigarettes and alcohol than do the unemployed and the uneducated living in public housing. The class cultures are reflected in the death differentials. It is rich and poor woven into North and South. The haves have a valid point when they say that the have-nots cannot forever multiply the subsidised care so long as they are voluntarily poisoning themselves with smokes and beer.

Vice is the stuff of which careers in social philosophy are made. Morals are a minefield. The British government has the legal right to deny income support to the 55 per cent of single mothers in severe hardship who smoke. They get through, on average, five packets of cigarettes a week. They are price-insensitive to a rise in tax. Nicotine is mother's little helper. It is self-medication that alleviates the boredom and the distress.

The British government might feel that it has a duty to wean deluded Penelope off a lifestyle that is so damaging to her health. It might say that five packets a week are not good for the women's welfare. The welfare mothers might reply that isolation and anxiety are even worse. Five packets are the subculture's way. And single parents are citizens too.

13.3.3 Melting the Pot

It may be cultural imperialism and it may be the social contract. Whatever it is, it can be done. Information, legislation, subsidies and taxes are four techniques that a tolerant but leaderly democracy can deploy to level the marginalised into the classless utopia of One Nation in Health.

Information gets the facts out. Only 19 per cent of Americans smoke. In England and France it is 27 per cent. In Germany it is 35 per cent. In Greece it is 38 per cent. Explaining the cultural disparities, Cutler calculates that up to one-half of the difference between the Old World and the New is due to the non-evolutionary force of belief-shaping paternalism. The State in America had pushed hard the message that cigarettes kill (Cutler and Glaeser, 2006).

National percentages are not, of course, socio-economic groups. Public information campaigns reach the health-conscious before they trickle down to the hard-to-reach. Traffic-light labelling of cigarettes and foodstuffs might have the greater impact on the suburbs who are already health-aware than on the less educated who are stuck in a rut. Even if all classes in the end smoke less and eat fresh, still it might be the privileged classes who are elevated more rapidly because they take the faster lift. In terms of health the conversion is of benefit to all. In terms of stratification it might be perverse. Inequality in health might become greater and not less.

Supplementing the flow of information, there are the laws, the bylaws and the rules. The State can refuse maternity benefit to a woman who has not attended her antenatal and well-baby clinics or proven that she has been to a talk on contraception. It can prohibit smoking in offices, restaurants and public places. It can ban commercial advertising and sponsorship of high-tar tobacco. It can shorten the licensing hours. It can rezone the saloons into the non-residential wasteland poorly served by public transport.

The State can back up its legislation with subsidies. Reducing the price, they induce prudent shoppers to substitute healthy bran for tooth-rotting sugar and to patronise public swimming pools which burn off the fat. Subsidies are an incentive to attend low-cost t'ai chi sessions that keep moodiness, stiffness, colon cancer and heart disease under control. An apple a day keeps the doctor away. The State can subsidise the apples. The wards and the clinics cost the nation so much more.

Subsidies to goods and services may upgrade the national health. Narrowing the gap is a different matter. In Britain fully 35 per cent of the highest occupational group but only 21 per cent of the lowest are consuming the recommended five portions of fruit and vegetables per day. Given the disparity, a subsidy, as with the dissemination of information, is likely to have a regressive impact (House of Commons Health Committee, 2009: 22). The intentions are good. The outcome, however, is unintended.

Taxes are similar to subsidies in that they have the power to skew. Apples can be taxed at a concessionary rate: pro-health discrimination steers deluded Ulysses into the greengrocer's shop. Alcohol can be taxed at a punitive rate: fiscal discouragement forces deluded Ulysses to ration his drinks. Taxation is extracurricular education. It is not just in the schoolroom but also in the High Street that Big Brother sets up his blackboard and begins to preach.

Taxes on sins price anti-health wants down to size. Higher cost may be a step in the direction of more equal outcomes. The lower classes, more prone to smoke but less able to pay, may be relatively more dissuaded by the lion in the path. Taxes are especially effective where, as Grossman says, they discourage most the impressionable young: 'Teenage price elasticities of demand for cigarettes are substantial and much larger than the corresponding adult price elasticities ... It follows that, if future reductions in youth smoking are desired, an increase in the federal excise tax is a potent policy to accomplish this goal' (Grossman, 1982: 194). It is more economical to condition the price-sensitive, the malleable and the inexperienced than it is to reacculturate the far-gone.

Young people have limited spending power. A tax on cigarettes, impeding their access at a time when they are economically as well as emotionally vulnerable, is likely over time to enrich the proportion of adults on higher incomes who could, if they wished, afford to smoke. Middle age begins at 20. People become set in their ways. Fiscal brainwashing has the great attraction that it rewashes the cultural patterns. Not all commodities lend themselves as well as cigarettes to conservatism by consent. Illicit drug-taking, multiple sexual partners and unprotected adolescent intercourse are notoriously difficult to tax.

13.4 INCOME

Money is the means to the end. People whose incomes are good can pay for a wholesome diet, good-quality housing, health club memberships and proper medical treatment. People whose incomes are inadequate must scrape along in threadbare clothing and unfit hovels where infectious diseases breed.

For individuals and countries at the lowest levels of affluence a small increment in purchasing power can lead to a major improvement in health. Once, however, the basic necessities have become easily affordable, the causal relationship becomes tenuous: 'Whether income affects adult health remains an open question' (Cutler et al., 2011b: 145). It may actually be flat-of-the-curve: 'Within developed countries, the relationship between mortality and income is ... tending to disappear, except for those at the lowest income levels' (Fuchs, 1974b: 181). The poorest of the poor are still unable to afford the oily fish, green vegetables and fresh tofu that would inject much-needed nutrients into their diet, raise their average productivity and shield their offspring from birth-born debility. Above that floor, however, the inadequate commons of the poverty trap are giving way to the modest comforts of the new-style lower deciles that have central heating, a refrigerator, a television, a computer and sometimes a car.

Poverty is not what it was in the poor developing country that is the main character in Dickens's *Hard Times* and Marx's *Capital*. A rise in absolute income, except for the shipwrecked stranded in the lower depths, no longer makes the difference between sickness and health. Preston found that only about 12.2 per cent of the improvement in life-expectancy in a worldwide scatter was actually associated with a rise in the standard of living (Preston, 1975: 237). Wilkinson made the piggy-backing no more than 10 per cent (Wilkinson, 1996: 36). In the richer countries the proportion will have been even less. Whatever else a decent income can buy, it is less and less likely to buy the income-earner health.

13.4.1 Relief and Empowerment

The rich do not normally need relief and empowerment. The higher deciles will normally have income, wealth and insurance sufficient for their health-related needs. If anything, the association between purchasing power and health indicators for them will turn perverse. Overeating, overwork, a sedentary lifestyle, luxury absinthe are the price of affluence that the economic vanguard is paying through hypertension, gout, skin cancer, duodenal ulcers and extreme sports in a yacht that might sink.

Apart from information, legislation, subsidies and taxes, there is a limit to what a health-conscious democracy can do to prevent an obese executive from grabbing a hamburger in his car when he ought to have been eating boiled lentils or doing keep-fit in the gym. There are few class-specific levers that the government can pull to make prosperous backsliders pro-health against their will. The higher deciles in any case already enjoy a superior health status. They are not in urgent need of relief and empowerment. The main target is the absolutely deprived. They are the deciles that governments in most countries say they want to raise up to the mean.

Most of our people are travelling upward on the moving staircase of growth. Some of our people, however, are being left behind. Excluded and forgotten, often new immigrants, often from an ethnic minority, often without a family network or a marketable skill, their income and wealth are not enough to buy them essential complements to good health. Children born into poverty, suffering from parasitic infections and impaired cognitive development, cannot realistically be expected to pull themselves up by their bootstraps in line with the success ethic of Samuel Smiles and Horatio Alger. Where public opinion is not comfortable with islands of destitution in a sea of prosperity, the voters, stung into action by the humanitarian spillover, will put pressure on the State to do for the marginalised what market capitalism cannot.

The policy instruments to relieve absolute misery are the familiar arsenal of cash handouts, earmarked payments and benefits in kind. Food vouchers, means-testing, income supplementation, unemployment benefits, medical insurance, vaccination campaigns, child allowances, concessionary eye-tests, earnings-linked pensions, cold-weather supplements, thermal insulation, part-paid school meals, free school milk, free school fruit, public housing, rent rebates, halfway hostels, home helps for the disabled, sheltered housing for the elderly, reverse discrimination in favour of ethnic minorities, selective discrimination in favour of geographical black spots, well-equipped local clinics with high-quality staff, fluoridation of drinking water, tax zero-rating for food staples and a winter coat, gas and electricity rebates, concerned social workers who counsel the underintegrated on the take-up of their stigma-free citizenship rights – these and other levers are all ways in which a welfare society can bring the less healthy up to the threshold entitlement that public opinion calls socially acceptable and proclaims the badge of citizenship.

Not all of the absolutely deprived are desperate rejects queuing up for help. Some of them are the poor-in-work. They have low-wage jobs that do not afford them a threshold standard of income and health. Their prospects are bleak unless churches, charities and the humanitarian State come to their aid. Should the consensus demand that mutual aid be made a national concern, there are a number of non-market instruments that the State can draw from its locker. These include the minimum wage, apprenticeship schemes, retraining grants, security of tenure, curbs on retrenchment, support to geographical mobility, the prohibition of racial discrimination, a quota system for the occupationally under-represented. The State can legislate for flexible work rosters, child care leave, child-minding facilities that enable women to remain in work. It can ensure free television licences and inexpensive public transport so that even the poorest lumps of labour will have access to the nation and the world.

Relief of distress is often regarded as a good thing in itself. Even better must be the empowerment that facilitates the escape from distress: 'What is required is not so much a safety net which allows the individual to reestablish their habitual life, but a "springboard" which repairs the damage caused by past disadvantage and equips the individual to enter, perhaps for the first time, a socially normal life' (Blane, 1999: 77). A new trajectory must be established if the disadvantaged are to escape from past neglect and their children be rescued from self-perpetuating despair.

Life-course is a cumulative process. One thing builds on another. In the same way that success breeds success, the never-was carries forward the tradition of the might-have-been. The scorched earth of long-term unemployment and half-starved ancestors is longitudinal, intergenerational and long term. If children are to be rescued from the dead end of a blighted start, the State would do well to invest in complements to occupational mobility such as education, housing and healthcare. Children need food that helps them to concentrate, a quiet place in which to study and medical care to stem the tuberculosis, hookworm and diarrhoea that will stunt their economic growth. Where the family income is too low to afford them an unimpeded life-course, it is usually the State with a mandate from the consensus that brings them closer to the mean.

13.4.2 Economic Welfare

Economic policy is social policy. It has an effect on people's incomes, their lifestyle and also their health. Deprived areas are deprived people. One way of raising up the people is to uplift the economic base. The State can provide concessionary interest rates, preferential licences, fast-track infrastructure and selective tax incentives to firms, domestic or multinational, which bring labour-intensive technology to areas where manpower is underemployed, unemployed, progressively unemployable.

The work will come to the workers. A geographical master plan is microeconomic welfare. As well as creating new incomes, regional policy revitalises local communities. Social networks would be badly affected if the young and the mobile had to move out in search of a job. There is not much community support where everyone left behind is sad, lonely and without ambition.

Unemployment itself can be a cause of absolute deprivation. People who are out of work are out of earnings. Where the unemployment is frictional or short-term search, it will be self-correcting once new information has been collected, new signals scanned and new contracts concluded. Where it is structural or demand-deficient, on the other hand, it can be associated with multiple stressors that may manifest themselves in physical and mental ill-health.

At the structural level, unemployment might reflect a decline in opportunities for the manual unskilled because computer-driven robots are automating their routines, immigrants are undercutting locals and free trade agreements are moving the work offshore. The new jobs that are open to the shake-out will often be insecure, temporary or part-time. Contract employment will often involve long hours, antisocial shifts, limited fringe benefits, little protection against redundancy. Workers in this sector have been called the 'precariat'. Not only are their wages low, but they never know how long the job will last.

In the case of demand-deficient unemployment, a macroeconomic downswing or an austerity budget leads to wage cuts and staff shrinkage. Dismissals may be compared to a regressive tax that imposes the greatest burden on the least advantaged. Particularly exposed will be the unskilled, the disabled, the poorly educated, the chronically ill, the older worker not yet of pensionable age, the new school leaver seeking an entry-level opportunity, the single parent whose choices are limited by the caring role. It is the marginal and not the thrust who are the more likely to end up first in the Marxian reserve army that, keeping wages low, make it possible for home exporters to compete in the world market.

Unemployment is often believed to be a threat to health. It is the loss of a regular income, with all of the negative knock-ons both for the laid-off and their dependants. It is the loss of professional identity, loss of a recognisable role, loss of contact with a support system of workmates, loss of access to the bush telegraph that grapevines word-of-mouth tips on new openings. For many if not most, it means isolation, purposelessness, worry and spoiled self-image. Heart disease, depression and suicide are psychosocial indicators of how body and mind can be affected when human beings see themselves as surplus to requirements.

Halliday in the United States found that a 'one percentage point increase in the unemployment rate increases the probability of dying within one year of baseline of working-aged men by 6 per cent' (Halliday, 2014: 21). Gardner and Oswald in Britain showed that, for men at least, each additional year without a job raises the probability of premature death by 1.4 per cent (Gardner and Oswald, 2004: 1191). Interest rates are lethal. Quantitative tightening is bad for the heart. Full employment is good for the heart. Keynesian macroeconomics is a part of the Welfare State. Supply-side economics blocks up the National Health.

Association does not, of course, distinguish the chicken from the egg. Poor health might have been the cause and not the effect of prolonged joblessness. The unemployed might have turned to drink to keep themselves sane. Bad habits make it harder for them to get back into work.

More confusing is the fact that even the facts do not speak with a single voice. Ruhm found evidence that a moderate amount of unemployment could actually have a positive effect on the nation's health. A one percentage point rise in cyclical unemployment had been associated with a 0.5 per cent fall in the total death rate in the United States over the period from 1972 to 1991. It had been associated with a 1.6 per cent reduction in bed-days, a 3.9 per cent decline in acute morbidities and a 4.3 per cent decrease in ischaemic heart disease.

Less work means fewer accidents at work. Less travel to work means fewer injuries on the road. Mainly, Ruhm says, the improvement was due to a change in lifestyle: 'Risky behaviours become less common when the economy deteriorates' (Ruhm, 2005: 351). Pubbing and clubbing are priced out when discretionary income goes west. Home-cooked meals take the place of carbohydrates and gristle in the canteen. Exercise and sport fill up some at least of the involuntary leisure.

Neoclassical economists will see it as rational choice. Unemployment makes investment in good health less costly. When the price falls, the quantity demanded goes up. While a transitory fall should not be mistaken for a permanent one, Ruhm's evidence does suggest that bad habits are not impregnable. Unemployment can force people to experiment with new conventions. New customs might be a game-changer that improves the nation's health.

Long-term unemployment is the result of secular change or of cyclical downswing. Whatever the cause, it reduces the living standards of the cliff-dwellers afflicted first by the turbulence of forced readjustment. A social floor of unemployment transfers will at least protect the health status of the first-out. Welfare gives them the countervailing power to refuse a starvation wage where the alternative would be starvation itself. The promise alone shelters them from the insecurity which eats away at well-being: 'It is not only adverse life events themselves which affect health, but the anticipation of adversity ... This effect is mitigated where life changes do not have adverse financial implications' (Bartley et al., 1997: 1196).

Cuts in benefits have the opposite effect. Cuts lower the replacement ratio and with it the reservation wage. Benefits themselves carry the opprobrium of a scrounger's charter. Augmented by the indignity of a personal means-test, free-loading, self-perceived, may deter the self-respecting from claiming what is theirs. State surveillance of job applications as the quid pro quo for the Jobseeker's Allowance is unlikely to convince the out-of-luck that welfare is a right and not a concession.

13.5 INEQUALITY

There is poverty and there is distance. Economic growth may or may not be the tide that raises even the meanest peasant to a standard of comfort undreamt-of by Charlemagne or Henry VIII. A society may be able to spend its way out of absolute deprivation. Relative deprivation is different. The gap in income, wealth, power and control is becoming greater with growth. The differences may be showing up in health.

13.5.1 Income and Health

At the national level, the distribution of the national income and not just the crude per capita take-home would appear to be closely correlated with the rate of mortality: 'The greater the spread, the larger the net loss' (Preston, 1975: 242). Mexico and Colombia, countries with a considerable spread, 'have life expectancies which are 6.7 and 2.1 years respectively below the levels predicted on the basis of average incomes' (Preston, 1975: 242). A similar phenomenon has been reported in Asia: 'Where differences between rich and poor are lower (as they are in Kerala) life expectancy is higher' (Bartley, 2004: 116). While nothing is ever certain in statistics, cross-country comparisons do lend some support to the idea that, as well as the level of income, the visible dispersion in income was having a causal impact on the disparities in health: 'Internationally, life expectancy is related more closely to income distribution than to overall wealth as measured by gross national product' (Marmot et al., 1999: 108)

Third World or First World, it seems not to be the richest but the more egalitarian societies that report the best health outcomes. Japan has high taxes and narrow differentials. It also has the highest life-expectancy in the world. Its infant mortality rate is one-third that of the United States which has a much greater income inequality: 'Upwards of 14 million deaths (9.6 per cent) could be averted in 30 OECD [Organisation for Economic Co-operation and Development] countries by levelling the Gini coefficient below the threshold value of 0.3' (Kondo et al., 2009: 1181). About 884 000 of those 14 million deaths are occurring in the United States. Reducing measured inequality to 0.3 might reduce the number of premature deaths in the United States by one-third.

Correlations are never conclusive and other things are never constant. Even so, the observations do seem to put inferior health and a wider spread in the same place at the same time. In the United States, age-adjusted excess mortality in urban areas with high as compared with low income inequality was 139.8 deaths per 100 000 population in 1990:

'An appropriate comparison would be that this mortality difference exceeds the combined loss of life from lung cancer, diabetes, motor vehicle crashes, HIV infection, suicide, and homicide in 1995' (Lynch et al., 1998: 1079). Outcomes shadow distance: 'When you compare the most egalitarian state, New Hampshire, with the least egalitarian, Louisiana, the latter has about a 60 per cent higher mortality rate' (Sapolsky, 2004: 376). The correlations lend support to the conjectures. Relative deprivation is a health hazard. Competition is toxic waste. Invidious comparison can kill.

In France and Greece life-expectancy went up at a time when income inequality was declining. The improvement was more rapid than in Britain and Ireland where little was being done to retard the growing disparities (Wilkinson, 1996: 7, 130). In the former Soviet Union life-expectancy at age 15 went down by five years in the period between 1989 and 1997. The rise in deaths coincided with a sharp spike in the Gini coefficient (Marmot and Bobak, 2000: 1125). Singapore is the outlier. It combines above-average inequality with above-average longevity. It is the exception. Overall, disparity and death seem to be taking the same train.

The threat to health is not inequality in itself but rather the perception that inequality is running wild. Moderate differentials are generally accepted as the fair day's wage for achievement, ambition and merit. It is not moderate but excessive differentials that are at the root of the frustration, resentment and Bad Egg. It is they that are responsible for the explosion into the evocative rallying cry, 'We are the 99 per cent'. Stiglitz is convinced that ordinary Americans have had enough: 'We've become increasingly a nation divided ... The top 1 per cent get in one week 40 per cent more than the bottom fifth receive in a year ... The wealthiest 1 per cent of households had 225 times the wealth of the typical American' (Stiglitz, 2012: 4, 8). Americans have no quarrel with hard work and upward mobility. It not reasonable distance but intolerable distance that is undermining their confidence in the American way.

Americans no longer see the road as open and unblocked. Nowadays, Stiglitz contends, they see their life-chances more and more as a function of family contacts, elite schooling and inherited wealth. They feel betrayed and cheated when they think that the ladder has been pulled up. They feel even more estranged from the American ideology when they conclude that their government has played an active role in making income and wealth cumulatively greater over time.

The State is believed to have unleashed the Gini. Stiglitz says that marginal influence and not just marginal productivity has been stamping its name on who has what. So does Piketty: 'The history of the distribution of wealth has always been deeply political, and it cannot be reduced to purely economic mechanisms' (Piketty, 2014: 21). The explanation is to be sought in politics even more than in economics. There are man-made multipliers wherever you look. The top rates of income tax have been reduced. Exemptions from capital gains and estate duty have been increased. Concessions have been granted to rent-seekers who donate generously to the ruling party. Public spending on welfare has been cut because the poor have only themselves to blame.

If Stiglitz and Piketty are right, then the politics of inequitable distance and perceived partiality is cultivating its own nemesis. The 99 per cent are suffering from 'political alienation and a sense of disempowerment and disillusionment' (Stiglitz, 2012: 131). They feel aggrieved that their representatives are speaking not for the great majority but for the top 1 per cent who have an Apartheid-like American Dream of their own. Stiglitz and Piketty warn that a market economy in alliance with a democratic State is not sustainable so long as the great majority believes it is being fobbed off with trivialities and tokenism.

Government can be the cause and effect of separation. It need not be so. Government can also be the fair-minded arbiter that is seen to defend the interests of the 100 per cent as a whole. If pecuniary inequalities are man-made and economically in excess of function, if social distance truly is gnawing away at the nation's health stock, then the government could become involved in taking in the slack.

Facial justice or social justice, the time-honoured route has been fiscal discrimination. The top can be levelled down through progressive taxes on income, property and intergenerational transfers. The bottom can be levelled up through a citizenship wage paid in cultural centres, buses and empowering services like comprehensive education. If it is feeling poor that is causing the heart attacks, then perhaps the answer is for the mansions to be squeezed until even the king has to cycle in to work: 'If everyone is poor ... then no one is' (Sapolsky, 2004: 373).

Governments that raise up the bottom and pull down the top are resettling 'a man's a man for a' that' on the common ground where there is neither conspicuous luxury nor manifest neglect. The movement towards the middle recalls Plato's jeremiad that excessive dispersion is incompatible with active citizenship. Plato believed that 'equality gives birth to friendship' (Plato, 1961 [c.348 BC]: 1137). Extreme opulence side by side with extreme deprivation did not. Putting Athens above the Athenians, he therefore recommended that the wealth gap separating the plutocrats from the peasants should not exceed a multiple of four to one (ibid.: 1329). Beyond that the surplus should be confiscated by the State in order to wash away any trace of Bad Egg. Collectivisation would be an investment in social capital and perceived integration. It would be entirely plus-sum. What more pleasure can a millionaire have than to know that his priceless porcelains are on display even to factory workers and plumbers' mates in his British Museum?

It is all very confusing. On the one hand there is malevolence and jealousy. The moral response to feelings of personal inadequacy and low self-esteem will not necessarily be to chop down the tall trees that are cornering the admiration. On the other hand there is perceived injustice and the bitter cry of equals robbed. The hospital drip may be the last refuge of the dispossessed once privatisation has deprived them of their citizenship commons. On the one hand it is the politics of envy. On the other hand it is the politics of equity. Democracy must be in tune with the consensus. Yet minority rights must be respected as well. Plumbers' mates are a minority. Millionaires are a minority. We are all the 1 per cent some of the time.

The government can strike at psychosomatic illness by squeezing the rich until the pips squeak. Whether it will be successful in squeezing out invidious comparison is more debatable. Widening reference groups and narrowing differentials may actually make the psychic wear-and-tear worse. Designer labels and positional consumption will not disappear once the tall trees have been pollarded. So long as people measure their relative success in terms of flagrant self-advertisement, they will never get themselves off the gin and the antipsychotics.

Economic growth will not get soul in shape. Yet there is a sense in which the shifting frontier may nonetheless be taking the edge off the resented relativities. The Preston Curve shows that the lifespan of the rich, although still greater than that of the poor, has been increasing at a slower rate. The mortality Gini has been going down at the same time that the income Gini has been going up. In this way economic growth has had a levelling impact: 'The changes in life expectancy represent not only a gain in welfare, by extending life on average, but have also contributed greatly to social equality' (Peltzman, 2009: 181). Money is fool's gold. Health is real wealth. Mortality and mortality are sugaring the pill. They are diluting the poison of Bad Egg.

13.5.2 Power and Control

Many are the cogs in the wheel who have to do as they are told. Their loss of operational latitude is a threat to their health. Marmot and his collaborators documented 'a steep inverse association' (Marmot and Theorell, 1988: 661) in the British civil service between coronary heart disease and the office-holders' location in the organisational chart.

Comparing top with bottom, fatal heart attacks, age-adjusted, stood in the ratio of 1:4. Achievable life lost at the bottom was approximately seven years. Morbidity was extra. Men in the lower grades took seven times more sick days than men in the higher grades. It is vertical inequality within a single hierarchy. The employer was the same. The hearts were not.

The lower grades were several times more likely to die prematurely. The higher grades, pressured and exposed as they were, had more discretion, more security, more variety in their daily tasks, more impact on their working environment, more control over their time management, more opportunity to learn new skills. They had more flexibility, more autonomy, more challenge, more power over others. It was their unspoiled identity that was keeping them alive despite the volume of work they had to get through and the tight deadlines they had to meet. Active functioning was the antidote to overload.

The higher grades had the freedom to choose. Freedom was defusing the negativity: 'Acute stress in such contexts provides challenges which often will be exciting, stimulating and, after the event, emotionally and intellectually satisfying' (Brunner and Marmot, 1999: 26). The lower grades, passive and invisible, were the ones who were the most at risk. Educated enough to expect to be consulted, insignificant enough to be treated as interchangeable parts, the order-executing grades were the ones most likely to be experiencing psychosocial symptoms brought on by monotonous work and the lack of support.

As many as 23 per cent of the clerical officers relied on cigarettes to get them through the day. They chain-smoked because they were overlooked, ignored, unpromotable, unsackable and stuck: 'Giving up smoking is easier when your self-esteem is high, you feel optimistic about life and you feel in control' (Wilkinson, 1996: 185). Fully 45 per cent of the lower grades (as opposed to 26 per cent of the higher ones) preferred an inactive to an active use of leisure. They watched soaps and television sports. They had fewer contacts with family and friends. They relied on comfort antidepressants like sweets. They put sugar in their caffeine. They were more likely to say that they 'see little purpose in life'. Marmot's Whitehall studies showed that 9 per cent of males in the highest occupational group had symptoms of depression. In the lowest occupational group it was 22 per cent.

Depression and obesity were the consequence and not the cause of their emptiness at work. Their American counterparts were just as down: 'Increasing levels of occupational prestige are associated with decreasing levels of depressive symptoms and decreasing rates of major depressive disorder ... The lowest stress levels [are] found in the highest occupational category' (Turner et al., 1995: 109–10, 114).

Financially speaking, the middle and lower grades were not absolutely deprived. Insufficient income was not the cause of poor health. They could afford decent food. They had job security. They had access to health care. They were seldom labouring to exhaustion. They were not practicing *karoshi*, which in Japan means death by overwork. Unlike the *salarymen* they were taking regular holidays. Although they had fewer employment or housing choices, they were not trapped. They were not ordinarily at physical risk. Life was good. The mind, however, is refractory to such Polyanna-ing. The fact is that relativities, subordination and hamster-wheel tedium at the place of work seem to have turned them against themselves. Their innate sense of fairness had been assaulted. It was sickening their minds and shortening their lives.

Rank rankles. Their peace of mind was being disturbed not so much by the pay differentials or the task-specific strain as by the power imbalance. The association is in line with Karasek's contention that is anger and exclusion more the physical stress experienced by a bus driver navigating rush-hour traffic that is doing the harm: 'Constraints on decision making, not decision making per se, are the major problem' (Karasek, 1979: 303).

Whitehall was bad for their health. The road to the operating theatre was paved with neuroendocrine pathways and biochemical reactions that link psychological stimuli to physiological responses. Structured dominance, musical chairs, the rat race and the pecking order trigger the release of adrenelin, cortisol and other hormones that raise blood pressure and put a strain on the heart. In small doses the fight-or-flight reflex will save the life of a zebra that spots a lion. Taken to excess, allostatic overload can lead to rheumatoid arthritis, diabetes and myocardial infarction: 'Chronic or repeated stressors make you sick' (Sapolsky, 2004: 16). Continuous fight-or-flight is Pavlovian and it is dangerous. Zebras do not get ulcers. Civil servants do.

Low-ranking baboons have few predators to fear. They have a plentiful supply of food. They consume no alcohol or cigarettes. They work no more than four hours a day. In spite of that, they suffer from high blood pressure. The reason is unequal standing and stratified control. Radical loss of confidence and the mortification of humiliating failure are the sand in the wheels that is weakening their immune system. Relative place is leaving its mark on disease: 'If you cling to the lowest rungs of the socioeconomic ladder, it can mean ... a five- to ten-year discrepancy in life expectancy' (Sapolsky, 2004: 367).

Poor health is a social phenomenon. Inequality, Wilkinson says, is unnatural to the human condition. Because the food chain shortens life rather than extending it, the shaming set pieces of repression, conflict and submission are out of keeping with the thrust of evolution. No one wants to see himself as a rejected second-rater who could not make the grade:

> To feel depressed, cheated, bitter, desperate, vulnerable, frightened, angry, worried about debts or job and housing insecurity; to feel devalued, useless, helpless, uncared for, hopeless, isolated, anxious and a failure: these feelings can dominate people's whole experience of life, colouring their experience of everything else. It is the chronic stress arising from feelings like these which does the damage ... Psychosocial stress can kill. (Wilkinson, 1996: 175, 215)

Psychosocial stress can kill. If it is the relativities that are costing the life-years, the inference would be that all the occupational groups stand to make a health-related gain from a narrowing in the power imbalance: 'Reducing inequality would increase the wellbeing and quality of life for all of us' (Wilkinson and Pickett, 2009: 33). Wilkinson believes that inequality is socially corrosive. The imbalance in power and control, he says, is eating away at the health status of the nation. It is doing the most harm to the health status of the least advantaged who are the most commodified and the most stifled by social competition.

The cause is power. The antidote is power-sharing. Bottom-up consultation and self-governing teamwork might be a superior alternative to the emergency clinic where the insecure, the insulted and the unfulfilled might otherwise go to be patched up. Nor will the doctors and the nurses ever be able to medicalise the cure:

> If the experience in Britain is a guide, even the achievement of universal access to medical care would not substantially reduce socio-economic differences in health and disease ... The determinants of inequalities in health lay elsewhere ... Attention must be paid to the circumstances in which people live and work. (Marmot et al., 1997: 901, 908)

Medicine is the superstructure. The economic basis is the foundation upon which the shaky palliatives must build.

Social epidemiology is national even as it is microscopic. Democracy exists because citizens do not like to be oppressed. The more responsive the leadership, the higher the level of health: 'Life expectancy was higher in democratically governed states than in authoritarian states throughout the 20th century' (Mackenbach, 2013: 143). Health and politics moved in step. Yet other things moved as well. Life-expectancy is not the only indicator and politics is not the only cause. Command societies may have been economically less developed than more consultative ones: poverty as well as power has an impact on health. Right-wing and left-wing autocracies will differ qualitatively in their Ministry of Health: a military junta is not the dictatorship of the proletariat. While it may be true that 'wealthy countries rarely evolve to become authoritarian states' (Muntaner, 2013: 110), morbidity and mortality are more difficult to weave into the political skein.

Aetiology is not easy to penetrate. Taken at face value, however, the link between health and control is likely to be the same link whether it is a national or a microscopic link. Basically, the position is this. If the boss is less bossy, the followers will live longer and feel more welcome in the organism of which they are a part.

13.5.3 Social Integration

The common culture is more than the common health. The good society does not stop short at prevention and cure. Yet social connectedness for all that is a topic in the health status production function. Communities promote mental and physical well-being. Tönnies's (2001 [1887]) *Gemeinschaft* and Putnam's (1995) social networks, free education for citizenship and Keynesian full employment make a social-ist contribution to the general perception that the citizens are all parts one of another. It was this sense of equal exposure to an enemy shared that made Buckingham Palace and the depressed East End of London stand as one when the bombings and the Blitz began. Resilience in the whole was resilience in the part. The part became stronger and healthier because it had found a homeland in the whole.

The Second World War, Titmuss writes, was an exercise in social engineering and nation-building. It was a cobweb of overlapping experience and team spirit. It bred a social valuation of belonging, cohesion, interaction, esteem, self-esteem, inclusion, camaraderie and unity which set limits to health-sapping individualism and the rationally marketeering mindset:

> The civilian war of 1939–45, with its many opportunities for service in civil defence and other schemes, also helped to satisfy an often inarticulate need; the need to be a wanted member of society ... The absence of an increase in neurotic illness among the civilian population during the war was connected with the fact that to many people the war brought useful work and an opportunity to play an active part within the community. (Titmuss, 1950: 347)

A community integrated in war remained a community integrated in peace. The warfare State became the Welfare State. Money was invested in common services because the British people had developed a culture of togetherness and a pattern of mutual support. It was not inevitable.

History could, as Szreter and Woolcock report, easily have taken a different course: 'Where urban neighbourhoods and rural communities (and particular sub-populations) are demonstrably low in social capital, residents report higher levels of stress and isolation, children's welfare decreases, and there is a reduced capacity to respond to environmental health risks and to receive effective public health service interventions' (Szreter and Woolcock, 2004: 651).

Social capital is status as well as contract. Each person becomes another person's resource. Its material expression may be voluntary service in an old people's home, sequential contracting in a business relationship, or bowling in a sports club as a less reclusive, less companionless alternative to bowling alone. The ties that bind, emotional, practical, informational, financial, have a positive effect on physical health and subjective well-being: 'Marriage and family, ties to friends and neighbours, workplace ties, civic engagement (both individually and collectively), trustworthiness and trust: all appear independently and robustly related to happiness and life satisfaction, both directly and through their impact on health' (Helliwell and Putnam, 2004: 1444).

Physical health, self-reported, is improved by social capital and involvement with others: 'All forms of social connectedness have strong positive effects on physical health' (Helliwell and Putnam, 2004: 1443). No doubt there are dis-welfares too: 'The most common things which friends share or give each other are cigarettes, alcoholic drinks, and the proverbial "cup of sugar" ... not to mention AIDS. Hardly a recipe for good health!' (Wilkinson, 1999: 261). On balance, however, it appears to be the case that people cushioned by a dense network of social connections and interpersonal support are less likely to experience excess morbidity and mortality. Integration can prolong life. Isolation can bring it prematurely to an end. Anomic suicide occurs because people are alone (Durkheim, 1952 [1897]).

Prima facie it is not an argument for the State. If informal networks can spontaneously foster trust and promote cooperation, then the State is less necessary because the pieces of the puzzle are finding their own way into place. Yet there may be a role nonetheless for a third party in inculcating the communitarian values that over time will become self-sustaining. It might be a *deus ex machina* like a war. It might also be the pump-priming impetus of comprehensive education, a common health service and peacetime conscription.

State intervention can be the precondition for devolution and decentralisation. It need not be top-down crowding-out that leaves no room for self-help and good-neighbourliness. It might be no more than the initial nudge that releases the latent momentum of self-sustained participation.

Involvement and volunteering have unexpected consequences. They may in the end be the antidote to migraine, cirrhosis, insomnia and heart attacks among civil servants, because heartless Whitehall is indifferent to what they have to share.

14. Equalising medical care

There is more to good health than formal care. Marked inequalities in health status

> are caused by the unequal distribution of power, income, goods, and services, globally and nationally, the consequent unfairness in the immediate, visible circumstances of peoples' lives – their access to health care, schools, and education, their conditions of work and leisure, their homes, communities, towns, or cities – and their chances of leading a flourishing life. (World Health Organization, 2008: 1)

The social gradient is always multidimensional. It is often unjust. The structural conditions of daily life and not the formal care inputs alone must all be thrown into the melting pot if a more equal society is to be forged.

A holistic approach is required that does not economise on the homes and the jobs. There is more to good health than uncaring economics, biased politics and medical solutions that are not enough to equalise the life-chances in illness and death. The health divide 'appears to have little to do with differences in health care systems. For example, the mortality differentials for the United States, which favors market-based health care (at least for the non-elderly), and Austria, where the government provides universal health care, are virtually identical' (Cutler et al., 2011b: 124). The same comparison may be made between the United States and England: 'Despite the universal health cover provided by the NHS [National Health Service] in England, its income gradient in health appears similar to that of the United States, where health care access is very uneven' (Martinson, 2012: 2054). Yet that is no reason to be complacent about the unequal sharing-out of scarce health care resources. The four sections of this chapter, 'Payment', 'Regulating the rules', 'The doctors and levelling up' and 'Proportionate universalism', explain what more can be done.

14.1 PAYMENT

Effective demand builds barriers that can keep equal citizens out. Bad risks might not be able to obtain private insurance. They might have to cover medical costs out of pocket. Where applicants do qualify, the premiums, co-payments, deductibles, prescriptions and top-ups are a discriminatory deterrent that is more likely to price the less affluent out of the demand curve. In the historic year of 2010, almost 20 per cent of insured adults under 65 in the United States were devoting more than 10 per cent of their total family income to premiums and add-ons (Department of Health and Human Services, 2015: 239). Individuals with private non-group insurance were the hardest hit.

Neoclassical economists interpret the demand curve as a single person's locus of expected satisfactions. A higher price per orange means that Jack will buy fewer oranges. Social economists see the demand curve as a queue and a procession. A higher price per orange means that no fewer oranges will be bought by Jack but that no oranges at all will be bought by Jill: 'For instance, a small fall in the price of hats or watches will not affect the action of every one; but it will induce a few persons, who were in doubt whether or not to get a new hat or a new watch, to decide in favour of doing so' (Marshall, 1949 [1890]: 83). Jill is forced by her economic circumstances to drop out of the market. Jill has not been elbowed out or crowded out. Jill has been priced out. Rationing is not just 'how much' but 'for whom'.

An equal charge is not an equal disincentive. That, as Beck established in his study of a small change in Saskatchewan, is in itself a reason for not raising the bar: 'The impact upon the poor ... is considerably greater than the reduction of service experienced by the entire population, which has been estimated at 6 to 7 per cent' (Beck, 1974: 140). The impact overall was 6 to 7 per cent. The impact on those below the national poverty line was 18 per cent. Even a very low charge of $1.50 for office visits led to a reduction of 14 per cent in the number of times the poor saw their general practitioners.

There may have been some overutilisation before the moral hazard was weeded out, and perhaps even some malingering through bogus requests for sick-notes. It is true by definition that Bad Samaritans can deplete the patrimony of the genuinely in need. A less Hobbesian reaction would, however, be that a health care system cannot be said to be protecting the national health where tuberculosis, glaucoma or fluid build-up in the inner ear are escaping timely detection because of an economic disincentive that is disproportionately a deterrent to the hand-to-mouth. No one welcomes the premature death from diphtheria or typhoid of a child whose parents could not afford to pay.

Public policy must steer a middle course between the Bad Samaritans and the premature deaths. Means-testing is sometimes believed to be a reasonable compromise. Then at least no one would be denied basic services because they could not pay.

The judgemental and the achievement-centred will insist that the basic standard should be set at the irreducible minimum. Higher taxes to pay for the dependent discourage the independent from doing their best. Free medical care meets a need that would otherwise have been satisfied by upward social mobility. Only failures expect charity to pick up the pieces. The concerned and the accepting, on the other hand, will argue that too little generosity is a greater shortcoming than too much feather-bedding. The economically disadvantaged should not be sent away with a pill and a promise. Instead, the fringes should be integrated into the common health culture that comes from and reinforces the bonds of community.

Means-testing in a system that is preponderantly private can take the form of price discrimination. Applying different scales for different income groups, waiving the fees where the patient is obviously down-at-heel, writing off bad debt as an unavoidable fact of life, the doctor or hospital is in effect performing its own cross-subsidisation of the needy. Different prices for different people only make sense where the services do not lend themselves to transfer, arbitrage or resale. While pharmaceuticals and appliances may be the exception, most medical services do tend to remain with the body-holder who experiences the intervention.

An alternative would be for the market sector to charge all patients the going rate but for the State to co-pay the bills of the most deprived. A trusting State will pay the cash directly to the patient on the assumption that even the poverty-stricken know what they need. A leaderly State, more proactive, will either settle the debt directly or employ the 'yes, but' middle way of earmarked vouchers. Vouchers are non-fungible coupons that can only be encashed for health and only at an approved outlet. Choosing only between the predigested alternatives, the consumer does not enjoy the unbounded autonomy of a full-blooded king. What they do have is the dignity of a constitutional monarch. Perhaps that is all that they want.

In the United States the government's Medicare, introduced in 1965, is not means-tested. The only criterion is that the recipient should be in the commercially unattractive age range of 65 and above. The elderly aside, income supplementation for health tends most definitely to reflect the inability to pay. Parents wishing to enrol their family in the Children's Health Insurance Program (CHIP) must be able to prove that their income hovers around the Medicaid line. Poor people wishing to access near-free Medicaid attention must be able to show that their income is no more than 138 per cent of the official poverty line. The cut-off is deliberately kept low. Individuals just above the threshold are on their own.

Before 2010 the rule was that single people and adult couples without dependent children were not eligible for Medicaid unless they were seriously disabled. Since 2010 all Americans who pass the means test have been able to apply. Cost-sharing is modest and there are no premiums. Yet income is a stumbling block. The working poor and the unemployed may have assets which disqualify them from the safety net. Besides that, inclusion or exclusion turn on an either/or. The unemployed may be afraid to take a job lest, in the absence of a sliding scale, they lose the whole of their entitlement at a stroke.

Means-testing can be as programme-specific as the Medicaid cut-off. It can also be as general as taxes and contributions. The overall incidence of direct and indirect tax, as was brought out in Chapter 9, is far from clear. Flat-rate subscriptions to a national insurance fund at any rate will be unambiguously regressive. The poor will be devoting a higher proportion of a lower income to a national health system that is free for all at the point of consumption.

Equal contributions are not equal burdens unless public policy builds in an element of pro-poor discrimination. One option would be to earnings-link the social contributions on the model of the personal income tax. Progressive banding would ensure that the rich pay more for what would remain an identical citizenship right. Another possibility would be the suppression of tax relief for private insurance. Levelling down, it would equalise citizens' access to *de facto* State support.

Indirect taxes could be zero-rated for the essential complements to good health. The sweat shop stiff would obtain their vitamins and their prunes tax-free. The same, of course, would be true of the sabretoothed wheeler-dealer on their way to the bank. Zero-rating treats the long-term unemployed and the property speculator as equal citizens with an equal right. It upgrades but it does not equalise. If the aim is to narrow the gap, then there is no alternative but selectivity in the shops. Value-added tax can be rebated to the mean but not to the posh. There is stigma in applying for and displaying a certificate of poverty; and the administrative overheads would keep an army of civil servants in work. But it could be done.

14.2 REGULATING THE RULES

It is not a question of the market versus the State. Sometimes it is enough for the State to regulate the market but not to take its place. Not substitutes but complements, sometimes good rules are the oil that makes an immobile chassis into a means of transport. Bad rules do the opposite. Few topics in political economy are more important than the normative environment within which supply and demand do their job.

14.2.1 Mandatory Insurance

The private sector can turn down bad risks, charge them prohibitive premiums or restrict their cover. Where they are not blanketed in by an occupational plan the excluded who cannot obtain or cannot afford free-market policies will have to pay out of pocket or do without. About 40 per cent of uninsured Americans have unpaid medical bills. Medical debt contributes to almost half of all bankruptcies in the United States. It must be a cause of considerable anxiety to have that volume of debt and still not be able to pay for necessary tests and procedures. Some will lose their homes. Some will lose their lives.

Historically, before the Patient Protection and Affordable Care Act in 2010, as many as 50 million Americans had no health insurance. It was about 15 per cent of the population. Particularly vulnerable were the unemployed, the freelance, the part-time, the low-paid just above the Medicaid floor, the late-middle-aged not yet old enough for Medicare. About a third of uninsured adults were skimping even on necessary attention. Hospital bills were the worst. The government estimated that the uninsured could afford to pay for no more than 12 per cent of their inpatient episodes (Department of Health and Human Services, 2015: 239). Insurance companies can negotiate discounts from all but the most prestigious hospitals. The uninsured are more likely to pay the rack rent.

Low-income Americans were four times as likely as high-income Americans to be without health insurance. There was a strong correlation with the ability to pay. About 61 per cent of uninsured adults told the Kaiser Commission that they had no health insurance because of the cost (Kaiser Commission, 2014).

The ability to pay was a barrier. The willingness to pay was, however, a choice. Some firms did not offer an occupational plan because they were small, new, family-run, on tight margins, squeezed by cutthroat competitors. Employees who took jobs in firms such as these did so because of compensating advantages such as high pay, job satisfaction, a blood link or a convenient location. Some liked the challenge of an entrepreneurial start-up that could become the next big thing. Taking a job without an occupational plan, they were revealing their preference. They were voting with their feet. They were saying that insurance to them was not the deal-maker.

Some could have applied for an individual plan on their own. Many made a conscious decision not to do so. Bundorf and Pauly found that no more than 0.36 per cent of Americans without health insurance were genuinely uninsurable. They also found that fully 30 per cent of uninsured adults had household incomes at least 300 percent above the poverty line (Bundorf and Pauly, 2006: 664).

While a third of the uninsured in America had incomes of $20 000 or less, 28 per cent breached the $50 000 mark (Gruber, 2008: 586). Between 25 per cent and 75 per cent of the uninsured were affluent enough to pay. The fact that they chose to remain uninsured lifts the curtain on their ranking scheme. They could have put their money into a merit good that would have alleviated their uncertainty. Instead they splashed out on gourmet meals and a cruise. There is no accounting for tastes. That is the way it is.

Affordability is not always the barrier that it seems. Even if it were, there is always the expectation that growth in living standards will bring health insurance within almost all the choice sets. In the short run the left-out will have the fall-back of Medicaid. In the long run they will be able to make their own choice. Some will buy health insurance. Some will not. People who are sane and over 21 generally value the freedom to choose for themselves.

Before 2010 the rules in America were generally in line with the freedom of choice. In 2010 the old rules gave way to the new. The Patient Protection and Affordable Care Act in 2010 required Americans not already protected by an occupational plan to take out private cover on their own. Companies with more than 50 employees were mandated to provide at least a basic package. Insurers were prohibited from imposing annual or lifetime caps. Premiums were made community-rated. They could no longer be shaded by age, gender, pre-existent condition or geographical location.

The government was regulating the rules but not running the shop. It was not national health insurance. In spite of that, the new system was a drain on public finance. The law specified that even the deprived had to pay their premiums. Where they could not afford to do so, the State committed itself to subsidise the invisible hand. Unlike Medicaid, it uses a sliding scale. The grant-in-aid only cuts off when the family income is four times the national poverty level. So respectable an entitlement cannot be called a workhouse test. About half the Americans buying private plans before 2010 became eligible for full or partial support.

Compulsory health insurance is a drain on the State where the State tops up the premiums of the deprived. Cutler estimated that it might cost the American government as much as $20 billion to buy the needy into private plans. While $20 billion is not a small sum, it would, Cutler said, be money well spent. The economic value of the life-years saved sums up to $33 billion. The quality of life purchased through better care would make the figure greater still. In other words: 'For every dollar spent, the benefits would be $1.50. There is thus an economic, as well as moral, case for universal insurance coverage' (Cutler, 2004: 65, 66).

Proper care saves lives: 'Uninsured individuals use only half as much medical care as the insured, and have a mortality risk that is 25 per cent higher, with over 18,000 people dying each year because of lack of insurance' (Gruber, 2008: 582). More Americans die each year from lack of health insurance than from kidney disease: 'Lack of health insurance is associated with as many as 44,789 deaths per year in the United States' (Wilper et al., 2009: 2294). Americans work hard and play hard. It is an alarming waste both of productive potential and of *joie de vivre* when 44 789 of them pass over before their time.

The introduction of national health insurance in Canada was associated with a 4 per cent decline in the infant mortality rate. It was associated with an 8.9 per cent decline in the incidence of low-birthweight babies among single mothers. Fiscal cuts and a reduction in entitlements have the opposite effect. Austerity is short-sighted where the axe falls on high-potential beneficiaries like children whose life-course is steered onto a reef.

The uninsured in the United States are less likely to be formally diagnosed with depression. They are less likely to have had a recent cholesterol test, to have had their blood pressure checked, to have been prescribed an anti-hypertensive drug. The uninsured have fewer and shorter consultations. The doctors they see will be less qualified and less experienced. Serious conditions are less likely to be detected at an early stage. They will not be offered a free intrauterine device (IUD) when at $800 the IUD would cost far less than a free Medicaid birth at US$13 000. The uninsured are on average less healthy than the insured. In spite of that they receive less care. The bill mounts up.

Hadley found for the United States that the uninsured were from 29 per cent (coronary artery bypass surgery) to 75 per cent (total knee replacement) less likely than the insured to receive expensive medical procedures (Hadley et al., 1991: 374, 377). Infant mortality rates among the uninsured were 40 per cent higher. Trauma patients without insurance were significantly less likely to have an operative procedure and 2.15 times more likely to die in hospital. Heart patients without insurance were 14 to 43 per cent less likely to receive arteriography, coronary bypass or angiography. For children, referral delay to a paediatric cardiologist was twice as long (Hadley, 2003: 41S, 43S, 48S). Delay costs money. Timely care saves lives.

Apart from the life-years and the quality of life, there is also the neighbourhood spillover. Without universal protection, communicable disease can spread. Whether this is an argument for mandatory insurance or simply mandatory vaccination, what is clear is that intervention costs money. Just as the recipients cannot be allowed to spend cash transfers on Sirens rather than treatments, so the taxpayers cannot opt out of their contributions in the expectation that their fellow citizens will altruistically satisfy the medical needs of the Atomic Bum. Compulsion by consent ensures that the rights and duties will be aligned. The rules in that sense are another name for freedom. Without the rules the pieces would not fall into place.

14.2.2 Culture and Compulsion

Perceptions vary with the median ideology of the nation in which they are embedded. The cultural resistance to mandates and subsidies varies from country to country. There are few universal propositions and even fewer eternal truths in public policy.

Thus the United States has a folk memory of personal responsibility. The American Dream colours its reaction to top-down government, up and doing. One study established that only 23 per cent of Americans agreed with the proposition that 'It is the responsibility of the government to take care of the very poor people who can't take care of themselves' (Rice, 2001: 32). Matter is curiously out of step with mind. The government has somehow become the largest single health insurer in the United States. Medicaid accounts for 15 per cent of national health expenditure and Medicare for 20 per cent. Other public projects are a further 7 per cent. Together the public involvement sums up to 42 per cent. Private health insurance reimburses only 33 per cent of the total (Moses et al., 2013: 1952).

Even so, the numbers in other countries are higher than the Americans' 42 per cent: 50 per cent in Germany, 56 per cent in Poland, 62 per cent in Britain and France, 66 per cent in Italy, and 71 per cent in Spain. The citizenship wage is alive and well in solidaristic Europe. It is a commitment to medical care. Social levelling is a different matter. Asked whether it is the mission of the NHS to knock the sharp edges off the distribution of income, three-fifths of British respondents said it was not. They felt that a health service should confine itself to good health alone (House of Commons Health Committee, 2009: 41). Three-fifths of British respondents reiterated that the government had a duty to level up the health status of the poor. As for income and wealth, the consensus was that the health service had more pressing concerns.

Absolute deprivation or relative deprivation, the 23 per cent in America compared with the three-fifths in Britain does indicate that the value systems are not the same. Commenting on the figures, Rice states that they

> graphically illustrate the very different social ethics that exist in the US vs. elsewhere. In a country like the US in which communitarian values are weak and markets are relied upon to distribute so-called 'merit goods' like health care, enacting reform like universal coverage is extraordinarily difficult. To do so it probably will be necessary for there to be a change in the prevailing social ethic, or – and this is perhaps the more likely route – to elect officials with this ethic who have the ability to pull the populace along with them. (Rice, 2001: 32)

It was not Attlee but the British social ethic that was responsible for the health care collectivism of the post-Dunkirk 1940s. In America the actualisation of Galbraithian social democracy would have to wait upon the charisma of John Kennedy or the single-mindedness of Barack Obama. Not least would this be so since not all Americans think alike. An early poll showed that 29 per cent of whites but 61 per cent of Hispanics and 91 per cent of blacks supported the 2010 Act. In terms of party politics, 11 per cent of the Republicans but 75 per cent of the Democrats were in favour (Pew Research Center, 2013). The President and Congress had to hammer consensus out of a multimodal distribution. After all the hammering the collective consciousness was still not there.

If the Americans feel as they do about compulsory private insurance, they are likely to be even more opposed to compulsory national health insurance, and still more so to free, non-exclusive medical services supplied directly by the State. The Patient Protection and Affordable Care Act is the gentler of the three slopes.

14.3 THE DOCTORS AND LEVELLING UP

It is normally the consumer who initiates the doctor–patient relationship. Since the lower-income groups have less information about the workings of the body than do the better-educated deciles, they are less likely to seek early diagnosis and treatment for asymptomatic or semi-asymptomatic conditions such as anaemia, colon cancer, high blood pressure or anal-retentive obsessiveness. They are less likely to recognise the hidden killers signposted by sudden weight loss, breathlessness or an unexpected faint. They are less likely to know about preventive injections or to demand a specific drug which was recommended in the press.

The lower-income groups are less likely to ask probing questions, to want longer consultations, to stand up to a middle-class professional, to call for a second opinion, to insist by name on a test or service, to appeal against a refusal: 'By virtue of their education, articulacy and general self-confidence, the better off may simply be better at persuading GPs that their needs can only be properly addressed by specialist services' (Dixon et al., 2007: 108). A stratified community produces a segregated demand function. Different groups make different requests. They end up with different services. They impose different costs.

Educational upgrading will help to equalise the knowledge stock. The spread of white-collar employment and middle-class culture will narrow the gap between those who demand explanations and those who do as they are told. Economic development is on the side of lifestyle convergence. Yet there will often be a need for the medical gatekeepers to take the lead if *de jure* access is to become *de facto* take-up. The suppression of the price deterrent by itself is not enough.

That is why it might actually be desirable for a proactive supplier to induce the demand. Patients' free choice can damage their health. At-risk occupational groups could be called in for a chest X-ray. All females in the target age-group could be offered a routine smear or a free mammogram. Old people living alone could be seen at least twice a year in their home or in the office. All children at school could be given comprehensive medical and dental check-ups.

Computers will facilitate the triage. Risk factors such as obesity, smoking, diet deficiencies, lack of exercise, irregular heartbeat, abnormal glucose can all be registered. They can be monitored before they lead to diabetes or a bypass. A centralised database can be used to identify those patients most likely to benefit from preventive and not just curative care. It is proactive universalism and it is patient-specific. Technology can cross-correlate the danger signs. It can calibrate the urgency of the need.

The doctors can invite. What is less certain is how the at-risk will respond. The health-deprived might not accept that the wild card of better health will compensate them for the inconvenience, the time lost and the discomfort that is the non-pecuniary price of a precautionary test. The health-conscious, accustomed to accumulating health capital, are less likely to fall through the net. Universalism is not needed for them to go on statins and aspirins in their middle years. It is a familiar pattern. A proactive health policy might have the unintended consequence of raising the average but still not reducing the amplitude. The gap might become greater.

The take-up can be addressed on the side of demand by making the visits and the tests mandatory, or by repaying voluntary walk-ins with priority points for public housing or a popular school. On the side of supply, the latent demand can be tapped through greater access to women doctors, doctors who were born working class and doctors from ethnic or religious minorities. Such pluralisation would ensure that patients had the chance to consult a medical professional who has an adequate overview of their subcultural baggage.

It can also protect them from racial discrimination and racial stereotyping. No sick person wants to be undermedicated because of his dreadlocks or her *hijab*. Nor do they want to be overmedicated because home-grown professionals mistake them for mad. Black inpatients in mental hospitals are four times as likely as whites to have been compulsorily admitted (Boyle, 2011: 325). The cues, the codes and the non-verbal language are not easy for an outsider to interpret.

Subcultures differ in their family networks, their interpretation of the sick role, their acculturated expectations of the doctor–patient dialogue. Koreans in New Zealand expect the doctor to be authoritative and decisive. They describe a doctor who hesitates as 'stupid' (Lee et al., 2010: 109). Subcultures do not all experience the same conditions. Afro-Caribbeans present with sickle-cell anaemia, Mediterraneans with thalassaemia, Ashkenazi Jews with Tay-Sachs Disease. They do not all have the same diet. Phytates in chapattis and tannin in tea can inhibit the absorption of vitamin D. Chapattis and tea can be the cause of iron-deficiency anaemia in lacto-vegetarian Indians.

Diet varies. So does language. Korean-American women who speak mainly Korean are given one-third fewer mammograms than Korean-American women who prefer to speak English (Department of Health and Human Services, 2015: 41). Professionals may find it difficult to empathise with the loneliness and confusion of a new-immigrant wife if she does not know English, is embarrassed by a physical examination and will not reveal what is wrong.

Multiculturalism is always bounded. At least 110 languages are spoken in the London borough of Tower Hamlets alone. There are at least as many cultures, subcultures and ways of life. No doctor can know everything about everyone. Respect for persons suggests nonetheless that all doctors in a rainbow society should know at least the basics about the exceptions.

14.4 PROPORTIONATE UNIVERSALISM

Marmot uses the phrase 'proportionate universalism' (Marmot and the Marmot Review Team, 2010) to encapsulate what Richard Titmuss described as 'positive discrimination without the infliction, actual or imagined, of a sense of personal failure and individual fault' (Titmuss, 1968: 135). All must share in the incremental endowment. Some, however, must be given a disproportionate share of the increase in order to bring their health status up to the national norm. It must be done without stigma. The heroes and the villains of the life-course are buried in an unmarked grave. We cannot go back. We can only go forward. We start from here.

14.4.1 Focusing the Increment

More beds and more doctors might not by themselves narrow the gap. Skewed marginalism within a broadly universalist system will be the plus-sum means to target the underprovided while not reducing the resources that reward and protect the health-conscious vanguard.

It would be a violation of equal respect if hospitals in the suburbs were to be closed in order that the bricks and mortar be freighted into the urban blight. It would be inconsistent with tolerance of diversity if the willing-to-pay were to be denied a private room, a convenient time or a branded drug merely because all sick people do not currently enjoy equal access to 'as much and as good'. Spiteful levelling down is not a good way of making equal citizens as equally healthy as they themselves would like to be. Constructive levelling up has the attraction that it is unashamedly plus-sum. Everyone gets more but the left-behind get even more still. They receive something extra in recognition of their special circumstances and of our expressed wish as a people that no one should fall short.

A personal means-test can single out and prioritise the most in-need. The byproduct of the fine-tuning is shame. Lone parents, the disabled, the old-elderly, the institutionalised, the long-term unemployed, the racially second-rate do not like to swear a poverty oath. They are embarrassed to state that they have failed the market test of earned livelihood. Geography is a less damaging heuristic. Underprovided areas flagged up by a national health map are given above-average funding. Poor areas stand in for poor people. No one's feelings are hurt. The downside is that maids in Beverley Hills are ranked with film stars who can afford to pay. That is the price of broad classification.

Travel is a deterrent. Because of the spatial concentration of supply, and because poor people are less likely to have a car, the fares and the timings, the potholes and the monsoons can ration demand by paring down the deprived. Incremental funding might take the form of a minibus shuttle, internet consultations, mobile mammography, dentistry units that travel out to areas of need. In the limit there are flying paramedics when the next big town is simply too far.

Subsidised or concessionary public transport would give the poor, the elderly and the disabled more choices in shopping and socialising as well as better access to medical services. Even if transport is cheap, still time costs lives: 'Increased distance to the nearest hospital is associated with higher mortality counts from emergent conditions, such as heart attacks and possibly from unintentional injuries' (Buchmueller et al., 2005: 759). A 1 mile increase in distance to the nearest trauma or emergency centre leads, in the United States, to a 6.5 per cent increase in deaths from cardiac arrest and up to a 20 per cent increase in deaths from injuries. Location matters. Sometimes the train is not quick enough. The 'golden hour' cannot be renewed.

The margin is clear. New hospitals should be constructed in under-bedded areas. Additional doctors should be recruited into underdoctored catchments. The economic solution would be differential capitations, tax exemptions and regional salary scales proportioned to the local parameters of supply and demand. The administrative solution would be manpower planning, compulsory posting and the bonding of medical students on scholarship to areas of red-button neglect. Assignment has the advantage over money that it can bring in a representative cross-section of professionals. The pecuniary incentive self-selects the most money-conscious. Some of them, already serving in another deprived area, may simply shift across for the bonus. It is only a net increase in the sense that it is a net increase in cost.

Medical education itself can increase the pool. A third of general practices in England and Wales have at least one vacancy. The poorer areas are even more desperate. The establishment of an outstanding medical school or teaching hospital in an underprovided area will increase the census of trained locals with personal knowledge of the turf. It will draw in family doctors and other professionals who will welcome the contact with colleagues, the in-service updating and the chance to participate in research. Better schools for their children and better policing to keep down crime would make it even more attractive for them to settle and stay.

Schools and policing widen the focus. It is an advantage of a national health service that it can coordinate its policies with social complements in order to ensure a minimum standard. A State system, collaborating with other ministries, can plan access on a countrywide basis. Still something is missing from the concerted campaign. The parallel sector, the private sector, is not a part of its unified net.

Rationing by price is an alternative currency. The affluent are better placed to avoid the queue by going private. They might drop out. Left to the invisible hand, the NHS might degenerate into a safety net for residuals who could not afford the inside track. If communitarian universalism is successfully to be combined with incremental discrimination, it is clear that the NHS must be made attractive to the poor and the prosperous alike. On top of care that is free at the point of consumption, there is a case for fixed appointments, house visits, evening and weekend clinics, widespread publicity so that local people can be made aware of what is available. So long as the convenience of the patient is not sacrificed to the throughput of the system, the affluent will join the national health service and will not drop out.

The prosperous must not be relegated to the footnotes and given the dregs. That way lies facial justice when the proper way is levelling up. At the margin, however, incremental resourcing should favour the backlog of uncorrected neglect. In this the wider welfare network will play an active role. Practice auxiliaries, volunteer translators and health visitors from a variety of backgrounds will provide support and counsel to the doctors and nurses. An integrated web of community complements will blend in the self-help groups, district nurses, accredited midwives, traditional midwives, child welfare officers, social workers, non-governmental organisations of all kinds. Non-medical professionals, visiting the hard-to-reach in their homes, will recognise the undetected pathologies simply by hearing about the symptoms, seeing the bruises, observing the baby-battering, spotting the dilated pupils and dodging the mice. The division of labour in this way helps to nip decay in the bud. Channels and funnels, complementing the coal face, play a part in assisting the self-effacing to gain a foothold in the system.

14.4.2 Targeting the Need

Targeting decomposes the macro-picture into its needs-based parts. Even if the global aggregate is flat-of-the-curve, a focused campaign might still be able to improve the health indicators. Rather than throwing money at an undifferentiated mass, it might be more health-effective to concentrate scarce resources on known medical needs. We are not all flat-of-the-curve.

Medicare guidelines specify an annual faecal blood test for colorectal cancer and an annual retinal eye examination for diagnosed diabetes. In spite of the benchmarks, Medicare enrollees receive in practice only 12 per cent and 45.3 per cent respectively of the Medicare services to which they are entitled (Wennberg and Cooper, 1999: 214, 215). The low reimbursement rate relative to the outside market meant that '17 per cent of doctors restricted the number of Medicare patients; among primary care physicians, a whopping 31 per cent did' (Goldman and Leive, 2013). Lower prices were the cause of neglect. The economics textbooks would make a comparison with rent controls which, they would warn, can decimate the housing stock.

Medicare, underfunded, is not living up to its promise. Medicaid too is stunted by an allocations constraint. A revaluation of the Medicaid minimum would save the lives of marginal newborns whose mothers would otherwise have been turned away: 'A 30-percentage-point increase in targeted eligibility would have been associated with an 11.5 percent decline in infant mortality' (Currie and Gruber, 1996: 1278). An 11.5 per cent decline cannot reasonably be described as flat-of-the-curve.

In Canada a 10 per cent increase in per capita medical spending was associated with a 0.4 to 0.5 per cent decrease in infant mortality (Hadley, 2003: 46S). A large number of Canadians alive today would have died as infants if their national health insurance had not treated them as an end in themselves. A borderline infant does, admittedly, put a strain on the budget. The price per infant life saved can be as high as $840 000. An infant life is a major expense.

One borderline infant costs far more than one child-year of schooling, more than one family-year on decent income maintenance. Economically speaking, it might not be a cost-effective purchase. In this case it is. Comparisons suggest that $840 000 is cheap at the price. Child-resistant cigarette lighters cost $3.15 million per child life saved, child restraint systems in cars $5.5 million, improvements in school bus safety in excess of $10 million. By that standard, borderline infants saved through Medicaid eligibility are a good buy. Equity and economics point in the same direction.

It is not always so. A society that can make 20 per cent on a new heart for a young executive would not be doing good business if it invested heavily in statistical loss-makers like underweight newborns who might not survive long enough for their payback: 'The introduction of the economic perspective leads to a quite different conclusion about the effects of neonatal intensive care than does consideration from a purely clinical perspective' (Boyle et al., 1983: 1335). It would be a waste of money to conduct a sixth stool test where the detection rate is only

0.0003 per 10 000 persons tested and the marginal cost per successful detection is $47 million (Neuhauser and Lewicki, 1975: 226). No one is worth $47 million. Economics is not a free good. For good economics the nation has to pay.

That is why macroeconomic policy must be handled with care. Although monetary and fiscal policy are public goods, available to all if they are available to any, they are also private bads. They are directional and finger-pointing even as they declare themselves to be impartial and even-handed. Libertarian monetarism in the 1980s set out to guarantee every American a stable cost of living. In doing so, austerity budgets had the unintended byproduct of starving the needy of their prenatal and neonatal care: 'The cutbacks coincided with a slowing in the decline of mortality rates, especially for blacks. For instance, from 1981 to 1982, the black neonatal mortality rate fell by 2.2 percent, and the white rate fell by 4.2 percent' (Corman et al., 1987: 340). Macroeconomic success rates fail to identify the black infants who without their incubators would not survive.

Demand-side policies seldom provide the exemptions and the escape clauses that would protect the victims of the nation's contrived disinflation. Policy cannot identify or insulate them. They are simply too numerous. The gradient becomes steeper and not flatter as a result. Expanding insurance coverage to the uninsured would reduce their mortality rate by 3.5 per cent to 7.5 per cent (Hadley, 2003: 62S). The reverse is also true. Cutting insurance coverage would for some be a sentence of death. Balancing the budget would be bad for their health.

Medical ethics says that a life in itself is always good. Economics says that some lives are cost-effective and some are low-return. Blacks earn less than whites. The unemployable earn nothing at all. Cash flow would be greater if the money were to be diverted to the mainstream while the forgotten were sentenced to remain forgotten because they had missed their sell-by date. Stalin sacrificed the *kulaks* to save the nation. It was a cost–benefit calculation. Altruists who are not prepared to throw excess baggage to the wolves will find their true vocation in the church. Stalin showed the way. Socialists and capitalists must follow where Stalin led. We are all economists nowadays.

15. The cost of care

The share of health care is rising. It is rising as a share of the domestic product, a share of total public spending and a share of the household budget. The phenomenon is across the board. It is happening in all countries, developed and developing alike.

Both the price tags and the units supplied have been going up. Prices have been the principal cause: 'Between 2000 and 2011, increase in price (particularly of drugs, medical devices, and hospital care), not intensity of service or demographic change, produced most of the increase in health's share of GDP [gross domestic product]' (Moses et al., 2013: 1949). The medical care consumer price index has 'outpaced general price inflation, in some cases substantially' (McGuire et al., 2012: 134). The unit price times the quantity supplied has had a tendency to escalate. Mainly because of the nominal variable but also because of the real magnitude, the health care sector, absolutely and relatively, is costing us more.

In America in 1950 total spending on health care was only 4.6 per cent of the gross domestic product. It is 18 per cent today. Health care in 1950 accounted for 3 per cent of the combined budget of the federal, state and local governments. Today, second only to defence, it has grown to 29 per cent. It is political economy as well as economics. A great deal of health-related spending is a charge on the State. Deficits have problems of their own.

In 1950 the typical American spent $500 on health care. Now it is $5615. Per capita personal income in the United States is $42 693. In 1950 it was $11 166. The typical American used to devote 4 per cent of their personal income to health. Now it is 13 per cent. It is serious money and a real threat. Health care is growing faster than the domestic product or income per capita. People want good health and good care. Yet they also want the other good things in life.

The concern is a general one. James Buchanan was speaking for many when he warned that the sorcerer's apprentice was slipping out of control:

> In the United States, a large and ever-increasing share of total economic value is directed toward outlay on medical or health care services ... It becomes

relatively easy to think of a share of one-quarter of the total value produced in the economy being devoted to medical and health care services ... The finitude of the resource base, the labor force and its complement of accumulated and natural capital, guarantees that the share of total value directed into medical services cannot continue to grow without limit. (Buchanan, 1990: 3, 10)

As much market failure as need satisfaction, the escalation of cost must be brought within the limits that the society believes to be appropriate.

This chapter is concerned with the escalation of cost. It provides the foundation for Chapters 16 and 17 on cost containment. The first three sections, 'Expenditure', 'Social trends' and 'Medicine: technology and structure', give the reasons for the rise. The fourth section, 'A fall in cost', is a reminder that some services are becoming more affordable even as others are threatening to break the bank.

15.1 EXPENDITURE

The countries with the best morbidity and mortality indicators are not the ones that put the most money per capita into care. The causal relationship between incremental spending and incremental health, at least for the richer countries, is loose and uncertain. But that is not the way that ordinary people see things. The vast majority of ordinary people regard money plunged into health as not the road to ruin but a characteristic of a civilisation that is getting its priorities right.

15.1.1 Income

In a poor country people commit their disposable income to basic necessities like food and shelter. Instead of seeing the doctor they rely on bed rest, herbs, traditional healers and over-the-counter medication. The body very often will return to normal given time. Where it does not, death is accepted as a fact of life. A higher level of pain is tolerated than would be the norm in a First World society. Psychoanalysis is not widely practised. Tranquillisers are not the first line of defence.

As the society becomes more affluent, people become better placed both to pay directly for care and to pay for health insurance that will share the expense. Rising incomes mean that anxious health-holders not only consult their doctor in an emergency but also can satisfy their precautionary demand for reassurance and early diagnosis. Even if corrective therapy will not be required, still they want the expert to tell them that they are in good health.

There is also a speculative demand. Rising real incomes mean that the consumer can chance a gamble. The likelihood of success may be low but the procedure of last resort may be all the hope that is left. It is more than idle curiosity. Learning the worst, the patients know that they can afford the cost of the sequence that comes next.

Ability to pay shifts the demand curve out. Rising affluence works against the disincentive of price. Richer people are willing and able to pay more for care. McGuire, surveying the evidence on the income elasticity of demand, reports 'a fairly accepted average elasticity at the aggregate level of around 1.3, implying that a 10 per cent increase in GDP will increase health expenditures by 13 per cent' (McGuire et al., 2012: 130).

Comparing the response over a cross-section of nations, Newhouse concluded that rising incomes account for about a quarter of the increase in real medical spending (Newhouse, 1992: 8). The link may be closer still. Parkin estimated that the income elasticity in the United States was 1.18. Looking back, he also found that changes in the domestic product could explain 87 per cent of the observed variance in medical spending (Parkin et al., 1987: 113).

15.1.2 Private Insurance

A rise in income facilitates more than the direct demand for care. Affluence is also associated with third-party payment, private and public. It is a smoking volcano. The price deterrent per intervention becomes the cost-share only and not the full marginal cost. If the co-payment is 10 per cent, it is the 10 per cent and not the 100 per cent that influences the quantity demanded.

The demand curve is not the true willingness to pay. Out-of-pocket spending in the United States accounts for only 11 per cent of total health expenditures. As recently as 1980 it was 23 per cent (Moses et al., 2013: 1949). In the case of inpatient care, it is 3 per cent. Financially at least, the system is responsible to pools and not to individuals. Prepayment and risk-sharing bring peace of mind. They are also contra-economic. The consumer with insurance is under no pressure to question whether the marginal utility is truly proportional to the full extra cost. The most expensive is also the cheapest where the consumer pays for an aspirin but not for magnetic resonance imaging (MRI).

Flat-of-the-curve medicine is made possible by a tap that is never turned off. The professional ethic is a mixed blessing. Where insurance automatically rubber-stamps the bill, there is no reason for the doctor to find out the true cost or to search for the best price. There is no reward for selecting a protocol which is economical as well as effective. There is no mechanism for standardising the practice variations. There is no incentive to incorporate the social spillovers as well as the private cost. There is no motive for the individual or the doctor to resist the temptations of moral hazard. Once in the club, it is the others who pay. Insurance, in short, is anti-economic. It is permissive toward the escalation in quantity and price.

More insurance means higher cost. Higher cost means more insurance. Martin Feldstein describes the vicious circle of defence and self-defence in the following way: 'For the community as a whole ... the spread of insurance causes higher prices and more sophisticated services which in turn cause a further increase in insurance. People spend more on health because they are insured and buy more insurance because of the high cost of health care' (Feldstein, 1973: 252). It is a ratchet effect. Marginal high-tech, low co-pays, supplier-induced demand and cost pass-through are laughing all the way to the bank.

Admittedly there is the rise in premiums when the policies come up for renewal. Manning and Marquis calculated that the price elasticity of demand for health insurance is –0.54 (Manning and Marquis, 1996: 629). When the price goes up by $1, the quantity demanded goes down by a moderate $0.54. It is positive but less than 1. Insurance is seen as necessary but not indispensable.

Limited responsiveness may reflect the institutional environment. Where the worker has contracted for an occupational plan the employer has limited freedom to curtail the benefit. An individual plan may be more sensitive to an increase in premiums. The annual premium for a family of four is not far different from the gross earnings of an American worker on the minimum wage. The worker does not have much room for manoeuvre when the numbers are so tight.

15.1.3 Social Insurance

Richer countries have more private insurance. They have more social insurance as well. The material and humanitarian externalities have increasingly been nationalised. The growth in the economy and in the tax take have made it possible for the nation as a whole to pay.

It is a double-edged sword. On the one hand the economies of scale and scope, the coordinated decision-making and the centralised plan keep the size of the medical budget within the limits set by public finance and competing claims. On the other hand there is the politicisation, the vote-seeking and the self-interested *homo economicus* of public choice.

Democracy is about elections. Health care is popular. Citizens push out governments who do not satisfy their appetite for more.

In Britain, which delivers payment and provision through the universalist National Health Service, public expenditure accounts for 83 per cent of the total health bill. In Japan it is 82 per cent. In Norway it is 85 per cent. In Mexico it is 50 per cent. Just below Mexico there is the United States. In the free-market United States the government share in health spending is 42 per cent. It is almost but not quite half.

Targeted explicitly at the disadvantaged, the friend-in-need mission of Medicare and Medicaid has been subverted both by a relative rather than an absolute definition of poverty and by the temptation on the part of families who can afford private insurance to opt for free or subsidised cover instead. The share of health in the State budget has gone up. So has the number of bodies (not all of them previously uninsured) for whom the State has assumed responsibility.

It is not just households that are inflating the public share. Firms are doing so as well. Where State insurance provides an acceptable package for lower-middle-income families, employers will have less of an incentive to offer a company plan. It is possible that they will put up remuneration to compensate their workers for the fringe benefit foregone. It is just as likely that they will retain the profits for themselves. Once the low-paid with insurance as well as the low-paid without have been sucked up into the generous Welfare State, the need is less for capital to pay directly for labour. The national health service is always there and it is free.

Compassion is expensive. Public opinion may be pressing the government to blanket in minority outsiders, relax its eligibility requirements and eliminate stigma in the form of the means-test. The end result might be a net transfer from the commercial sector. As well as new cost for new cover, it might be a straightforward socialisation of an existing cost that had previously been a private sector responsibility. Socialisation may be seen as a hidden subsidy to households and firms who can afford to pay. It might be 'Director's Law'. It might be the haves and not the have-nots who are inflating the public sector's share in health.

The middle classes will always be with us. The poor will be moved up by productivity, education and opportunity. One possible future might be reprivatisation into individual and occupational plans as a consequence of *embourgeoisement* and rising incomes. Selective schemes aimed explicitly at the lower-income groups might be self-liquidating. The share of health in the national product and in household budgets will continue to rise but at least the pressure on the State will be less.

It is one scenario. 'Director's Law' is another. The households and the firms, having grown accustomed to the subvention, might regard it as a citizen's wage. They might press for a rise in the Medicaid cut-off. They might demand a greater realism in the Medicare reimbursements. Patients are canny. They know when billable fees are so low that the doctors are shortening safety net consultations in order to invest scarce time in full-fee business.

One scenario is that social insurance will reprivatise itself into commerce. Another scenario is that social insurance will be ratcheted into an ever greater commitment. We are all middle class nowadays. We are all the stakeholders in 'Director's Law'. We are not prepared to sacrifice an endowment on which we have come to depend merely because the libertarian economists say that private purchase is best. The inference is clear. The share of the State will go up.

15.1.4 Fiscal Welfare

State protection is one part of the new collectivism. Private insurance is the other. Taken together, in the USA, these two risk-pooling mechanisms spend four times as much on medical care as do individuals and families (Cutler, 2004: x). The financial arrangements are not as sealed off as the ideological underpinnings would suggest. Apart from selective support to the lower-decile deprived, the State has been known to lease out State land at concessionary rentals and to subsidise the construction of private hospitals in underprivileged communities. It also provides fiscal welfare through tax relief.

Insurance that the employer can set against tax as an approved business expense is worth more to the employee than the equivalent value in taxable pay. Employees end up overinsured relative to the amount of cover they would have bought on a level playing field. Artificial cheapening below the market-clearing price may be expected to lead to an expansion in the quantity consumed. It puts up the cost of care.

Overconsumption of care would be reduced, using the economic benchmark, if health insurance were to be taxed as earned income or if the tax exemption were to be restricted to basic cover. A concession once granted is not, however, easy to withdraw. The resistance of employees and unions will be particularly strong where tax rates are high and tax bands progressive. A deduction is worth more to the prosperous than to the low-paid. It is the middle-class fiscal Welfare State. Nowadays we are all 'Director's Law'.

15.2 SOCIAL TRENDS

Economic growth, commercial insurance and State co-payment are social facts that have contributed to the rise in cost. They have been complemented by changes in culture, demography and technology that have exercised a cost-enhancing influence of their own.

15.2.1 A Common Culture

A common culture imposes an economic burden. The comfortable support the defenceless because the future is hidden behind a veil. The life they save may be their own. Rich and poor share common clinics in the State and sometimes also the private sector. That overlap in itself tends to mean that more money must be put into amenities and standards. At the same time, the revolution of rising expectations is displacing upwards the general definition of decency. Middle-classness is in the air. Patients are demanding the services that they believe to be the norm at the top. They are no longer prepared to put up with the bare minimum. Even Marx's proletariat nowadays expects a tolerable waiting time, an air-conditioned ward, a courteous welcome, a broadband link and a choice of food. Citizenship is upward convergence. Upward convergence is cost.

Early policymakers in the United Kingdom had called for a once-and-for-all campaign to clear the backlog. They had predicted that once the policy of 'universalising the best' had definitively integrated the neglected into the common health, the push would come to an end. After that the dose, much less, would be maintenance only.

Their expectations proved unrealistic. As the diseases of poverty became less prevalent, new demands took the place of the old. Patients requested more tests and referrals. They saw the doctor for minor aches that in the past they would have treated as a fact of life. They insisted upon equal quality irrespective of the cost. The result was an escalation of excellence which had not been anticipated in 1948.

A rising level of general education has played a part in the snowballing of demand. Schooling has made people more aware, more articulate and more critical. They are better able to read health-related articles and to understand the media broadcasts. No longer willing to take what they are given without a word, their new-found status of consumer rather than supplicant introduced a ratchet effect into the cost of care.

Better-educated people are more likely to look after their health. They recognise the need for iron supplements, aerobics and jogging. They know when it is time to approach a doctor for discretionary advice:

'More informed consumers are significantly more likely to visit a physician ... Poorly informed consumers tend to underestimate the marginal product of medical care' (Kenkel, 1990: 590). Information is high-powered. It puts up the cost of care.

The personal social services too have been active in getting the message out. Social workers integrate the marginalised into the mainstream. They ensure that the confused are made aware of their rights. The same is true of the medical professionals. Their job description is being broadened and socialised. The doctors and the nurses are increasingly being expected to counsel the drug addicts, alcoholic unemployables, bullied executives, despairing housewives and anorexic teenagers who in a less caring society would have been left to the priests, the Charity Organisation Societies, the police and the morgue. The social services and the clinicians are shifting outwards the demand for care. Doing so, they are also increasing the cost.

15.2.2 Demography

Changes in the population pyramid have contributed to the rise. As agriculture gives way to manufacturing and high-end services, there is a concomitant fall in the birth rate. In developed countries it seldom reaches even the replacement ratio of 2.1. Clinics, like schools, are under less pressure from the dependent young. That is the saving. There is also a cost. The cohort is smaller that will add value and pay tax.

The dependent young go down but the dependent old go up. Better food, housing and medical care mean that more are surviving to experience age-related pathologies such as macular degeneration, osteoporosis, prostate cancer and Alzheimer's dementia that impose a disproportionate burden on limited medical resources. In the poorer countries a death from malaria, diphtheria, pneumonia or cholera is a cheap way to go. In the First World, the epidemiological transition is at once an economic transition and a financial strain. More will have to be treated in their later years who in a poor country would already have died.

Debilitating old age is the price a society must pay for better health throughout the life cycle that begins before birth. Old people on average cost more. Yet the economic burden of old people should be seen in perspective:

> Medical costs are driven overwhelmingly by chronic illness at every age. Moreover, chronic illness among those younger than 65 years, not among the elderly, accounts for 67 per cent of spending. If trauma is added (including

assault, attempted suicide, and motor vehicle crashes), about 80 per cent of total US expenditure is for those younger than 65 years. (Moses et al., 2013: 1951)

Sick people cost more than healthy people. It is not, however, just the elderly who are imposing the cost. That poor thing broke her leg in the shower. Who is to say that that poor thing is not sweet 16 and simply slipped on the soap?

The statistics must be handled with care. In the United States about 55 per cent of total health care expenditures go to only 5 per cent of the population. About 69 per cent go to the sickest 10 per cent. At the other end of the scale the healthiest 50 per cent absorb a mere 3 per cent. They trigger annual expenditures of only $122. For the least healthy 5 per cent the equivalent figure is $56 459 (Berk and Monheit, 2001: 12, 13). Sick people cost a great deal of money.

Everyone knows that the sick cost money. About 27 per cent of health care spending in the United States is concentrated on only 1 per cent of the population (Aaron, 1991: 51). A statistic on the sick is not, of course, a statistic on the old. Even soccer players slip on the soap. Soccer players aside, the statistics do lend support to the stereotype. Unpacking the most costly 1 per cent, the truth emerges that retired people are soaking up fully 46 per cent of the whole (Berk and Monheit, 2001: 13). The last year of life is the most costly. The old on balance are more likely than the young to be approaching that costly last act when successive treatments successively fail until in the end the patient goes off the books.

A minority is causing an inequality. The chronic and degenerative diseases of the old-elderly are imposing a supernormal cost. Older people are admitted more frequently to hospital. Each inpatient episode is likely to last longer. Old people are more likely to be housebound or to require long-stay residential care. Old people are less likely to be able to cook a meal, wash unaided or use a toilet. Old people will not successfully age in place if their activities of daily life are so restricted by the depletion of their systems.

Social trends are not on their side. Industrialisation, urbanisation, the two-career couple, the revised self-perception of women, the preference for privacy, the high cost of spare bedrooms, second bathrooms, grab-rails and ramps all undermine the resolve and capacity of the multigenerational family to act as the primary care-giver. Unpaid relatives, sandwiched between their parents and their children, do not have the time to look after the incontinent, the vacant and the frail. Old people's homes, hospices, live-in attendants and meals-on-wheels fill the social void. So do expensive hospital beds when the aged have no family nucleus to which they can return.

Perhaps the imbalance between young and old should be seen not as a problem but as a fact of life. Considered as a journey, the life cycle is a risk-pooling scheme in which the odds evolve as the organism matures. Citizens who expect to grow old cannot reasonably opt out of contributions when they are young. Not everyone, however, sees the unfunded commitment in that light. Intolerant towards the irreversibly ill who impose an unsustainable burden, some complain that bed-blockers unfairly block the rest of us out: 'A highly concentrated spending distribution may indicate that some population groups are obtaining excessive care with benefits not commensurate with costs, that other groups may be underusing medical care, and that overall social welfare might be enhanced through a reallocation of resources from the former group to the latter' (Berk and Monheit, 2001: 10).

Reallocation is the R-word that the silver-haired in their golden years do not like to hear. No one would say that the feeding tube should be disconnected or the incurable abandoned on freezing mountaintops. The world has moved on from the hard-hearted cost-effectiveness of 'they who do not sow, neither shall they reap'. No one would say it. Many nonetheless will think it. Many, in line with Chapter 7, section 7.1, will think that the tail is wagging the dog. They are wondering if society really wants its health policy to be made by a minority. What nation wants to march in step with the Baptists, gays, Elks, Irish or blacks? Why should the old have any more influence than the ethnic Chinese?

The fear is that cost will escalate out of control unless society recognises that blockbuster services cannot be provided for all. Priorities will be needed. One selective standard will be to put patients who have not had their 'fair innings' above the grizzled and the rheumy whose quality of life is so badly spoiled that it is not much better than no life at all. Health policy may be at variance with public opinion where it makes longevity at any cost into its meta-objective. Inequality is already enshrined in insurance contracts which are capped at a lifetime ceiling and in hospital usages which move prime-time professionals to the head of the queue. The old and the ill may be subject to discrimination even in a society that on paper is committed to minority rights. It is not 'one treated as one'. At least it retards the escalation in cost.

15.3 MEDICINE: TECHNOLOGY AND STRUCTURE

Incomes, insurance, statism, inclusion, expectations, education and demography are pushing up the cost of care. They are magnified by the relentless mutation in medical technology. A timeless model that assumes away the novelty and the innovation gives a misleading impression of how science forever builds upon itself.

Kidney dialysis, coronary bypass, joint replacement, balloon angioplasty, pacemaker implants, cardiac catheterisation, genetic engineering, foetal monitoring, radiation therapy, the computerised scan, the linear accelerator, open-heart surgery, the life-prolonging AIDS cocktail, the 'smart drug' for colon cancer that costs £130 000 for a two-year course – the scientific revolution is pushing the stethoscope, the thermometer, the bedside manner and the hand-held pulse to the margins of total cost. Household names like research and development (R&D), CT, PET and MRI scans say it all. Advances in capital plus advances in pharmacology are inexorably inflating the medical bills.

It is not just like-for-like but more of the new that is swelling the outlay. High-tech costs more per case than routine management. Estimation is always approximate. Smith calculates that medical technology alone explains between 27 and 48 per cent of the 4.8 per cent annual rise in real per capita health spending in the United States between 1960 and 2007 (Smith et al., 2009: 1280). Even after allowing for a margin of error, one-quarter to one-half of a 4.8 rise, recurring, can only be described as a large sum of money.

Research done in the universities and the grant-funded institutes will be driven by *pro bono publico*, professional recognition and the thrill of the chase. Research done by the equipment manufacturers and the pharmaceutical majors will be planned with a view to lucrative patents that boost corporate dividends and capital gains. That is how profit-seeking activity serves the public interest. No one should disparage a desirable breakthrough like a cure for cancer merely because the research and development was a fishing trip expressly designed to make Big Pharma rich. At the same time, it puts up the cost.

Doctors and academics become caught up in the momentum of medical trials. New departures come onstream faster than the ability of the community to pay for them. The knowledge that so many new options are not being taken up must be a source of frustration to the citizen who wants to be well. That frustration, in a tax-financed health care system, expresses itself in pressure on the political leadership to increase the funding for health.

Some new techniques and drugs do lead to more and better recoveries. 'There may ... be no need to worry about long-term cost growth, if the new health spending is more valuable than spending in other areas' (Cutler, 1994: 18). Sometimes the outcomes will more than repay the seed money staked. It is not always so. Where the difference is medically trivial or economically cost-ineffective, the novelty can only be described as a waste.

Waste happens: 'The marginal value of some intensive cardiac procedures is close to zero ... Many medical technologies may be used excessively, inadequately, or inappropriately' (McClellan and Noguchi, 1998: 90, 95). As much as one-third of all medical care supplied in Europe is believed to be unsuitable or ineffective (Cutler, 1994: 14). While the salesmen may have been persuasive and the hospital administrators slow, it would be wrong to underestimate the force of demand-induced supply. What patients want might not be what patients need. Even policymakers, however, must dwell in the real world. In the real world, it can be wants and not needs that sway the balance of demand.

Patients tend to judge quality at least in part by vintage and investment. Shopping around for a clinic, the customers in a competitive market will want the most up-to-date equipment. Newest is best. They will not know or perhaps not care that it is underemployed capacity, an idle overhead that is pushing up the cost. What they will know is that it is state-of-the-art. Literacy and computer literacy are conducive to alertness and access. Democracy has the same effect on demand. The incumbent cannot afford to stop at thermometers when the opposition is pressing for a gamma knife.

Hospital management will often err on the side of conspicuous production. In a competitive market the executives will understand the extent to which expensive toys are status symbols that sell the product. The patients aside, the prestige associated with glamorous capital and cutting-edge science will make it easier to attract donations and enlist well-known consultants.

Machinery increases the cost. Manpower does so as well. The number of doctors and the doctor–patient ratio drift up. The proportion of expensive specialists to general practitioners tends to rise. Supplier-induced demand is a theoretical possibility. It may result from the overproduction of medical professionals in countries that allow private medical schools to make the number of places demand-led.

Besides that, there is the physical inelasticity of the listening ear. Despite the scientific management and the microelectronics, health care remains a labour-intensive industry. Newhouse is right to say that medical productivity can and does go up: 'The treatment of heart attacks has certainly changed more than haircuts or the performance of Mozart string quartets' (Newhouse, 1992: 9). The problem is that efficiency in the manufacturing sector goes up even faster.

In health care, because of the person-to-person component, output per unit of input cannot increase beyond a point without debasing the quality of the product. The lightning consultation is simply not as effective as the two-way exploration of the patient's unique circumstances. The service sector is handicapped by its relative inability to absorb rising wages through rising throughput. Simultaneously, however, the pay it offers must be competitive and comparable if it is to recruit and retain. It is the 'Dutch disease'. Two sectors are competing for the same scarce endowment. One sector can raise productivity. The other sector has no alternative but to put up the price.

The cost of care is bid up by the relative inability to take in the slack. It is high as well because of a plethora of market imperfections. Professional associations, entry barriers, extended in-service internships, restricted accreditation of new medical schools all lengthen the obstacle race. They limit the supply of practitioners even as growth in demand is producing a bottleneck. They reinforce the upward pressure on fees.

The evidence, perhaps surprisingly, only partially bears out the expectation of ransom, booty or supra-functional surplus. A study in the United States in the 1990s suggested that the internal rate of return on investment in medical education was 15.9 per cent for general practitioners, 20.7 per cent for dentists and 20.9 for specialists. While 20.9 or even 15.9 per cent seems high in absolute terms, it was actually less than the comparable figure for lawyers (25.4 per cent) and much less than the return to business graduates (29 per cent) (Weeks et al., 1994: 1280).

The pay-back in 2009 was not very different. There were outliers like 35.3 per cent for non-invasive radiology but also bunching in the middle from 13 per cent for general surgery and 15.3 per cent for family medicine to 17.4 per cent for immunology and 18.1 per cent for cardiology (Roth, n.d.: 19). Medical training was a profitable placement; and the supernormal rewards were undoubtedly a part of care cost inflation. Specialists were earning 5.8 times the average national wage (Cutler and Ly, 2011: 11). In spite of that, other sheepskinned professionals were continuing to cream off an even higher rent. The fact that the doctors were failing to match the opportunity cost is a socio-economic *curiosum* in itself. It is as if they knew that they had unexploited economies of power but that, like Hippocrates, they deliberately held themselves back from tapping all the traffic would bear.

The monopoly power of the doctors may have been exaggerated. That, however, is not how it looks from outside. The newsflash that striking professionals are letting their patients suffer and die, the saloon-bar imputation that fee-seekers are milking their punters for unneeded placebo, is a threat to the doctor–patient relationship. The breakdown in trust is reflected in a tendency to demand (and pay for) a second opinion. There is also the malpractice action if something is believed to have gone wrong.

The possibility of a lawsuit forces the doctor into precautionary ('defensive') tests and medicines of low cost-effectiveness or doubtful clinical value. Excessive caution imposes an avoidable burden on the system that bears a superficial resemblance to supplier-induced demand. The consequences may be similar but the motivation is not. Supplier-induced demand is gain maximisation. Excessive caution is loss minimisation. All that the doctor wants is to keep on the right side of the judge.

It has been estimated that 75 per cent of American doctors in low-risk and 99 per cent in high-risk specialities will face at least one malpractice claim in the course of their career (Jena et al., 2011: 629). Mean damages are $274 887 but the banner awards cross the $1 million mark. The fear of litigation will sometimes cause medical professionals to refuse business altogether where the outcome is especially uncertain, negligence a grey area and the probability of legal action high. Gynaecology, obstetrics and aesthetic surgery have often been neglected for this reason. Even 'frivolous litigation', with the associated publicity and time wasted in court, can damage a professional's reputation. When the payouts become larger and the liability insured approaches 100 per cent, the malpractice premiums go up. The cost of care rises when these liabilities are passed on to the final consumer.

The effect on total cost is not in the event very large. Defensive tests and self-protective procedures are no more than 3 per cent of total health care spending in the United States. Malpractice actions add only another 1 per cent (Cutler, 1994: 16). But that is not to say that caps on compensation and the abolition of punitive damages would not make a worthwhile contribution. Kessler and McClellan estimate that the cost saving by means of ceilings and norms could be as much as $50 billion and that quality indicators such as mortality and complications would not be adversely affected (Kessler and McClellan, 1996: 386). Even small savings in the vicinity of $50 billion should not be rejected merely because they are small.

15.4 A FALL IN COST

This chapter on the rise in cost should not end on a note of despair. There are counteracting forces within the system which have a tendency to slim down the deadweight without the need for public policy.

Economic growth itself may be keeping the rise in check. Obesity and inactivity, salt and sugar are the ugly face of affluence. Yet affluence at the same time is a vote for affordable housing, underground sewers and adequate heating. Lifestyle is changing. People know when and where to go for help. They know how to use the internet to shorten a time-consuming search. If they require treatment, urbanisation reduces the complementary cost of travel.

Universal education, a response to the expansion in middle-class job opportunities, is making even the rural, the elderly and the deprived relatively more sensitive to prevention and cure. They know more about nicotine and preservatives. They are more likely to present for antenatal care which can save as much as $16 800 per birth monitored (Gray, 2001: 683). Early detection reduces the long-term burden of medical attention. Urine checks discover pre-symptomatic diabetes. Blood pressure warns of a stroke. Self-examination picks up a cyst or a lump.

One could even say, in line with Grossman, that the productivity of medical care when it is actually delivered will be higher because the body-capital will have been well maintained. Body-holders drilled to invest in their follow-ups and their take-ups will have a lower incidence of debility and death. While upgrading into a more homogeneous society may make the included less passive, more articulate and more demanding, they will also be more likely to complete a course of drugs or comply with the regimen that closes the case. It has not happened yet: 'The World Health Organization estimates that as many as 50 per cent of patients do not adhere fully to their medication treatment, leading to 125,000 premature deaths and billions in preventable health care costs' (Department of Health and Human Services, 2015: 215). It has not happened yet. Demand, however, is evolving. Health alertness is in the air. Health awareness is favourable to the containment of cost.

On the side of supply, there is the therapeutic transformation. Pharmacists review medication to minimise duplication, contraindications and discarding. Drugs and talking therapies take the place of the long-stay mental ward. Stomach ulcers can be treated without surgery. Generics are frequently as good as big-name brands. The contraceptive pill and the polio vaccine eliminate the need for an inpatient stay. Cholesterol can be reduced with statins and diabetes managed with insulin. Beta-blockers prescribed after a heart attack mark down the odds of a second heart attack by a quarter. Wearable technology monitors the heartbeat through a smart watch. A fibre-optic mattress checks the blood pressure at night. Genetic decoding allows the at-risk to opt for a just-in-case mastectomy in preference to a more costly operation later on.

Routine medical procedures are being devolved from expensive doctors to paramedics, physician's assistants, nurses, nurse-practitioners, hospital auxiliaries and community pharmacists. General practitioners using miniaturised kit are supplying chemotherapy and dialysis at the primary level. Telemedicine permits consultation without travel. Budget airlines make cheaper interventions accessible in the intra-national and international market. Subsidiarity, in short, is generating an unbroken chain of joined-up care. It cuts the cost.

Laparoscopic surgery reduces the average stay. Cataracts, hernias and varicose vein stripping are being dealt with on the less expensive day-case basis. About 70 per cent of all British National Health Service surgery is now ambulatory. More will follow as the same-day clinic builds up its reputational capital: 'Of the almost 1 million procedures in England in 2009/10 that could potentially have been performed as day cases, just over one-fifth were *not* carried out as day cases. This is equivalent to around 220,000 patients treated as inpatients who could have been treated as day cases' (Appleby et al., 2011: 17). Outpatient surgery is minimising the costly overnights. This is true even in Japan where hospital stays, traditionally for rest (*ansai*), are the longest in the Organisation for Economic Co-operation and Development (OECD). Private insurers as well as the National Health are under pressure to select the less-expensive procedure.

Capital itself is value for money. Better equipment makes possible better diagnosis, earlier intervention, fewer complications and a reduced incidence of pricy recidivism. Although the investment will initially entail a cost, plant in the long run may cut the total burden of the curative sequence to the extent that it raises the average productivity of the clinician and the hospital. Total cost may rise. The cost per case may fall.

Institutions are changing. Some of the changes are keeping the cost down. Thus managed care, unknown in the past, is bringing together the primary and the inpatient stages. The managed-care organisation has a tendency to limit the hospital stays and to refer within the group.

Simultaneously, there has been a movement away from solo towards multi-speciality practices that spread the overheads and share out the aides. The productive economies are so great that scale and scope may be an argument even for a multi-speciality group of more than 100 doctors

(Marder and Zuckerman, 1985: 173). Good doctoring can be good economics as well.

Efficiency in the modern age has become the axial value. Its intellectual hegemony may be detected in all areas of social life. It contains the cost of care. In medicine, the pursuit of efficiency has meant that randomised control trials are being conducted to define what is meant by a 'necessary' hospital stay or the 'best possible' standard of treatment. Science-based medicine leads to convergence. It reduces the amplitude of practice variation.

In economics, efficiency has meant that cost-effectiveness and cost–benefit analysis are being used to estimate the value for money of a new drug or therapy. Even where scrutiny does not reduce the total cost in absolute terms, the economic calculus homes in on the novelty that is the best buy for the clinical pay-off.

In administration, efficiency has meant that bureaucratic inertia is being challenged by unsentimental managers trained in business schools to eliminate internal slack. Skilled executives squeeze out avoidable error and 'x-inefficiency' caused by motivational slippage (Leibenstein, 1987: 4). The CAT scanner is in service round the clock. The patient flow in theatre is maximised with operational research. The notes and files are put online. Information technology (IT) is used to coordinate the fragmented departments. Telephone bookings are outsourced to call-centres abroad. Technology is cold and unfeeling but it cuts the cost.

Economic efficiency can complement administrative efficiency. League tables and the retention of surplus even within a single national health service can bring about an incentive structure in the not-for-profit hospitals that closely resembles the objective-function of competitive private business. Administrators adapt to the free-market discipline. Rivalry, the economists say, will get the unit costs down.

There is, however, a major obstacle. It is the social philosophy in which the health system is embedded. The electorate may regard the new commercialisation as a cuckoo in the nest. It may reject the calculative marketeering and the economical mindset because it believes that the peddler principle is incompatible with the inclusive citizenship and the inviolable entitlement that are the time-hallowed cornerstones of social medicine

Democratic consultation is a troublesome old beast. Commodification, profit-seeking, quasi-markets and the market-clearing price will only fulfil a cost-containing function if the social consensus is willing to accept the new belief system. Sometimes it will not. Even convinced libertarians would concede that in health the ideological sea change has not yet occurred.

The electorate will at the very least require proof that what worked for the Coal Board and British Rail will also work for the National Health Service. Evidence is hard to find. No one can say for certain whether transparency and rivalry will be able to vanquish any residual sluggishness that prevents a nationalised monolith from matching the unit costs of private capital: 'It is not self-evident that private sector bureaucracies are better controlled than public sector ones ... The case for privatization as a method of cost control or an agent for the promotion of efficiency is thus uneasy' (Culyer, 1989: 28). All that can be said for certain is that the social valuation of efficiency will presumably lead even the not-for-profit sector to innovate, to experiment and to counteract the escalation in cost.

16. Cost containment

The share of care is going up. It is going up as a share of the gross domestic product (GDP), of total public expenditure and of the median household budget. There is nothing wrong with that. If society wants better health, and if it is convinced that more care is the best means to the end, then it ought to welcome the rise. We do not cut or curtail the cost of something that is doing us good. The question is simply whether an equivalent health status can be delivered at a lower unit cost. This chapter explores the possibility that it can.

There is no consensus on medical effectiveness, value for money or clinical priority. There is no consensus on the target share of health. Where there is consensus is that spending is escalating and that the price times the quantity is becoming a threat. Choice in health must extend to the choice of cost: 'Health care expenditures cannot grow at rates 2 per cent or 3 per cent higher than GDP indefinitely' (McGuire et al., 2012: 140). At some point the members of the community must call a halt. What that point will be is, however, not a matter for doctors or even economists to prescribe: 'Ultimately ... the level of expenditure will be determined by the preferences for health care displayed by individual countries' (McGuire et al., 2012: 142). Each country's consensus is the *suprema lex*. Agreement is all. Without agreement it would be civil war.

The debate is not about whether mature adults in a liberal democracy should be allowed access to consumer goods and investment opportunities that make a difference to their felt well-being. The debate is about whether extra care at the margin should be allowed to push out other choices that purposive individuals, if fully informed, would have ranked more highly. If the citizens decide that there is no need for the genie to be kept in the bottle, then there is no need for this chapter. If, however, the citizens are convinced that health care should be restricted and circumscribed, then there is a role for public policy. That role is discussed in the following four sections on 'The demand side: price', 'The demand side: time', 'The supply side: purchase and containment' and 'The supply side: size and cost'.

16.1 THE DEMAND SIDE: PRICE

Neoclassical microeconomics posits a downward-sloping demand curve. An increase in the price reduces the quantity demanded. If the percentage increase exceeds the percentage reduction, the total cost will fall. If the percentage increase is less than the percentage reduction, the total cost will rise. It is all a question of the elasticity of demand.

16.1.1 A Market-Clearing Price

Where an artificially low price is immobilised in a fixed disequilibrium limbo, the result is that sick people will demand more services than the treatment centres are willing to supply. In a free market the price would drift upwards until both blades of the scissors were cutting the same cloth. In the market for health there are administered distortions in the form of targets and ceilings.

Imbalance breeds dissatisfaction. Consumers are frustrated because the quantity supplied of their price-regulated service does not proceed to the point where their marginal private utility like their marginal user fee will be equal to zero. Taxpayers are resentful because the shared encumbrance of their taxes, premiums and contributions is becoming an intolerable albatross without ever delivering the quantity to which they as citizens believe they have purchased an entitlement.

It is primitive communism. Jekyll is unhappy. Hyde is unhappy. The rational solution, James Buchanan insists, can only be a free-market payment that reunites the two sides of a single identity: 'The inconsistency between demand-choice and supply-choice must be eliminated ... The individual, as the ultimate chooser, must be placed in positions where the two parts of what is really a single decision are not arbitrarily separated' (Buchanan, 1965: 16). The negotiated price would make the exchange nexus transparent. It would bring to an end the contrived cheapness that is turning all the traffic lights red.

The libertarian solution is the invisible hand. Policy, however, must start from here. The trade in health is not virgin soil. Instead, it is an established garden of entrenched conventions. Sometimes health care is provided free at the point of use. Sometimes the fees and charges are controlled by professions, associations and ministries. Sometimes the paying arm reimburses the whole or a part of the price. In the market for health what is more common than the market-clearing price is the pseudo-price. It is a symbol and a gesture. No one would say that a prescription lump sum covering no more than the cost of the bottle is a homeostatic mechanism that succeeds as a gatekeeper in eliminating overuse.

Each charge that emerges in the regulated order is a philosophical affirmation of the value the decision-makers wish to assign to a particular group or activity. Charges can be needs-tested to target the specific circumstances of pregnant women, young children and the carriers of an infectious virus. Charges can be means-tested so as to enfold bottom-decile marginals such as welfare recipients living alone. Charges can be as general as a 20 per cent excess across the board, as service-specific as a co-payment for an eye test or an after-hours consultation, as outcome-related as a concessionary levy imposed for a drug with a high therapeutic pay-off. Always, however, the charge falls short of the invisible hand. A charge is not a full-cost price that would make demand and supply the same.

A charge is a halfway house. It educates the consumer to think twice before making a claim on the pool. It teaches the shopper that there is no such thing as a free drug. It acts as a quasi-tax (the more polemical name is 'creeping privatisation') that generates finance for reinvestment in health. But it is not a market-clearing signal. The information conveyed through the preferences revealed cannot be taken to be a perfect photograph of the invisible mind.

16.1.2 The Nature of the Slope

So pervasive are third-party reimbursement, State-subsidised provision and market rigidities that real-world data on the price-elasticity of demand is not easy to interpret. There is general agreement, however, that the inverse relationship does exist. The gradient has been estimated both for the nation as a whole and for the microeconomic subsectors which have unique characteristics of their own.

At the national level, Manning found that the response of quantity to price lay in the range from -0.17 to -0.22. A 10 per cent increase in the price of all medical services would be followed by approximately a 2 per cent decrease in the quantity demanded (Manning et al., 1987: 268). Some people would give up. Most would pay up. Most people do not take chances with their health.

Some response rates are national aggregates. Others describe the reactions and sensitivities in specific submarkets. For surgery the elasticity of demand was between -0.14 and -0.17 (Cromwell and Mitchell, 1986: 304). For office consultations it was -0.16 for urgent and serious conditions, -0.35 for marginal and general check-ups (Wedig, 1988: 152, 159). The reduction in demand was extremely small. Cardiac arrest, a grumbling appendix or a broken leg is not something that the patient postpones because of the price. Catastrophes do not take well to economics.

Cosmetic surgery or elective top-ups, luxuries rather than necessities, are likely to register a higher proportionate response. The same is true of commodities with close substitutes and alternatives. For nursing home beds the response of quantity demanded to a rise in price lay in the range between −0.69 and −2.40 (Chiswick, 1976: 307). The high values reflect the cross-elasticity of demand. Residential care faces competition from day centres, home nurses and dutiful children. Prices can be increased but more than proportionate business will be lost. Charges matter:

> We estimate that with no cap on out-of-pocket spending, those with 100 percent coinsurance (that is, no insurance) would spend about half as much as those with free care, those with 50 percent coinsurance would spend about 63 percent as much as those with free care, and those with 25 percent coinsurance would spend about 71 per cent as much. (Newhouse and Insurance Experiment Group, 1993: 82)

Newhouse was generalising on the basis of the RAND Health Insurance Experiment. Conducted between 1974 and 1982, it tracked the experience of 2750 American families assigned at random to insurance plans with different co-pays.

The investigators found that payment influenced conduct. Adults whose care was free had 34 per cent more dental visits and spent 46 per cent more money on dentistry than adults co-insuring at a rate of 95 per cent on their own. Teeth are sensitive to price. Mayerhoefer calculates that a movement from out-of-pocket payment to a dental insurance plan would increase the probability of preventive check-ups by 19 per cent and major dental work by 11 to 16 per cent (Mayerhoefer et al., 2014: 14). RAND found sensitivity not just in teeth but in prescription drugs, doctor visits and discretionary stays in hospital. All varied inversely with the price the final consumer had to pay.

When the price goes up, the quantity goes down. The free market would seem to be the ideal tool for a nation seeking to contain the cost of care. In fact it is a mirage. Most medical services are necessities. The elasticity of demand for essential services is low. The quantity demanded falls proportionately less than the percentage rise in price. A rise in price does not contain the share of care but rather increases it. A fall in price would be the more economical option. It may be a price ceiling and not the invisible hand that is the better way to cap the cost of care.

16.1.3 Beyond Deterrence

Charges deter but medicine heals. The economic orientation does not capture the clinical and social externalities which differentiate the market for health from the market for pins. There is more to health than price. You get what you pay for. Penny-pinching would be a false economy if the hidden cost were to be worsening health status and expensive chronic care. A cheese pared can be a slippage magnified. Cost rises in the long run because cost falls in the myopic here-and-now.

Cheese-paring can bring out the rats. It need not be so. Longitudinal data from the RAND experiment suggests that life-expectancy, maternal mortality and other primary indicators were insensitive to the co-pays: 'The reduced service use under the cost-sharing plans had little or no net adverse effect on health for the average person' (Newhouse et al., 1993: 339). Vision and blood pressure had deteriorated slightly over time. Otherwise, despite the fact that families registered in the least generous plan were spending 30 per cent less on care, there was no apparent correlation between more insurance and better outcomes. On that basis at least, some people are likely to have been overinsured.

If RAND is right, if health status outcomes are not sensitive to price, then there may be an argument in terms of moral hazard for making medical care more expensive. Charges are a reason to invest in body maintenance. An apple a day keeps the doctor away. Prevention is a luxury that requires a monetary sacrifice. Treatment is a necessity that is free on demand on the National Health Service (NHS). The deterrence is skewed and asymmetrical. It is also counter-productive. Consumers who do not splash out on an apple a day are more likely to become chronic cases who raise the total cost of care.

Charges reduce the care consumed. The economics may sound but the sociology is shaky. A lump-sum charge by definition is not an equal burden on all income classes. A fixed fee, being a higher proportion of a lower income, is regressive and in that sense unfair. Chapter 14 made clear that a demand curve is better seen as a demand queue. The prosperous do not reduce the number of tests they consume. The statistical reduction is due to the poor who cancel all their appointments. A smaller quantity is consumed. Yet the reduction in demand is entirely due to the scapegoated periphery that has the greatest need.

The poor cannot pay. It is a fact. A study of impoverished Medicaid recipients in Utah revealed that the introduction of a modest $2 co-payment reduced the number of office visits from 600 per 1000 enrollees to fewer than 500. It caused the utilisation of prescription medicines to fall by 8 per cent (Ku et al., 2004). Yet it can never be in the interests of good health for diabetics to be forced to space out their insulin or the bipolar to cut back on their antipsychotics. It is never sensible to price away a precautionary consultation when early detection might save the patient's leg or eyesight.

Charges reduce the quantity demanded. They curtail consumption but they are inconsistent both with good health and with even-handed equity. A compromise would be for co-pays to be shaded through a household income test or kept low so as not to screen out the most vulnerable. Moderation is humane but it may not contain the cost. Special cases are risky. Only economics is safe. People who are priced away from dentists never demand any fillings. The edentulous are cheap. It is the intensive who impose the cost. A downward-sloping demand curve is bad for your teeth if you are poor.

16.2 THE DEMAND SIDE: TIME

Waiting times limit the flow. Travelling times guard the gate. Lists are an alternative to the pecuniary price. They ration the take-up without money changing hands.

16.2.1 Delay and Demand

Time price is different from money price in that the *quid* of one trading partner never becomes the *quo* of the other. The time paid by the patient is not a remittance pocketed by the doctor. It never augments the supplier's net wealth. It never enters into the producer's incentive structure. There is no link between the two sides of the circular flow.

No one likes to wait. Even free care is not free. Patients signal their dissatisfaction through verbal feedback which does not limit resource use and through uptake abandoned which does. Coffey found that 'a 10 per cent increase in the time required to obtain care leads to about a 1 per cent decline in the probability of seeking care' (Coffey, 1983: 422). The crowds were not much thinned out but at least the demand curve sloped down.

Acton established that the time-price elasticity of demand for outpatient visits was –0.14 (Acton, 1975: 607). Mueller and Monheit arrived at the same figure for dental care. At –0.14, the time-price elasticity was only slightly less than the money-price elasticity of –0.18 (Mueller and Monheit, 1988: 68). The molars may have had caries but at least the cost was being capped.

Gravelle showed that cataract removal in the National Health Service was a function of distance. The travel-time elasticity was −0.35. An increase in distance of 10 per cent reduced the admissions demanded by −3.5 per cent. With respect to waiting times, the elasticity was −0.25 (Gravelle et al., 2001: 446). Cataract surgery, like hernia repair or a precautionary electrocardiogram, is a non-emergency procedure. It is not elective but neither is it urgent. Its status in the eyes of the consumer is proven by its time-price responsiveness of demand. Elasticity was low but not zero.

The same seems to have been true of the time-price paid for goitre and epilepsy. Although medical attention was indispensable, immediate management was discretionary. When the time-price went up the quantity demanded went down. Lindsay and Feigenbaum estimated the relevant elasticity at between −0.55 and −0.64 (Lindsay and Feigenbaum, 1984: 406).

Inconvenience makes the service less valuable in the eyes of the patient. Delay is like a discount rate that reduces the pressure of excess demand: 'Market clearance is brought about by the fact that the utility derived from the consumption of the good declines the longer the individual has to wait' (Martin and Smith, 1999: 142). Some sufferers will abandon their search. They will become accustomed to intermittent pain in their knees and hips. Some will seek treatment from family doctors and outpatient clinics. Some will recover naturally because the body is built that way. Some will die while waiting for their turn. Attrition thins out the ranks. Evaporation contains the cost.

Unless, of course, there is a parallel route that bypasses the clock. A hegemon is not a monopolist and the NHS is not the only shop. Patients who abandon an intolerable wait may only be doing so because they are shifting to fast-track supply. Private medicine gives the impatient the freedom to purchase the same expected gain at a cost paid in money and not in discomfort. It is an escape valve that extends the sick person's range of choice.

The parallel route dilutes the cost containment. Where the disillusioned re-privatize their search, other patients immediately occupy their beds. In the State sector as in the private sector, a built bed is a filled bed: 'There is relatively little impact of health care supply on the demand for health care in England' (Martin and Smith, 1999: 158). Augmenting the supply does not markedly influence the occupancy.

Private care does not alleviate the strain in the public sector. What private care does is to increase the total endowment that is being allocated to the two sectors taken together. The increment may be small where doctors curtail their hours in the public sector in order to accommodate frustrated customers wanting an escape from the queue. The increment may be substantial where the superscale back door is offering expensive add-ons like magnetic resonance imaging and wonder-drugs that State providers do not find cost-effective. The waits may be containing the cost. The parallel route might be putting up the total.

A parallel sector is sometimes said to be a violation of citizenship equality. Time is money. The affluent, aware that private insurance reimburses for spend but not for deferral, are in a position to purchase a more congenial priority. The deprived, as passive in the doctor's office as they are on the production line, must put up with physical presence in a waiting room and the non-market sorting-hat of a protracted waiting list. Prices and waits are sometimes said to proxy the difference between rich and poor. If the distinction is a valid one, then it might be equitable as well as cost-containing to limit or even suppress the private sector in medicine.

The argument is a blind alley. Not only is it impossible to win consensus for the nationalisation of all roads to good health, but it is also by no means obvious that the queue-jumpers will necessarily be top-quintile plutocrats arrogantly striving to leap-frog the disadvantaged. Some of the queue-jumpers will be relatively deprived. Paid by the hour or by the piece, the poor in work will often be making the greatest sacrifice when they have to down tools in order to toe the line. The marginal utility of low incomes is high. The bottom deciles might not be able to afford the opportunity cost of unpaid leave.

The unemployed, the retired and the indigent will arguably prefer a wait to a price. Not so the freelance handyman or the taxi driver desperate for extra shifts. The queue is not always and everywhere the friend of the low-waged and the insecure. Payment in time is not a guaranteed means of preventing unequal income from translating itself into unequal health. Payment in money might be the poor person's friend.

16.2.2 Acceptable and Excessive

People complain about waits and queues. Anxious about possible glaucoma and embarrassed to walk with a frame, they find it distressing when they are put on a non-emergency list and told that their turn will come. As sympathetic as one must be to their spoiled quality of life, still the disappointed have only limited grounds for complaint. If they have agreed to a national health system that rations by time and not by price, then they cannot realistically demand that their waits be reduced to zero. Allocation is a fact of life where resources are not infinite. All that the members of the community can say is that their waits are excessive relative to the multi-period benchmark that was agreed upon in advance.

Implicit or implicit, a constitutional contract lays out the entitlements. It forms the basis for reasonable and consensual expectations. We as a society believe that stage 4 cancer and a ruptured appendix should be treated without delay, but that snoring and astigmatism can safely be put on a list. We as a society want shorter waits for the young and the educated, longer waits for the past-it and the infirm. We as a society think that three to six months is a tolerable wait for a trapped nerve but that more than six months is too long. On Pluto the foreigners say two months. On Saturn the aliens say two years. In Clapham we say six months. Six months is the way we do things around here.

An acceptable wait is the delay that is broadly in keeping with the social compact. An excessive wait is a wait that ordinary men and women find at variance with their shared perception of what ought to be. 'Excessive' is more than a word in the dictionary. 'Excessive' is encoded in social attitudes and the spirit of the place. Imprecise and diffuse, policymakers must use proxies and indicators to lay down norms which most of the people most of the time will take to be right.

One way of identifying an 'excessive' wait might be in terms of the number of patients who, having paid for the narrower gate, are willing to pay a second time for a fast-track refuge. An acceleration in sector-crossing may be seen as a signal that more and more people are finding the postponement unacceptable. If they could get their knee replaced on the NHS, they would not have had to go private in Harley Street or Chennai.

Desertion may be an indicator of dissatisfaction. Yet it is a messenger with a forked tongue. By itself it does not mean that the core offerings are underfunded or that there ought to be an early increase in capacity. All that desertion might be saying is that shoppers in a rush might be going ad hoc by taxi when usually they would be taking the bus. It is a positive feature of the dual system that minorities and majorities will have the opportunity to reveal preferences of this kind.

Economic growth and rising incomes give patients the freedom to cross and recross at will. While a stampede for the door might suggest that a national health promise has not properly been honoured, a one-off mix-and-match might only mean that in normal circumstances patients are happy with the bus but that in exceptional cases they prefer something else.

'Excessive' may be defined in terms of desertions not reversed by re-entry. Yet the desertions in themselves may be reflecting something more basic than whimsical preference. Outcome indicators transmit objective information on the medical history of the patients who pay by time. Retention might be the death certificate. Rational people might be crossing to money price while they still have the chance.

The professionals may be uncovering evidence of sustained discomfort, deterioration of function, threat of contagion and declining life-expectancy which proves that the time-price system is out to lunch. The bureaucrats may be citing inputs and outcomes in comparable societies which confirm that the NHS is letting the nation down. Ordinary men and women might be learning from the experts that the trend is underperforming and that the deviations disappoint. The NHS website My NHS at least ensures that the required statistics will be easy to access.

Objective indicators may lie at the root of subjective dissatisfaction. Ordinary men and women might be concluding that outside alternatives offer not just shorter waits but better quality. Like is not being compared with like. People might be deserting the time-price sector for what they believe to be higher standards outside. They might be rejecting the institutions that practice time-price because in their view the time-price sector has lost its sheen. Excessive waits are secondary. When people complain with their feet, the real reason might be that they do not regard the time-price sector as up to the mark.

People always complain. Public opinion demand-pulls the entitlements because wants resemble needs and me-first is in pain. The fundamental fact is that no system can meet all the demands. It is the self-imposed mission of supply-side paternalists to limit the overuse of scarce resources even when there is no money-price to stem the buffet syndrome. Time-price is one way of keeping expenditure within the boundaries set by the budget. People always complain. If, however, they have chosen the time-price system, they cannot really object when they are asked to wait.

16.3 THE SUPPLY SIDE: PURCHASE AND CONTAINMENT

There is the payment side and there is the treatment side. The payment side, private or State, can exercise its countervailing power to press for constrained utilisation in combination with satisfactory outcomes. The payment side is in a strong position to discourage the treatment centres from inflating the quantities and padding the prices. The individual does not have the time or expertise to recognise when misplaced trust is being abused. The payment pool fills the functional gap.

16.3.1 Information

The insuring agency has overview sufficient to identify the median standard. It can advise the consumer on the choice of doctor and clinic. It can counsel the patient on price, quantity, quality and risk. It has a personal and private incentive to keep the cost of care down. Since commercial providers have the opposite incentive, the net result might be that the biases will cancel out.

The insuring agency is accountable to its shareholders, its trustees or the political leadership. It is compelled by the logic of its position to make itself familiar with clinical trials of efficacy and with economic measures of efficiency. It profiles the doctors to identify practice variation in prescription patterns and referral rates. It investigates the hospitals to pick up dispersion in professional–patient ratios, median waits, medical errors, on-call specialisms, flexibility in scheduling, staff–patient ratios, hotel and catering facilities, rates of cross-infection, post-operative complications, five-year survival rates, average bill per standardised case and average length of impatient stay.

Where costs are out of line, unique circumstances may be recorded in extenuation. These might include an abnormally polluted locality, an abnormally elderly catchment or a deliberate policy of minimal inpatient convalescence in order to maximise the surgical throughput. Costs can, of course, also fall below the norm. Doctors replicating a standard procedure, hospitals with specialised capital, have a higher success rate and fewer expensive readmissions.

Monitoring can have the desired effect. Feldstein cites evidence to show that utilisation review was able to reduce hospital admissions by 12.3 per cent, hospital inpatient days by 8 per cent, total hospital spending by 11.9 per cent and total medical spending by 8.3 per cent. At a discount rate of 5 per cent, this means that a company plan covering 1000 employees would typically make a net saving of $633 000 over a five-year period (Feldstein et al., 1988: 1314). Putting trade secrets into the public domain clearly had the potential to keep down the cost.

Utilisation review must, of course, be complemented by medical audit lest poor workmanship be mistaken for quality. Cost-cutting through tranquillisers and painkillers might imply that the doctors were too inexperienced or too tired to conduct a proper examination or to make an evidence-based evaluation. Sustained cross-infection might indicate that a particular hospital was economising on post-operative hygiene. Medical success indicators such as these educate by means of comparison. A knowledge of the mean and the median can shame underachievers into improving their relative position.

Best practice saves money. Estimating preventable hospitalisations in terms of the best achievable standard, the United States Department of Health calculates that whites would have 590 000 fewer episodes and would save the system $4.8 billion. For blacks the equivalent figures were 470 000 and $3.9 billion (Department of Health and Human Services, 2015: 208). Convergence on best practice clearly has social and economic as well as medical advantages: 'There is little evidence that greater spending brings better health ... In other words, the "cure" for underservice ... appears to be better management of resources, not more spending' (Wennberg and Cooper, 1999: 238).

The fact that insurers are relying on utilisation review to identify overtreatment and overcompensation is a financial incentive for preferred providers to protect their eligibility. Doctors, however, are in two minds about the publicity. While most are opposed to ineptitude and waste, many also feel that the standard practice inhibits their discretion to do their best for their own unique patient. Clinical trials and evolving techniques mean that professional convergence itself must move with the times. Doctors will express the fear that the knee-jerk duplication of the tried-and-tested is a vote against creative deviance that might in the long run deliver a better product. Yet it is conservatism that pays the rent. Being excluded from the insurers' list is almost as bad for the doctor's economic survival as being struck off the medical register.

Data collection makes transparent how well the peers and the cohorts are performing. Yet it also means a leakage from care into administration. Multiple organisations impose parallel burdens. Completeness and complexity generate additional overheads. Marginal cost must be distinguished from average cost. An adjustment must be made for self-correcting excess capacity. Recoveries must be tracked in order to pick up later relapses and delayed readmissions. It all costs money. The policing overhead might exceed the financial gain. Free-marketeering itself might be putting up the cost of care.

Cost-effectiveness and cost–benefit analysis complement the medical evidence. The introduction of new drugs and technologies is made contingent on the demonstration that they are worth the next-best foregone. At the same time, cross-country studies are being conducted on the correlation between health status and financial outlays in a variety of delivery systems. International comparisons do not prove that one system is better than another. The differences in culture and circumstances are too great. They are, however, a shadow on the wall. They provide an indication of what can and cannot be done.

New departures are putting a strain on budgets. Economic analysis might nonetheless establish that improved outcomes are more than justifying the extra cost. Fewer fatalities from heart attacks and cancers mean more productive days at work. Early treatment of cataract and depression improve the body-holder's enjoyment of life. More means less. A short-run rise in cost might reward the initial investment with a competitive surplus.

Cutler and Richardson demonstrated for the United States that high cost can be a bargain at the price. Between 1970 and 1990 the present value of lifetime health capital for a newborn child, discounted at 3 per cent, increased by $95 000. For the over-65s who were living longer due to improved cardiovascular units the rise was even greater. It was $169 000. Crucially, the incremental cost of medical care was only $19 000 for the infants and $34 000 for the elderly. The gain far exceeded the cost: 'The increase in health capital is greater than the increase in medical spending; thus, the return to medical care could be very high' (Cutler and Richardson, 1998: 99). Cost-effectiveness and cost–benefit analysis enabled the community not to mistake a good buy for a deadweight loss that had urgently to be contained.

16.3.2 Reimbursement

Payment that is open ended is a black hole. Providers can supply unnecessary services and bill at will. Where cost pass-through is permissive, suppliers have a licence to print profits and mint revenues. It is the task of the paying agencies to ensure that they do not shelter behind the medical mystique or betray the community's trust.

With respect to quantity, the paying agency might insist on pre-admission certification for all but emergency cases. It might refuse its approval for a more expensive package if it felt that outpatient management, significantly less costly, would meet the clinical need. It might ask to inspect the X-rays and the reports before it accepted liability. It might insist on a second opinion from its own doctor or nurse-auxiliary.

The patient once admitted, the purchasing arm might call for itemised billing. It might demand that medical attention, hotel facilities and pharmaceuticals be invoiced separately. Even more, it might insist that each test in a sequence be individually costed. Abnormal doses and scans might have to be justified in words.

In hospital, the insurer might keep the patient under constant and concurrent review. It will want to ensure that the next step really is cost-effective and that good money is not being thrown after bad. Out of hospital, the insurer might check the paperwork carefully to satisfy itself that nothing had been supplied which had not been agreed.

If the transactions are numerous and the sums involved small, comprehensive monitoring might not repay the investment. It is the usual pattern. In the United States, '82 percent of the population spends less than $5,000 on health care annually ... They account for only 29 percent of the dollars spent' (Cutler, 1994: 16). The minnows do not cover the bait. The whales are more appetising. Because only 18 per cent of the population is accounting for 71 per cent of the cost, it is economical business practice for the insurer selectively to squeeze its gains from the bias. It will concentrate its search on the big bills. It will leave small reimbursements for spot checks and random sampling.

With respect to price, the insurers might substitute prospective for retrospective payment. Where the remuneration is not fixed in advance, the supplier has no financial incentive to pare its fees and limit its mark-ups. Open-ended billing is an invitation to inflate the services. Prices for surgical procedures are normally only estimates until the service is delivered. Prospective payment alters the game. A fixed rate is agreed upon in advance. It is the same fixed rate whether the supplier makes a profit or a loss.

The predetermined indemnity reflects the median experience of the representative patient. It is not a rubber yardstick that is permissive towards the 'usual, customary and reasonable', but a pre-announced sum that is not open to further negotiation. Unexpected complications can occur and the costs can overrun. Where they do, the unanticipated overhang will be entirely at the charge of the supplier.

Prospective payment shifts the burden of uncertainty not just from the patient to the insurer but also from the insurer to the provider. The treatment centre becomes *de facto* the insurer's reinsurer. The prospective contract forces the supply side and not just the demand side to limit its extravagance. Suppliers become cost-aware. Their new-found sensitivity to workload and productivity has a tendency to put a lid on the cost per episode. The maximum fee is also the minimum. All that the provider can do is to eliminate the waste.

The evidence confirms the conjecture. Rosko and Broyles compared prospective with retrospective payment in 160 American hospitals. The cost per admission under prospective payment was 14.1 per cent lower (Rosko and Broyles, 1987: 97–8). It is not quite a happy end. While the cost per admission may go down, the total annual cost may not. Hospitals that have agreed prepayment per episode can circumvent the purpose of the cap by expanding the number of the episodes. Although the cost per admission was 14.1 per cent lower when prospective payment was adopted, Rosko and Broyles established that the number of admissions had actually risen by 11.7 per cent (Rosko and Broyles, 1987: 97–8).

Assuming that the case mix remained the same, the cost that was contained could not have exceeded 2.4 per cent.

So long as there is little dispersion in the severity of each condition, the treatment centres will not raise any objection to a standard rate. Where, however, there are high-risk outliers that can be spotted in advance, the provider paid prospectively will have an economic incentive to refuse chronic cases that will cost more than the norm. A flat rate can starve out the most in-need. It is undeniable that it is cost-containing to turn away the above-average pathologies. Yet exclusion is not a good way to help the sick.

A flat rate can lead to a periphery of rejections. The problem is not market failure but simply the logic of supply and demand. Known loss-makers are unattractive to commercial profit-seekers. The only way to shelter the loss-makers from the actuaries is for the refusal of cover to be proscribed by law.

The law might demand that the flat rate be high enough to reflect special needs within the pool. Savings made on the less complicated cases would then be recycled to cross-subsidise the more severe, the more expensive ones. A devolved and commercial alternative would be for the insuring agency to shade its prospective rate where it is clear that a specific patient, exceptionally ill, will require repeated transfusions, patented drugs and long stays that the hospital would otherwise have had to cover on its own.

Alongside abnormal outgoings, payment over the odds might also be offered to compensate the treatment centre for local heterogeneities such as above-average wages, a teaching commitment or active outreach. A large nation will encompass a multiplicity of variations. Expense will vary from one submarket to another. One size might not fit all.

The insuring agency, private or public, might have to show some flexibility in its prospective payments. At the same time, it must not be too accommodating lest it open the floodgates to special pleading and greed-driven expense. A middle way would be for supplementary compensation to be released only after the above-average burden had reached an overhang of 10 per cent or more. This threshold is analogous to the deductible in a private contract. The purchaser is forcing the provider to absorb some at least of the supernormal cost.

If an identical indemnity per diagnostic-related group is quoted for all institutions in a definable category, the level must be high enough to ensure normal profits for the least efficient. The marginal provider, economically substandard, will not have to cut its costs to survive. The intra-marginal enterprise, already superstandard, will continue to earn a windfall profit. Support prices in agriculture have long been confronted with a similar trade-off between conditioned-reflex inertia and dynamic efficiency. Costs do not go up but neither do they go down. It is a compromise. A low indemnity would shake out the barely economic. In business terms it would make sense. It would, however, be political suicide for a government to allow a succession of small, local hospitals to be converted into luxury flats.

All claims for special treatment will have to be carefully scrutinised. It will have to be demonstrated that it really is the intricacy of the bypass or the high rents in Manhattan that are giving rise to the exception. It must be shown that the claim is not an excrescence of supplier-induced demand, unwarranted practice variation or the internal inefficiency of a thoroughly confused management. Defend itself as it will, the knowledge that the wall is also a door is an invitation to moral hazard. In the limit the pragmatically allocated extras might subvert altogether the end of cost containment. Too many exceptions would undermine the rule.

Cost escalation is not the only risk. As with all fixed-fee systems, prospective payments can result in undertreatment. Money can be saved by economising on the seniority or the number of the attending physicians, reducing the battery of tests and prescriptions, making the inpatient stay dangerously brief. The relationship between inputs and outcomes is not always clear-cut. Even so, the temptation to omit the failsafes and the double-checks is not reassuring to the patient who expects the clinical optimum and does not want a make-do. Patient confidence is undermined by so undignified a display of avarice. Patients can nonetheless take some comfort from the insurer's quality control and the prospect of repeat business. They are checks and balances built into the system which ensure that flagrant corner-cutting will not be widespread.

Prospective payment proceeds on the basis not of a single patient but of a diagnostic-related group (DRG). The classifications, each of them 'clinically coherent', simplify the task of administration and reimbursement. Weighting patients by their DRG, a case mix index for the hospital as a whole can be constructed. It is tidy but it does not always contain the cost. In terms of prices, there is 'DRG creep' whereby a patient with several conditions is automatically put into the highest-paying group. In terms of quantities, payment by DRG does nothing to limit the number of interventions. The solution might be for the insurer to complement price controls with volume controls. It might not be a sustainable strategy. Ceilings to police ceilings will make the system top-heavy and cumbersome. There is, moreover, a limit beyond which sick people cannot be disappointed merely because aggravated haemophilia is bad business.

16.3.3 Selective Incentives

Purchasing agencies are in a position to issue guidelines that keep the cost of care down. Hospitalisation will not be reimbursed where there is a domiciliary alternative. Minor surgery should be performed by a general practitioner. All tests must be completed pre-admission. Operations must be scheduled within the first 24 hours. Home visits must be restricted in favour of office-based consultations. Guidelines are more than moral suasion. They are sanctioned with rewards and penalties. Providers who want to be paid are nudged in the direction of the least expensive option. There is no guarantee that this will be the outcome that would have been ground out either by medical efficacy or by consumer sovereignty. Cost containment is not the only test that the health care system is functioning well.

Targeted incentives encourage suppliers to perform certain tasks and to phase out others. Performance bonuses and special-needs concessions, as was discussed in Chapter 6, section 6.3, complement the three core modes of remuneration. They alter the rules of the game. Because they nip ill-health in the bud, they are instances where money is spent in order that money might be saved: 'Only one-quarter of people with hypertension have their blood pressure successfully controlled, despite a wealth of effective medications ... What we do not prevent, we wind up treating later, frequently at higher cost' (Cutler, 2004: xi).

Early detection reduces the medium-term cost. Cost falls because cost has risen. It is sound business sense. Or is it? The fewer the patients who die young, the more who will live on to experience the degenerative diseases of old age. Cost rises because cost has fallen. The life cycle becomes a business cycle. Subprime people become the harbinger of a crash. It is best not to think that way.

Bonuses for positive patient feedback can encourage professionals to invest in courtesy and attentiveness. Bonuses for antenatal monitoring can reduce the lifetime costs of perinatal compromise. Bonuses for the follow-up of prescription antidepressants can cut the incidence of attempted suicide. Bonuses for below-average complications or above-average recoveries can stimulate the surgeons and the hospitals to race their counterparts for the prize.

Incentives have both clinical and economic objectives. For both reasons they have the potential to keep down the cost of care. Providers would think differently if the risk profile were to be shaken up by economics: 'If there were additional income to be earned by making sure cholesterol tests were performed, doctors would figure out how to increase testing' (Cutler, 2004: 101). If there were to be special payments for the hardest-hit deciles, doctors would have an economic stake in the reduction of the health care divide: 'If the relative benchmarks are set correctly, insurers will not want to take the rich over the poor. Indeed, the poor could even be prized enrollees' (Cutler, 2004: 109).

We welcome the filthy when they come bearing lucre. Doctors would send out reminders. Doctors would programme their computers. Their motivation may be self-interest but the end-state is affordable health. Adam Smith's herring men, subsidised by the State, set themselves the objective of 'catching, not the fish, but the bounty' (Smith, 1961 [1776]: II, 25). It was the bounty and not the fish that made them put out to sea. Yet, as if guided by an invisible hand, the fish were caught and the nation was fed. Selective incentives were enough for the herring men. Medical professionals are human too.

Selective incentives can be targeted at the patient as well as the supplier. Thus the insurer might suspend the deductible if the patient agrees to day-case rather than inpatient surgery. It might cancel the cost-shares if the patient goes to a lower-cost hospital abroad. It might quote a lower premium for an applicant who, neither a smoker nor a drinker, reveals that they are investing prudently in their own health capital. It might deny reimbursement to a patient who consults a specialist without a first assessment and a referral from a family doctor.

Aware that prevention is cheaper than cure, the insurer might offer discounts on occupational plans where the employer sponsors fitness memberships, runs stress-management sessions and retains an on-site nurse. Aware that early detection is cheaper than the asymptomatic time-bomb, the insurer because of narrow economising might make annual check-ups compulsory and require all diabetics to present for blood-sugar monitoring. Insurance, in short, can be active rather than passive. If moral hazard is believed to aggravate the risk profile, then immoral hazard may be said to improve it.

Business is business. Cost containment can be the result. Adam Smith said that bureaucrats on a salary were seldom known for their cost-conscious good husbandry. The fault lay not in the character of the civil servants but in the incentive structure that had led them to stagnate into carelessness and indolence. That, however, is the key: 'Public services are never better performed than when their reward comes only in consequence of their being performed, and is proportioned to the diligence employed in performing them' (Smith, 1961 [1776]: II, 241). Ultimately, as Cutler says, money talks: 'The medical system works the way the incentives steer it. Rather than fight the system or plead for it to be otherwise, we should instead line the incentives up right so the system gives us what we want' (Cutler, 2004: 46). Money talks. It is the task of the payment arm to design incentive structures that enlist self-interest in the service of good health.

It is not very easy. The danger is that suppliers might select only those means that enable them to score well on a standard test. Practitioners who qualify for a bonus when blood in urine goes down will register only responsible adults who can afford the tablets. Hospitals which receive above-average subsidies for above-average survivals will turn away patients in ambulances who are by inspection a wasting asset. The incentives can turn perverse. They can turn malign. Automaticity does not guarantee an optimum. Payment systems that drive out the sick are no better than insurance plans that cream-skim the healthy because it is efficiency and not equity that makes the share values rise.

16.4 THE SUPPLY SIDE: SIZE AND COST

The average cost is a function of scope and scale. Other things being equal, a rational society will want a system that minimises the unit cost of health. Other things are seldom equal. Health policy does the best it can.

16.4.1 Integration

Mergers and acquisitions, demergers and buy-outs, expansion and contraction are common in all areas of economic life as enterprises seek out their optimum size. Health care is an economic activity like any other. In health care, as in transportation, banking and communications a fine course must be charted between 'too small' and 'too large'.

The underdeveloped organisation will be high-unit-cost because it has not yet exploited its economies of scope. The overdeveloped organisation will be high-unit-cost because it has already exhausted its internal economies of scale. Somewhere between the minnow and the whale there will be the lowest point on a U-shaped curve. An organisation that settles at the lowest point on its U is an organisation, other things being equal, that is contributing what it can to the containment of cost.

The cost of production is more than the cost of manufacturing alone. Alongside the physical cost of transforming iron into steel there are the transaction costs of collecting information, negotiating contracts and monitoring deception. Williamson, acknowledging the familiar argument for spreading the fixed overheads without incurring communication slippages, takes the view that the two kinds of cost are not equally important. The cost of producing, he says, is 'rarely decisive'. It is the cost of doing business that better explains whether the organisation will be small or large: 'Transactional considerations, not technology, are typically decisive in determining which mode of organization will obtain in what circumstances and why' (Williamson, 1975: 2, 248).

In tracing the *raison d'être* of the unified organisation back to the relative cost, Williamson was echoing the contention of the founding father Coase that 'the distinguishing mark of the firm is the supersession of the price mechanism' (Coase, 1937: 389). Every organisation has to decide what it will produce in-house and what it will buy in from outside. Coase used neoclassical microeconomics to demonstrate that it is all a matter of comparative cost. Market exchange or intra-organisational supply, ideology breaks down in the face of applied economics: 'When we are considering how large a firm will be the principle of marginalism works smoothly. The question always is, will it pay to bring an extra exchange transaction under the organising authority?' (Coase, 1937: 404).

On the one hand there are the butcher, the brewer and the baker who buy and sell on their own account. On the other hand there are the multinationals, the monoliths and the ministries who like to keep their swaps within the family. A priori there is no way of adjudicating between them. Smith on exchange or Weber on hierarchy, it all depends on the 'comparative costs of planning, adapting and monitoring task completion under alternative governance structures' (Williamson, 1981: 1544). Nothing is ever clear in advance of play. Sometimes the Coca-Cola Company will be the better buy. Sometimes the economic choice will be the barrow boy who sells apples in the street. Institutional survival alone will decide.

Coase and Williamson are insistent that the choice between exchange and organisation is one that can only be made pragmatically, impartially, case by case. Yet it is one that is being made every day, and the field of health is no exception. Vertically and horizontally, integration is taking place. Coase and Williamson would say that it is sensible to have an open mind. Others, less cautious, would suggest that both the physical plant and the transaction costs are already voting for the whale and not for the minnow that can no longer compete.

Vertically, a health care conglomerate can integrate backwards into orthopaedic prostheses and research laboratories. It can integrate forwards into health insurance and retail pharmacies. It can buy out small competitors providing radiology and imaging services. It can insource helplines previously operated by small independents. It can operate its own nursing school to ensure adequate supplies of a bottleneck input. Internalising its value chain, it is building a wall around its business. Whatever may happen to the industry and the world, at least those of us inside the wall will be safe.

Vertical integration is a way in which the organisation can hedge its bets. Diversification and synergy protect its resources and its markets from the vagaries of an outsider organisation's business plan. An established brand name is a reliable shelter that keeps the marginal cost of market penetration down. The hospital and the airline come under the umbrella of the fizzy drink. New lines are trusted because old lines have not let their customers down. Meanwhile, the profits from old lines can be used to subsidise the new departures until they have consolidated their market position.

Horizontally, a health care corporation can amalgamate with a troublesome rival. Sideways expansion enables it to reduce its uncertainty, minimise its excess capacity, enhance its bargaining position, invade a new territory and enrich its market share. A sideways sweep would allow it to expand without deserting its core business. Teeth in India is teeth in Kenya. The organisation has name recognition for teeth. It builds on the reputation it has already won.

Corporate growth through mergers and acquisitions means that it can retain its stranglehold over its 'proprietory assets' (Caves, 2007: 106). These might include a unique way of doing budget surgery, a one-off patent or an unusual business model which it does not want to fall into the hands of an interloper. Integration in this sense becomes an entry barrier. The first-mover multiplies its advantage to such an extent that a second-mover can no longer mount a credible challenge. The result may be a takeover that reduces the average cost.

At some point the sum of the technological and the transaction costs will be at their minimum. That is the theory. The practice is the fog. Destruction is creative. Aiming at the most efficient point on a familiar U, the firm ends up at a less efficient point on an even lower U. Entrepreneurship is a kaleidoscope that makes every optimum into a flux. Identifying the lowest point and manoeuvering the organisation into the appropriate slot is in itself an entrepreneurial act. It is a leap of faith. No one knows what the future will bring.

Perhaps the hierarchy will compete away the market: 'Changes like the telephone and the telegraph which tend to reduce the cost of organising spatially will tend to increase the size of the firm' (Coase, 1937: 397). Perhaps, however, it will be the small organisation that will be dealt the winning cards. Hiving off might allow a hospital to concentrate on its core business of making sick people well. Call centres abroad, blood supply capitalists at home, perhaps a mix of globalisation, microelectronics and the division of labour will have a role to play in keeping the cost of care down.

Yet costs are not prices and prices are not bills. Even if the costs fall, hospitals might not pass the savings on to the paying agency. Oligopolists are notoriously unwilling to share their profits with the community. Where price cuts are inevitable, they might compensate by amplifying the number of treatments they supply. Seen from the perspective of the nation as a whole, the cost of care will not have been contained.

16.4.2 A Coordinated Matrix

The paying partners might take the view that the providing partners are too numerous and too small. Big is beautiful. Anarchic competition is not: 'Large tasks require large organizations. That is how it is' (Galbraith, 1977: 277). The payers might take the view that the providers could reduce their average cost if they rationalised their wasteful duplication. The payers might demand that the providers combine their capacity in order to get the average cost down.

The payers can combine. The providers can combine. There is something more. The payers and the providers might combine with each other across what might increasingly be seen as artificial split. Whether through a health maintenance organisation or a national health service, the marriage of finance with delivery might be able to produce a whole that is more economical than the sum of the parts.

Bisectoral amalgamation means that the organisation that pays is also the organisation that treats. The two pockets are one. A unicameral structure has an incentive to track and control its preferred providers. It has an incentive to practice preventive medicine as a bulwark against expensive surgery. It has an incentive to minimise medical error. The incentive has fed through into the costs. Manning in America found that enrollees in managed care were experiencing more well-child and gynaecological examinations combined with 40 per cent fewer hospital admissions and hospital days than were their counterparts seen under piecework fee for service (Manning et al., 1984: 1508). The substitution of capitation for fee for service must have contributed something to the comparative performance. It is the contention of Manning and others that the united structure must have contributed even more.

Bisectoral concentration may be cutting costs in the health maintenance organisation. If so, then it is likely to be even more effective in the case of a national health service. A single hierarchy has an overview of its own delivery centres and its own cash flow. The fact that there is a single payment arm makes clear to the single provision arm that the budget is fixed unless and until the government readjusts the premiums or the subsidies.

A joined-up network simplifies the task of utilisation review and internal comparison. Member institutions can be identified that are above average in outgoings or below average in medical efficacy. Guidelines, rewards and sanctions can be cross-correlated with differentiating characteristics such as case mix, location and utilisation of capacity.

A system-wide database disentangles the patchwork of costing, billing, accountancy and management. Institution-specific misdiagnosis, cross-infection, readmission or complaints come to light. Follow-up data becomes available that in a multi-supplier environment might have disappeared into parallel files, all of them confidential. Supplier-induced and supplier-reduced demand are thrown into relief. Sustained incompetence and occasional malversation are investigated within the system itself.

A national system is more than a national spreadsheet. Proactive rather than passive, it can standarise policy on waiting times, salaries, promotions, retirement and recruitment. It can plan system-wide for out-of-area referrals in place of the geographical inequity that ties NHS patients to local providers. It can shade hospital budgets in recognition of shorter waits. It can emulate international best practice. It can make legally binding the evidence-based recommendations of authoritative assessors such as, in the United Kingdom, the National Institute for Health and Care Excellence (NICE). In the devolved United States system extra spending seems to have no relationship to better outcomes (Fisher et al., 2003). The excessive spending in the United States represents money crying out to be saved: 'If 30 per cent of medical spending is not necessary, then the potential waste is more than $700 billion annually' (Cutler and Ly, 2011: 5). The NICE targets in Britain seek to limit that open-handed generosity of outlier practice variation.

Medical efficacy aside, a national system on top of the single-payer function can redirect the doctoring pool towards family doctors and away from metropolitan specialists. It can manage the build-up or run-down of the nation's bedstock. It is easier to close an uneconomic hospital if it is known where the neighbourhood spillover of its inpatients and outpatients will lie. Redundant staff can be reposted without threatening their security of employment.

A national system can arrange for hospitals to share underemployed equipment that would otherwise have been unaffordable. Joint operation has the additional advantage that it protects specialist skills from atrophy through disuse. In the private sector individual institutions can copy this model by means of a consortium. Commercial rivals may make a short-run commitment but still their status as competitors is a disincentive to long-term collaboration. The members of a national health system are more receptive to cooperation. Their budget is only marginally affected by the volume of paying business they can snatch from one another.

A national system can link up its members. It can redistribute over-ordered drugs that would otherwise have gone out of date. It can, more ambitiously, bring insider institutions into broader social net. State hospitals can liaise with social workers in order to provide a complete package that prevents a relapse brought on by malnutrition, hypothermia or a near-fatal fall.

The complete package can ensure the smooth transfer of long-stay patients from expensive hospital beds to sheltered housing that costs so much less. The National Health is a part of the Welfare State. The same, however, can be said of the private sector. Even private hospitals can make contact with the ministries and the local authorities to ensure that their patients, when discharged, have somewhere to go. Health and welfare are two sides of a coin. Private or public, the social services are a part of the web.

A national health organisation is a near-monopoly to its customers, a near-monopsony to its suppliers. Being national, there is a presumption that its policies will be broadly consonant with public opinion as refracted through political democracy. A heterogeneous private sector cannot be expected to match its success in conforming to the consensus. Being powerful, a national system can negotiate as a bloc with non-member general practitioners, trade unions, pharmaceutical multinationals and cross-border authorities such as the European Union. It can utilise its countervailing power to buy in bulk at a quantity discount. Near-monopsony can, in short, keep the cost of care down: 'Centralized control of health care budgets seems to result in lower spending levels than otherwise would be expected' (Culyer, 1989: 28). Control succeeds. Planning succeeds. Perhaps the cacophony of competition is only a second-best.

16.4.3 Administration

Yet competition has the great advantage that it keeps the bureaucrats on their toes. The economics textbook teaches that same-side rivalry is a spur. If the free-marketeers are correct, then an obese national hierarchy will be a locus of organisational slack while a multiplicity of lean-and-mean rivals will be driven by their circumstances to keep sterile administration to a minimum.

That is the conjecture. The test is more difficult. A national health service is national insurance sealed in with national delivery. Payment is twinned with provision to make up an ambitious and unique joint product. Not every country, however, fights ill-health with the same double-edged sword. If administrative waste is to be compared, than some subdivision of the broad health kingdom must be found in which both public and private have a presence. Such a subdivision is insurance. Insurance is unambiguous and it is universal. Intertemporally and internationally, insurance is an area in which meaningful similarities can be found.

Richard Titmuss compared private health insurance in the United States with national health insurance in the United Kingdom. His conclusion was that the slippage in American capitalism had become so great that 'the consumer now gets less than half his dollar back in medical care' (Titmuss, 1963: 258). Competition in America had not been on the side of the consumer. Nationalisation in Great Britain had been the better buy:

> The administrative costs of private Workmen's Compensation Insurance were of the order of 30 to 40 per cent of the premiums collected. Such figures can now be compared with the administrative costs of the Department of Health and Social Security in administering the present system of National Insurance against Industrial Injuries and Diseases. These costs are in the neighbourhood of 5 to 10 per cent. The private market was many times more costly in terms of administrative efficiency. (Titmuss, 1974: 82)

Titmuss was not saying that the whole of purchase-plus-provision was many times less costly than the institutional arrangements that had preceded it. His evidence relates exclusively to the national insurance function. Here, even allowing for the passage of time that separates the bowler hat from the Beatles, he is announcing that he has demonstrated the superiority of hierarchy over exchange. On the one hand there was 30 to 40 per cent. On the other hand there was 5 to 10 per cent. Administrative savings on the delivery side might still further have strengthened his case. The evidence he cited confirmed his long-standing ideological bias. Public costs less than private. Public is the cost-containing choice.

Administration is a parasite that is forever on the take. Underwriting, correspondence, reinsurance, monitoring, advertising, marketing, paper, printing, software, hardware, billing, appeals, staff training, auditing, record-keeping, book-keeping, business strategy, paying commissions, checking credentials, estimating contingencies, collecting premiums, collecting co-payments, communicating with clients, managing claims, satisfying the regulators, filling in the forms – all of this creams money off the top.

There is more to follow. The statistic on administration does not include the supra-competitive bonuses that senior management pays itself. It does not include the private administration that is performed in-house by companies with a group plan. It does not include the personal administration that is down to individuals when they fight their way through the forms, the options and the spreadsheets. Profits are extra. It is not clear if they should be classified as administrative waste, a private tax or a necessary incentive.

Administration can be regarded as a hand in the till. Importantly, it can also be seen as a social benefactor that has a cost-containing function. Services such as risk appraisal, detection of fraud, verification of eligibility, utilisation review and case management keep the long-run cost of care down. Information is provided to doctors and pharmacists about unwarranted practice variation, potential overuse and harmful cross-indications. Reminders are sent to patients to take their drugs. Reserves are held idle to smooth the cash flow. Micro-costs such as these ultimately make the macro-costs less. They are a gain and not a drain. They are a *memento mori* to the possibility that administrative costs in the public sector might have been too low relative to the benefits that they might have occasioned. Complexity can be good. Cost containment can be a false economy.

There are the benefits but there is the deadweight too. Part of administration is a genuine loss for which no improvement in insurance or health status is ever returned. Comparisons bring the achievable economies into sharp relief. Woolhandler estimates that operational overheads are 11.7 per cent of total cost in American private insurance but only 3.6 per cent for Medicare and 1.3 per cent in the Canadian national scheme (Woolhandler et al., 2003: 768). There seem to be 44 per cent more administrators in pluralistic America than in single-payer Canada. Administration accounted for 39 per cent of the difference in cost (Cutler and Ly, 2011: 6).

The United States Congress confirmed the public–private divide: 'Administrative costs and return on investment account for about 11 per cent of private plans' costs of delivering Medicare benefits, whereas the administrative costs of the fee-for-service Medicare program ... account for less than 2 per cent of its expenditures' (Congressional Budget Office, 2006: 12). Goldman and Leive felt that Congress if anything had been too kind. They raised the 11 per cent to 17 per cent (Goldman and Leive, 2013). Pauly and Percy raised it still further to 34 per cent for a group health insurance policy, 44 per cent for a single or family contract (Pauly and Percy, 2000: 20).

In Taiwan the administrative costs of the national health insurance scheme, modelled on American Medicare, are, like American Medicare, 2 per cent. The administrative costs in the private health insurance sector are 16 per cent. In the Netherlands they are 4.4 to 4.9 per cent in the public sector, 10.4 per cent in the private sector. In Switzerland they are 5.0 to 6.1 and 16.1 per cent respectively. In Mexico they are 16.9 per cent and 32 per cent. For Bangladesh the figure in the public sector is not known. In the private sector it is 53 per cent (Nicolle and Mathauer, 2010: 6, 7, 8). For Bangladesh at least, Titmuss was right. The consumer now gets back less than half his dollar in medical care.

In Australia in the private sector the leakage into administration is 15.8 per cent. In the German private sector it is 20.4 per cent (Woolhandler et al., 2003: 773). In Britain the loading, defined as the excess of premium income over claims expenditure is, aggregated for the private insurance industry as a whole, not far short of 25 per cent (Boyle, 2011: 93). While some of the evaporation into duplication might have been cost-containing, some of it was an incubus that would have been better employed to make sick people well: 'Removing this gap would provide an attractive means of saving a large amount of money, money that could be recycled to cover the uninsured' (Gruber, 2008: 585).

If that is so, then a single-payer system would be far and away the better buy. The problem is that it might not be so. Geeks, nerds, wonks, sophisters and economists alone know the truth. All that the rest of us know is that the figures can be presented in a variety of ways using a variety of techniques to support a variety of conjectures. Different reporting methods, different statistical methods, different time periods, different levels of domestic product all make both intra-national and international comparisons an art rather than a science.

The world is a very big place. Services, culture, coverage and infrastructure are not all the same. A corrupt society requires more monitors than a self-policing one. A dispersed population without good microelectronics costs more to administer than a city-State with top-notch computers. A country which makes its contributions income-related will require more inspectors than a country which falls back on an undifferentiated flat rate. A country with a labour shortage will spend more on skilled manpower than a country that opens its doors to foreigners.

Like must be compared with like. The world, however, is a labyrinth of unlikeness. Sometimes but not always, the premiums for health insurance are collected at the same time as house insurance, social security or general taxation: how should the overheads be apportioned? Sometimes but not always the State system is for the destitute while the private system is for the prosperous: since the chronic consume more services, is it any surprise that Medicare fixed overheads fall as a proportion of the throughput? It is all so different.

Plato makes it the task of the philosopher-ruler to govern in accordance with the truth. That is why the post of philosopher-ruler is not easy to fill. The truth does not speak for itself. Its representatives, however, have been more than willing to speak on its behalf.

Nicolle and Mathauer, speaking for the truth, contend that administrative costs in private health insurance systems are 'on average nearly 3 times higher than for public ones' (Nicolle and Mathauer, 2010: 11). Paul Krugman, also speaking for the truth, calculates that extending Medicare to all Americans as a State-run national insurance scheme would reduce the share of health care in the national product from 18 per cent to 14 per cent:

> In international perspective, the United States spends nearly six times as much per capita on health care administration as the average for Organization for Economic Cooperation and Development [sic] (OECD) nations. Nearly all of this discrepancy is due to the sales, marketing, and underwriting activities of our highly fragmented framework of private insurance, with its diverse billing and review practices. (Krugman, 2009)

Overlapping bureaucracies, Krugman states, are not cost-effective. Since life-expectancy in the United States is less than that in the European social democracies that offer 'universal Medicare', there would be still more gains in terms of health status and social equality.

Robert Book, also speaking for the truth, makes an equally persuasive calculation. He contends that 'on a per-person basis Medicare's administrative costs are actually *higher* than those of private insurance ... Switching the more than 200 million Americans with private insurance to a public plan will not save money but will actually increase health care administrative costs by several billion dollars' (Book, 2009). Several billion dollars is a considerable sum of money.

Now at last the truth is out. Administration costs more in the public sector. Administration costs more in the private sector. Administration costs more in both sectors. The only cheap alternative is not to have administration at all.

17. State, market and cost

Laws shape choices. Natural law gravitates to the market equilibrium as if guided by an invisible hand. It is one law but it is not the only law. This chapter is about the balance between automaticity and plan when the invisible hand has demonstrably failed to contain the cost.

Section 17.1, 'An internal market', is about the compromise solution of quasi-markets within a State-owned system. Section 17.2, 'Controls', discusses the role of ceilings and licences when free enterprise is thought unable to stop the rise. Section 17.3, 'Liberalisation', is about deregulation. Some observers have contended that decentralisation is an untapped resource that can put all the clocks right. Section 17.3 says that nothing in the world can put all the clocks right. There is no pill for every ill, but some pills can cure some of the ills some of the time. Section 17.3 asks if the return of autonomy from the whole to the part is such a pill.

17.1 AN INTERNAL MARKET

The previous chapter explained that large tasks require large organisations. Complete physical, mental and social well-being is a large task. A national health service is a large organisation. Monoliths have economies and monopolies contain costs. Under Stalin, Russian railways ran on time. It would have been a waste to lay duplicate tracks side by side so long as these railways satisfied the Russians' reasonable expectations. Are duplicate beds any different? Prima facie it is an argument for a unified network.

It would be premature, however, to say that a single web will necessarily grind out value for money in combination with decent client satisfaction. In the textbook free market it is supply-side competition and demand-side search that induce the butcher, the brewer and the baker to deliver a quality product at an affordable price. In the administered system of silos and hierarchies the incentive structure is different. It might happen that an unaccountable rubric and an impenetrable flowchart will come between patients and the complete good health that the World Health Organization has made theirs by right. If a national health service does not satisfy the democratic groundswell, then pressure is bound to build for the monoliths to be privatised and the monopolies broken up.

A national service has a social mandate to safeguard the nation's health. While parliaments and politicians will not always be able to provide the continuous and informed scrutiny that is required, still the answer is not inevitably the de-nationalisation of the titles. Private ownership may not be the precondition so long as there is workable competition. All that is required is that the single shareholder should actively create an internal market.

17.1.1 The National Budget

The revenues are the taxes, fees, charges, contributions and borrowing. The disbursements are the allocations paid for specific activities. The government is the valve that manages the flow. Even public spending is effective demand. No commitment can ever be open-ended. There is always a resources constraint.

Where the national budget is single-period, it is likely to be pushed upward year on year by the lobbies, the interest groups and the electorate. Democracy is not cheap. The share of the budget going to health is especially likely to rise. Even if medicine is flat-of-the-curve, still citizens are seduced by the mystique into thinking that more inputs will improve their health.

Where the national budget is multi-period, there at least there will be a constitutional cap that blocks off the politicising impact of special pleading. Time is a veil of uncertainty. Fixed limits agreed upon in advance mean that citizens choose the binding constraint in radical ignorance of their own personal history-to-come. They may later discover that the budget was pitched too high or too low for their needs: 'If so, a binding cost ceiling might well impose a welfare loss, by preventing medical care consumers and providers from making mutually advantageous exchanges' (Newhouse, 1992: 19). Regret is endemic where choices are being made in unknowledge. The alternative, however, is in-period struggle for concession; and that way lies the escalation in cost.

17.1.2 The Practice Budget

Once the national budget has been approved, once the subdivision for health care has been agreed, the paying arm must either make its own purchases or decentralise its choices to its delegates. If the money is devolved to the level of the patient, each body-holder becomes their own payer. Shoppers are given vouchers which they may be allowed to top up.

They use those vouchers to buy services from a socially validated range of medical providers. Information asymmetry can, however, waste the taxpayers' transfers; and that is why the licence to spend is more commonly distributed to the general practitioners. Fund-holding family doctors then use their practice budgets to buy all outpatient and inpatient services on behalf of the clients who are on their list.

The size of each practice budget is determined by the funding body. The formula will reflect the number of patients for whom the family physician is the primary purchaser. It will take into account the demographic composition of the list and the cost of referrals in the locality. One-off supplementation may be granted for a catastrophic episode where without a piecemeal top-up the practice budget would be exhausted. Supernormal capitations may be paid for high-risk hard cases likely to impose an above-average drain.

Social values will play a part. Most of all will society have an impact in a politically sensitive national health system. If there is a strong consensus that the unmet needs of the absolutely deprived should be given a high priority, the practice budgets might be levelled up where doctors take their citizenship commitments to heart. Without the add-on, the budget-holders might be led by their duty to their median patient to turn away the neglected.

The money follows the patient who follows the practitioner. Acting as a medical professional, the primary doctor makes a diagnosis and outlines the scenarios. Acting as a small business, the fund-holder then costs the clinics and scans the specialists. The agent acts and the principal fits in. Cash-limited and calculative, the family doctor knows that resources are finite. The knowledge that there is a limit focuses the mind on value. It also makes rival hospitals price more competitively. Each is trying to attract the practice budgets into the shop.

The hidden assumption is that the doctor has an MBA mindset and a feel for a deal. While some professionals can no doubt function simultaneously as a healer and a tradesman, others will find it out of keeping with their Hippocratic self-image that they should be required to make the money stretch. They will complain that the trade-off between the best possible and the most affordable involves them in a debasing conflict of loyalties. They will assert that cost-consciousness can never be the proper maximand in a caring profession such as health. A compromise might be for the agents to hire subagents of their own to take over the accountancy, the computing and the small savings made at the margin. Out of sight is out of mind. Morally speaking, the sanctimonious transfer of the poisoned chalice leaves much to be desired but at least the practice budget is kept in the black.

As always, there is a risk. Expensive referrals might be dodged. Returning loss-makers might be dropped. The cost of convalescence might not be eliminated but cynically shifted from the medical services to supportive family members, meals-on-wheels, private taxis, community services and charity shelters. Even if no false economies actually make the news, the patient is not a fool.

The principal might be especially concerned where the budget-holder is allowed to retain the annual underspend. The residual windfall, the equivalent of the private sector's profit motive, is a focused incentive for the alert and the entrepreneurial to search prudently and bargain hard. It may not be a strong enough reason to make the patient well.

The disgruntled can transfer their capitations to another practitioner. They can lodge a vague, perhaps unprovable complaint. They can abandon State medicine for fee-for-service private care. Other than that there is not a lot the alienated can do if they suspect that their national health portal is pursuing a private and personal agenda. Alienation is antithetical to the bedrock of trust in the doctor–patient relationship. Free-marketeers put their faith in the complementary self-interest of the butcher, the brewer and the baker. Kidney patients might not.

It is commercialisation, consumerism and commodification. Yet a medical consultation is qualitatively different from meat, beer and bread. What is suitable for marketisation in one area of life might not be suitable in all. Historically, the medical nexus has been fragmented down to the level of one caring doctor, one ailing patient. Ethics may not allow for shopping around.

An internal market is both the consequence and the cause of a cultural receptiveness to the invisible hand. Freedom of exchange is not just an allocative mechanism but a mentality, an ideology and a window on the world. Hegemonic as it is, the primacy of interest does not appeal equally to all observers. An internal market has been criticised for its tendency to shift attention from medicine to consumer's choice and cost-effectiveness: 'The myth of efficiency, productivity, and accountability trumps the myth of trustworthy expertise applied altruistically to the needs of patient … client … I mean customers. It is the master myth of modern society' (Light, 2000: 971). Light says that the master myth is driving out the alternative myth that disinterested service has intrinsic value in itself.

17.1.3 'Market Socialism'

The previous section showed that, on the demand side, an internal market devolves choices to the family doctor and the practice budget. This section is concerned with the supply side. It demonstrates that even within a nationalised system the constituent providers can compete with one another for payment by results. Each National Health hospital becomes a wolf to every other.

If the global budget for each hospital is a fixed allocation, the institutions have no financial incentive to improve efficiency or throughput. There is even the perverse incentive to extend inpatient stays so as to reduce the frequency of costly surgery. The situation is different when the institutions are obliged to earn their living through sequential contracts. Free-standing managements have to differentiate their product. They have to experiment and innovate. They have to keep their costings keen and their delivery dates competitive. They have to earn their budget. In the absence of an annual allocation their funding is linked directly to customer satisfaction and work coming in.

Rivalry comes at a price. The British experience indicates that management had no choice but to let quality standards slip: 'Hospitals located in more competitive areas had higher death rates' (Propper et al., 2008: 165). Hospitals in less competitive areas had fewer patients who left in a box. People died but at least the queues went down: 'We estimate the cumulative impact of competition on death rates to have more or less negated the fall in death rates that the whole sector experienced during the time period due to technological change' (Propper et al., 2008: 139).

An internal market is competition but it is not privatisation. The right of ownership remains firmly vested in the State. Enthoven calls it 'market socialism' (Enthoven, 1985: 40). Market socialism presumes that the State-owned institutions will have hands-off discretion to set their own prices and fix their own salaries. There will not be sensitive market signalling if the component units do not have operational independence. Where practice budgets can be spent for private as well as public treatment, the whole of the health care industry will see itself as one interconnected matrix. Publicly owned or privately owned, all are fellow gain-seekers chasing the same pot of gold.

An internal market can be created not just between the national health institutions but within them as well. If each department were to become a self-contained budget-holder, buying from and selling to its confederates, it would then expand or contract, pay bonuses or cut wages, depending on the fee income that it brings in. Internal billing rather than an automatic pro rata focuses the mind on performance and efficiency. A section that fails to earn a living for itself goes to the wall. Thus does the kaleidoscope of Coase slim down the capital.

There are exceptions. Some divisions such as the emergency room will always be unprofitable. A hospital which wants to retain them will have to cross-subsidise them. Outside the hospital, the national authorities might earmark additional funding for loss-making departments that meet a named social need. No one wants an epidemic or a plague to spread. Where the isolation ward does not return a profit, the social consensus will be unanimous in calling upon the State to cover the externality. A special case is, however, the exception. Expediency is the rule.

Market socialism relies on financial incentives to stimulate productivity. So does market capitalism. It is possible to see the internal market as a disequilibrium stage on the road from the National Health to full, gain-seeking, State-less private enterprise. Some people would say that the transition is as inevitable and as evolutionary as the collapse of Soviet planning and the triumph of individual-based homeostasis. The Electricity Board has gone. The Coal Board has gone. The Health Board is safe. The Berlin Wall belongs to the past. The future belongs to the Royal Free. Why?

17.1.4 State Capitalism

Once an internal market has been adopted the role of the single property-owner becomes ambiguous. It may be a misnomer to speak of a national health service at all when there is no clear distinction between a stable of State-owned competitors and a network of managed care organisations.

All treatment centres, public or private, have to conform to the law. National health or commercial health, all are bound by the baselines and the guidelines that have been laid down by the State. What is central to the logic of the internal market is that nationalised competitors cannot be encumbered by additional guidelines which would make the playing field uneven. An internal market is a fight to earn budgets. If a single shareholder insists on a single market, it cannot also insist that its National Health should make a citizenship investment in the social fabric. That is not how business is done.

There is no reason why a hands-on government should not restrict hospital-building in overprovided areas or legislate for affirmative action in employment and promotion. Social engineering is a time-hallowed function of public policy. What it cannot do in the internal market is to make selective use of its medical assets to push through its social reforms. The laws must be the same for all. The public sector cannot be made subject to uneconomic burdens merely because its capitalist is the State.

It is all very confusing. Nationalised enterprise has often been legitimated with the argument that absentee owners cannot plan or coordinate.

The internal market stands the case for service-wide direction on its head. In the internal market the providers must have operational freedom. The State should be scrupulously hands-off. Politicians and civil servants lack knowledge and incentives. Hospital administrators know better. It is not clear whether the private market knows best. If it does, then it might be time for State capitalism to be auctioned off.

It is already happening. Catering, cleaning and gardening are contracted out to profit-seekers whose short-lease monopoly is renewable only if their performance is competitive. Bookings, accounts, blood banks, blood tests, maintenance and laundry are franchised to independent specialists tasked to keep the price down. Hospital doctoring is subcontracted on a rolling basis to locum agencies with a track record to defend. Air ambulances are put out to sequential suppliers quoted on the Stock Exchange. Hospital pharmacies are leased to High Street companies that every patient knows and trusts. Surgeons commission their cyberknife from a multinational corporation that has never sworn a Hippocratic Oath rather than from an in-house manufactory that has never been sullied by an invisible hand. It is already happening. Rolling reappraisal is already here.

On the one hand there are the Adam Smithian brewers and bakers who serve us out of self-interest. On the other hand there are Bevanite socialists who want to help the sick. The borders between capitalism and socialism are shifting sands in the whirlwind of applied economics. If nutritious food and clean sheets can be privatised on the model of the hospital fruit-stall, then it may be just as efficient for intensive care and the recovery room to be hived off from the State capitalist who knows best.

17.2 CONTROLS

The model is the doctor who does battle with cruel nature to save the patient's life. If it were left to laissez-faire, the patient would have died. The great lawmaker is just such a doctor. Regulations that reshape the quantity and channel the price are alternatives to libertarian automaticity. Active rather than passive, the artificial and the manufactured distort the balance of nature. They do this because great lawmakers, like great doctors, will often refuse to equate the social optimum with the natural equilibrium when, as in the case of cost, the 'is' and the 'ought to be' may not be the same.

17.2.1 Output

Inflation in the price of care may be likened to a polluting externality. As with the public bad of an unfiltered chimney, State intervention may be needed to correct a market failure.

Flexible prices are attractive because they identify an imbalance and set in train a correction. Medical care is different. In the case of medical care, never-satisfied demand tends always to outstrip supply. Administered prices cap the bills because, in medicine at least, there is no market-clearing equilibrium that is not distorted by information asymmetry and producer power.

The State, in consultation with the medical profession, can appoint a regulatory commission to fix the reimbursements. The schedules may not be enough to contain the cost. Suppliers may still be able to induce demand through marginal tests and unneeded interventions. Discretionary extras, through additional volume, compensate the clinicians for the ceiling on price. Some specialisms will be left unregulated. The State sector may be capped but not the private sector. Total cost might be shifted but not reversed or reduced.

Price controls are handicapped by complexity. Prices and quantities are difficult to police. There is no economic way to plug all the loopholes, inspect all the invoices and identify all the add-ons. No office consultation or precautionary procedure is ever standard-sized. Besides that, different regions have different costs. A national schedule would become a matrix of exceptions.

Statutory schedules go out of date when new technology comes onto the market. Accelerated obsolescence may itself be a byproduct of non-price competition. Treatment centres have to invest in state-of-the-art capital in order to differentiate their product. In that way price controls may put up the cost of care.

The height of the hurdle is a stumbling block. The maximum price, where it is set too low, can lead to hospital closures, lengthening queues and even rationing by lottery. The maximum price, where it tracks the average, will be above the rate that would have been quoted by the go-ahead and the ambitious. They retain the right to price below the average in order to expand market share. Yet human nature is weak and a higher price is a temptation. A price intended to be a maximum can in that way become ossified into a minimum and a target. Serving both as a ceiling and a floor, the spread will be narrowed and allocative efficiency lost.

A cost-plus system is no better. Where the commission fixes the rate of return at some notional opportunity cost, suppliers such as pharmaceutical corporations will have no incentive to cheapen their process or to improve their quality. Whatever they do, the profit per unit supplied will always be the same. Dynamic efficiency is sacrificed to the determination to control.

17.2.2 Input

The price of final services can be regulated. So can the price of the factors of production. Health care is a labour-intensive industry. First and foremost it will be the wage bill that will have to be controlled. In the State sector this can be done through civil service pay scales. It is an advantage of a centralised health service that its manpower plan will integrate remuneration with staff numbers and internal efficiency. In the private sector the payments will have to be contained through an incomes policy, mandatory and permanent.

Incomes policy can be evaded: a promotion can be offered instead of a rise. It can be inequitable: the low-paid prefer a lump sum but the higher deciles prefer a percentage. It can be inefficient: payment below the opportunity cost may make recruitment difficult. It can be subverted: rent-seekers exaggerate their case because they have their eye on special concessions. Public choice is not the same as public interest.

Capital is the other input that may be regulated. Too many hospitals means high average cost. An arms race means that rival institutions will not be able to spread their fixed overheads or optimise their factor-combinations. Quality standards may slip. Supplier-induced demand may be inevitable as underemployed suppliers seek to drum up business. Too few suppliers, however, mean high retail price. Powerful oligopolies will gouge out whatever the traffic will bear. A rule of reason is clearly required if open-minded regulators are to steer a middle course between the anarchic arms race on the one hand, the restrictive practice on the other.

Excessive competition can be stemmed through entry barriers. Limits on the number of medical schools, protracted placements and internships, stringent licensing for medical staff trained abroad, all limit the volume of business. They do this by limiting the manpower complement without which the treatment centres could not function. As for the centres themselves, new hospitals could be denied access to or expansion in a market catchment unless they had obtained a certificate of need confirming that they would not be flooding the area with idle capacity or wastefully duplicating existing potential.

Such barriers contain the bedstock and the equipment. They may, however, be doing so at the expense of novelty, managerial, professional and technological, that might refresh a frozen industry. Medicine stagnates where settled incumbents are never challenged by hungry interlopers. The just-adequate are sealed in. The very promising are blocked out. It is not easy to promote the survival of the fittest if the fittest are simultaneously being excluded lest they upset a fragile equilibrium.

New entry can be kept out. Winners can be picked and losers denied a permit. Existing players can at the same time be merged and consolidated. A regulatory commission can be a marriage broker that proactively links up the underutilised and the uneconomic. Combination and concentration lower the average cost. Horizontal integration eliminates redundant slack. Vertical integration generates a rational network. A government board empowers firms to trade at their minimum cost.

But not, apparently, the minimum price: 'When consolidation occurs among hospitals geographically close to one another, price increases have been substantially larger, as much as 40 per cent or more' (Holahan and Blumberg, 2008: 3). Cost of production may have gone down but the price to the consumer went up. It is not an obvious way to keep down the share of health.

17.3 LIBERALISATION

The share of health can be inflated by excessive competition. It can also be inflated by inadequate rivalry that may have to be challenged by the State.

17.3.1 Pro-Competitive Regulation

Antitrust watchdogs and competition commissions have traditionally intervened in the public interest where natural monopolies, price leadership, market-making cartels and collusive conspiracies 'in restraint of trade' have refused to translate the economies from scale and scope into discounted prices at the retail stage. Imperfect competitors may be strong-arming the price of output up and the price of input down. Oligopolists may be dividing up the territory, earning surplus profits and gaming new entry. They may be blocking valuable innovations with the spurious justification that without managed markets all could so easily end up bankrupting each. They may, in short, be restricting the supply of doctoring and putting up the price.

Inadequate competition may be self-correcting through laissez-faire. Where, however, the market is not contested, the State can lean against the prevailing winds. It can monitor high-cost institutions and decertify poor performers. It can break a consolidated supply chain into its constituent parts. It can offer tax rebates, start-up grants and investment subsidies to new entrants. It can withdraw tax exemptions and preferential rentals from over-bedded incumbents. It can even allocate permits by auction in order to promote cost-conscious productive efficiency while transferring the monopoly rent to the State. The problem is information. The regulators are dependent on the regulated for the facts, the opinions and the advice. It can lead to the regulatory capture of the policing panel by the special-pleaders. If the health care market is to become more competitive, then the regulatory board cannot stop short at the private sector alone. It must also ensure that the State sector enjoys no especial advantages nor experiences any sector-specific handicaps.

The handicaps, discussed in the first section, relate to the dual function of the National Health in medicine and in social policy. The advantages are just as much of a problem if cross-sector competition is to be used to contain the cost. The public sector has a head start. It is the familiar status quo. Many patients, aware of information asymmetry, are more comfortable with non-profit medicine and more comfortable still with political accountability. There is also the economic calculus. If the State providers are subsidised out of tax, then patients who go private are effectively paying twice for care. It is a sound reason to remain with the devil they know.

17.3.2 A Rational Choice

The free market presumes informed consent. Shoppers must be in a position to make a non-random choice. The newspapers and the internet provide across-the-board background. Hospital websites describe their facilities and their success rates. Family doctors and commercial facilitators fine-tune general knowledge to the specific needs of the medical one-off. Information is all around.

Disclosure is good business where the suppliers are led by self-interest to publicise their unique selling points. Company secrets do not get the good word out. A practice will want to make known that it can advise on diet, allergies and natural childbirth, that it works to a fixed roster of appointments, that it sees patients in the evenings and on Sundays, that it is conveniently situated for public transport, that it has subsidiary expertise in non-standard treatments, that its staff speak minority languages, that its doctors attend refresher courses. Pro-competitive legislation is not needed to induce the rivals to cry their wares. What is needed is a free market in which transparency has an economic value.

A pro-competitive State can supply complements to the free market. It can publish composite tables giving the age, gender, qualifications, referral patterns and experience of local doctors. It can name and shame where professionals have been found guilty of serious misconduct or where there have been substantiated complaints. Most of all, a pro-competitive State can seek to eliminate traditional and functionless restrictions which keep necessary information out of the reach of the consumers. Surgeons must be obliged by law to disclose how often they have performed a specific procedure. They must provide audited feedback from previous customers. Hospitals must be required to post their utilisation reviews and document their median charges. A Freedom of Information Act is in the consumer's interest. The body-holder has a right to know if anyone does.

Commercial advertising can play a role in the diffusion of information and the comparison of alternatives. Pro-market salesmanship can reduce the cost. Kwoka found that the lifting of restrictions on advertising was associated with a decline of more than 20 per cent in the price of optometric services (Kwoka, 1984: 216). It was also associated with shorter consultations on the part of the firms that chose to advertise. Firms that did not were spending up to 11 minutes longer on their examinations. Longer consultations could be a proxy for better eyesight. Alternatively, they could mean no more than flat-of-the-curve. In the absence of any information on the long-term outcomes, the most that can be said is that at least the consumer is being given a choice.

Pro-competitive legislation can mean a free market in the advertising of the facts. It can also mean the half-truth distortions of tasteless manipulation, image creation, film-star endorsements or unrepresentative testimonials. The fear motive dictates that the cowboys and the pirates must be sidelined first. Not all citizens, however, are in the market for minimax. Medical professionals will frequently practice self-regulation as an investment in the integrity of their good name. The advertising industry itself conforms to a self-imposed code which proscribes fraudulent exaggeration and downright mendacity. Sometimes the free market will generate its own warranty. Where it does not, a pro-market State may establish a media watchdog to ensure that informed consent is not sacrificed to the selling imperative.

Publicity can lead to a greater spread in services and prices. It can also mean the opposite in the form of retrenchment and conservatism. The name recognition of a trademark surgeon or a brand-name hospital might push the consumer into the knee-jerk inelasticity of a habitual rut. The return to the tried-and-tested might be a defensive reaction to the information overload which makes people feel insecure and confused in an economic world where time too has a cost: 'In a market with complex information conditions ... advertising may inhibit rather than promote competition' (Rizzo and Zeckhauser, 1990: 498). Name and image are blinkers which restrict search and inhibit competition. New entrants might find it difficult to break in. The barrier of differentiation can put up the cost of service.

So can the elasticity of the pool. In some cases, as with broken bones, the total quantity of procedures supplied cannot be manipulated but the patient flow can be redistributed. In other cases, as with cosmetic surgery, the advertising of the service draws in a first-time clientele and the total volume goes up. Where the numbers are plus-sum rather than zero-sum, the impact of the sales effort is clear. The budget for health goes up.

17.3.3 Gateways and Funnels

Incumbent oligopolies can be challenged and information can be more widely diffused. There is a third form that liberalisation can take. A pro-competitive State can legislate for a greater variety of gateways and funnels. Medical schools and medical qualifications can become a spectrum and not a point. Choice may contribute to the containment of cost.

Accreditation could be granted to private medical schools with a differentiated curriculum. Some could admit school-leavers, others degree-holders, others less-schooled applicants with practical experience, others mid-career professionals seeking a second start. Foreign-trained doctors could be allowed to practice without spurious recertification that resembles a non-tariff barrier. Professional associations could phase out artificial lines of demarcation that prevent a nurse from prescribing an anti-malarial, taking out stitches or delivering a baby. It is an economic waste for practitioners to be overtrained relative to the difficulty of the procedure they are being asked to perform. A less-qualified paramedic will often supply the same service at a significantly lower price.

An unneeded standard of quality artificially inflates the cost. This was demonstrated by Kleiner and Kudrle in their comparison of dentistry in selected American states. Stricter occupational licensing did not improve the clinical outcomes as measured directly by tooth decay and indirectly by complaints and malpractice premiums. What it did do was to constrict the pipeline of new dentists and boost the rents of the professionals:

'Dentists in the most regulated states earn a statistically significant 12 percent more than practitioners in the least regulated states' (Kleiner and Kudrle, 2000: 573–4). Patients in high-regulation California pay $1630 more for a standardised correction than they would in low-regulation Kentucky. A more liberal marketplace would reduce the unit cost.

Demand-led pluralisation would undermine the comfortable traditionalism of conventional standards hallowed into canon by doctors' trade unions and professional cartels. Fewer entry barriers would encourage substitutability and availability at the margin. Whether a wider range of standards and services would actually reduce the share of medicine in the budgets is less certain. Even if it reduced the price per unit, a larger number of practitioners might still manufacture a larger number of wants.

The replacement of occupational licensure by simple registration might open the floodgates to quacks, fakes, charlatans, incompetents and butchers whose clumsy workmanship would later have to be put right at a cost. As opportunism succeeded to paternalism, so quality might deteriorate, the patients' health suffer and contagious diseases rage unchecked. No one wants that. Rationing by price is suspect where the cut-price article is cheap because it is not very good.

Yet free markets do have built-in correctives. Malpractice suits, interpersonal networks, multi-period referrals, personal recommendations, reputational capital, all of these are checks and balances that fulfil the same function as a government's rigid hurdle or a professional body's threat of striking off. Where a department store clinic wishes to maximise its return on capital it cannot afford to employ substandard doctors, however certified, who will frighten off the paying customers. Institutional signalling and corporate image can consign the irresponsible and the short-terming to the margins. As far as Milton Friedman is concerned, the most sensible course is to let the buyers and the sellers do what they do best: 'Licensure has reduced both the quantity and quality of medical practice … Licensure should be eliminated as a requirement for the practice of medicine' (Friedman, 1962: 158).

18. Conclusion

There are no easy answers. This book has shown that health policy is a labyrinth of tangles. Each of them is a crossroads. Not one of them is the gold standard. Not one of them is universally right or eternally wrong. The choice is unambiguous. It all depends.

An obsession with single answers, like the quest for 'complete physical, mental and social well-being', is an uncompromising El Dorado that brings out the fanatic and the megalomaniac in us all. Titmuss (n.d.) was right to warn that there is 'something unhealthy about the perfection of the absolute'. The truth will be a mix of different perceptions and a multiplicity of conflicting viewpoints. There is no algorithm that can predict the sines and cosines of fair-minded exchange of opinion. Agreement is all. Without give and take it would be Hobbes all the way to the Apocalypse.

There is no panacea that will resolve for all time the tension between individual and society, consumption and investment, duty and preference, authority and exchange, community and liberty, Richard Titmuss and Adam Smith. Health policy is an 'and' and a compromise like all the rest. That is just the point: 'The most important concept in political economy is the *and*. The most important asset in the study of the mixed economy is an open mind' (Reisman, 2005: 14). All students of health policy must adapt their tools not just to the 'is'-ness but to the 'and'-ness which is all around.

References

Aaron, H.J. (1991), *Serious and Unstable Condition*, Washington, DC: Brookings Institution.

Abel-Smith, B. (1959), 'Whose welfare state?', in N.I. Mackenzie (ed.), *Conviction*, London: MacGibbon & Kee, 55–73.

Abelson, P. (2003), 'The value of life and health for public policy', *Economic Record*, 79, Special Issue, S2–S13.

Acton, J.P. (1973), *Evaluating Public Programs to Save Lives: The Case of Heart Attacks*, Research Report R-950-RC, Santa Monica, CA: Rand Corporation.

Acton, J.P. (1975), 'Nonmonetary factors in the demand for medical services: some empirical evidence', *Journal of Political Economy*, 83, 595–614.

Akerlof, G.A. (1970), 'The market for "lemons": quality uncertainty and the market mechanism', *Quarterly Journal of Economics*, 84, 488–500.

Andersen, T.F. and G.H. Mooney (1990), 'Medical practice variations: where are we?', in T.F. Andersen and G.H. Mooney (eds), *The Challenges of Medical Practice Variations*, London: Macmillan, 1–15.

Appleby, J., V. Raleigh, F. Frosini, G. Bevan, H.Y. Gao and T. Lyscom (2011), *Variations in Health Care: The Good, the Bad and the Inexplicable*, London: King's Fund.

Arrow, K.J. (1973 [1963]), 'The welfare economics of medical care', *American Economic Review*, 53, reprinted in M.H. Cooper and A.J. Culyer (eds), *Health Economics*, Harmondsworth: Penguin Books, 13–48.

Association of Community Health Councils (1990), *Health and Wealth: A Review of Health Inequalities in the UK*, London: Association of Community Health Councils.

Auster, R., I. Leveson and D. Sarachek (1969), 'The production of health: an exploratory study', *Journal of Human Resources*, 4, 412–36.

Baker, L.C. and K.S. Corts (1996), 'HMO penetration and the cost of health care: market discipline or market segmentation?', *American Economic Review (Papers and Proceedings)*, 86, 389–94.

Bambra, C. (2011), *Work, Worklessness, and the Political Economy of Health*, Oxford: Oxford University Press.

Bartley, M. (2004), *Health Inequality: An Introduction to Theories, Concepts and Methods*, Cambridge: Polity Press.

Bartley, M., D. Blane and S. Montgomery (1997), 'Health and the life course: why safety nets matter', *British Medical Journal*, 314, 1194–6.
Beck, R.G. (1974), 'The effects of co-payment on the poor', *Journal of Human Resources*, 9, 129–42.
Bergson, A. (1938), 'A reformulation of certain aspects of welfare economics', *Quarterly Journal of Economics*, 52, 310–34.
Berk, M.L. and A.C. Monheit (2001), 'The concentration of health care expenditures, revisited', *Health Affairs*, 20 (2), 9–18.
Bernoulli, D. (1738 [1954]), 'Exposition of a new theory on the measurement of risk', transl. L. Sommer, *Econometrica*, 11, 22–36.
Bevan, A. (1958), Speech in the House of Commons, 30 July, in *Parliamentary Debates (Hansard)*, Cols 1382–98, London: HMSO.
Bevan, A. (1961 [1952]), *In Place of Fear*, London: MacGibbon & Kee.
Biddle, J.E. and G.A. Zarkin (1988), 'Worker preferences and market compensation for job risk', *Review of Economics and Statistics*, 70, 660–67.
Blane, D. (1999), 'The life course, the social gradient, and health', in M. Marmot and R.G. Wilkinson (eds), *Social Determinants of Health*, Oxford: Oxford University Press, 64–80.
Blaxter, M. (1976), 'Social class and health inequalities', in C.O. Carter and J. Peel (eds), *Equalities and Inequalities in Health*, London: Academic Press, 111–25.
Blaxter, M. (1990), *Health and Lifestyles*, London: Routledge.
Blendon, R.J., M. Kim and J.M. Benson (2001), 'The public versus the World Health Organization on health system performance', *Health Affairs*, 20, 10–20.
Blomquist, G. (1979), 'Value of life saving: implications of consumption activity', *Journal of Political Economy*, 87, 540–58.
Blomquist, G. (1982), 'Estimating the value of life and safety: recent developments', in M.W. Jones-Lee (ed.), *The Value of Life and Safety*, Amsterdam: North-Holland, 27–40.
Book, R.A. (2009), 'Medicare administrative costs are higher, not lower, than for private insurance', http://www.heritage.org/research/reports/2009/06, accessed 17 May 2015.
Borland, S. (2013), 'Thousands of elderly are losing their sight as NHS rations cataract surgery', *Daily Mail*, 15 July, http://www.dailymail.co.uk/news/article-2363857, accessed 28 June 2015.
Boulding, K.E. (1966), 'The concept of need for health services', *Milbank Memorial Fund Quarterly*, 44, 202–21.
Boulding, K.E. (1969), 'Economics as a moral science', *American Economic Review*, 59, 1–12.

Boyle, M.H., G.W. Torrance, J.C. Sinclair and S.P. Horwood (1983), 'Economic evaluation of neonatal intensive care of very-low-birth-weight infants', *New England Journal of Medicine*, 308, 1330–37.

Boyle, S. (2011), *Health Systems in Transition: United Kingdom (England)*, Brussels: European Observatory on Health Systems and Policies.

Braybrooke, D. (1987), *Meeting Needs*, Princeton, NJ: Princeton University Press.

Brennan, H.G. and J.M. Buchanan (1980), *The Power to Tax*, Cambridge: Cambridge University Press.

Brennan, H.G. and J.M. Buchanan (1985), *The Reason of Rules*, Cambridge: Cambridge University Press.

Brickman, P., D. Coates and R. Janoff-Bulman (1978), 'Lottery winners and accident victims: is happiness relative?', *Journal of Personality and Social Psychology*, 36, 917–27.

Brook, R.H., J.B. Kosecoff, R.E. Park, M.R. Chassin, C.M. Winslow and J.R. Hampton (1988), 'Diagnosis and treatment of coronary disease: comparison of doctors' attitudes in the USA and the UK', *Lancet*, 331, 750–53.

Brooks, S.K., C. Gerrada and T. Chalder (2011), 'Review of literature on the mental health of doctors: are specialist services needed?', *Journal of Mental Health*, 20, 1–11.

Broome, J. (1978), 'Trying to value a life', *Journal of Public Economics*, 9, 91–100.

Brunner, E. and M. Marmot (1999), 'Social organization, stress, and health', in M. Marmot and R.G. Wilkinson (eds), *Social Determinants of Health*, Oxford: Oxford University Press, 17–44.

Buchanan, J.M. (1965), *The Inconsistencies of the National Health Service*, London: Institute of Economic Affairs.

Buchanan, J.M. (1975), *The Limits of Liberty*, Chicago, IL: University of Chicago Press.

Buchanan, J.M. (1986), *Liberty, Market and State*, Brighton: Wheatsheaf.

Buchanan, J.M. (1990), *Technological Determinism Despite the Reality of Scarcity*, Little Rock, AR: University of Arkansas for Medical Sciences.

Buchanan, J.M. and R.L. Faith (1979), 'Trying again to value a life', *Journal of Public Economics*, 12, 245–8.

Buchanan, J.M and G. Tullock (1962), *The Calculus of Consent*, Ann Arbor, MI: University of Michigan Press.

Buchmueller, T.C., K. Grumbach, R. Kronick and J.G. Kahn (2005), 'The effect of health insurance on medical care utilization and implications for insurance expansion: a review of the literature', *Medical Care Research and Review*, 62, 3–30.

Bundorf, M.K. and M.V. Pauly (2006), 'Is health insurance affordable for the uninsured?', *Journal of Health Economics*, 25, 650–73.

Bunker, J.P., H.S. Frazier and F. Mosteller (1994), 'Improving health: measuring effects of medical care', *Milbank Quarterly*, 72, 225–58.

Carlin, P.S. and R. Sandy (1991), 'Estimating the implicit value of a young child's life', *Southern Economic Journal*, 58, 186–202.

Caves, R.E. (2007), *Multinational Enterprise and Economic Analysis*, 3rd edn, Cambridge: Cambridge University Press.

Chaloupka, F. (1991), 'Rational addictive behavior and cigarette smoking', *Journal of Political Economy*, 99, 722–42.

Chantler, J.K., A.J. Tingle and R.E. Petty (1985), 'Persistent rubella virus infection associated with chronic arthritis in children', *New England Journal of Medicine*, 313, 1117–23.

Chassin, M.R., R.H. Brook, R.E. Park, J. Keesey, A. Fink, J. Kosecoff, K. Kahn, N. Merrick and D.H. Solomon (1986), 'Variations in the use of medical and surgical services by the Medicare population', *New England Journal of Medicine*, 314, 285–90.

Chassin, M.R., J. Kosecoff, C.M. Winslow, K.L. Kahn, N.J. Merrick, J. Keesey, A. Fink, D.H. Solomon and R.H. Brook (1987), 'Does inappropriate use explain geographic variations in the use of health care services?', *Journal of the American Medical Association*, 258, 2533–7.

Chiswick, B.R. (1976), 'The demand for nursing home care: an analysis of the substitution between institutional and noninstitutional care', *Journal of Human Resources*, 11, 295–316.

Christie, L. (2003), 'America's most dangerous jobs'. CNNMoney.com, http://money.cnn.com/2003/10/13/pf/dangerous jobs, accessed 5 January 2015.

Clemens, J. and J.D. Gottlieb (2014), 'Do physicians' financial incentives affect medical treatment and patient health?', *American Economic Review*, 104, 1320–49.

Coase, R.H. (1937), 'The nature of the firm', *Economica*, 16, 386–405.

Cochrane, A.L. (1972), *Effectiveness and Efficiency*, London: Nuffield Provincial Hospitals Trust.

Cochrane, A.L., A.S. St Leger and F. Moore (1978), 'Health service "input" and mortality "output" in developed countries', *Journal of Epidemiology and Community Health*, 32, 200–205.

Coffey, R.M. (1983), 'The effect of time price on the demand for medical-care services', *Journal of Human Resources*, 18, 407–24.

Collard, D. (1978), *Altruism and Economy*, Oxford: Martin Robertson.

Colle, A.D. and M. Grossman (1978), 'Determinants of pediatric care utilization', *Journal of Human Resources*, 13, 115–58.

Collinson, P. (2014), 'Surgeons and GPs more likely to cause car accidents than other workers', *Guardian*, 1 September, http://www.theguardian.com/money/2014/sep/01, accessed 12 June 2015.

Congressional Budget Office (2006), *Designing a Premium System for Medicare*, Washington, DC: Congress of the United States.

Contoyiannis, P. and A.M. Jones (2004), 'Socio-economic status, health and lifestyle', *Journal of Health Economics*, 23, 965–95.

Cooper, P.F. and A.C. Monheit (1993), 'Does employment-related health insurance inhibit job mobility?', *Inquiry*, 30, 400–416.

Corman, H., T.J. Joyce and M. Grossman (1987), 'Birth outcome production function in the United States', *Journal of Human Resources*, 22, 339–60.

Cromwell, J. and J.R. Mitchell (1986), 'Physician-induced demand for surgery', *Journal of Health Economics*, 5, 293–313.

Cropper, M.L., N.B. Simon, A. Alberini, S. Arora and P.K. Sharma (1997), 'The health benefits of air pollution control in Delhi', *American Journal of Agricultural Economics*, 79, 1625–9.

Crosland, C.A.R. (1974 [1971]), *A Social-Democratic Britain*, Fabian Tract 404, in C.A.R. Crosland, *Socialism Now*, London: Jonathan Cape.

Culyer, A.J. (1971), 'The nature of the commodity "health care" and its efficient allocation', *Oxford Economic Papers*, 23, 189–211.

Culyer, A.J. (1976), *Need and the National Health Service*, London: Martin Robertson.

Culyer, A.J. (1982), 'The NHS and the market: images and realities', in G. McLachlan and A. Maynard (eds), *The Public/Private Mix for Health: The Relevance and Effects of Change*, London: Nuffield Provincial Hospitals Trust, 25–55.

Culyer, A.J. (1989), 'Cost containment in Europe', *Health Care Financing Review*, 10, Annual Supplement, 21–32.

Culyer, A.J. (2005), *The Dictionary of Health Economics*, Cheltenham, UK and Northampton, MA, USA: Edward Elgar Publishing.

Culyer, A.J. and A. Wagstaff (1993), 'Equity and equality in health and health care', *Journal of Health Economics*, 12, 431–57.

Currie, J. (2009), 'Healthy, wealthy, and wise: socioeconomic status, poor health in childhood, and human capital development', *Journal of Economic Literature*, 47, 87–122.

Currie, J. and J. Gruber (1996), 'Saving babies: the efficacy and cost of recent changes in the Medicaid eligibility of pregnant women', *Journal of Political Economy*, 104, 1263–96.

Currie, J. and E. Moretti (2003), 'Mother's education and the intergenerational transmission of human capital: evidence from college openings', *Quarterly Journal of Economics*, 118, 1495–532.

Cutler, D.M. (1994), 'A guide to health care reform', *Journal of Economic Perspectives*, 8, 13–29.

Cutler, D.M. (2004), *Your Money or Your Life: Strong Medicine for America's Health Care System*, New York: Oxford University Press.

Cutler, D.M. and E.L. Glaeser (2006), *Why Do Europeans Smoke More than Americans?*, Working Paper 12124, Cambridge, MA: National Bureau of Economic Research.

Cutler, D.M., F. Lange, E. Meara, S. Richards-Shubik and C.J. Ruhm (2011a), 'Rising educational gradients in mortality: the role of behavioral risk factors', *Journal of Health Economics*, 30, 1174–87.

Cutler, D.M. and A. Lleras-Muney (2006), *Education and Health: Evaluating Theories and Evidence*, Working Paper 12352, Cambridge, MA: National Bureau of Economic Research.

Cutler, D.M., A. Lleras-Muney and T. Vogel (2011b), 'Socioeconomic status and health; dimensions and mechanisms', in S. Glied and P.C. Smith (eds), *The Oxford Handbook of Health Economics*, Oxford: Oxford University Press, 124–63.

Cutler, D.M and D. Ly (2011), 'The (paper)work of medicine: understanding international medical costs', *Journal of Economic Perspectives*, 25, 3–25.

Cutler, D.M. and S.J. Reber (1998), 'Paying for health insurance: the trade-off between competition and adverse selection', *Quarterly Journal of Economics*, 113, 433–66.

Cutler, D.M. and E. Richardson (1998), 'The value of health: 1970–1990', *American Economic Review (Papers and Proceedings)*, 88, 97–100.

Daly, E., A. Gray, D. Barlow, K. McPherson, M. Roche and M. Vessey (1993), 'Measuring the impact of menopausal symptoms on quality of life', *British Medical Journal*, 307, 836–40.

Daniels, N. (1985), *Just Health Care*, Cambridge: Cambridge University Press.

Dardis, R. (1980), 'The value of a life: new evidence from the marketplace', *American Economic Review*, 70, 1077–82.

Dartmouth Atlas of Health Care (2015), www.dartmouthatlas.org, accessed 25 March 2015.

Department of Health (UK) (2006), *The Health Profile of England*, London: Department of Health.

Department of Health (UK) (2011), *The NHS Atlas of Variation in Healthcare: Reducing Unwarranted Variation to Increase Value and Improve Quality*, London: Department of Health.

Department of Health (UK) (2012), *Long Term Conditions Compendium of Information*, 3rd edn, London: Department of Health.

Department of Health and Human Services (USA) (2015), *2014 National Healthcare Disparities Report*, AHRQ Publication No. 14-0006, Rockville, MD: Agency for Healthcare Research and Quality.

Dixon, A., J. Le Grand, J. Henderson, R. Murray and E. Poteliakhoff (2007), 'Is the British National Health Service equitable? The evidence on socioeconomic differences in utilization', *Journal of Health Services Research and Policy*, 12, 104–9.

Doblhammer, G. and J.W. Vaupel (2001), 'Lifespan depends on month of birth', *Proceedings of the National Academy of Sciences of the United States of America*, 98, 2934–9.

Donnelly, L. (2014), 'Age discrimination laws mean patients should not be denied procedures on grounds of age', http://www.telegraph.co.uk/news/health/news/10942295, accessed 15 July 2015.

Dowd, B. and R. Feldman (2006), 'Competition and health plan choice', in A.M. Jones (ed.), *The Elgar Companion to Health Economics*, Cheltenham, UK and Northampton, MA, USA: Edward Elgar Publishing, 137–46.

Downs, A. (1957), *An Economic Theory of Democracy*, New York: Harper & Row.

Doyal, L. and I. Gough (1991), *A Theory of Human Need*, London: Macmillan.

Drummond, M., G. Torrance and J. Mason (1993), 'Cost-effectiveness league tables: more harm than good?', *Social Science and Medicine*, 37, 33–40.

Dubos, R. (1959), *Mirage of Health*, New York: Harper & Row.

Durkheim, E. (1952 [1897]), *Suicide*, transl. J.A. Spalding and G. Simpson, London: Routledge.

Durkheim, E. (1984 [1893]), *The Division of Labor in Society*, transl. W.D. Halls, New York: Free Press.

Dworkin, R. (1988), *The Theory and Practice of Autonomy*, Cambridge: Cambridge University Press.

Economist Intelligence Unit (2015), *The NHS: How Does It Compare?*, London: The Economist.

Eddy, D.M. (1990), 'Screening for cervical cancer', *Annals of Internal Medicine*, 113, 214–26.

Ellis, R.P. (1998), 'Creaming, skimping and dumping: provider competition on the intensive and extensive margins', *Journal of Health Economics*, 17, 537–55.

Elo, I.T. and S.H. Preston (1996), 'Educational differentials in mortality: United States, 1979–85', *Social Science and Medicine*, 42, 47–57.

Enthoven, A.C. (1980), *Health Plan*, Reading, MA: Addison-Wesley.

Enthoven, A.C. (1985), *Reflections on the Management of the National Health Service*, London: Nuffield Provincial Hospitals Trust.

Evans, R.G. (1974), 'Supplier-induced demand: some empirical evidence and implications', in M. Perlman (ed.), *The Economics of Health and Medical Care*, London: Macmillan, 162–73.

Evans, W.N. and J.D. Graham (1990), 'An estimate of the lifesaving benefit of child restraint use legislation', *Journal of Health Economics*, 9, 121–42.

Evans, W.N. and J.S. Ringel (1999), 'Can higher cigarette taxes improve birth outcomes?', *Journal of Public Economics*, 72, 135–54.

Fang, P.Q., S.P. Dong, J.J. Xiao, C.J. Liu, X.W. Feng and Y.P. Wang (2010), 'Regional inequality in health and its determinants: evidence from China', *Health Policy*, 94, 14–25.

Feldstein, M.S. (1973), 'The welfare loss of excess health insurance', *Journal of Political Economy*, 81, 251–80.

Feldstein, P.J. (1988), *Health Care Economics*, 3rd edn, New York: Wiley.

Feldstein, P.J., T.M. Wickizer and J.R.C. Wheeler (1988), 'Private cost containment: the effects of utilization review programs on health care use and expenditures', *New England Journal of Medicine*, 318, 1310–14.

Festinger, L. (1962 [1957]), *A Theory of Cognitive Dissonance*, London: Tavistock.

Fisher, E.S., D.E. Wennberg, T.A. Stukel, D.J. Gottlieb, F.L. Lucas and E.L. Pinder (2003), 'The implications of regional variations in Medicare spending. Part 1: the content, quality, and accessibility of care', *Annals of Internal Medicine*, 138, 273–88.

Fogel, R.W. (1986), 'Nutrition and the decline in mortality since 1700: some preliminary findings', in S.L. Engerman and R.E. Gallman (eds), *Long-Term Factors in American Economic Growth*, Chicago, IL: University of Chicago Press, 439–555.

Frey, B.S. and F. Oberholzer-Gee (1997), 'The cost of price incentives: an empirical analysis of motivation crowding-out', *American Economic Review*, 87, 746–55.

Friedman, M. (1962), *Capitalism and Freedom*, Chicago, IL: University of Chicago Press.

Friedman, M. and L.J. Savage (1948), 'The utility analysis of choices involving risk', *Journal of Political Economy*, 56, 279–304.

Fuchs, V.R. (1973 [1966]), 'The contribution of health services to the American economy', *Milbank Memorial Fund Quarterly*, 44, reprinted in M.H. Cooper and A.J. Culyer (eds), *Health Economics*, Harmondsworth: Penguin Books, 135–71.

Fuchs, V.R. (1974a), *Who Shall Live?* New York: Basic Books.

Fuchs, V.R. (1974b), 'Some economic aspects of mortality in developed countries', in M. Perlman (ed.), *The Economics of Health and Medical Care*, London: Macmillan, 174–93.

Fuchs, V.R. (1986 [1978]), 'The supply of surgeons and the demand for operations', *Journal of Human Resources*, 13, reprinted in V.R. Fuchs, *The Health Economy*, Cambridge, MA: Harvard University Press, 126–47.

Fuchs, V.R. (1996), 'Economists, values, and health care reform', *American Economic Review*, 86, 1–24.

Galbraith, J.K. (1958), *Journey to Poland and Yugoslavia*, Cambridge, MA: Harvard University Press.

Galbraith, J.K. (1977), *The Age of Uncertainty*, London: British Broadcasting Corporation and André Deutsch.

Garber, A.M. and J. Skinner (2008), 'Is American health care uniquely inefficient?', *Journal of Economic Perspectives*, 22, 27–50.

Gardner, J. and A. Oswald (2004), 'How is mortality affected by money, marriage and stress?', *Journal of Health Economics*, 23, 1181–207.

Gillon, R. (1985), *Philosophical Medical Ethics*, Chichester: Wiley.

Goldman, D. and A. Leive (2013), 'Why "Medicare-for-All" is not the answer', *Health Affairs Blog*, 14 May, healthaffairs.org/blog/2013/05/14, accessed 16 May 2015.

Granovetter, M. (1985), 'Economic action and social structure: the problem of embeddedness', *American Journal of Sociology*, 91, 481–510.

Gravelle, H., M. Dusheiko and M. Sutton (2001), 'The demand for elective surgery in a public system: time and money prices in the UK National Health Service', *Journal of Health Economics*, 21, 423–49.

Gray, B. (2001), 'Do Medicaid physician fees for prenatal services affect birth outcomes?', *Journal of Health Economics*, 20, 571–90.

Green, T.H. (1941 [1879]), *Lectures on the Principles of Political Obligation*, London: Longmans.

Greenspan, A.M., H.R. Kay, B.C. Berger, R.M. Greenberg, A.J. Greenspon and M.J. Spuhler (1988), 'Incidence of unwarranted implantation of permanent cardiac pacemakers in a large medical population', *New England Journal of Medicine*, 318, 158–63.

Grossman, M. (1972), 'On the concept of health capital and the demand for health', *Journal of Political Economy*, 80, 223–55.

Grossman, M. (1982), 'Government and health outcomes', *American Economic Review (Papers and Proceedings)*, 72, 191–5.

Gruber, J. (2008), 'Covering the uninsured in the United States', *Journal of Economic Literature*, 46, 571–606.

Guralnik, J.M., K.C. Land, D. Blazer, G.G. Fillenbaum and L.G. Branch (1993), 'Educational status and active life expectancy among older blacks and whites', *New England Journal of Medicine*, 329, 110–16.

Hadley, J. (2003), 'Sicker and poorer – the consequences of being uninsured: a review of the research on the relationship between health insurance, medical care use, health, work and income', *Medical Care Research and Review*, 60, Supplement, 3S–75S.

Hadley, J., E. Steinberg and J. Feder (1991), 'Comparison of uninsured and privately insured hospital patients: condition on admission, resource use, and outcome', *Journal of the American Medical Association*, 265, 374–9.

Halliday, T.J. (2014), 'Unemployment and mortality: evidence from the PSID', *Social Science and Medicine*, 113, 15–22.

Ham, C. (1988), *Health Care Variations*, London: King's Fund Institute.

Ham, C. (2005), *Health Policy in Britain*, 5th edn, Basingstoke: Palgrave Macmillan.

Harris, J. (1985), *The Value of Life: An Introduction to Medical Ethics*, London: Routledge.

Harsanyi, J.C. (1982 [1977]), 'Morality and the theory of rational behaviour', in A. Sen and B. Williams (eds), *Utilitarianism and Beyond*, Cambridge: Cambridge University Press, 39–62.

Hartley, L.P. (2014 [1960]), *Facial Justice*, London: Penguin Books.

Hayek, F.A. (1948), *Individualism and Economic Order*, Chicago, IL: University of Chicago Press.

Health and Social Care Information Centre (HSCIC) (2015), 'Statistics of smoking, England – 2015 (NS)', http://www.hscic.gov.ukl/searchcatalogue?productid=17945&returnid=3945, accessed 27 June 2015.

Helliwell, J.F. and R.D. Putnam (2004), 'The social context of well-being', *Philosophical Transactions: Biological Sciences*, London: Royal Society, 1435–46.

Hirschman, A.O. (1982), *Shifting Involvements*, Oxford: Basil Blackwell.

His Majesty's Stationery Office (1942), *Social Insurance and Allied Services* (The Beveridge Report), Cmd. 6404, London: His Majesty's Stationery Office.

Holahan, J. and L. Blumberg (2008), 'Can a public insurance plan increase competition and lower the costs of health reform?', Washington, DC: Urban Institute Health Policy Center, www.healthpolicycenter.org, accessed 18 May 2015.

House of Commons Health Committee (2009), *Health Inequalities*, London: House of Commons.

Howard, D.H., L.C. Richardson and K.E. Thorpe (2009), 'Cancer screening and age in the United States and Europe', *Health Affairs*, 28, 1838–47.

Hughes, M.E. and L.J. Waite (2009), 'Marital biography and health at mid-life', *Journal of Health and Social Behavior*, 50, 344–58.

Illich, I. (1977), *Limits to Medicine*, Harmondsworth: Penguin Books.

Jena, A.B., S. Seabury, D. Lakdawalla and A. Chandra (2011), 'Malpractice risk according to physician speciality', *New England Journal of Medicine*, 365, 629–36.

Johannesson, M. and U.-G. Gerdtham (1996), 'A note on the estimation of the equity–efficiency trade-off for QALYs', *Journal of Health Economics*, 15, 359–68.

Johannesson, M. and P.-O. Johansson (1997), 'Is the valuation of a QALY gained independent of age? Some empirical evidence', *Journal of Health Economics*, 16, 589–99.

Johnson, M.L. (1977), 'Patients: receivers or participants?', in K. Barnard and K. Lee (eds), *Conflicts in the National Health Service*, London: Croom Helm, 72–98.

Jones, I.G. and D. Cameron (1984), 'Social class analysis: an embarrassment to epidemiology', *Community Medicine*, 6, 37–46.

Jones, S. (2013), 'Great British class survey finds seven social classes in UK', *Guardian*, 3 April, http://www.theguardian.com/society/2013/apr/03, accessed 15 July 2015.

Jones-Lee, M.W. (1989), *The Economics of Safety and Physical Risk*, Oxford: Basil Blackwell.

Jones-Lee, M.W., M. Hammerton and P.R. Philips (1985), 'The value of safety: results of a national sample survey', *Economic Journal*, 95, 49–72.

Jones-Lee, M.W. and M. Spackman (2013), 'The development of road and rail transport safety valuation in the United Kingdom', *Research in Transportation Economics*, 43, 23–40.

Joyce, T., A.D. Racine and N. Mocan (1992), 'The consequences and costs of maternal substance abuse in New York City', *Journal of Health Economics*, 11, 297–314.

Kahn, M. (1998), 'Health and labor market performance: the case of diabetes', *Journal of Labor Economics*, 16, 878–99.

Kaiser Commission on Medicaid and the Uninsured (2014), 'Key facts about the uninsured population', www.kff.org/uninsured/fact, accessed 17 March 2015.

Kant, I. (1961 [1785]), *Groundwork of the Metaphysic of Morals*, transl. H.J. Paton, in H.J. Paton (ed.), *The Moral Law*, London: Hutchinson, 53–148.

Kaplan, R.M. (1995), 'Utility assessment for estimating quality-adjusted life years', in F.A. Sloan (ed.), *Valuing Health Care: Costs, Benefits, and Effectiveness of Pharmaceuticals and Other Medical Technologies*, Cambridge: Cambridge University Press, 31–60.

Karasek, R.A. (1979), 'Job demands, job design latitude, and mental strain: some implications for job redesign', *Administrative Science Quarterly*, 24, 285–308.

Kenkel, D. (1990), 'Consumer health information and the demand for medical care', *Review of Economics and Statistics*, 72, 587–95.

Kessler, D. and M. McClellan (1996), 'Do doctors practice defensive medicine?', *Quarterly Journal of Economics*, 111, 353–90.

Keynes, J.M. (1973 [1936]), *The General Theory of Employment, Interest and Money*, London: Macmillan.

Kind, P., R.M. Rosser and A. Williams (1982), 'Valuation of quality of life: some psychometric evidence', in M.W. Jones-Lee (ed.), *The Value of Life and Safety*, Amsterdam: North-Holland, 159–70.

Klarman, H.E., J.O. Francis and G. Rosenthal (1973 [1968]), 'Cost effectiveness analysis applied to the treatment of chronic renal disease', *Medical Care*, 6, reprinted in M.H. Cooper and A.J. Culyer (eds), *Health Economics: Selected Readings*, Harmondsworth, Penguin Books, 230–40.

Kleiner, M.M. and R.T. Kudrle (2000), 'Does regulation affect economic outcomes? The case of dentistry', *Journal of Law and Economics*, 43, 547–82.

Knetsch, J.L. and J.A. Sinden (1984), 'Willingness to pay and compensation demanded: experimental evidence of an unexpected disparity in measures of value', *Quarterly Journal of Economics*, 99, 507–21.

Knight, F.H. (1971 [1921]), *Risk, Uncertainty and Profit*, Chicago, IL: University of Chicago Press.

Knight, F.H. (1997 [1935]), *The Ethics of Competition*, New Brunswick, NJ: Transaction Publishers.

Kondo, N., G. Sembajwe, I. Kawachi, R.M. van Dam, S.V. Subramanian and Z. Yamagata (2009), 'Income inequality, mortality and self-rated health: a meta-analysis of multilevel studies', *British Medical Journal*, 339, 1178–81.

Kravdal, O. (2001), 'The impact of marital status on cancer survival', *Social Science and Medicine*, 52, 357–68.

Krugman, P.R. (2009), 'Administrative costs', *New York Times*, 6 July, http://krugman.blogs,nytimes.com/2009/07/06, accessed 15 May 2015.

Ku, L., E. Deschamps and J. Hilman (2004), 'The effects of copayments on the use of medical services and prescription drugs in Utah's Medicaid program', Washington, DC: Center on Budget and Policy Priorities, http://www.cbpp.org/research, accessed 18 June 2015.

Kunreuther, H.C., M.V. Pauly and S. McMorrow (2013), *Insurance and Behavioral Economics: Improving Decisions in the Most Misunderstood Industry*, Cambridge: Cambridge University Press.

Kwoka, J.E. (1984), 'Advertising and the price and quality of optometric services', *American Economic Review*, 74, 211–16.

Lakdawalla, D. and T.J. Philipson (2006), 'Economics of obesity', in A.M. Jones (ed.), *The Elgar Companion to Health Economics*, Cheltenham, UK and Northampton, MA, USA: Edward Elgar Publishing, 72–82.

Laudicella, M., L. Siciliani and R. Cookson (2012), 'Waiting times and socioeconomic status: evidence from England', *Social Science and Medicine*, 74, 1331–41.

Le Grand, J. (1978), 'The distribution of public expenditure: the case of health care', *Economica*, 45, 125–42.

Le Grand, J. (1982), *The Strategy of Equality*, London: George Allen & Unwin.

Le Grand, J. (1991), *Equity and Choice: An Essay in Economics and Applied Philosophy*, London: HarperCollins.

Le Grand, J. and M. Rabin (1986), 'Trends in British health inequality, 1931–1983', in A.J. Culyer and B. Jönsson, (eds), *Private and Public Health Services: Complementarities and Conflicts*, Oxford: Basil Blackwell, 112–27.

Lee, Y., R.A. Kearns and W. Friesen (2010), 'Seeking affective health care: Korean immigrants' use of homeland medical services', *Health and Place*, 16, 108–15.

Leibenstein, H. (1987), *Inside the Firm: The Inefficiencies of Hierarchy*, Cambridge, MA: Harvard University Press.

Light, D.W. (2000), 'Sociological perspectives on competition in health care', *Journal of Health Politics, Policy and Law*, 25, 969–74.

Lindsay, C.M. and B. Feigenbaum (1984), 'Rationing by waiting lists', *American Economic Review*, 74, 404–17.

Lleras-Muney, A. (2002), *The Relationship between Education and Adult Mortality in the United States*, Working Paper 8986, Cambridge, MA: National Bureau of Economic Research.

Locke, J. (1993 [1689]), *Second Treatise on Government*, in D. Wootton (ed.), *John Locke: Political Writings*, Harmondsworth: Penguin Books, 261–386.

Loomes, G. and L. McKenzie (1989), 'The use of QALYs in health care decision making', *Social Science and Medicine*, 28, 299–308.

Lynch, J.W., G.A. Kaplan, E.R. Pamuk, R.D. Cohen, K.E. Heck, J.L. Balfour and I.H. Yen (1998), 'Income inequality and mortality in metropolitan areas of the United States', *American Journal of Public Health*, 88, 1074–9.

Lynch, J.W., G.A. Kaplan and J.T. Salonen (1997), 'Why do poor people behave poorly? Variation in adult health behaviours and psychosocial characteristics by stages of the socioeconomic lifecourse', *Social Science and Medicine*, 44, 809–19.

Mackenbach, J.P. (2013), 'Political conditions and life expectancy in Europe, 1900–2008', *Social Science and Medicine*, 82, 134–46.

Manning, W.G., A. Leibowitz, G.A. Goldberg, W.H. Rogers and J.P. Newhouse (1984), 'A controlled trial of the effect of a prepaid group practice on the use of services', *New England Journal of Medicine*, 310 (23), 1505–10.

Manning, W.G. and M.S. Marquis (1996), 'Health insurance: the tradeoff between risk pooling and moral hazard', *Journal of Health Economics*, 15, 609–39.

Manning, W.G., J.P. Newhouse, N. Duan, E.B. Keeler, A. Leibowitz and M.S. Marquis (1987), 'Health insurance and the demand for medical care: evidence from a randomized experiment', *American Economic Review*, 77, 251–77.

Marder, W.D. and S. Zuckerman (1985), 'Competition and medical groups: a survivor analysis', *Journal of Health Economics*, 4, 167–76.

Marin, A. and G. Psacharopoulos (1982), 'The reward for risk in the labor market: evidence from the United Kingdom and a reconciliation with other studies', *Journal of Political Economy*, 90, 827–53.

Marmot, M. and M. Bobak (2000), 'International comparators and poverty and health in Europe', *British Medical Journal*, 321, 11.

Marmot, M., C.D. Ryff, L.L. Bumpass, M. Shipley and N.F. Marks (1997), 'Social inequalities in health: next questions and converging evidence', *Social Science and Medicine*, 44, 901–10.

Marmot, M., J. Siegrist, T. Theorell and A. Feeney (1999), 'Health and the psychosocial environment at work', in M. Marmot and R.G. Wilkinson (eds), *Social Determinants of Health*, Oxford: Oxford University Press, 105–31.

Marmot, M. and T. Theorell (1988), 'Social class and cardiovascular disease: the contribution of work', *International Journal of Health Services*, 18, 659–74.

Marmot, M. and the Marmot Review Team (2010), 'Fair society, healthy lives: strategic review of health inequalities in England post-2010', http://www.marmotreview.org, accessed 6 January 2015.

Marshall, A. (1949 [1890]), *Principles of Economics*, London: Macmillan.

Marshall, A. (1966 [1907]), 'Social possibilities of economic chivalry', in A.C. Pigou (ed.), *Memorials of Alfred Marshall*, New York: Augustus M. Kelley, 323–46.

Marshall, T.H. (1981 [1965]), 'The right to welfare', *Sociological Review*, 13, reprinted in T.H. Marshall, *The Right to Welfare and Other Essays*, London: Heinemann Educational Books, 83–94.

Marshall, T.H. (1992 [1950]), *Citizenship and Social Class*, London: Pluto Press.

Martin, S. and P.C. Smith (1996), 'Explaining variations in inpatient length of stay in the National Health Service', *Journal of Health Economics*, 15, 279–304.

Martin, S. and P.C. Smith (1999), 'Rationing by waiting lists: an empirical investigation', *Journal of Public Economics*, 71, 141–64.

Martinson, M.L. (2012), 'Income inequality in health at all ages: a comparison of the United States and England', *American Journal of Public Health*, 102, 2049–56.

Marx, K. (1973 [1844]), *Economic and Philosophical Manuscripts of 1844*, transl. M. Milligan, London: Lawrence & Wishart.

Marx, K and F. Engels (1848 [2011]), *The Communist Manifesto*, London: Penguin Books.

Maslow, A.H. (1968 [1962]), *Toward a Psychology of Being*, 2nd edn, Princeton, NJ: Van Nostrand.

Maslow, A.H. (1970 [1954]), *Motivation and Personality*, 2nd edn, New York: Harper & Row.

Mayerhoefer, C.D., S.H. Zuvekas and R. Manski (2014), 'The demand for preventive and restorative dental services', *Health Economics*, 23, 14–32.

McClellan, M. and H. Noguchi (1998), 'Technological change in heart-disease treatment: does high tech mean low value?', *American Economic Review (Papers and Proceedings)*, 88, 90–96.

McGuire, A., J. Henderson and G.H. Mooney (1988), *The Economics of Health Care*, London: Routledge & Kegan Paul.

McGuire, A., V. Serra-Sastre and M. Raikou (2012), 'How are rising health care expenditures explained?', in A. McGuire and J. Costa-Font (eds), *The LSE Companion to Health Policy*, Cheltenham, UK and Northampton, MA, USA: Edward Elgar Publishing, 129–43.

McKeown, T. (1979), *The Role of Medicine*, 2nd edn, Oxford: Blackwell.

McKinlay, J.B. and S.M. McKinlay (1977), 'The questionable contribution of medical measures to the decline of mortality in the United States in the twentieth century', *Milbank Memorial Fund Quarterly*, 55, 405–28.

Menger, C. (1976 [1871]), *Principles of Economics*, transl. J. Dingwall and B.F. Hoselitz, New York: New York University Press.

Mill, J.S. (1974 [1859]), *On Liberty*, ed. Gertrude Himmelfarb, Harmondsworth: Penguin Books.

Miller, R.H. and H.S. Luft (1997), 'Does managed care lead to better or worse quality of care?', *Health Affairs*, 16 (5), 7–25.

Ministry of Health (UK) (1944), *A National Health Service*, Cmd 6502.

Mirrlees, J.A. (1982), 'The economic uses of utilitarianism', in A. Sen and B. Williams (eds), *Utilitarianism and Beyond*, Cambridge: Cambridge University Press, 63–84.

Mishan, E.J. (1971), 'Evaluation of life and limb: a theoretical approach', *Journal of Political Economy*, 79, 687–705.

Mooney, G.H. (1977), *The Valuation of Human Life*, London: Macmillan.

Mooney, G.H. (1991), 'Communitarianism and health economics', in J.B. Davis (ed.), *The Social Economics of Health Care*, London: Routledge, 40–60.

Moore, M.J. and W.K. Viscusi (1988), 'Doubling the estimated value of life: results using new occupational fatality data', *Journal of Policy Analysis and Management*, 7, 476–90.

Moses, H., D.H.M. Matheson, E.R. Dorsey, B.P. George, D. Sadoff and S. Yoshimura (2013), 'The anatomy of health care in the United States', *Journal of the American Medical Association*, 310, 1947–63.

Mueller, C.D. and A.C. Monheit (1988), 'Insurance coverage and the demand for dental care', *Journal of Health Economics*, 7, 59–72.

Muntaner, C. (2013), 'Democracy, authoritarianism, political conflict, and population health: A global, comparative, and historical approach', *Social Science and Medicine*, 86, 107–12.

Murray, C.J.L. (1996), 'Rethinking DALYS', in C.J.L. Murray and A.D. Lopez (eds), *The Global Burden of Disease*, Cambridge, MA: Harvard University Press, 1–98.

Murray, C.J.L. and A.K. Acharya (1997), 'Understanding DALYs', *Journal of Health Economics*, 16, 703–30.

Musgrave, R.A. and P.B. Musgrave (1980), *Public Finance in Theory and Practice*, 3rd edn, New York: McGraw-Hill.

Needleman, L. (1980), 'The valuation of changes in the risk of death by those at risk', *Manchester School*, 48, 229–54.

Neuberger, J., D. Adams, P. MacMaster, A. Maidment and M. Speed (1998), 'Assessing priorities for allocation of donor liver grafts: survey of public and clinicians', *British Medical Journal*, 317, 172–5.

Neuhauser, D. and A.M. Lewicki (1975), 'What do we gain from the sixth stool guaiac?', *New England Journal of Medicine*, 293, 226–8.

Newhouse, J.P. (1978), *The Economics of Medical Care*, Reading, MA: Addison-Wesley.

Newhouse, J.P. (1992), 'Medical care costs: how much welfare loss?', *Journal of Economic Perspectives*, 6, 3–21.

Newhouse, J.P. and L.J. Friedlander (1980), 'The relationship between medical resources and measures of health: some additional evidence', *Journal of Human Resources*, 15, 200–218.

Newhouse, J.P. and Insurance Experiment Group (1993), *Free for All? Lessons from the RAND Health Insurance Experiment*, Cambridge, MA: Harvard University Press.

Nicolle, E. and I. Mathauer (2010), *Administrative Costs of Health Insurance Schemes: Exploring the Reasons for Their Variability*, Geneva: World Health Organization.

Niskanen, W. (1971), *Bureaucracy and Representative Government*, Chicago, IL: Aldine.

Nozick, R. (1974), *Anarchy, State, and Utopia*, New York: Basic Books.

Nussbaum, M.C. (1993), 'Non-relative virtues: an Aristotelian approach', in M.C. Nussbaum and A.K. Sen (eds), *The Quality of Life*, Oxford: Clarendon Press, 242–76.

Office for National Statistics (UK) (2014), *Life Expectancy at Birth and at Age 65 by Local Areas in the United Kingdom, 2006–08 to 2010–12*, London: Office for National Statistics, http://www.ons.gov.uk/rel/subnational-health4, accessed 26 June 2015.

Olson, C.A. (1981), 'An analysis of wage differentials received by workers on dangerous jobs', *Journal of Human Resources*, 16, 167–85.

Organisation for Economic Co-operation and Development (OECD) (2011), *Health at a Glance: OECD Indicators*, Paris: OECD.

Parkin, D., A. McGuire and B. Yule (1987), 'Aggregate health care expenditures and national income: is health care a luxury good?', *Journal of Health Economics*, 6, 109–27.

Pauly, M.V. (1968), 'The economics of moral hazard: comment', *American Economic Review*, 58, 531–7.

Pauly, M.V. (1988), 'A primer on competition in medical markets', in H.E. Frech III (ed.), *Health Care in America: The Political Economy of Hospitals and Health Insurance*, San Francisco, CA: Pacific Research Institute for Public Policy, 27–71.

Pauly, M.V. (1994), 'Universal health insurance in the Clinton Plan: coverage as a tax-financed public good', *Journal of Economic Perspectives*, 8, 45–53.

Pauly, M.V. and A.M. Percy (2000), 'Cost and performance: a comparison of the individual and group health insurance markets', *Journal of Health Politics, Policy and Law*, 25, 9–26.

Pearson, R.J.C., R. Smedby, R. Berfenstam, R.F. Logan, A.M. Burgess and O.L. Peterson (1968), 'Hospital caseloads in Liverpool, New England, and Uppsala: an international comparison', *Lancet*, 2, 559–66.

Peltzman, S. (1974), *Regulation of Pharmaceutical Innovation*, Washington, DC: American Enterprise Institute.

Peltzman, S. (2009), 'Mortality inequality', *Journal of Economic Perspectives*, 23, 175–90.

Pew Research Center (2013), 'Wide partisan gap over health care law predates passage', http://www.people-press.org/2013/09/16, accessed 12 February 2014.

Phelps, C.E. (1988), 'Death and taxes: an opportunity for substitution', *Journal of Health Economics*, 7, 1–24.

Phelps Brown, H. (1988), *Egalitarianism and the Generation of Inequality*, Oxford: Clarendon Press.

Pigou, A.C. (1932 [1920]), *The Economics of Welfare*, 4th edn, London: Macmillan.

Piketty, T. (2014), *Capital in the Twenty-First Century*, transl. A. Goldhammer, Cambridge, MA: Harvard University Press.

Plato (1961 [c.348 BC]), *The Laws*, in E. Hamilton and H. Cairns (eds), *The Collected Dialogues of Plato*, Princeton, NJ: Princeton University Press, 1225–513.

Plato (2012 [c.380 BC]), *The Republic*, ed. C. Rowe, London: Penguin Books.

Pope, A. (2006 [1732]), 'An epistle to Allen Lord Bathurst', in *Alexander Pope: The Major Works*, Oxford: Oxford University Press, 250–64.

Preston, S.H. (1975), 'The changing relation between mortality and level of economic development', *Population Studies*, 29, 231–48.

Pritchett, L. and L.H. Summers (1996), 'Wealthier is healthier', *Journal of Human Resources*, 31, 841–68.

Propper, C., S. Burgess and D. Gossage (2008), 'Competition and quality: evidence from the NHS internal market 1991–9', *Economic Journal*, 118, 138–70.

Putnam, R.D. (1995), 'Bowling alone: America's declining social capital', *Journal of Democracy*, 6, 65–78.

Rawls, J. (1972 [1971]), *A Theory of Justice*, Oxford: Clarendon Press.

Rawls, J. (1982), 'Social unity and primary goods', in A. Sen and B. Williams (eds), *Utilitarianism and Beyond*, Cambridge: Cambridge University Press, 159–85.

Reichman, N.E. and M.J. Florio (1996), 'The effects of enriched prenatal care services on Medicaid birth outcomes in New Jersey', *Journal of Health Economics*, 15, 455–76.

Reisman, D.A. (1993), *Market and Health*, London: Macmillan.

Reisman, D.A. (2001), *Richard Titmuss: Welfare and Society*, 2nd edn, Basingstoke: Palgrave.

Reisman, D.A. (2002), *The Institutional Economy: Demand and Supply*, Cheltenham, UK and Northampton, MA, USA: Edward Elgar Publishing.

Reisman, D.A. (2005), 'Exchange and authority: the mixed economy', *American Review of Political Economy*, 3 (2), 1–15.

Reisman, D.A. (2006), 'Payment for health in Singapore', *International Journal of Social Economics*, 33 (2), 132–59.

Reisman, D.A. (2007), *Health Care and Public Policy*, Cheltenham, UK and Northampton, MA, USA: Edward Elgar Publishing.

Reisman, D.A. (2015), *James Buchanan*, Basingstoke: Palgrave Macmillan.

Rice, T. (2001), 'Should consumer choice be encouraged in health care?', in J.B. Davis (ed.), *The Social Economics of Health Care*, London: Routledge, 9–39.

Richards, C. (1989), *The Health of Doctors*, London: King Edward's Hospital Fund.

Rizzo, J.A. and R.J. Zeckhauser (1990), 'Advertising and entry: the case of physician services', *Journal of Political Economy*, 98, 476–500.

Roemer, M.I. (1961), 'Bed supply and hospital utilization', *Hospitals: Journal of the American Hospital Association*, 35 (November), 36–42.

Rosko, M.D. and R.W. Broyles (1987), 'Short-term responses of hospitals to the DRG prospective pricing mechanism in New Jersey', *Medical Care*, 25, 88–99.

Rosser, R.M. and P. Kind (1978), 'A scale of valuation of states of illness: is there a social consensus?', *International Journal of Epidemiology*, 7, 347–58.

Roth, N. (n.d.), 'The costs and returns to medical education', www.econ.berkeley.edu/sites/default/files/roth_nicholas, accessed 25 February 2015.

Rousseau, J.J. (2012 [1762]), *The Social Contract*, in *The Major Political Writings of Jean-Jacques Rousseau*, Chicago, IL: University of Chicago Press, 153–272.

Ruhm, C.J. (2005), 'Healthy living in hard times', *Journal of Health Economics*, 24, 341–63.

Sackett, D.L. and G.W. Torrance (1978), 'The utility of different health states as perceived by the general public', *Journal of Chronic Diseases*, 31, 697–704.

Saffer, H. (1991), 'Alcohol advertising bans and alcohol abuse: an international perspective', *Journal of Health Economics*, 10, 65–79.

Sandel, M.J. (2012), *What Money Can't Buy: The Moral Limits of Markets*, New York: Farrar, Straus & Giroux.

Sapolsky, R.M. (2004), *Why Zebras Don't Get Ulcers*, 3rd edn, New York: Owl.

Schelling, T.C. (1973 [1968]), 'The value of preventing death', in S.B. Chase (ed.), *Problems in Public Expenditure Analysis*, reprinted in M.H. Cooper and A.J. Culyer (eds), *Health Economics*, Harmondsworth: Penguin Books, 295–321.

Schuster, M.A., E.A. McGlynn and R.H. Brook (1998), 'How good is the quality of health care in the United States?', *Milbank Quarterly*, 76, 517–63.

Schwartz, J. and D.W. Dockery (1992), 'Increased mortality in Philadelphia associated with daily air pollution concentrations', *American Review of Respiratory Diseases*, 145, 600–604.

Sen, A. (1999), *Development as Freedom*, Oxford: Oxford University Press.

Shackle, G.L.S. (1972), *Epistemics and Economics*, Cambridge: Cambridge University Press.

Simon, H.A. (1959), 'Theories of decision-making in economics and behavioral science', *American Economic Review*, 49, 253–83.

Simon, H.A. (1979), 'Rational decision making in business organizations', *American Economic Review*, 69, 493–513.

Smith, A. (1961 [1776]), *The Wealth of Nations*, Vols. I and II, ed. E. Cannan, London: Methuen.

Smith, A. (1966 [1759]), *The Theory of Moral Sentiments*, New York: Augustus M. Kelley.

Smith, D.R. and P.A. Leggat (2007), 'An international review of tobacco smoking in the medical profession: 1974–2004', *BMC Public Health*, 7, www.biomedcentral.com, accessed 11 February 2015.

Smith, J.P. (1999), 'Healthy bodies and thick wallets: the dual relation between health and economic status', *Journal of Economic Perspectives*, 13, 145–66.

Smith, S., J.P. Newhouse and M.S. Freeland (2009), 'Income, insurance, and technology: why does health spending outpace economic growth?', *Health Affairs*, 28, 1276–84.

Spencer, N. (2007), 'Behaving badly? Smoking and the role of behaviour change', in E. Dowler and N. Spencer (eds), *Challenging Health Inequalities: From Acheson to 'Choosing Health'*, Bristol: Policy Press, 157–74.

Starr, P. (1986), 'Health care for the poor: the past twenty years', in S.H. Danziger and D.H. Weinberg (eds), *Fighting Poverty: What Works and What Doesn't*, Cambridge, MA: Harvard University Press, 106–32.

Stationery Office (1998), *Independent Inquiry into Inequalities in Health: Report* (The Acheson Report), London: The Stationery Office.

Stigler, G.J. (1970), 'Director's Law of public income redistribution', *Journal of Law and Economics*, 13, 1–10.

Stiglitz, J.E. (2012), *The Price of Inequality*, New York: Norton.

Strombom, B.A., T.C. Buchmueller and P.J. Feldstein (2002), 'Switching costs, price sensitivity and health plan choice', *Journal of Health Economics*, 21, 89–116.

Sturm, R. (2002), 'The effect of obesity, smoking, and drinking on medical problems and costs', *Health Affairs*, 21, 245–53.

Szreter, S. and M. Woolcock (2004), 'Health by association? Social capital, social theory and the political economy of public health', *International Journal of Epidemiology*, 33, 650–67.

Tawney, R.H. (1964 [1931]), *Equality*, London: George Allen & Unwin.

Tawney, R.H. (1966), *The Radical Tradition*, Harmondsworth: Penguin Books.

Thaler, R.H. (1991), *Quasi Rational Economics*, New York: Russell Sage Foundation.

Thompson, M.S. (1986), 'Willingness to pay and accept risks to cure chronic disease', *American Journal of Public Health*, 76, 392–6.

Titmuss, R.M. (1950), *Problems of Social Policy*, London: His Majesty's Stationery Office and Longmans, Green & Co.

Titmuss, R.M. (1963), *Essays on 'The Welfare State'*, 2nd edn, London: George Allen & Unwin.

Titmuss, R.M. (1968), *Commitment to Welfare*, London: George Allen & Unwin.

Titmuss, R.M. (1970), *The Gift Relationship: From Human Blood to Social Policy*, London: George Allen & Unwin.

Titmuss, R.M. (1974), *Social Policy: An Introduction*, ed. B. Abel-Smith and Kay Titmuss, London: George Allen & Unwin.

Titmuss, R.M. (n.d.), Unpublished lecture, in Papers of Richard Titmuss, British Library of Political and Economic Science, London School of Economics, Box 3/370. Cited by permission of Ann Oakley.

Titmuss, R.M., B. Abel-Smith, G. Macdonald, A. Williams and C. Ward (1964), *The Health Services of Tanganyika*, London: Pitman Medical Publishing.

Tobin, J. (1970), 'On limiting the domain of inequality', *Journal of Law and Economics*, 13, 263–77.

Tönnies, F. (2001 [1887]), *Community and Civil Society*, transl. J. Harris and M. Hollis, Cambridge: Cambridge University Press.

Torrance, G.W. (1986), 'Measurement of health state utilities for economic appraisal', *Journal of Health Economics*, 5, 1–30.

Townsend, P. (1979), *Poverty in the United Kingdom*, Harmondsworth: Penguin Books.

Townsend, P. (1987), 'The geography of poverty and ill-health', in A. Williams (ed.), *Health and Economics*, London: Macmillan, 37–67.

Townsend, P. and N. Davidson (1982a), 'Introduction to the Pelican Edition', in P. Townsend and N. Davidson (eds), *Inequalities in Health: The Black Report*, Harmondsworth: Penguin Books, 13–34.

Townsend, P. and N. Davidson (eds) (1982b), *Inequalities in Health: The Black Report*, Harmondsworth: Penguin Books.

Townsend, P., P. Phillimore and A. Beattie (1988), *Health and Deprivation*, Beckenham: Croom Helm.

Tu, J.V., D. Naylor, D. Kumar, B.A. DeBuono, B.J. McNeil and E.L. Hannan (1997), 'Coronary artery bypass graft surgery in Ontario and New York State: which rate is right?', *Annals of Internal Medicine*, 126, 13–19.

Tudor Hart, J. (1971), 'The inverse care law', *Lancet*, 297, 405–12.

Tullock, G. (1976), *The Vote Motive*, London: Institute of Economic Affairs.

Turner, R.J., B. Wheaton and D.A. Lloyd (1995), 'The epidemiology of social stress', *American Sociological Review*, 60, 104–25.

Tversky, A. and D. Kahneman (1981), 'The framing of decisions and the psychology of choice', *Science*, 211, 453–8.

Vayda, E. (1973), 'A comparison of surgical rates in Canada and in England and Wales', *New England Journal of Medicine*, 289, 1224–9.

Viscusi, W. Kip (1992), *Fatal Tradeoffs: Public and Private Responsibilities for Health*, New York: Oxford University Press.

Viscusi, W. Kip (1993), 'The value of risks to life and health', *Journal of Economic Literature*, 31, 1912–46.

Viscusi, W. Kip and J.E. Aldy (2003), 'The value of a statistical life: a critical review of market estimates throughout the world', *Journal of Risk and Uncertainty*, 27, 5–76.

Wadsworth, M.E.J. and D.J.L. Kuh (1997), 'Childhood influences on adult health: a review of recent work from the British 1946 national birth cohort study, the MRC National Survey of Health and Development', *Paediatric and Perinatal Epidemiology*, 11, 2–20.

Wagstaff, A. and E. van Doorslaer (2000), 'Equity in health care finance and delivery', in A.J. Culyer and J.P. Newhouse (eds), *Handbook of Health Economics*, Vol. 1B, Amsterdam: Elsevier, 1803–62.

Walzer, M. (1983), *Spheres of Justice: A Defence of Plurality and Equality*, Oxford: Martin Robertson.

Wasserman, J., W.G. Manning, J.P. Newhouse and J.D. Winkler (1991), 'The effects of excise duties and regulations on cigarette smoking', *Journal of Health Economics*, 10, 43–64.

Weber, M. (1948 [1922]), 'Bureaucracy', in H.H. Gerth and C.W. Mills (eds), *From Max Weber: Essays in Sociology*, London: Routledge, 196–244.

Wedig, G.J. (1988), 'Health status and the demand for health: results on price elasticities', *Journal of Health Economics*, 7, 151–63.

Weeks, W.B., A.E. Wallace, M.M. Wallace and H.G. Welch (1994), 'A comparison of the educational costs and incomes of physicians and other professionals', *New England Journal of Medicine*, 330, 1280–86.

Weisbrod, B.A. (1991), 'The health care quadrilemma: an essay on technological change, insurance, quality of care, and cost containment', *Journal of Economic Literature*, 29, 523–52.

Wennberg, J.E. and M. Cooper (1999), *The Quality of Medical Care in the United States: A Report on the Medicare Program (The Dartmouth Atlas of Health Care in the United States)*, Chicago, IL: American Health Association Press.

Wennberg, J.E., E.S. Fisher and J.S. Skinner (2002), 'Geography and the debate over Medicare reform', *Health Affairs*, 13 February, W96–W114.

Wennberg, J.E., J.L. Freeman and W.J. Culp (1987), 'Are hospital services rationed in New Haven or overutilised in Boston?', *Lancet*, 1, 1185–8.

Wennberg, J.E. and A. Gittelsohn (1973), 'Small area variations in health care delivery', *Science*, 182, 1102–8.

Westert, G.P., A.P. Nieboer and P.P. Groenewegen (1993), 'Variation in duration of hospital stay between hospitals and between doctors within hospitals', *Social Science and Medicine*, 37, 833–9.

Wicksell, K. (1958 [1896]), 'A new principle of just taxation', selection from *Finanztheoretische Untersuchungen*, transl. J.M. Buchanan, in R.A. Musgrave and A.T. Peacock (eds), *Classics in the Theory of Public Finance*, London: Macmillan, 72–118.

Wilkinson, R.G. (1996), *Unhealthy Societies: The Afflictions of Inequality*, London: Routledge.

Wilkinson, R.G. (1999), 'Putting the picture together: prosperity, redistribution, health, and welfare', in M. Marmot and R.G. Wilkinson (eds), *Social Determinants of Health*, Oxford: Oxford University Press, 256–74.

Wilkinson, R.G. and K. Pickett (2009), *The Spirit Level: Why More Equal Societies Almost Always Do Better*, London: Penguin Books.

Williams, A. (1997), *Being Reasonable about the Economics of Health: Selected Essays by Alan Williams*, ed. A.J. Culyer and A. Maynard, Cheltenham, UK and Northampton, MA, USA: Edward Elgar Publishing.

Williams, A. and R. Cookson (2000), 'Equity in health', in A.J. Culyer and J.P. Newhouse (eds), *Handbook of Health Economics*, Vol. 1A, Amsterdam: Elsevier, 1863–910.

Williams, B. (1973 [1962]), 'The idea of equality', in B. Williams, *Problems of the Self: Philosophical Papers 1956–1972*, Cambridge: Cambridge University Press, 230–49.

Williamson, O.E. (1975), *Markets and Hierarchies*, New York: Free Press.

Williamson, O.E. (1981), 'The modern corporation: origins, evolution, attributes', *Journal of Economic Literature*, 19, 1537–86.

Wilper, A.P., S. Woolhandler, K.E. Lasser, D. McCormick, D.H. Bor and D.U. Himmelstein (2009), 'Health insurance and mortality in US adults', *American Journal of Public Health*, 99, 2289–95.

Winslow, C.M., D.H. Solomon, M.R. Chassin, J. Kosecoff, N.J. Merrick and R.H. Brook (1988), 'The appropriateness of carotid endarterectomy', *New England Journal of Medicine*, 318, 721–7.

Woolf, S.H., R.E. Johnson, G.F. Fryer, G. Rust and D. Satcher (2004), 'The health impact of resolving racial disparities: an analysis of US mortality data', *American Journal of Public Health*, 94, 2078–81.

Woolhandler, S., T. Campbell and D.U. Himmelstein (2003), 'Costs of health care administration in the United States and Canada', *New England Journal of Medicine*, 349, 768–75.

World Bank (2015), 'HealthStats', Washington, DC: World Bank, http://databank.worldbank.org/data/view/variableSelection, accessed 16 June 2015.

World Health Organization (1962 [1946]), *Constitution of the World Health Organization*, in WHO, *Basic Documents*, Geneva: WHO, 1–18.

World Health Organization (2008), *Closing the Gap in a Generation: Health Equity through Action on the Social Determinants of Health*, Geneva: World Health Organization.

World Health Organization (2010), *Human Resources for Health: Country Profile Thailand*, Bangkok: Regional Office for South-East Asia, World Health Organization.

Yip, W.C. (1998), 'Physician response to Medicare fee reductions: changes in the volume of coronary artery bypass graft (CABG) surgeries in the Medicare and private sectors', *Journal of Health Economics*, 17, 675–99.

Index

Abel-Smith, B. 212
ability to pay 7, 8, 110, 171, 175, 185, 256, 258, 272
absolute rights 183, 190, 192, 193–4
acceptable waits 295–7
access *see* equal access
accountability 137, 319, 326
accreditation 51, 328
Acharya, A.K. 18
Acheson inquiry 204, 205, 209–210
Acton, J.P. 27, 293
actuarialism 181, 182–3
administration 286, 311–15
adverse retention 160
adverse selection 5, 143, 144, 146, 157, 158, 160, 167, 170
advertising 327, 328
affluence 57, 239, 271, 272, 284
affordability 259
Africa 53, 214
age discrimination 125
age-standardisation 12, 208, 216
ageing population 7
ageism 123
aggregate index of inputs 52–4
aggregated data 13
agitation 58
air pollution 63, 217
airborne contagions 65
alcohol misuse 55
alcohol-related fatalities 60, 236
alcohol-related hospital admissions 234
alcoholism 230–31
allocation 8, 18, 90, 122, 125, 132, 188, 203, 229, 295
altruism 6, 103, 121, 128, 129, 192, 198, 269
Andersen, T.F. 107
anger 249

Appleby, J. 109
appraisals (practitioner) 96–7
Aristotelians 82–3, 86
ascription 120–25, 201
Asia 53, 214, 215, 244
aspirations 80
Association of Community Health Councils 210–211
at-risk occupational groups 263
attitudes 15, 65, 120, 173, 174, 234
Auster, R. 229
austerity 242, 260, 269
Australia 214, 222, 314
authority 51–2
autocracies 250–51
autonomy 86, 119, 155, 221
availability 50, 64, 112

Bad Samaritans 121, 171, 255, 256
Baker, L.C. 167
Bangladesh 215, 314
baseline remuneration 98
basic health 188
Beck, R.G. 255
belief(s) 1, 120
benefit cuts 243
benevolence 200
Bernoulli, D. 30, 142
best practice 95, 106, 299
Bevan, A. 132, 172, 204, 205, 218
Beveridge Report (1942) 203
Biddle, J.E. 43
biology 183, 228
bipartism (insurance) 168–9
birth weight 61, 207, 210, 214, 231, 260
bisectoral amalgamation 309
Black, D. 211
black–white differences
  birth weight 207

355

compulsory hospital admittance 264
education 207, 227, 231
life expectancy 213
medical care 207
mortality rates 207, 227–8, 269
preventable hospitalisations 299
Blaxter, M. 10, 211
Blendon, R.J. 54
Blomquist, G. 46
blood donation 84, 131–2
bonuses 106, 304, 313
Book, R.A. 315
Boulding, K. 118
bounded rationality 20, 77, 145
Braybrooke, D. 132, 181
Broome, J. 22, 23
Broyles, R.W. 301
Buchanan, J.M. 23, 30, 134, 174, 197, 198, 270, 289
Bundorf, M.K. 259
Bunker, J.P. 69
bureaucrats 134

Canada 107, 109, 112, 115, 214, 260, 268, 313
capitalism 65, 167, 312, 322
capitation 97–9, 106, 113
care *see* health care; medical care
caring externality 128–30, 199
category, risk rating by 145–6
Census 13
certainty 21–2
Chaloupka, F. 60
Chamberlain, J. 64
Chassin, M.R. 114
child mortality 11, 66
Children's Health Insurance Program (CHIP) 256–7
China 215, 223
choice
  abrogation of responsibility 82
  allocation of health care 122
  evidence-based medicine 115
  exercise of 77
  and inequality 184, 221
  of insurance 155
  political economy and 147
  private medicine and 294
  public transport and 266
  unknowledge and regret 317
  valuation of life 23
  see also consumer choice; freedom of choice; rational choice
chronic illness 56, 148, 158, 209, 211, 242, 277
citizenship 183, 193, 276, 286
citizenship rights 193–5
citizenship wage 246, 261
clinical decision-making 101
clinical disasters 69
clinical freedom 117, 152, 164, 166
clinical trials 298, 299
co-insurance 153
co-payment(s) 153, 163, 167, 256, 292
Coase, R.H. 307
Cochrane, A.L. 67, 70
Coffey, R.M. 293
cognitive bias 39
cognitive dissonance 18–19
collective action 1, 64
collective agreements 40
collective bargaining 39
collective need 121
collectivisation 246–7
collectivism 262, 275
collectivity 81, 194
common culture 6, 176, 203, 251, 256, 276–7
communism, through effective demand 149–51
community rating 7, 147, 148
compassion 6, 128, 132, 198–200, 274
competition 320, 324
complete health 9, 10, 15, 16, 33, 41
comprehensive model (NHS) 173–4
compulsory insurance 162–3, 171, 258–61
compulsory screening 13
condition money 36–7
confidentiality 13
conformity (practitioner) 112–13
conscience collective 122
consensus 4, 115, 133–4, 138, 173, 198
conservatism 19, 131, 238, 299, 327
consultation 81–2, 102
consumer choice 62, 76–7, 118, 135

consumer culture 53
consumer knowledge 75
consumer sovereignty 3, 32, 80–82, 99, 102, 119, 304
consumption 59
contingent valuation 23, 28
contract employment 242
contribution, equality of 180–83, 257
control 247–51
controls 322–5
conventions 20, 131, 234
Cooper, M. 111
Cooper, P.F. 161
cooperation 252
coordination 309–311
Corts, K.S. 167
cost(s)
   quality-adjusted life years 124
   of smoking during pregnancy 61
   see also opportunity costs; transaction costs
cost of care 7, 93, 270–87
   alcohol misuse 55
   excess neonatal 231
   expenditure and rising 271–9
   fall in 284–7
   and health capital 300
   insurance and rising 152
   medicine, technology and structure 280–83
   social trends 276–9
cost containment 288–315
   demand side 289–97
   in health insurance 142, 169
   selective criteria and 97
   supply side 297–315
   and value for money 286
cost–benefit analysis 27–8, 29, 150, 269, 286, 299, 300
cost-consciousness 164, 188, 305, 318, 326
cost-cutting 298
cost-effectiveness 159, 167, 286, 299, 300
cost-plus systems 324
cost-sharing 106, 153, 167, 257
countervailing forces (marketplace) 102–6

Crosland, C.A.R. 57
cross-subsidisation 5, 140, 148, 158, 162, 170, 177, 180, 256, 302, 321
culpable negligence 182
cultural heterogeneity 14
cultural imperialism 234–6
cultural need 72
culture
   and compulsory health insurance 261–2
   impact on the 'normal' 79–80
   narrowing the gap in inequality 232–8
   residualism 175
   survival of personal taste 131
   and values 118
   see also common culture; consumer culture; multiculturalism; subcultures
Culyer, A.J. 75, 128, 129
Currie, J. 214
Cutler, D.M. 114, 163, 237, 260, 300, 305

daily satisfaction survey, dialysis patients 31–2
damage-averter 195–6
danger money 36, 38
Daniels, N. 79, 187–8
Dardis, R. 33–4, 46
data collection 11, 13, 299
death certificates 12
death(s)
   alcohol-related 60, 236
   cancer-related 235
   doctors' non-emphasis of 92
   from hospital errors 51
   from lack of health insurance 260
   smoking-related 235
   and socio-economic status 236
   supply of beds as a predictor of 111
   willingness to pay to avoid 28
   see also mortality; mortality rates; premature death(s)
decennial recertification 115
decentralisation 32, 252
decision-making 20, 21, 77, 101, 103, 159, 249

deductible insurance 153
defensive tests 283
delay 294
demand
  for health care 3
  see also effective demand;
    supplier-induced demand;
    supply and demand
demand curve 89, 100, 101, 105, 255, 272, 289, 292, 293
demand-side policies 269
democracy 126, 136–8, 168, 179, 189, 247, 250, 281
demography 277–9
Denmark 54, 95, 228
dentists/dentistry 215, 217, 219, 266, 282, 291, 293, 328, 329
dependency 69, 87
depression 248, 260
deprivation 218, 241, 262
the deprived 217, 236, 240, 259, 295
desertion 296
detection 154, 164, 228, 260, 268–9, 284, 293, 304, 305
deterrence 292–3
devolution 1, 32, 252
diagnostic criteria 12
diagnostic-related group (DRG) 303
dialogue 86
dialysis patients, daily satisfaction survey 31–2
difference principle 122
differentiation 81, 148, 155–6, 160, 167, 207
direct tax 171, 257
Director's Law 212, 274, 275
disagreement, in medicine 107, 108
disclosure 62, 63, 78, 326
disease(s)
  affluence and 57
  airborne 65
  Galenian concept 10
  see also illness; morbidity
dissatisfaction 130–31, 289, 293, 296, 297
dissensus 136–8
distance to hospital, mortality and 266
disutility supplement 40

division of labour 51, 87, 221, 223, 267, 308
divorce 56
Dockery, D.W. 63
doctor–patient ratio 281
doctor–patient relationship 70, 89, 99, 104, 161, 166, 262, 283, 319
doctors
  lawsuits and malpractice claims 283
  and levelling up 262–4
  per population(s) 214
  see also practitioners
the double void 78–80
Dowd, B. 167
Downs, A. 134
Drummond, M. 124
Durkheim, E. 117

earmarked fees 98
economic efficiency 2, 129, 286
economic growth 57, 72, 120–21, 201, 247, 284, 296
economic policy 241
economic status 43, 218
economic welfare 241–3
economics 45, 72, 90, 94, 95, 126, 200–201
education 57, 65, 207, 226–32, 263, 266, 276–7
effective demand 8, 29, 64, 83, 110, 129, 139, 149–51, 186, 187, 197, 255, 317
efficiency 201, 223, 282, 286, 287, 319, 326
  see also economic efficiency; inefficiency
Elo, I.T. 228
emotion 20
employees, and insurance 158, 159, 160, 161, 169
employer-paid medical treatment 177
employer-sponsored health insurance 5, 158–63, 169
employment see contract employment; full employment; unemployment
employment dismissals 242
empowerment 85, 239–41
emptiness at work 248

end of life 125–6
Enthoven, A.C. 320
entrepreneurship 308
equal access 6, 187, 188, 203
equal need
  equal access for 203
  equal treatment for 185–9
equalisation 200, 201, 202, 203, 210, 219
  see also levelling up; medical care, equalising
equality 47, 246
  of contribution 180–83, 257
  democracy and 179
  economic justification 200–201
  as equity 194
  of expenditure 180
  in health 203
  of outcome 183–5
  of respect 183
  of sacrifice 181, 182
  of treatment 185–9
equity 120, 122–3, 147, 179–202
evidence-based medicine 115
excessive medical care 99–100
excessive waits 295–7
exclusion 249
experience, and quality of care 51–2
experience-rated premiums 158
explanatory manuals 55
externalities 127–30

facial justice 219, 246
factoring down 1, 131
fair innings argument 122–3, 279
fairness 136, 147, 179, 201
Faith, R.L. 23
false consciousness 39
family 252
fear 16, 19, 20, 38, 41, 78, 97, 140, 197, 198, 225, 283, 327
fee for service 94–5, 106
Feldman, R. 167
Feldstein, M.S. 273
Feldstein, P.J. 159, 298
Festinger, L. 18–19
fight-or-flight reflex 249

financial incentives 5, 75, 96, 97, 98, 99, 101, 102, 113, 145, 146, 152, 229, 299, 302, 321
  see also subsidies
Finland 228, 230
firms, and health 56
'first past the post' 134
fiscal brainwashing 238
fiscal discrimination 246
fiscal federalism 137
fiscal socialism 197
fiscal welfare 154, 275
Fisher, E.S. 111
fitness, occupations and standards of 15
fixed fees 292, 303
flat rates 302
flexible prices 323
Fogel, R.W. 64
food 57, 62, 64
foreknowledge 141
France 54, 214, 237, 245, 261
free care 291, 293
free market 1, 7–8, 291, 326, 327, 329
freedom 6, 69, 155, 183
  to become 82–6
  of choice 72, 77, 92, 174, 221, 248, 259, 263
  of exchange 319
  see also clinical freedom; liberty; unfreedom(s)
Friedlander, L.J. 68, 229
Friedman, M. 30, 80, 174, 329
Fuchs, V.R. 67, 100, 155, 229
full employment 57, 159, 242, 251
functioning 79
functioning body 191, 192
fundamental rights 196, 219, 220

Galbraith, J.K. 174
Galenian concept, of disease 10
Gardner, J. 242
gender
  and health inequalities 205
  see also women
general case vs specific exception 186
General Household Survey 212
general will 133
generalisation 42, 46

generosity 198–200
geographical location 6, 214–18, 236, 265
Germany 95, 214, 237, 261, 314
Gillon, R. 192
Gini mortality rate 247
goal attainment 51
Golden Rule 195, 234
Goldman, D. 313
good health 3, 9–24
   contribution of households to 55–6
   definition 9–10
   infrastructure and 65
   as met needs 72
   nutrition and 64
   objective and subjective aspects 15–17
   perceptions of 2, 15, 31
   probability 21–4
   rational choice 17–21
   representative samples 42–3
   self-determination and 85
   social context 14–15
goodwill 105
'government by groundswell' 126
Granovetter, M. 105
Gravelle, H. 294
Greece 223, 237, 245
Green, T.H. 194
Greenspan, A.M. 114
Grossman, M. 226, 229, 238, 284
group insurance plans 158–63
group model (HMOs) 163
Gruber, J. 214
guaranteed renewal (insurance) 148
Guralnik, J.M. 227

Hadley, J. 260
Halliday, T.J. 242
Ham, C. 109, 217
happiness 92, 124
Harsanyi, J.C. 88
health
   background knowledge 74
   income and 244–7
   inequalities 6–7, 203–218, 254
      geographical location 214–18
      narrowing the gap 219–53

   social distance 204–214
   as unnatural to the human condition 249
   influence on occupation 209
   perceptions of, and actual health status 18
   Platonic model 10
   receptiveness to education 231
   unemployment and 242
   see also basic health; good health; ill health; right to health
health capital 164, 178, 201, 226, 229, 263, 300, 305
health care
   beyond medicine 54–8
   choice and allocation of 122
   cost see cost of care; cost containment
   demand for 3
   equality in see equality
   expenditure
      equality of 180
      national preferences 288
      rising cost of care 271–9
      socio economic group and 212
      see also individual countries
   financial incentives and supply of 102
   health insurance and health status 68
   household expenditure 55
   ill health and valuation of 44
   informed decisions 77
   as labour intensive 281
   as a primary good 196
   rapid expansion of 7
   special properties 2
   as a special social good 188
health divide 205
health insurance 5, 139–56
   as care beyond medicine 57
   claims, insurers' scrutiny of 152
   combinations and permutations 153–6
   compulsory 162–3, 171, 258–61
   contracts 146, 151, 154, 166, 279
   cost containment 142
   health care and health status 68
   lock-in 148
   moral hazard 149–53

morbidity data 13
overinvestment in 20
payment beyond 176–8
and price 106
risk rating 142–9
risk and uncertainty 140–42
willingness to pay 35
see also national health insurance; private health insurance
health maintenance organisations (HMOs) 163–6
health policy(ies)
alleviation of misery 240
as collective action 1
as nation-building 199
and needs 84
pooled 2
proactive 264
redirection of total spending 8
refusal to treat as illness policy 10
as a response to the shared and felt 2
use of visible proxies to define 'good health' 17
health status 2
as an intergenerational bequest 230–32
behavioural component 232
biology and 183
and demand for health care 3
as economic status 218
financial outlays and 299
health insurance, health care and 68
perceptions of one's health and actual 18
sensitivity to price 292
health workers 65
Healthcare Facilities Accreditation Program (HFAP) 51
height, and unemployment 231
Heisenberg Principle 35
herd instinct 113
heterogeneity 14, 53, 180, 189
hierarchy of needs 83–5
high income 182, 212, 258
Hippocratic Oath 93, 103, 152, 191, 322
Hirschman, A.O. 130
Holland 113
home economics 228

horizontal equity 185
horizontal integration 307, 308, 325
hospital admissions 111, 234, 235, 264, 301–2
hospital beds 99–100, 111, 214
hospital errors, deaths due to 51
hospital management 281
hospital staff 217
household expenditure, health care 55
households, contribution to health 55–6
humanitarian spillover 128–30, 162, 240
hypothecation 128, 168, 170, 174, 182

ideal doctor 89, 91
ideology 1
ignorance 3, 18, 22, 48, 73–8, 88, 89, 112, 122, 138, 140, 197
ill health
distribution of care 186
knowledge and ignorance 74–5
perceptions of 13
and valuation of care 44
Illich, I. 68, 69, 70
illness
self-inflicted 181, 235
subcultures and 264
see also chronic illness; mental illness; psychosomatic illness
immunisation 64–5, 66
imperfect information 21
impulse 199
income
and health 244–7
and health care expenditure 271–2
narrowing the gap in inequality 238–43
and smoking 235–6
uninsured adults 259
user charges as a source of 177
see also high income; low income; rising income
income-related insurance contributions 169
inconvenience 294
Independent Inquiry into Inequalities in Health (Acheson) 204, 205, 209–210

India 63
indirect tax 171, 257
individual(s) 71–86
   as the best of judge of their own well-being 3
   freedom to become 82–6
   information asymmetry 78–82
   knowledge and ignorance 73–8
   needs and wants 71–3
   perceptions of health 18
   versus the tribe 125–7
individual insurance plans 157, 273
individualism 1, 25, 84, 88, 117, 204, 251
inefficiency 52, 204
inequalities
   in health *see* health, inequalities
   of outcomes 184
   social conscience and 186
inequity 204
infant mortality 11
   cross-country comparisons 54
   decline in 59–60, 205, 260
   education and 227–8, 231
   geographical location 214, 215, 216
   health care expenditure and 268
   health insurance and 260
   income and 66, 244
   legislation and 59–60
   social distance 210, 211
informal networks 252
information
   advertising and diffusion of 327
   cost containment 298–300
   questionnaires and misuse of 27
   and the rising cost of care 277
   withholding of 78
   see also imperfect information; perfect information
information asymmetry 3, 4, 18, 78–82, 89, 94, 143–4, 170, 323, 326
information campaigns 237
information overload 42, 160, 328
information sharing 104
infrastructure 57, 64, 65
inputs 2–3, 49–70
   care beyond medicine 54–8
   controls 324–5
   equalisation 203
   increments and totals 67–70
   jurisdiction and legislation 58–63
   medical care 49–54, 212, 217
   prosperity and progress 63–7
insecurity 243
insurance *see* health insurance; social insurance
integration
   as an end and a means 202
   collectivisation and 247
   and cost containment 306–309, 325
   need for 84, 199
   in sickness and health 201
   social 251–3
intellectual biases, in studies 30
intergenerational bequest 230–32
intergenerational multiplier 209
internal market 316–22
interpersonal transfers 177
interpersonal valuation 46
intuition 20
invisible curriculum 228–9
invisible hand 1, 7, 152, 193, 213, 259, 289, 316
invisible mind 25–48
involvement 253
Ireland 222, 245
isolation 252
Italy 54, 95, 223, 261

Japan 54, 214, 244, 249, 274, 285
job risks 36–7, 38, 40–41, 43, 224
Joint Commission International (JCI) 51
The Joint Commission (TJC) 51
Jones Lee, M.W. 18, 28, 34
Joyce, T. 231
justice 93, 136, 186, 192, 198
   see also facial justice; social justice

Kahneman, D. 30
Kaiser Permanente 163
Kant(ianism) 121, 155, 195
Karasek, R. 223, 224, 249
Kessler, D. 283
Keynes(ianism) 141, 242, 251
Kind, P. 26, 92

Kleiner, M.M. 328
Knight, F.H 141
knowledge 73–8, 92, 195, 197, 263
  see also foreknowledge;
    unknowledge
Krugman, P.R. 315
Kudrle, R.T. 328
Kwoka, J.E. 327

laissez-faire 59, 127, 156, 193, 322, 326
lawsuits 283
Le Grand, J. 182, 208, 212
legislation 58–63, 63, 127, 225, 236, 237, 327
Leive, A. 313
levelling 196, 247, 261–2
levelling down 219, 257, 265
levelling up 188, 197, 202, 203, 219–53, 262–4, 265
liberal democracy 1, 16, 21, 25, 41, 45, 77, 81, 120, 288
liberal individualism 32–3, 45, 87
liberalisation 325–9
libertarianism 59, 60, 155, 193, 212, 234, 269, 275, 286, 289
liberty 187, 191
licensure 329
life *see* end of life; life; right to life; value of life
life chances 6, 79, 188, 209, 227, 245, 254
life expectancy 205
  co-payment and 292
  comparisons 11–12, 54
  democracy and 250
  economic growth 247
  education and 227
  geographic location 214, 216
  happiness ranked above 92
  income and 244, 245
  nutrition and 64
  and standard of living 239
  see also individual countries
life-course 241
lifestyle 56, 66, 110–11, 145–6, 227, 232, 243
Locke, J. 190–91, 192, 193
long-term unemployment 243

love 84
low birth weight 61, 207, 214, 231, 260
low income 7, 154, 182, 210, 212, 213, 233, 238–9, 241, 259, 262–3, 274
lower classes 225, 238
lump-sum charges 292

McClellan, M. 283
McGuire, A. 272
McKeown, T. 63, 66, 68
McKinlay, J.B. 65
McKinlay, S.M. 65
macroeconomic policy 269
macroeconomic stability 57
majority rule 126
malpractice claims 283
managed care 163–6, 285, 309
manifest preferences 88
Manning, W.G. 150, 273, 290, 309
marginal utility 31, 43, 72, 142, 150, 181, 272, 295
Marin, A. 43
market competition 137, 143, 158, 165
market economics 32, 55
market economy 139, 190, 201, 246
market failure, state intervention 7, 61, 127–8, 323
market incentives 130
market liberals 83, 135
market socialism 319–21
market-clearing price 289–90
Marmot, M. 247, 248, 265
Marquis, M.S. 273
marriage 56, 252
Marshall, A. 36, 129, 208
Marshall, T.H. 117, 184, 194
Marx/Marxism 59, 206, 223, 224, 276
Maslow, A. 83–5
maternal education 231, 232
maternal mortality 214, 292
Mathauer, I. 315
maximin 195–8
maximum possible 90
maximum price 93, 323
Mayerhoefer, C.D. 291
means-testing 182, 256, 257, 265, 274, 290

Medicaid 213, 214, 257, 259, 261, 268, 274, 292
medical care 49–54
  effectiveness 63–4, 65
  equalising 254–60
    doctors and levelling up 262–5
    payment 255–7
    proportionate universalism 265–9
    regulation 258–62
  excessive 99–100
  inequalities in 207, 213
  payment beyond insurance 176–8
  pre-paid 5
  unsuitability/ineffectiveness 281
  variation in, UK 217
  see also cost of care
medical debt 258
medical education 266, 282
medical opinion 14
medical procedures, devolved 285
medical savings accounts (MSAs) 177–8
medical schools 328
medical services 4
  and access 187
  fixed indemnities 153
  and mortality rates 63, 67
  non-traditional 55
medicalisation 69
Medicare 111, 114, 207, 213, 214, 256, 261, 268, 274, 313, 315
medicine
  care beyond 54–8
  disagreement in 107, 108
  evidence-based 115
  patient-based 80–82
  rising the cost of care 280–83
  see also preventive medicine; private medicine
medicine man, appeal of 3
membership 199
mental hospitals, compulsory admittance 264
mental illness 211
mental mutilation 223
mental well-being 9, 251
mergers and acquisitions 306, 308
merit goods 5, 117–18, 154

metering 181
methodological individualism 26, 29, 34
Mexico 244, 274, 314
middle classes 14, 57, 212, 263, 276
Mill, J.S. 3, 126, 127
minimal State 191, 192
minimax 20, 169, 197
Ministry of Health 104
misadventure, death by 12
mobility 37, 148, 161, 162, 208, 209, 240, 241, 245, 256
monetarism 269
Monheit, A.C. 161, 293
Mooney, G.H. 107
Moore, M.J. 36
moral agents 89
moral hazard 5, 35, 39, 149–53, 181
moral obligation 186
moral philosophy 45
morbidity/rate(s) 6, 12–14, 34, 67, 211, 218
mortality/rate(s) 6, 11–12, 34
  air pollution 63
  austerity and 269
  competition and 320
  by country *see individual countries*
  data on 11, 12
  deprivation and 218
  distance to hospital and 266
  education and 228
  Gini coefficient 247
  income and 238–9, 244–5
  medical breakthroughs and 65
  medical services and 63, 67
  nutrition and decline in 64
  social distance and 207, 210, 211
  unemployment and 242, 243
  widows 56
  see also child mortality; death(s); infant mortality; maternal mortality; neonatal mortality
Mueller, C.D. 293
multi-speciality practices 285–6
multiculturalism 264
multiple-pool market 166–8
Murray, C.J.L. 18
Musgrave, R.A. 117–18

nannying 128, 235
nation-building 6, 199, 251
national budget 6, 317
national health insurance 5, 168–72
   Canada 260
   self-funding model 168–71
   Taiwan 314
   tax-subsidised model 171–2
   see also Children's Health Insurance Program; Medicare
National Health Service (NHS) 172–6
   caring externality 129
   collective conservatism 131
   comprehensive model 173–4
   contributions dilemma 182
   minimax 197
   morals and ethics dilemma 123
   as other-regarding public policy 198
   and policy coordination 266–7
   as proof of a caring community 199
   public expenditure 274
   redistributive aspect 172
   residual supplier model 175–6
   social values 126, 132
National Institute for Health and Care Excellence (NICE) 310
nationalisation 8, 45–8, 312, 321
natural order 191
natural rights 190–93
Needleman, L. 36
needs 71–2, 73
   doctor's perspective of 91
   payment and 94–9
   separation of wants and 119–20
   targeting 267–9
   see also collective need; equal need; hierarchy of needs; validated need
needs-testing 290
neighbourhood spillover 261, 310
neoclassical economics 129, 243, 255, 289, 307
neonatal care, cost of excess 231
neonatal mortality 269
Netherlands 314
network model (HMOs) 163–4
new hospitals 266, 324
Newhouse, J.P. 68, 229, 272, 281, 291

Nicolle, E. 315
Niskanen, W. 134
non-prescription drugs 55
non-rational preferences 30
non-traditional medical services 55
'normal opportunity range' 190
normal species functioning 79
normalcy 14, 16, 31, 79–80
North–South divide 216
Norway 56, 274
Nozick, R. 191, 192, 193, 195
Nussbaum, M.C. 86
nutrition 64, 230, 231

obesity 61–2, 248
occupation
   at risk groups 263
   and inequalities in health 6, 205–214, 247–8
      narrowing the gap 220–25
   legislation 59
   morbidity and mortality 207
   and standards of fitness 15
   wage-risk trade-off 36–7, 38, 40–41
occupational health plans 158–63, 258
occupational injury 225
occupational stress 57
old people 123, 124, 125, 169, 277–8
Olson, C.A. 40, 41
open-ended billing 301
opportunity costs 15, 23, 81, 96, 120, 150, 229, 232, 282, 295, 324
Oswald, A. 242
other-regarding 133, 198
ought-ness 186
out-of-pocket payment 35, 55, 141, 150, 164, 177, 255, 258, 272, 291
outcomes 49
   approximation 2
   care inputs and 67, 68
   equalisation 210
   equality of 183–5
   non-rational preferences for feel good 30
   quality of care 51
overconsumption 5
overtreatment 95

parallel sector 295
Pareto, V. 3
Parkin, D. 272
pass-through reimbursement 95, 151
paternalists 87, 117, 135–6
path dependence 130–32
Patient Protection and Affordable Care Act (2010) 258, 259, 262
patient-based medicine 80–82
Pauly, M.V. 77, 147, 155, 259, 313
pay-productivity nexus 40
payment
   cost containment 300–303
   equalisation of care 255–7
   influence on conduct 291
   and need 94–9
   see also ability to pay; co-payment(s); out-of-pocket payment; prospective payments; retrospective payments; third-party payments
peer groups 232–3
peer pressure 60, 103–4, 222
perceived distance 201
perceived probability 39
perceptions
   of good health 2, 15, 31
   of normalcy and malfunction 16
   of one's own health 18
   salience and biased 19
Percy, A.M. 313
perfect certainty 21
perfect information 75
person-centred care 70
personal responsibility 261
personality 113
philosopher-ruler 58, 135, 202, 315
philosophy 45, 93, 121, 286
physical externality 127–8
physical health 252
physical well-being 9, 251
physiological needs 71–2, 83–4
Pigou, A.C. 61, 127
Piketty, T. 245–6
Plato 10, 85, 246, 315
pluralism 14, 22, 133, 174, 186, 234, 264, 313, 329
Poland 214, 261

political economy 132–8, 147
political income 135
poll tax 171–2
pollution 63, 217
poor-in-work 240, 257
Pope, A. 107
positive discrimination 185, 265
possessions, right to 191
poverty 239, 250
power 247–51
practice budget 317–19
practice variation 76, 106–113, 125
practitioners 87–116
   accidents and ill-health 222
   countervailing forces 102–106
   knowledge and expertise 91–3
   payment and need 94–9
   practice variation 106–113
   professional assessment 88–91
   supplier-induced demand 99–102
   trimming the fat 115–16
   value for money 113–15
   see also doctors
praise 103
pre-paid care 5
pre-paid insurance 163, 164, 165, 166
precariat 242
precautionary tests 283
preference, democracy and 189
preference reversal 20
preferences
   differences in 137
   true and manifest 88
   wants as 72
   see also non-rational preferences; revealed preferences
pregnant women 60–61, 231, 234
prejudice(s) 124, 145
premature death(s) 29, 36, 55, 56, 61, 242, 248, 256, 284
premiums (insurance) 141, 142, 143, 147, 149, 154, 158, 165, 169, 273, 314
Preston Curve 247
Preston, S.H. 228, 239
preventive medicine 51, 66, 98, 164, 213, 228, 292, 305
price 267, 289–93

price controls 323
price differentiation 167
price discrimination 103, 177, 256
price dispersion 105
primary goods 196
principal–agent relationship 69, 101
private enterprise 223
private health insurance 5, 157–68, 261, 275
   differential contributions 182
   group plans 158–63
   health care expenditure 272–3
   individual plans 157
   managed care (case study) 163–6
   size and cost 312, 313, 314, 315
   suppression of tax relief 257
private medicine 129, 294–5
privatisation 287
pro-competitive regulation 325–6
probability, good health 21–4
producer sovereignty 77–8
product differentiation, in insurance 155–6, 160
production function 3, 49–50, 56, 58, 63, 68, 229, 251
productivity 96–7, 164, 223, 281, 284, 319, 321
professional assessment 88–91
professional bodies, and practice variation 112
professional certification 104
professional ethic 4, 103, 272
professionalism 117
profit-seeking 164, 223, 280
progress 63–7
'proper ground', distribution of care 186, 187
property 192
proportionate universalism 265–9
prospective payments 106, 152, 301, 302, 303
prosperity 63–7
proximate cause (of death) 12
Psacharopoulos, G. 43
psychic income 103
psychological pitfalls, in studies 30
psychometrics 26–7
psychosocial stress 250

psychosomatic illness 72, 247
public expenditures 212
public information campaigns 237
public opinion 4, 14, 30, 120, 126, 182, 240, 297
public policy 1, 46–7, 120
   see also social policy
public transport 266
publicity 327–8
the public 117–38
   externalities 127–30
   path dependence 130–32
   political economy 132–8
   social values 118–27
purchase, and cost containment 297–306
Putnam, R.D. 251

quality of care 50–52, 104–5, 165, 281
quality of life 47, 93, 114, 250, 260
quality-adjusted life years 47, 122, 124, 125
quantity, and price 290–91
questionnaires 26–32

Rabin, M. 208
race, and inequalities in health 207
racial discrimination 91, 240, 264
radical uncertainty 22, 141
Rand Health Insurance Experiment 68, 291, 292
rank 249
ranking, of alternatives 196
rational choice 1, 17–21, 74, 97, 195, 197, 243, 326–8
rationing by price 267
Rawls, J. 44, 48, 87, 122, 136, 195, 196, 197, 198
reallocation 57, 279
reason 190
rebates 182, 257
reciprocal obligation 194
reciprocity 198
Registrar General 11
regret 317
regulation 4, 258–62, 325–6
relevant attributes, representative samples 42–3

relief 239–41
religion, and health 58
religious values 6
representative samples 13, 41–8
repression 223
residential segregation/sorting 207, 217
residualism 6, 175–6
resources *see* allocation; reallocation
respect 4, 16, 32, 45, 121, 131, 155, 183, 264
   see also self-respect
responsibility(ies) 6, 78, 82, 261
retrospective payment 301
return on investment, medical education 282
revealed preferences 18, 19, 21, 22, 23, 34, 106, 118, 123, 135, 142
Rice, T. 262
Richardson, E. 300
right to health 190–202
   citizenship rights 193–5
   generosity and compassion 198–200
   maximin 195–8
   natural rights 190–93
   structural imperative 200–202
right to life 191
rights *see* absolute rights; citizenship rights; fundamental rights; natural rights; social rights
rising income 7, 57, 64, 65, 271, 272, 296
risk
   and insurance 140–42
   see also job risks
risk appetite 23, 28, 43, 110
risk aversion 16, 18, 30, 43, 113, 142, 196
risk factors 263
risk intensive employments 43
risk pooling 180, 275, 279
risk premium 36, 40
risk profile/profiling 145–6, 150
risk rating 142–9
risk segmentation 167
risk tolerance 197
risk-tolerant employees 43
risky behaviours 243
risky choice 19

Roemer, M.I. 99–100, 111
role models 2–3
roles 80
Rosko, M.D. 301
Rosser, R.M. 26
Rousseau, J.J. 133
Ruhm, C.J. 243
rules 198

Sackett, D.L. 31, 44
sacrifice 35, 122, 181, 182, 229
safety needs 84
salary (doctors) 96–7, 106, 113
salience, and biased perceptions 19
Samaritanship 103
Sandel, M.J. 129, 130
Savage, L.J. 30
savings, funding of treatment 177
Say's Law 100
Schuster, M.A. 114
Schwartz, J. 63
scientific revolution 65
Second World War 6, 251
security needs 84
segregation 207
selection satisficing 20
selective criteria 97
selective incentives 304–6
selective inclusion 162
self-actualisation 84–5
self-deception 19
self-determination 85, 119, 131
self-esteem 84
self-funding model, national health insurance 168–71
self-inflicted illness 181, 235
self-interest 1, 134, 135, 152, 196, 319, 322
self-medication 13, 222, 236
self-rating, health states 31
self-regulation 104, 327
self-respect 84, 196
self-selection 144
Sen, A. 83
sentiment 200
service ethic 94, 196
Shackle, G.L.S. 141
shame 265

side-effects 69, 114
Sierra Leone 54
Simon, H.A. 20, 145
Singapore 54, 214, 245
single-issue referendums 47
single-payer system 314
sleep deprivation 55
Smith, A. 1, 2, 3, 36, 103, 223, 305
Smith, S. 280
smoking 60–61, 223, 233, 235–6, 237, 238, 248
social capital 247, 252
social connectedness 252
social conscience 186, 187
social context, good health 14–15
social contract 126, 183, 235, 236
social control 90–91, 126
social democracy 59, 262
social distance 204–214, 236, 245, 246
social duty 182, 198
social economists 255
social engineering 175, 234, 251, 321
social engineers 202
social ethic 262
social good(s) 186, 188, 195
social gradient 254
social guarantee 196
social insurance
  differential contributions 182
  and health care expenditure 273–5
  see also national health insurance
social integration 251–3
social justice 4, 246
social philosophy 286
social policy 1
  see also economic policy; health policy
social rights 183, 194
social services 277
social values 118–27, 128, 318
social wage 212
social welfare function 119
social well-being 9
social-ism 117, 126, 129, 131, 251
socialism 5, 58–9, 64, 65, 174, 204, 212, 223, 322
  see also fiscal socialism; market socialism

societal change 53
socio-economic status 205
  see also lower classes; middle classes
socio-psychological inheritance 230
solidarity 6, 117, 121, 132, 169, 176
soup kitchen medicine 174
special capitations 98–9
specific egalitarianism 186
specific exception, general case vs 186
staff model (HMOs) 163
standards of fitness 15
standards of living 65, 204, 239, 243
state capitalism 321–2
state intervention
  devolution and decentralisation 252
  distress relief 240, 241
  in insurance 148–9
  in market failure 7, 61, 127–8, 323
stewardship 191
Stigler, G.J. 212
Stiglitz, J.E. 245, 246
stranger-gifts 84, 128, 131–2, 177, 198
stress 57, 58, 222, 250, 252
Strombom, S. 160
structural imperative 200–202
subcontracting 322
subcultures 6–7, 14, 235, 264
subscriptions (MSAs) 177–8
subsidies 57, 148, 180, 236, 237
  see also cross-subsidisation
substitution 27
suicide 12, 210
supplier-induced demand 3, 99–102, 105, 324
supplier-induced extravagance 106
supply and demand 1, 89–90, 99–100, 188, 302
surveys 13, 26–32
Sweden 95, 122, 124, 214, 215, 228
Switzerland 129–30, 214, 314
symptoms 14
Szreter, S. 64, 252

Taiwan 231, 314
targeting need 267–9
Tawney, R.H. 58, 59, 179, 180
tax relief 154, 158, 257, 275

tax-subsidised model, national health insurance 171–2
taxation 59–60, 62, 128, 181, 236, 237–8, 256, 257
Taylor, F.W. 223
technology 7, 51, 53, 280–83, 323
Thaler, R.H. 82
third-party payments 5, 7, 149, 272, 290
Thompson, M.S. 29
'thou shalt not harm' 191
thresholds, of normalcy and malfunction 16
time factor, in studies 30–31
time price 293–7
Titmuss, R.M. 1, 2, 10, 122, 129, 130, 131, 132, 133, 154, 174, 176, 185, 198, 199, 212, 251, 265, 312
tobacco 56
Tobin, J. 186, 187
toddler fatalities, reduction in 59–60
Tönnies, F. 133, 251
Torrance, G.W. 17–18, 31, 44
Townsend, P. 215–16, 217–18
training, and practice variation 112
transaction costs 37–8, 142, 160, 306, 307, 308
transparency 62, 97, 165, 169, 287, 299, 327
travel 266
travel time 294
treatment
  adherence to 284
  equal 185–9
treatment centres
  funding 6
  nationalisation 8
true preferences 88
trust 99, 102, 252
Tullock, G. 30, 134, 135
Tversky, A. 30

unanimity 137–8
uncertainty 3, 5, 138, 140–42
  see also radical uncertainty; veil of uncertainty
underutilisation 106
unemployed 169, 221–2, 242, 257, 295

unemployment 161–2, 218, 231, 241–2, 243
unfreedom(s) 58, 69, 83
the uninsured 175, 258, 259, 260
United Kingdom
  doctors 95, 214, 222
  health care expenditure 68, 217
  inequalities in health 210, 215–18
  life expectancy 68, 210, 211, 214, 216
  mortality rates 210, 216, 242
  obesity 61–2
  occupational injury 225
  practice variation 109–110, 125
  private health insurance 312, 314
  smoking 233, 235, 237
United States
  doctors 92, 214, 222–3, 283
  health care
    expenditure 7, 53, 270, 272, 274, 278, 301, 310
    heterogeneity of 189
    high cost, and health capital 300
    international league table 53–4
  health insurance 153, 258–61, 262, 275
    private 158, 161, 162, 163–4, 167–8, 261, 312, 313, 314
    see also Children's Health Insurance Program; Medicare; RAND Health Insurance Experiment
  inequalities in health 210
  life expectancy 213, 214, 227
  low birth weight 231
  medical debt 258
  mortality rates 207, 214, 215, 227–8, 242, 244–5, 254, 260, 266
  obesity 61, 62
  perception of life chances 245
  personal responsibility 261
  practice variation 107–109, 111, 112
  smoking 233, 237
  value for money 113, 114, 115
universalism 6, 131, 176, 201, 263–4, 265–9
unknowledge 21, 48, 74, 101, 140, 141, 147, 197, 198, 317
user charges 177, 290

utilisation 50
utilisation review 8, 142, 298, 299
utilitarianism 22, 137, 200
'utilitarianism of rights' 195
utility maximisation 32, 44

validated need 188
valuation of care 44
value judgements 33
value of life 22, 23, 33–4, 35–6, 37, 40, 43, 46, 93, 121
value for money 113–15, 152, 285
value systems 4–5, 262
value-added tax 257
values *see* religious values; social values
veil of ignorance 48, 122, 138, 197
veil of uncertainty 181, 199, 317
veil of unknowledge 74, 147
vertical integration 163, 307, 308, 325
Viscusi, W.K. 36, 37, 43
visible hand 8
volunteering 253

wage-risk trade-off 36–7, 38, 40–41
waiting time 294, 295–7
Walzer, M. 186, 199
want(s) 72, 73, 119–20, 186
want-creation 62–3, 102, 106
Wasserman, J. 60
waste 281
wealth gap 246
Weber, M. 134
welfare 243
Welfare State 6, 91, 197

well-being 1, 3, 9, 250, 251, 252
Wennberg, J.E. 108, 111, 114
Westert, G.P. 113
White Paper (1944) 203
Whitehall studies (Marmot) 247–8
Wicksell, K. 133
Wilkinson, R.G. 239, 249–50
Williams, A. 92
Williams, B. 186–7
Williamson, O.E. 306, 307
willingness to earn 35–41
willingness to pay (spend) 2, 19, 22, 27, 28, 29, 32–5, 55, 121, 258
willingness to sacrifice 122
women
    alcoholism 230–31
    and education 227, 232
    health inequalities 204
    inputs to national health 57
    and mental illness 211
    see also pregnant women; widows
Woolcock, M. 64, 252
Woolf, S.H. 207
Woolhandler, S. 313
working class 211, 264
Working Group on Inequalities in Health 211
World Health Organization (WHO) 9, 33, 54, 196, 219, 219–20, 284, 316

Yip, W.C. 100

Zarkin, G.A. 43
zero-rating 257